THE EUROPEAN CUP

THE EUROPEAN CUP

AN ILLUSTRATED HISTORY

Rab MacWilliam

AURUM PRESS

ACKNOWLEDGEMENTS

I would like to thank Anne Beech, Kevin Connolly, Daniel Fine, Tim Webb and Adam Ward for their help in the preparation of this book.

As I could find nothing up-to-date, accessible and in print in the English language on the history of the European Cup, I decided to fill the gap with this book. There have been some excellent histories of the tournament – including Brian Glanville's *Champions of Europe* and John Motson and John Rowlinson's *The European Cup, 1956–1980* – and they were essential background reading. Ron Hockings' *Hockings' European Cups* and Anton Rippon's *The European Cup* were also useful references.

Other, more general, volumes – such as Chris Nawrat and Steve Hutchings' *Sunday Times Illustrated History of Football*, Norman Barrett's *Daily Telegraph Football Chronicle*, Kier Radnedge's *Ultimate Encyclopedia of Football*, Phil Soar's *Hamlyn Encyclopedia of World Football*, John Ballard and Paul Suff's *Dictionary of Football* and my own *Great Football Moments of the Twentieth Century* – helped remind me of the wider context. And few football books can be written without the constant presence to hand of the *Rothman's Soccer Yearbook* and, in terms of European football, Mike Hammond's unparalleled *European Football Yearbook*. The entertaining *Rough Guide to European Football* also contained much interesting information.

There is a plethora of books on British football teams and players – too many to list here – but, among others, I found useful Hamlyn's official club histories and player-by-player series. There are also specific titles referring to British clubs in Europe, such as Stephen Kelly's *Liverpool in Europe* and Jon Ladd's *Up for the Cup!* UEFA also publish regular guides to the competition as well as statistical publications, including their annual *Statistical Handbook*, the *Champions' League All-time Players' Records* and *Directory of Finalists in European Competitions*, which proved invaluable in confirming facts and settling arguments.

I also watched various videos and surfed innumerable club and general football websites on the Internet, of which the star – for the purposes of this book – was *www.rssf.com*, the Rec Sport Soccer Statistics Foundation, which must be the definitive source of European football statistics on the world-wide web. Other websites worth a visit include *www.worldfootball.org* and, of course, UEFA's own site, *www.uefa.com*.

Finally, and apart from my fading and unreliable memory, my other main sources of information were back issues of various newspapers, particularly *The Scotsman*, the *Daily Telegraph* and *The Times*, and magazines, the most helpful by a long way being the essential and magisterial *World Soccer*.

Picture credits: All photos Colorsport except 14, 33 and 50 (Hulton Getty) and 17, 31, 36 and 37 (Popperfoto).

First published in Great Britain
2000 by Aurum Press Ltd
25 Bedford Avenue, London WC1B 3AT

A catalogue record for this book is available from the British Library.

ISBN 1 85410 715 1

1 3 5 7 9 10 8 6 4 2
2000 2002 2004 2003 2001

Design by Robert Updegraff
Printed and bound in Italy by LEGO SpA

Title page photo: **The stadium at Bari just before the kick-off of the 1991 European Cup Final between Red Star Belgrade and Marseille.**

Introduction

The European Cup – or, more precisely, the European Champion Clubs' Cup – came into being in 1955 partly through English insularity.

The post-war British consensus was that foreign football was all very well, but the game's truest expression, the standard by which it should be judged, lay in English and Scottish league and cup tournaments and the Home Championships. Indeed, the British football associations had rejoined FIFA as late as 1946, having resigned in 1928 in a dispute about professionalism, and England did not bother to enter the World Cup until 1950. Even the ensuing humiliation of being beaten 1-0 by the USA's part-timers did not shake England's belief in their natural pre-eminence in the world game.

However, three years later at Wembley the myth of their invincibility was shattered by a marvellous Hungarian team – featuring Puskas, Czibor and Kocsis – who took England apart 6-3, and the Mighty Magyars emphasised the huge superiority in continental skill and tactics by winning again in Budapest 7-1 six months later. More sophisticated observers began to suggest that the future lay in competition with Europe, although the obdurate English football authorities were to take some convincing.

Earlier European Cup Tournaments

The **Mitropa Cup** was initiated in 1927 by Hugo Meisl and was a knockout, home and away competition between clubs from Austria, Hungary, Czechoslovakia and Yugoslavia, with clubs from Italy and Switzerland joining later. It flourished between the Wars, but declined in importance and by 1980 was limited to second division winners.

The **Latin Cup** had a similar format and was first played in 1947 by teams from France, Italy, Portugal and Spain. It withered away in 1957 with the arrival of the European Cup.

Kenny Dalglish celebrates his Quarter-final goal for Liverpool against Benfica in 1978.

At British club level, there had been several post-war friendlies, mostly against Eastern European sides, with teams like Arsenal, Chelsea, Hibernian and Wolves showing the most enlightened choice of opposition. On 14 December 1954, Wolves, the robust, long-ball English champions, played top side Honved under their new Molineux floodlights and recovered from 2-0 down to beat the Hungarian wizards 3-2. *The Times* commented, 'Wolverhampton did British football proud under the night sky.' Wolves having earlier routed Spartak Moscow 4-0, the *Daily Mail* went further, proclaiming them 'Champions of the World' – a characteristically triumphalist reaction conveniently forgetting that these were home wins in non-competitive games.

The gauntlet, however, had been thrown down, and was gratefully accepted by one Gabriel Hanot, ex-French international footballer and editor of the French sports paper *L'Equipe*. A long-term proponent of European club competition, he suggested, in the paper, a new European tournament. To be played in midweek between nominated clubs from each country on a home-and away basis, with points awarded in the usual manner, it would decide beyond dispute who really was the best in Europe.

Responses from European football associations were mixed, with the English Football League predictably complaining about the potentially harmful impact on domestic fixtures. However, Hanot was sufficiently heartened to convene a meeting of fifteen European clubs in Paris on 2 April, which agreed to present the idea, reformulated to a knockout rather than league system, to FIFA for approval.

José Altafini scores in AC Milan's 1963 victory over Benfica at Wembley.

Ole Gunnar Solskjaer (centre) scores Manchester United's second goal in injury time in the 1999 Final.

Although formally charged with responsibility for national rather than club football, on 7 May FIFA ratified the new European Cup, which UEFA, its European body, was to take responsibility for running – something of a relief to *L'Equipe*. The first-round draw included clubs such as Chelsea and Hibs who were not necessarily national champions, but from the second season, FIFA stipulated, champions only would compete. The new European Champion Clubs' Cup, with clubs from sixteen countries, kicked off in September 1955.

UEFA
(Union of European Football Associations)

The governing body for European football, it was formed in 1954 under the auspices of FIFA. Its main tournaments are the European Cup, UEFA Cup and the European Championships and it has 51 member countries. Its current President is Lennart Johansson and its headquarters are in Nyon, close to Geneva.

From such modest and speculative beginnings was born the tournament that has thrilled millions of football fans across Europe over the last forty-five years. The stunning 1960 Final between Real Madrid and Eintracht Frankfurt, Celtic's exuberant dethroning of Herrera's Inter Milan in 1967, the 'total football' artistry of Ajax in the early 1970s, the five-year dominance of English clubs, the majesty of Berlusconi's AC Milan and Manchester United's last-minute destruction of an unbelieving Bayern Munich in 1999 – these are only some of the unforgettable memories from this proud competition.

It has also had its blacker side: rioting, violence and, notably, the Heysel disaster of 1985. Bribery and corruption have never been too far away. And changes to the format in recent years have provoked dissent and controversy, particularly over the introduction of the Champions League and its emphasis on money.

But, in spite of the arguments and disputes, Hanot's pioneering spirit lives on in the famous stadia of Europe each year as the great teams gather to contest football's most coveted club prize, the European Cup.

The match which kicked off the new European Cup tournament was played between Sporting Lisbon and Partizan Belgrade on a warm afternoon in Lisbon on 4 September 1955. This landmark game in the history of European football resulted in a toughly-contested 3-3 draw. In the second leg in Belgrade in October, three goals from the 19-year-old Yugoslav striker Milos Milutinovic helped Partizan to a 5-2 victory and a meeting in the Quarter-finals with Real Madrid.

Under club president Santiago Bernabeu, whose energy and vision had led to the construction of the magnificent 125,000 capacity Bernabeu Stadium, Real were evolving into the European team of the decade. The incomparable Alfredo Di Stefano was supported in attack by inside-left and fellow Argentinian Hector Rial and the speedy left-winger Paco Gento. The impeccable defence included Marcos Marquitos and Juan Zarraga, with captain Miguel Munoz in the role of attacking wing-half.

Real began their unparalleled five-year dominance of European football with a 7-0 aggregate victory over Servette Geneva in the first round. Servette, managed by Karl Rappan, the inventor of the 'bolt' defence which was later to evolve into the stultifying *catenaccio* system, were beaten in Geneva by goals from Munoz and inside-forward Rial, and Real added five more at home. On Christmas Day in Madrid, they faced Partizan Belgrade in the Quarter-final and swept the Yugoslavs aside 4-0. In the second leg in a freezing Belgrade they were defeated 3-0, two coming from the high-scoring Milutinovic, but Real squeezed through on aggregate to the semis, where they met AC Milan.

Milan, with such international talents as the international Uruguyan striker Juan Schiaffino and the Swedish forward Nils Liedholm, started the tournament surprisingly badly by squandering a 3-1 lead against Saarbrücken to go down 4-3. However, they won the second leg in Milan 4-1 and in the Quarter-finals demolished Rapid Vienna 7-2 in the second leg, having drawn 1-1 in Austria.

The Semi-final first leg in Madrid between Real and Milan ended in a 4-2 victory for the Spaniards, and a second leg 2-1 win for Milan, secured by two penalties from Dal Monte, was not enough to keep the Italian side in the tournament. Real were through to the Final and their opponents were to be French champions Reims.

Managed by Albert Batteux, and starring French international players such as the stylish defender Robert Jonquet and the brilliant forward Raymond Kopa, Reims had knocked out Aarhus of Copenhagen 4-2 in the first round, Leon Glovacki scoring three. Against Hungary's Mitropa Cup holders Voros Lobogo, a dazzling performance from Kopa overshadowed his opposite number, Nandor Hidegkuti, the master schemer of the Hungarian national team, and Reims won 4-2. In Budapest, the Hungarians came back from 4-1 down to draw 4-4, with three second-half goals. Reims, however, moved through to the semis, where they beat Hibs 3-0.

In the meanwhile, it had been announced that Kopa had agreed to join Real Madrid in the forthcoming season, but his next meeting with Real was to be at the Parc des Princes on 13 June in the first-ever European Cup Final.

Results

First Round	1st leg	2nd leg	Agg
Aarhus v Reims	0-2	2-2	2-4
AC Milan v Saarbrücken	3-4	4-1	7-5
Djurgarden v Gwardia Warsaw	0-0	4-1	4-1
Rapid Vienna v PSV Eindhoven	6-1	0-1	6-2
Rot Weiss Essen v Hibernian	0-4	1-1	1-5
Servette v Real Madrid	0-2	0-5	0-7
Sporting Lisbon v Partizan Belgrade	3-3	2-5	5-8
Voros Lobogo v Anderlecht	6-3	4-1	10-4
Quarter-finals			
Hibernian v Djurgarden	3-1	1-0	4-1
Rapid Vienna v AC Milan	1-1	2-7	3-8
Real Madrid v Partizan Belgrade	4-0	0-3	4-3
Reims v Voros Lobogo	4-2	4-4	8-6
Semi-finals			
Real Madrid v AC Milan	4-2	1-2	5-4
Reims v Hibernian	2-0	1-0	3-0

BRITISH CLUBS

Chelsea, under the chairmanship of Joe Mears, were enthusiastic about the potential of the European Cup, and they had sent a delegate to the April 1955 meeting in Paris. In the first round they were drawn against the Swedes Djurgarden. However, the hostile and suspicious Football League, apparently concerned about the problem of fixture congestion, 'advised' Chelsea to withdraw from the fledgling tournament, which the club reluctantly did. Their place was taken by Gwardia Warsaw.

Hibernian, with the encouragement of the Scottish League (whose chairman Harry Swain was also conveniently chairman of Hibs), had no such qualms and entered the tournament. Although they only finished fifth the previous season, Hibs, with their 'famous five' forward line, were regarded as the top Scottish team of the time and had regularly played friendlies against leading foreign clubs.

In their first game against Rot Weiss Essen in Germany, in front of several thousand British army troops, Hibs won 4-0, Eddie 'Cannonball' Turnbull becoming the first British player to score in a competitive club game in Europe. He followed this up with another goal, and centre-forward Lawrie Reilly and winger Willie Ormond, a future Scotland manager, completed the rout. Back at Easter Road, they drew 1-1 and faced Djurgarden in the Quarter-final. It was the middle of the Swedish winter and their pitch was unplayable, so

Alfredo Di Stefano

Djurgarden moved their home fixture to Partick Thistle's Firhill ground in Glasgow. Hibs comfortably won 3-1, although the Swedes scored first in the 2nd minute, and they ensured their journey to the Semi-final with a 1-0 victory at Easter Road. In the first leg of the semi in Paris against Reims, Hibs faced the legendary Raymond Kopa and winger Michel Hidalgo, who was to manage France in the 1978 World Cup finals. Michel Leblond and Réné Bliard both scored for Reims with Hibs unable to reply and, in the second leg at Easter Road, in front of nearly 45,000 fans, Hibs' departure from the tournament was sealed by a goal by Glovacki from a Kopa pass.

Hibs had blazed the trail for British clubs in the European Cup, a trophy which was to be in British hands ten times by the end of the century.

Alfredo Di Stefano (1926). One of the finest players ever to grace the game, the Argentinian-born Di Stefano left Millionaros of Bogota to join Real Madrid in 1953. Alternating between midfield and centre-forward, Di Stefano was the driving force and inspiration behind the Spanish club's domination of European football between 1956 and 1960. Revered by the fans as the 'blond arrow', he was the aristocrat of Real Madrid. His finest moment was his hat-trick against Eintracht Frankfurt in the 1960 European Cup Final and, by the time of his departure to Espanol in 1964, he had scored 49 goals in the European Cup, a record which still stands. He was European Footballer of the Year in 1957 and 1959. He received 7 Argentinian and 2 Colombian caps and also made 31 appearances for Spain. He later managed Boca Juniors, Sporting Lisbon, Valencia and Real Madrid.

1956

THE FINAL

French polish but Real shine

Real Madrid (2) 4   Reims (2) 3

Parc des Princes, Paris, 13 June 1956
Attendance: 38,000
Referee: Ellis (England)

Home to Paris St Germain and for many years the French international football stadium, the Parc des Princes had been selected as the stage for the first European Cup Final. For Reims, the game was virtually a home fixture, and they began the match with confidence and assurance. Within 12 minutes from the kick-off, the favourites Real unexpectedly found themselves two goals down. In the sixth minute Leblond headed in a Kopa free kick, although Real protested that it had not crossed the line, and four minutes later left-winger Jean Templin added another. A few minutes later, however, Di Stefano ended a run from his own half with a fine shot from the edge of the penalty area past goalkeeper Jacquet to score Real's first goal. With half an hour gone, Rial equalised with a header from a corner. Two-all at half time.

Early in the second half a goal from Real's right winger Joseito was ruled offside by English referee Ellis, and Reims went ahead shortly after, Hidalgo heading in another Kopa free kick. Madrid's equaliser in the 67th minute came from an unlikely quarter, the big defender Marquitos making his way up the pitch to score with a deflection off the leg of Templin.

With just over ten minutes of an exciting game remaining, Gento, the left-winger who was to become the veteran of Real's European campaigns, laid on the winner for Rial. Although a Templin shot against the crossbar briefly raised Reims' hopes, the French club had left it too late and Real Madrid had won the inaugural European Cup.

The teams
Real Madrid: Alonso, Atienza, Lesmes, Munoz, Marquitos, Zarraga, Joseito, Marchal, Di Stefano, Rial, Gento (manager: Villalonga) [Di Stefano 15, Rial 30, 79; Marquitos 67]
Reims: Jacquet, Zimny, Giraudo, Leblond, Jonquet, Siatka, Hidalgo, Glovacki, Kopa, Bliard, Templin (manager: Batteux) [Leblond 6, Templin 10, Hidalgo 62]

As the 1956/57 tournament got under way, it was clear that the inaugural European Cup had been a great success. The competition had been watched by nearly one million spectators and had provided 127 goals – just under 4.5 per game. The clubs were also finding it a prestigious and profitable adjunct to their domestic business.

In 1956, the champions of a further six countries entered – Luxembourg, Czechoslovakia, Romania, Bulgaria, Turkey and England – making a total of 22 clubs. After a preliminary round, the first round proper saw the champions Real Madrid forced to a play-off against Rapid Vienna, having succumbed to a hat-trick, comprising two free kicks and a penalty, from centre-back Ernst Happel in Vienna. A £25,000 payment from Real to the Austrian club was sufficient inducement to stage the play-off in Madrid, and Real duly won 2-0.

In the same round, top Hungarian team Honvéd had travelled to Spain to play Athletic Bilbao days before the Russian tanks rolled into Budapest to crush the Hungarian Revolution. Clearly, the minds of their players – including Ferenc Puskas and Zoltan Czibor – were not focussed on football, and Honvéd lost 6-5 on aggregate, their 'home' leg being played in Brussels.

Real progressed to the Quarter-finals where they disposed of Nice, who had in turn eliminated Scottish champions Rangers. Manchester United, who had annihilated Anderlecht 12-0 and narrowly defeated Borussia Dortmund, also made it through to the semis with a victory over Bilbao.

Italian champions Fiorentina reached the last four by beating Norrköping and Grasshoppers Zurich but displayed the defensive obduracy which would become typical of Italian football in the 1960s. In the Semi-final, Real defeated Manchester United and Fiorentina knocked out Red Star Belgrade, scoring only eight goals in six games. The winners were to meet in the Final in Madrid on 30 May.

Results

Preliminary Round

	1st leg	2nd leg	Agg
Aarhus v Nice	1-1	1-5	2-6(a)
Porto v Athletic Bilbao	1-2	2-3	3-5
Anderlecht v Manchester United	0-2	0-10	0-12
Borussia Dortmund v Spora Luxembourg	4-3	1-2	5-5 7-0 (b)
Dynamo Bucharest v Galatasaray	3-1	1-2	4-3
Slovan Bratislava v CWKS Warsaw	4-0	0-2	4-2

Byes: Real Madrid, Rapid Vienna, Rangers, Honved, Rapid Heerlen, Red Star Belgrade, CDNA Sofia, Grasshoppers Zurich, Fiorentina, Norrköping.

(a): 1st leg in Copenhagen; (b): play-off in Dortmund

First Round

	1st leg	2nd leg	Agg
Athletic Bilbao v Honved	3-2	3-3	6-5(e)
CDNA Sofia v Dynamo Bucharest	8-1	2-3	10-4
Fiorentina v Norrköping	1-1	1-0	2-1(f)
Manchester United v Borussia Dortmund	3-2	0-0	3-2
Rangers v Nice	2-1	1-2	3-3 1-3(d)
Rapid Heerlen v Red Star Belgrade	3-4	0-2	3-6
Real Madrid v Rapid Vienna	4-2	1-3	5-5 2-0(c)
Slovan Bratislava v Grasshoppers Zurich	1-0	0-2	1-2

(c): play-off in Madrid; (d): play-off in Paris; (e): 2nd leg in Brussels; (f) 2nd leg in Rome

Quarter-finals

	1st leg	2nd leg	Agg
Athletic Bilbao v Manchester United	5-3	0-3	5-6
Fiorentina v Grasshoppers Zurich	3-1	2-2	5-3
Real Madrid v Nice	3-0	3-2	6-2
Red Star Belgrade v CDNA Sofia	3-1	1-2	4-3

Semi-finals

	1st leg	2nd leg	Agg
Real Madrid v Manchester United	3-1	2-2	5-3
Red Star Belgrade v Fiorentina	0-1	0-0	0-1

BRITISH CLUBS

Rangers qualified as Scottish champions and received a bye in the preliminary round. They were drawn against Nice in the first round and won 2-1 in the first leg at Ibrox, the scorers being Max Murray and Billy Simpson. In a scrappy and bad-tempered game in Nice, Rangers went 1-0 up through a Johnny Hubbard penalty only to lose two goals in quick succession and have left-half Willie Logie sent off for fighting. They were beaten 3-1 in the play-off in Paris, their solitary goal coming from a French defender.

Manchester United's Busby Babes were the young hopefuls of English football. Half-backs Eddie Colman and the powerful, hugely talented Duncan Edwards, along with forwards Dennis Viollet and Tommy Taylor, were at the heart of the team that had stormed the English league championship by an 11-point margin. United had decided to accept UEFA's offer to take part in the tournament in spite of the misgivings of the Football League. 'This is where the future of the game lies', said prescient manager Matt Busby.

Drawn against Anderlecht in the preliminary round, United won 2-0 in Belgium and, in the return leg at Maine Road (the Old Trafford floodlights were not yet ready), they produced one of their finest-ever European displays to crush Anderlecht 10-0, with Dennis Viollet scoring four. In the first leg of the first round at Maine Road, United went 3-0 up against Borussia Dortmund, but defensive errors reduced the final score to 3-2. In the return leg, a solid defensive performance by United produced a 0-0 draw.

They faced Athletic Bilbao in freezing conditions in Spain in the second round and, although 3-0 down at half-time, they fought back to a 5-3 defeat, their third coming from a magnificent solo goal from Whelan. In the return at Maine Road, a defensive Bilbao tried to maintain their lead but goals from Viollet, who finished the tournament as top scorer with nine, Tommy Taylor and an 84th-minute strike from Johnny Berry, put United into the Semi-final against Real Madrid.

In the first leg in Madrid, played in front of 120,000 spectators, Real were simply too good for United, finishing 3-1 ahead with goals from Rial, Di Stefano and Mateos. In the return at Old Trafford, two goals created by Gento for Kopa and Rial put Real further in front. United replied with two from Taylor and Bobby Charlton, playing his first game in Europe, but they were not enough to keep United in the tournament. However, Manchester United's dreams of European glory were far from over.

THE FINAL

Fiorentina no match for Spanish masters

Real Madrid (0) 2 Fiorentina (0) 0

Santiago Bernabeu Stadium, Madrid, 30 May 1957
Attendance: 124,000
Referee: Horn (Netherlands)

Real's second European Cup Final took place at their stadium in Madrid in front of over 120,000 of their fans.

Their opponents, Italian league champions Fiorentina, possessed players – such as the strong Brazilian right-winger Julinho and the Argentinian inside-forward Miguel Montuori – who were fast, creative and skilful, although not perhaps a match for the legendary ball-artists of Madrid. However, Fiorentina were also a cautious and defensive team, and difficult to break down.

The game was something of a dour stalemate until the 70th minute when Real's inside-right Enrique Mateos sprinted clear towards goal and, although a linesman immediately waved his flag for offside, referee Leo Horn awarded a penalty when Mateos was brought down in the Fiorentina penalty area. Di Stefano gleefully converted the spot-kick. Six minutes later, Raymond Kopa sent a through ball to Gento who held his nerve and beat the Italian goalkeeper Giuliano Sarti.

Real had retained the European Cup and Miguel Munoz again collected the trophy, this time from Generalissimo Franco, himself a supporter of the club.

The teams
Real Madrid: Alonso, Torres, Marquitos, Lesmes, Munoz, Zarraga, Kopa, Mateos, Di Stefano, Rial, Gento (manager: Villalonga) [Di Stefano 70, Gento 76]
AC Fiorentina: Sarti, Magnini, Orzan, Cervato, Scaramucci, Segato, Julinho, Gratton, Virgili, Montuori, Bizzarri (manager: Bernardini)

'Paco' Gento (1933). Francisco Gento joined Real Madrid from Santander in 1953, and became an integral part of that legendary side. An outside-left with electric pace and the dribbling skill to tease and torment defenders, he was supplier to Puskas and Di Stefano and scored many important goals himself, including the winner in the 1958 European Cup Final. He played in all eight of Real's European Finals between 1956 and 1966, and won six European Cup winner's medals, a collection yet to be surpassed.

By the start of the 1957/58 tournament, the European Cup had already established its credentials with the supporters and clubs. Nearly twice as many spectators had watched the 1956/57 competition as had watched in 1955/56, and more new countries – Northern Ireland, Eire and East Germany – had entered their champions.

Ajax and Benfica – both to be future winners of the trophy – were in the draw, although neither progressed very far this year. Benfica went out in the first round to Seville. Ajax, with a bye in the first round, were eliminated in the Quarter-finals 6-2 by Hungarian side Vasas.

Real Madrid, the undisputed champions of Europe and rapidly becoming one of the greatest club sides in the history of the game, had a new manager in the shape of ex-Nice coach Luis Carniglia, and their captain Munoz had retired, although he was soon to reappear at the Bernabeu as successor to Carniglia. The arrival of the tall and technically gifted defender Jose Santamaria from Uruguay was to provide more strength and direction at the back and to supply the forwards, particularly Di Stefano, with even more attacking options.

Busby Babes die at Munich

On 6 February 1958, on their way back from their 5-4 aggregate Quarter-final win over Red Star Belgrade, the Busby Babes' twin-engined Elizabethan aircraft stopped to refuel at Munich. In the snowy conditions, two take-off attempts were abandoned. On the third attempt, the plane could not gain altitude, left the runway, hit a house and burst into flames. Roger Byrne, Geoff Bent, Mark Jones, David Pegg, Liam Whelan, Eddie Colman and Tommy Taylor were killed instantly, and Duncan Edwards died of his injuries two weeks later. Matt Busby was also critically injured. All of European football was shocked by the tragedy and, although Busby eventually recovered, it took him another ten years to rebuild his team into the champions of Europe.

Real and Di Stefano, who was to end the competition as top scorer with ten goals, were in free-scoring form, Di Stefano scoring two in their win over Antwerp in Belgium and four in the 8-0 drubbing of Seville in Madrid. A Semi-final 4-0 victory over Vasas at home, with Di Stefano claiming another hat-trick, was enough to get them to the Final, although Vasas pulled two back in Hungary.

AC Milan needed a play-off to overcome Rapid Vienna but cruised through in the second round against Rangers. A fine away result against Borussia Dortmund took them to the Semi-final against the tragically depleted Manchester United, who could not contain the fast-moving Italians in the away leg at the San Siro.

Spain and Italy were going to be facing each other in a Final again, this time in Brussels' Heysel Stadium on 28 May.

Results

First Round

	1st leg	2nd leg	Agg	
Aarhus v Glenavon	0-0	3-0	3-0	
AC Milan v Rapid Vienna	4-1	2-5	6-6	4-2 (a)
CDNA Sofia v Vasas	2-1	1-6	3-7	
Gardia Warsaw v Wismut Karl-Marx-Stadt	3-1	1-3	4-4	1-1 (b)
Rangers v St Etienne	3-1	1-2	4-3	
Seville v Benfica	3-1	0-0	3-1	
Shamrock Rovers v Manchester United	0-6	2-3	2-9	
Stade Dudelange v Red Star Belgrade	0-5	1-9	1-14	

a) Play-off in Zurich; b) Play-off in East Berlin; Wismut progressed on the toss of a coin. Byes: Ajax, Antwerp, Borussia Dortmund, CCA Bucharest, Dukla Prague, Norrköping, Real Madrid, Young Boys Berne.

Second Round

Antwerp v Real Madrid	1-2	0-6	1-8	
Borussia Dortmund v CCA Bucharest	4-2	1-3	5-5	3-1 (c)
Manchester United v Dukla Prague	3-0	0-1	3-1	
Norrköping v Red Star Belgrade	2-2	1-2	3-4	
Rangers v AC Milan	1-4	0-2	1-6	
Seville v Aarhus	4-0	0-2	4-2	
Wismut Karl-Marx-Stadt v Ajax	1-3	0-1	1-4	
Young Boys Berne v Vasas	1-1	1-2	2-3	

c) Play-off in Bologna.

Quarter-finals

Ajax v Vasas	2-2	0-4	2-6
Borussia Dortmund v AC Milan	1-1	1-4	2-5
Manchester United v Red Star Belgrade	2-1	3-3	5-4
Real Madrid v Seville	8-0	2-2	10-2

Semi-finals

Manchester United v AC Milan	2-1	0-4	2-5
Real Madrid v Vasas	4-0	0-2	4-2

BRITISH CLUBS

Glenavon did well to hold Aarhus to a 0-0 draw in the first leg, but were comfortably disposed of by the Danes 3-0 in the second leg in Belfast.

Rangers, in the competition for the second year running, beat French champions St Etienne 4-3 in the first round and were unfortunate to find themselves facing AC Milan in the second. A Max Murray goal early on kept Rangers ahead 1-0 at Ibrox, until the last fifteen minutes when Milan moved up a gear and scored four by the final whistle through Argentinian Ernesto Grillo (2), Dino Banuffi and Gastone Bean. Rangers' 2-0 defeat at the San Siro was virtually a formality, and the Scottish champions were beginning to discover just how difficult it was to compete with Europe's best.

Manchester United, however, were on song. Relatively unimpressive at home, they were making up for it in Europe. Brushing aside Shamrock Rovers 9-2 in the first round, they took on the great Czech midfielder Josef Masopust's Dukla Prague and made it through to the Quarter-final 3-1. Red Star Belgrade were next and, although the Yugoslavs went 1-0 up at Old Trafford, Bobby Charlton and right-half Eddie Colman scored in the second half. The away leg in Belgrade was a thriller. Viollet opened the scoring in the 2nd minute and young Charlton added two more, one a 30-yard rocket, to make the score 3-0 at half-time. The frantic crowd willed on Belgrade, and the team responded by bringing the score to 3-3. The match finished a draw and United were on course to play AC Milan in the Semi-final.

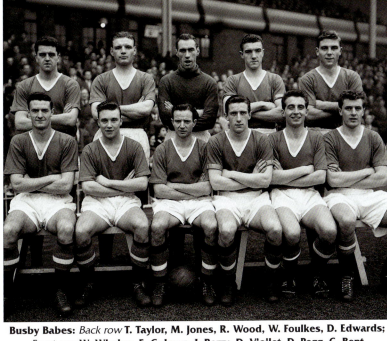

Busby Babes: *Back row* **T. Taylor, M. Jones, R. Wood, W. Foulkes, D. Edwards;** *Front row* **W. Whelan, E. Colman, J. Berry, D. Viollet, D. Pegg, G. Bent**

The horror of the Munich air crash on the way back from Belgrade ended the era of the Busby Babes. Red Star suggested that the Cup be abandoned and the trophy awarded to United, but UEFA decided that the competition had to continue. In early May at Old Trafford a makeshift United side went 1-0 down to Milan after 23 minutes to a goal from Schiaffino, but rallied in the second half with strikes from Viollet and Taylor. They took the 2-1 advantage to the San Siro but the intimidation of the 60,000 crowd, who pelted the players with fruit and vegetables, and the after-effects of the crash contributed to a 4-0 defeat by Milan, two of the goals coming from Schiaffino.

United were not to appear again in the European Cup until the mid-1960s, when Busby's team were to become again a formidable presence in the tournament.

THE FINAL

Gento ensures hat-trick for Real

Read Madrid (0) 3   AC Milan (0) 2 (after extra time)

Heysel Stadium, Brussels, 28 May 1958
Attendance: 70,000
Referee: Alsteen (Belgium)

Played for the first time in a neutral ground, the 1958 Final was a closely-fought struggle between two of the giants of European football.

Marshalled at the back by Cesare Maldini, and possessing forwards with the skill and explosive shooting power of Argentinian Ernesto Grillo and Schiaffino, Milan were at least a worthy match for Di Stefano, Kopa, Gento and Santamaria.

The first half was an edgy, tense affair, neither side wishing to make the mistake which could turn the game against them. In the 59th minute, however, a pass from Liedholm found Schiaffino and the ball was in the net. Di Stefano, whose tireless efforts kept Real in the game, equalised in the 74th minute, only for Grillo to put Milan

ahead again a few minutes later. Within a minute, Rial levelled the score, and it stayed that way until the end of normal time.

Milan nearly went ahead again in extra time when a shot from outside-left Tito Cucchiaroni hit the crossbar. In the 17th minute of extra time, Gento shot at goal, the ball rebounded off a defender, he shot again and the ball bounced into the net past goalkeeper Soldan. Real held onto their lead to claim the European Cup for the third year in succession.

The teams
Real Madrid: Alonso, Atienza, Santamaria, Lesmes, Santisteban, Zarraga, Kopa, Joseito, Di Stefano, Rial, Gento (manager: Carniglia) [Di Stefano 74, Rial 79, Gento 107]
AC Milan: Soldan, Fontana, Beraldo, Bergamaschi, Maldini, Radice, Danova, Liedholm, Schiaffino, Grillo, Cucchiaroni (manager: Puricelli) [Schiaffino 59, Grillo 78]

Juventus, funded by the Agnelli family, the owners of the Fiat car company, were Italian champions and one of the favourites to reach the Final. With the small, elusive Argentinian forward Omar Sivori in attack and the big, powerful Welshman John Charles alternating between centre-forward and centre-half, Juventus were scoring a lot of goals in the Italian league. In the first leg of the qualifying round against Austria's Wiener Sport-Club, Sivori netted a hat-trick. However, in Austria Wiener shocked Juve fans by putting seven goals past the Italians without reply. English champions Wolverhampton Wanderers fared little better and also went out in the first round.

In their hunt for a fourth consecutive trophy, Real Madrid had produced a master-stroke and acquired the tubby, 31-year-old Hungarian genius Ferenc Puskas, now exiled in Europe after the Hungarian Revolution, to line up alongside Kopa and Di Stefano. Real progressed by beating Besiktas 3-1 in the first round (with Di Stefano sent off) and conquerors of Juventus, Wiener, in the Quarter-final 7-1, Di Stefano claiming four goals and Puskas being sent off for retaliation. The dismissals of these two not overly-physical players can perhaps be seen as an indication of the frustration felt by gifted individuals at the increasingly close marking and defensive play being adopted by many clubs.

Atlético Madrid, who qualified as runners-up in the Spanish league, were Real's opponents in the semi-final. Atlético,

Zarraga, the captain of Real Madrid, holds up the European Cup after his team have beaten Reims 2-0 in the final. A beaming Di Stefano looks on.

Results

Qualifying Round	1st leg	2nd leg	Agg	
Ards v Reims	1-4	2-6	3-10	
Atlético Madrid v Drumcondra	8-0	5-1	13-1	
Dynamo Zagreb v Dukla Prague	2-2	1-2	3-4	
Utrecht v Sporting Lisbon	3-4	1-2	4-6	
Jeunesse Esch v IFK Gothenburg	1-2	1-0	2-2	1-5(a)
Juventus v Wiener Sport-Club	3-1	0-7	3-8	
KB Copenhagen v Schalke 04	3-0	2-5	5-5	1-3(b)
Polonia Bytom v MTK Budapest	0-3	0-3	0-6	
Standard Liège v Hearts	5-1	1-2	6-3	
Wismut Karl-Marx-Stadt v Petrolul Ploiesti	4-2	0-2	4-4	4-0(c)

a) Play-off in Gothenburg; b) Play-off in Enschede; c) Play-off in Kiev. Walkovers for Besiktas and Young Boys Berne. Olympiakos and Manchester United withdrew. Byes: Helsinki Palloseura, Real Madrid, Wolverhampton Wanderers.

First Round	1st leg	2nd leg	Agg	
Atlético Madrid v CDNA Sofia	2-1	0-1	2-2	3-1(a)
IFK Gothenburg v Wismut Karl-Marx-Stadt	2-2	0-4	2-6	
MTK Budapest v Young Boys Berne	1-2	1-4	2-6	
Reims v Helsinki Palloseura	4-0	3-0	7-0	
Real Madrid v Besiktas	2-0	1-1	3-1	
Sporting Lisbon v Standard Liège	2-3	0-3	2-6	
Wiener Sport-Club v Dukla Prague	3-1	0-1	3-2	
Wolverhampton Wanderers v Schalke 04	2-2	1-2	3-4	

a) Play-off in Geneva.

Quarter-finals	1st leg	2nd leg	Agg	
Atlético Madrid v Schalke 04	3-0	1-1	4-1	
Standard Liège v Reims	2-0	0-3	2-3	
Wiener Sport-Club v Real Madrid	0-0	1-7	1-7	
Young Boys Berne v Wismut Karl-Marx-Stadt	2-2	0-0	2-2	2-1(b)

(b) Play-off in Amsterdam.

Semi-finals	1st leg	2nd leg	Agg	
Real Madrid v Atlético Madrid	2-1	0-1	2-2	2-1(c)
Young Boys Berne v Reims	1-0	0-3	1-3	

c) Play-off in Zaragoza.

although second-best in the Spanish capital, could still parade a strike-force of the Brazilian Vava, scorer of two goals in the 1958 World Cup Final, Portugal's Mendonca and Spain's scheming inside-forward Joaquim Piero. In the first leg in the Bernabeu, Chuzo put Atlético ahead, Rial equalised, Puskas scored from a penalty and Vava had his penalty saved by new Real goalkeeper Rogelio Dominguez. Two-one to Real. In the second leg, a Collar goal for Atlético was sufficient to force a playoff in Zaragoza, where a goal from Puskas just before half-time proved to be the winner for Real.

Reims, who lost to Real in the first Final, were to meet them again in Stuttgart on 3 June. The French double winners now had in their attack Just Fontaine, scorer of 13 goals in the 1958 World Cup finals. In the Semi-final, they took a 1-0 away defeat by Young Boys Berne back to France and won 3-0. Reims were back in the Final.

BRITISH CLUBS

Ards from Northern Ireland were drawn against eventual Finalists Reims. In the first leg of the qualifying round at Windsor Park, the prolific Just Fontaine scored four before Ards replied through Lowry. Ards lost 6-2 in the second leg.

Scottish champions **Hearts** had won the league by 13 points, aided by their international players, the dashing centre-forward Alex Young and the tough, skilful right-half Dave Mackay. They faced Standard Liège in the qualifying round and were comprehensively beaten 5-1 in Belgium, Crawford gaining their solitary goal. Two goals from centre-forward Willie Bauld at Tynecastle were only consolation strikes, and yet again a Scottish club was outfoxed at an early stage in Europe.

Manchester United were invited by a sympathetic UEFA to compete but, after initial approval from the FA, a curmudgeonly joint Football League and FA committee ruled against their involvement, citing the fact that they were not champions. United withdrew.

Wolverhampton Wanderers were English champions and had recent experience of playing top European teams, beating Moscow Spartak, Moscow Dynamo and Honvéd in a famous series of 'floodlit friendlies' at Molineux. Led by England's captain Billy Wright, Wolves received a bye in the qualifying round and in the first round they drew German side Schalke 04 at home.

Down 1-0 at half-time, Wolves scored two through Broadbent but Koslowski equalised for Schalke. In the second leg, Schalke went 2-0 up and Wolves could only score once through Jackson. The game generated some animosity between the clubs, the Germans accusing Wolves of over-physical play and Wolves complaining of time-wasting. In any event, Wolves were out.

Raymond Kopa

Raymond Kopa (1931). Born in France to a Polish immigrant family named Kopaszewski, Kopa joined Reims in 1950. An inside-forward, he led Reims to the first European Cup Final and joined Real Madrid shortly after, moving to the right wing to accommodate Di Stefano. Kopa was one of the stars in France's 1958 World Cup campaign in Sweden when they finished in third place, and he was named European Footballer of the Year the same year. He was capped 45 times for France. He rejoined Reims in 1959 and retired from football in 1967.

THE FINAL

Reims capitulate to Real in dour final

Real Madrid (1) 2   Reims (0) 0

Neckarstadion, Stuttgart, 3 June 1959
Attendance: 72,000
Referee: Dusch (West Germany)

This was a lacklustre and uninspiring Final, with Reims and manager Batteux loudly criticised in France for their performance.

Puskas did not play, as he was nursing an injury. Real went ahead in the second minute from a goal by Mateos, who later in the half had his penalty well saved by Colonna. Kopa was injured early on, fouled by the Reims winger Jean Vincent, and played little part in the game. Shortly after half-time Di Stefano scored a second for the Spaniards, continuing his record of scoring in every Final, and the final score was 2-0.

Kopa had never really settled into the right-wing position for Real and found it difficult to escape from the shadow of Di Stefano. This was his last game for Real. That summer he moved back to Reims and French football, which was not to see another French club in the European Cup Final until St Etienne in 1976.

The teams
Real Madrid: Dominguez, Marquitos, Santamaria, Zarraga, Santisteban, Ruiz, Kopa, Mateos, Di Stefano, Rial, Gento (manager: Carniglia) [Mateos 2, Di Stefano 47]
Reims: Colonna, Rodzik, Giraudo, Jonquet, Penverne, Leblond, Lamartine, Biliard, Fontaine, Piantoni, Vincent (manager: Batteux)

The 1959/60 European Cup campaign is remembered chiefly for its climax, which is still often described as the greatest game ever played.

Real Madrid had added to their squad with the acquisition of Didi, Brazil's 1958 World Cup finals playmaker, his countryman Canario and Luis del Sol, a hard-working, tricky inside-forward from Real Betis. Manager Carniglia had gone and had been replaced as coach by the erstwhile captain Miguel Munoz.

All-conquering as Real had been in Europe, however, domestically they had come second the previous season to a resurgent Barcelona side who had also won the Spanish Cup. Managed by the obsessive disciplinarian Helenio Herrera, Barcelona were playing fast, attractive football with an attacking line-up of Puskas' old Hungarian teammates Sandor Kocsis, Zoltan Czibor and Ladislav Kubala, as well as the young Luis Suarez (soon to be a superstar with Inter) and the Brazilian Evaristo.

Real had been given a bye in the qualifying round and, in the first round, crushed Luxembourg's Jeunesse Esch 12-2. In the Quarter-final, they eased past Nice 6-3. In the Semi-final they were drawn against Barcelona, who began the competition in similar rampant form with an 8-4 victory over CDNA Sofia and a 7-1 humiliation of Italian champions AC Milan. In the Quarter-final, Barca demonstrated the superiority of European club football over the English game when they handed out a 9-2 footballing lesson to Wolves.

For the first leg of the Semi-final, Herrera dropped crowd favourites Kubala and Czibor, owing partly to a disagreement over bonuses, and Barcelona suffered as a result. Real won both legs 3-1, with Puskas scoring three and Di Stefano two, and Herrera moved to Inter Milan shortly after, his reputation tarnished in Spanish football. In a few years time, however, Herrera would be back at the peak of European football.

Real's opponents were to be Eintracht Frankfurt, the first German side to reach the Final. Frankfurt had eliminated Young Boys Berne and Wiener Sport-Club on their way to the Semi-final, where they out-played and out-thought Rangers to run up an embarrassingly emphatic 12-4 scoreline. Their experienced and talented squad, included veteran inside-left and captain Alfred Pfaff, outside-right Richard Kress and the young centre-forward prodigy Erwin Stein.

Results

Qualifying Round

	1st leg	2nd leg	Agg
ASK Vorwaerts v W. Wanderers	2-1	0-2	2-3
CDNA Sofia v Barcelona	2-2	2-6	4-8
Fenerbahce v Csepel	1-1	3-2	4-3
Jeunesse Esch v LKS Lodz	5-0	1-2	6-2
Linfield v IFK Gothenburg	2-1	1-6	3-7
Nice v Shamrock Rovers	3-2	1-1	4-3
Olympiakos v AC Milan	2-2	1-3	3-5
Rangers v Anderlecht	5-2	2-0	7-2
Red Star Bratislava v Porto	2-1	2-0	4-1
Wiener Sport-Club v Petrolul Ploiesti	0-0	2-1	2-1

Walkover: Eintracht Frankfurt. Withdrew: Kuupio Palloseura. Byes: Odense, Real Madrid, Red Star Belgrade, Sparta Rotterdam.

First Round

AC Milan v Barcelona	0-2	1-5	1-7
Fenerbahçe v Nice	2-1	1-2	3-3 1-5(a)
Odense v Wiener Sport-Club	0-3	2-2	2-5
Rangers v Red Star Bratislava	4-3	1-1	5-4
Real Madrid v Jeunesse Esch	7-0	5-2	12-2
Red Star Belgrade v W. Wanderers	1-1	0-3	1-4
Sparta Rotterdam v IFK Gothenburg	3-1	1-3	4-4 3-1(b)
Young Boys Berne v Eintracht Frankfurt	1-4	1-1	2-5

a) Play-off in Geneva. b) Play-off in Bremen.

Quarter-finals

Barcelona v W. Wanderers	4-0	5-2	9-2
Eintracht Frankfurt v Wiener Sport-Club	2-1	1-1	3-2
Nice v Real Madrid	3-2	0-4	3-6
Sparta Rotterdam v Rangers	2-3	1-0	3-3 2-3(c)

c) Play-off in London.

Semi-finals

Eintracht Frankfurt v Rangers	6-1	6-3	12-4
Real Madrid v Barcelona	3-1	3-1	6-2

BRITISH CLUBS

Linfield began promisingly in the qualifying round at Windsor Park with a 2-1 win over IFK Gothenburg, both goals coming from Jackie Milburn. This narrow margin was soon overturned in Sweden, with Gothenburg dispatching the Northern Ireland club 6-1, including five goals from Ove Ohlssun.

Rangers were back again in the tournament, and attempting to improve their record in a competition which, to date, had been an unhappy one for the club. They started well, with a 7-2 qualifying round victory over Anderlecht and a 5-4 first round elimination of Red Star Bratislava in a couple of bad-tempered games. In the Quarter-final they needed a play-off at Highbury in March to see off Sparta Rotterdam on aggregate 3-2, the big inside-forward Sammy Baird scoring two, with the other an own goal.

Rangers had reached the Semi-final and their footballing reputation had been restored within Europe. However, this did not last for long. They were simply swept aside by Eintracht Frankfurt in Germany and again at Ibrox, losing 12-4 on aggregate to a team whose speedy wing play, midfield domination and overlapping movement bewildered the Scots and awakened the players and spectators to the obvious superiority of the continental game and the equally glaring deficiencies of Scottish domestic football.

A similar gap between the tactical sophistication of English and continental football had been observed two months earlier at Molineux where Barcelona, following a 4-0 victory in Spain, gave **Wolves** a 5-2 thrashing in the Quarter-finals. Wolves, admittedly without the central figure of Billy Wright, now retired, discovered that their muscular long-ball game, so successful in England, was easily exposed by top European teams. Barcelona's intelligent and patient defending, and their speed on the counter-attack, were too much for the brave but naïve Midlanders. In the game at Molineux, the brilliant Kocsis scored four, the other coming from Villaverde.

Ferenc Puskas slots home Real's fourth goal from the penalty spot.

Magical Real Madrid thrill Hampden

Read Madrid (3) 7   Eintracht Frankfurt (1) 3

Hampden Park, Glasgow, 18 May 1960
Attendance: 127,000
Referee: Mowat (Scotland)

One of the finest displays of artistic and attacking football ever witnessed, the 1960 European Cup Final was a breathtaking game which thrilled the huge crowd at Scotland's national stadium.

Although Frankfurt had proved they were one of the top teams in Europe, they were quite unable to deal with the imagination and wizardry of the magnificent Spaniards, in particular Di Stefano and Puskas. Although Frankfurt scored first after 20 minutes through a Kress volley at the near post, a Di Stefano shot from a Canario cross soon levelled the score. Three minutes later Di Stefano pounced again from close range, and just on half-time a crashing left-foot angle shot from Puskas made it 3-1.

Ten minutes into the second half, a Puskas penalty sent the German goalkeeper Loy the wrong way, and shortly after it was Puskas again with an improbable header from a Gento cross. Then Puskas picked up his fourth goal, spinning round and blasting a shot into the top corner of the net. A Stein goal 15 minutes from time restored some respectability to the Germans, but almost immediately a Puskas pass to Di Stefano made it three for the Argentinian master and seven for Real. Two minutes later Stein took advantage of a Real defensive blunder to grab a consolation goal for Frankfurt. However, the energetic and skilful German side, who had played well enough

probably to have beaten any other side in Europe, had been completely outclassed by the sheer brilliance of Real Madrid.

Real went on a lap of honour around the old stadium, and the crowd rose in salute. It was to prove a magnificent swansong for Real, as the club's period of dominance was passing and the young pretenders of Benfica were waiting to seize the European crown. For Frankfurt, it was to be their last appearance in the European Cup.

The teams
Real Madrid: Dominguez, Marquitos, Pachin, Vidal, Santamaria, Zarraga, Canario, Del Sol, Di Stefano, Puskas, Gento (manager: Munoz) [Di Stefano 26, 29, 74; Puskas 45, 54, 60, 72]
Eintracht Frankfurt: Loy, Lutz, Eigenbrodt, Hofer, Weilbacher, Stinka, Kress, Lindner, Stein, Pfaff, Meier (manager: Osswald) [Kress 20, Stein 74, 76]

Ferenc Puskas (1927). Puskas was one of the greatest footballers of the 20th century. His stocky figure belied his artistry and he was a master-finisher for Hungary and Real Madrid. Known as the 'Galloping Major' after his time playing for Hungarian Army team Honved, he captained Hungary in their 6-3 and 7-1 routs of England in 1953 and joined Real Madrid in 1958. An inside-left, his explosive left foot brought him four goals in the 1960 European Cup Final and a hat-trick in Real's 5-3 defeat by Benfica in the 1962 Final. With Di Stefano, he formed the strike force of that marvellous Real team and, although he retired from playing in 1966, he scaled European heights again in 1971 when he managed Panathinaikos to the 1971 European Cup Final. He made his first appearance for Hungary at the age of 18 and scored 83 goals in 84 international appearances.

Barcelona keeper Ramallets thwarts a Benfica attack in the 1961 Final in Berne.

THE *1960-61* SEASON

Results

Preliminary Round

	1st leg	2nd leg	Agg	
Aarhus v Legia Warsaw	3-0	0-1	3-1	
Barcelona v Lierse	2-0	3-0	5-0	
Fredrikstad v Ajax	4-3	0-0	4-3	
HJK Helsinki v Malmö	1-3	1-2	2-5	
Hearts v Benfica	1-2	0-3	1-5	
Juventus v CDNA Sofia	2-0	1-4	3-4	
Limerick v Young Boys Berne	0-5	2-4	2-9	
Rapid Vienna v Besiktas	4-0	0-1	4-1	
Red Star Belgrade v Ujpest Dózsa	1-2	0-3	1-5	
Reims v Jeunesse Esch	6-1	5-0	11-1	

Walkovers: Wismut Karl-Marx-Stadt, Spartak Kralove. Withdrawn: Glenavon, CCA Bucharest. Byes: Hamburg, Burnley, Panathinaikos, Real Madrid.

First Round

	1st leg	2nd leg	Agg	
Aarhus v Fredrikstad	3-0	1-0	4-0	
Benfica v Ujpest Dózsa	6-2	1-2	7-4	
Burnley v Reims	2-0	2-3	4-3	
Malmö v CDNA Sofia	1-0	1-1	2-1	
Rapid Vienna v Wismut Karl-Marx-Stadt	3-1	0-2	3-3	1-0
Real Madrid v Barcelona	2-2	1-2	3-4	
Spartak Kralove v Panathinaikos	1-0	0-0	1-0	
Young Boys Berne v Hamburg	0-5	3-3	3-8	

Quarter-finals

	1st leg	2nd leg	Agg	
Barcelona v Spartak Kralove	4-0	1-1	5-1	
Benfica v Aarhus	3-1	4-1	7-2	
Burnley v Hamburg	3-1	1-4	4-5	
Rapid Vienna v Malmö	2-0	2-0	4-0	

Semi-finals

	1st leg	2nd leg	Agg	
Barcelona v Hamburg	1-0	1-2	2-2	1-0(a)
Benfica v Rapid Vienna	3-0	1-1	4-1	

a) Play-off in Brussels

The European Cup was now the continent's major footballing event, with over two million spectators attending the 52 matches the previous year. Real Madrid's glorious exhibition of football at Hampden Park had been a fitting finale to what had been a successful and popular season.

However, the balance of football power had now begun to shift in Europe and, like all great teams, Real were discovering just how difficult it was to sustain their exalted position. The main threat to European clubs still came from the Iberian peninsula, but in this tournament Barcelona and Lisbon, rather than Madrid, were to provide the top teams and the Finalists.

For the second successive year, Barcelona had won the Spanish championship, this time under new coach Ljubisa Brocic, and they started their campaign with a 5-0 victory over Lierse. Real had a bye in the preliminary round and, in a repeat of the previous season's Semi-final, they were drawn against Barcelona in the first round.

With centre-half Santamaria injured, and with new signing Swedish centre-forward Agne Simonsson ineligible, nonetheless Real went ahead through Mateos within two minutes in the Madrid first leg. Suarez equalised with a free kick and Gento made it 2-1 to Real. Just before the end, Kocsis fell in the penalty area and, in spite of Real's protestations, English referee Arthur Ellis awarded a penalty to Barcelona, which was converted by Suarez.

The match finished 2-2: the first time Real had not won a home game in the European Cup. The kings of European football were no longer invincible. The point was reinforced in the second leg when, with the score 1-0 to Barca, a flying Evaristo header ten minutes from time put Real out of the competition, in spite of a late Canario goal.

The Catalans swept aside Spartak Kralove 5-1 and met Hamburg, conquerors of Burnley, in the Semi-final in April.

A Barcelona 1-0 home win, with the goal from Evaristo, was followed by Hamburg going 2-0 up at home. Barca were rescued by a header from Kocsis, which took the clubs to a play-off in Brussels. Another Evaristo goal separated the teams, and Barcelona were in the Final, where they were to meet Benfica.

Benfica, the 'Eagles of Lisbon', were emerging as one of the best and most exciting sides in Europe. Under the management of their much-travelled and widely-respected Hungarian manager Bela Guttman, they had a formidable line-up of talented players – indomitable, lavishly moustachioed centre-half Figueiredo Germano, Europe's finest goalkeeper Costa Pereira, the high-scoring centre-forward and captain Jose Aguas, outside-right Jose Augusto and the inside-left and playmaker Mario Coluna. They were an attacking side, often playing five up front.

They progressed through the tournament with easy wins over Hearts, Ujpest Dózsa and Aarhus, and met Rapid Vienna in the Semi-finals. The Austrians went down 3-0 in Lisbon, with goals from Coluna, Aguas and winger Domiciano Cavem, and in Vienna, with the score 1-1 in the second half, the English referee Reg Leafe turned down Rapid's appeal for a penalty. A riot ensued with players and spectators fighting on the pitch, and the game was abandoned. UEFA awarded the game to Benfica and banned Rapid from playing home European games in the stadium for three years. This was the first instance of crowd trouble in the tournament but was not to be the last.

BRITISH CLUBS

Glenavon were drawn against East German side Wismut Karl-Marx-Stadt but, as East Germans were not allowed visas to travel to Great Britain, they had to find another 'home' ground. The potential financial and logistical problems were such that they withdrew from the competition.

Hearts, with recently-arrived right-winger Gordon Smith who had played for Hibs in the 1955/56 tournament, faced the eventual champions Benfica in the preliminary round. Although Alex Young scored, Hearts went down 2-1 at Tynecastle. A 3-0 defeat in Lisbon marked their last-ever appearance in the European Cup.

Burnley, with a bye in the preliminaries, met a Fontaine-less Reims at home in the first round. Goals from Robson within 45 seconds and another from McIlroy gave them a 2-0 lead at Turf Moor. In Paris, a 33rd-minute Robson goal put them one ahead at half time. Reims (this time without Kopa) then scored three, but a Connelly strike ensured a 4-3 aggregate victory to the Lancastrians.

Hamburg, with the great international centre-forward Uwe Seeler leading the attack, were the opponents for the Quarter-final. In January, in front of a 32,000 crowd at Turf Moor, Burnley went ahead after eight minutes, scored another with a Pilkington 20-yard shot and grabbed a third through Robson, before Dorfel scored for Hamburg.

By March, however, fixture congestion had caught up with Burnley, and a tired team contested the second leg in Germany. Three-nil down shortly after half-time, Burnley's hopes were raised by a 55th-minute Harris goal, but Hamburg scored another through Seeler, and Burnley's European Cup run was halted 4-5 on aggregate. Burnley, like Hearts, have never played in the competition since.

THE FINAL

Lisbon Eagles swoop to conquer

Benfica (2) 3 Barcelona (1) 2

Wankdorf Stadium, Berne, 31 May 1961
Attendance: 27,000
Referee: Dienst (Switzerland)

Although the attendance was disappointing, those who did watch this game between the two Iberian giants witnessed an enthralling and absorbing contest.

Barca's forward line – Kubala, Kocsis, Evaristo, Suarez and Czibor – was feared throughout Europe, but they faced a commanding defence in Costa Pereira and Germano, as well as, in Coluna, Augusto and Cavem, players who could turn the game in a flash of inspiration.

As Benfica's manager Guttman had feared, Barcelona took an early lead through a Kocsis diving header in the 19th minute, but the anticipated flood of Spanish goals did not materialise. In fact, Barcelona were rocked by two goals in two minutes. The first came from Aguas after goalkeeper Antonio Ramallets had left his line too quickly to cover Cavem, and the second was again down to Ramallets, when

the keeper punched a headed backpass against the crossbar and the ball bounced behind the goal line.

In the 55th minute, Benfica went further ahead with a Coluna volley from a cross from Cavem. With the score now 3-1 to Benfica, Barcelona threw themselves into attack. They surged forward and Kocsis and Kubala both hit the post, but Costa Pereira dealt with virtually everything that was on target. He was, however, beaten by a fine strike from Czibor, who shortly after saw another shot rebound off the post. Benfica held on and, at the final whistle, the European Cup had left Spain for the first time.

The teams
Benfica: Costa Pereira, Mario Joao, Angelo, Neto, Germano, Cruz, Jose Augusto, Santana, Aguas, Coluna, Cavem (manager: Guttman) [Aguas 30, Ramallets (o.g.) 32, Coluna 55]

Barcelona: Ramallets, Foncho, Gracia, Verges, Gensana, Garay, Kubala, Kocsis, Evaristo, Suarez, Czibor (manager: Orizaola) [Kocsis 19, Czibor 75]

Results

Preliminary Round

	1st leg	2nd leg	Agg
ASK Vorwaerts v Linfield	3-0 (a)		
CCA Bucharest v FK Austria	0-0	0-2	0-2
CDNA Sofia v Dukla Prague	4-4	1-2	5-6
Gornik Zabrze v Tottenham Hotspur	4-2	1-8	5-10
IFK Gothenburg v Feyenoord	0-3	2-8	2-11
Monaco v Rangers	2-3	2-3	4-6
Nuremberg v Drumcondra	5-0	4-1	9-1
Panathinaikos v Juventus	1-1	1-2	2-3
Servette v Hibernians Malta	5-0	2-1	7-1
Spora Luxemburg v Odense	0-6	2-9	2-15
Sporting Lisbon v Partizan Belgrade	1-1	0-2	1-3
Standard Liège v Fredrikstad	2-1	2-0	4-1
Vasas v Real Madrid	0-2	1-3	1-5

a) Linfield withdrew after first leg. Byes: Fenerbahçe, Valkeakosken Haka, Benfica.

First Round

	1st leg	2nd leg	Agg
ASK Vorwaerts v Rangers	1-2	1-4	2-6(b)
FK Austria v Benfica	1-1	1-5	2-6
Odense v Real Madrid	0-3	0-9	0-12
Fenerbahçe v Nuremberg	1-2	0-1	1-3
Feyenoord v Tottenham Hotspur	1-3	1-1	2-4
Partizan Belgrade v Juventus	1-2	0-5	1-7
Servette v Dukla Prague	4-3	0-2	4-5
Standard Liège v Valkeakosen Haka	5-1	2-0	7-1

b) Played in Malmo, Sweden. ASK Vorwaerts denied entry to UK.

Quarter-finals

	1st leg	2nd leg	Agg	
Dukla Prague v Tottenham Hotspur	1-0	1-4	2-4	
Juventus v Real Madrid	0-1	1-0	1-1	1-3(c)
Nuremberg v Benfica	3-1	0-6	3-7	
Standard Liège v Rangers	4-1	0-2	4-3	

c) Play-off in Paris

Semi-finals

	1st leg	2nd leg	Agg
Benfica v Tottenham Hotspur	3-1	1-2	4-3
Real Madrid v Standard Liège	4-0	2-0	6-0

As the 1961/62 tournament began, some observers were suggesting that Real Madrid, although again Spanish champions, were becoming an ageing side and losing the pace to continue at the highest level of European football. Heresy, indeed, to question the abilities of Di Stefano, Gento and Puskas, but they could not stay at the top for ever.

Their early performances, however, indicated otherwise. A 5-1 victory over Vasas in the preliminary round was followed by a 12-0 aggregate trouncing of Odense, with Di Stefano scoring a hat-trick in Madrid. In the Quarter-finals, Di Stefano scored the only goal against Juventus in Turin, but in the return in the Bernabeu a stunned Spanish crowd of 72,000 saw Sivori do likewise, with a sidefoot shot from a Charles cross. Till that point, Real had not been beaten at home in the European Cup, and this seemed further evidence that the old order was changing.

However, in the play-off in Paris they put together a convincing performance to win 3-1 and progress to the Semi-finals against Belgium's Standard Liège, against whom a 6-0 aggregate victory ensured Real's appearance in the Final.

Benfica had unveiled Guttman's latest signing shortly after the previous year's Final. Eusebio da Silva Ferreira, an 18-year-old striker from Mozambique, had been pinched from under the noses of rival Sporting Lisbon, and was to prove Benfica's and Portugal's finest-ever player.

The club began the defence of their title with a convincing 6-2 win over FK Austria and faced Nuremberg in the Quarter-final. Eusebio was injured for the first leg in Germany but Guttman introduced another signing, the 17-year-old Antonio Simoes, a fast and exciting winger. Benfica were surprisingly beaten 3-1 but got their revenge in Lisbon where a recovered Eusebio scored twice in a 6-0 victory, with Benfica two goals up in the first four minutes. They were drawn against English champions Tottenham Hotspur in the Semi-finals.

Benfica took a 3-1 home win to White Hart Lane, where a spirited and fighting performance from the home side was not enough to break down the Portuguese team's firm but skilful defending, and Benfica were through to the Final for the second year in succession.

BRITISH CLUBS

Linfield, drawn against ASK Vorwaerts in the preliminary round, were defeated 3-0 in the first leg in East Berlin. The difficulties encountered in arranging visas resulted in Linfield pulling out of the second leg.

The performances of the two mainland British teams in the tournament, however, went some way to restoring the image of the British game in European eyes.

Rangers, with brilliant left-half Jim Baxter, predatory forwards Jimmy Millar and Ralph Brand, goal-scoring winger Davie Wilson and arch-schemer Ian McMillan, were fielding what many feel was their greatest-ever side. Under manager Scot Symon, they were dominating the Scottish game.

They started in the preliminary round with a 6-4 defeat of AS Monaco, with three coming from right-winger Alex Scott, and were drawn away in the first leg of the first round to Vorwaerts. They won the tie 2-1, with a penalty from left-back and captain Eric Caldow and a Ralph Brand goal, but, due to the refusal of the government to grant the East

Germans a visa, Rangers played their 'home' tie in Malmö a week later. By half-time Rangers were a goal up, but the fog closed in and the referee abandoned the game. With all the pressures of a busy domestic season, Rangers wanted the tie over with quickly and agreed to play the next day. A cold Swedish morning saw Rangers win 4-1, two coming from inside-right McMillan.

In the Quarter-finals in February they met Standard Liège, who had conceded only two goals in their previous two ties, and a 4-1 defeat in Belgium made the Semi-finals a distant prospect for the Scots. A 2-0 victory at Ibrox against a well-organised and defensive Liège, with goals again coming from Brand and Caldow, was not sufficient for Rangers to progress further that year.

Tottenham Hotspur had just won the English cup and league 'double', the first team to do so in the 20th century and, like Rangers, had probably the best team in their history. Captained by the visionary Danny Blanchflower, and with a forward line containing speedy winger Cliff Jones, bustling centre-forward Bobby Smith and Scottish playmaker John White, Spurs were the English team of the era.

In the preliminary round against Gornik Zabrze, Spurs were shaken to find themselves 4-0 down after 60 minutes, but Jones and winger Terry Dyson each replied to make the score 4-2. A thrilling 8-1 victory at White Hart Lane, initiated by a Blanchflower penalty and including a hat-trick from Jones, took the club to the first round against Feyenoord, whom they beat 3-1 in Holland and with whom they drew 1-1 at home.

By now the prolific goalscorer Jimmy Greaves had arrived from an unhappy spell at AC Milan and, although he was ineligible for the Quarter-finals, Spurs overcame Dukla Prague, a 4-1 win at home in blizzard conditions negating a 1-0 defeat in Czechoslovakia. Cup-holders Benfica awaited Spurs in the Semi-final.

In the first leg in Lisbon in March, with Greaves making his European debut for the club, a storming onslaught from the home side saw Simoes and Jose Augusto put Benfica 2-0 ahead within 20 minutes. A Bobby Smith headed goal was followed by a similar strike from Augusto, and Benfica won 3-1, although Spurs protested about two disallowed goals.

In a frantic, pulsating return game at White Hart Lane, Aguas put the Portuguese further ahead within 16 minutes, but the lead was cut back by Smith and Blanchflower. Although Spurs hit both posts, and towards the end a shot from right-half Dave Mackay cannoned off the crossbar, Benfica finished 4-3 winners on aggregate. The magnificence of Costa Pereira in goal and the dominant figure of centre-half Germano had prevented the first appearance of a British club in the Final.

Eusebio

Eusebio (da Silva Ferreira) (1942). Certainly Portugal's greatest ever player, Eusebio – the 'Black Pearl' – was born in Mozambique and made his debut for Benfica at the age of 19 in 1961, the year he earned his first cap. A prodigious goal scorer, Eusebio won the Golden Boot at the 1966 World Cup with nine goals, four coming in Portugal's fightback against North Korea, and appeared five times for Benfica in the European Cup Final, winning twice. In 1965 he was awarded the honour of European Footballer of the Year and he made 64 appearances for Portugal. He finished his playing career in North America and came back to coach Benfica in 1977.

THE FINAL

Eusebio strikes to retain Cup for Benfica

Benfica (2) 5   Real Madrid (3) 3

Olympic Stadium, Amsterdam, 2 May 1962
Attendance: 61,000
Referee: Horn (Netherlands)

With two of the great attacking sides of Europe competing for the European Cup, this game promised much. In the event, it more than lived up to expectations, and was a joyous and exhilarating exhibition of fast and fluid football, capped by eight goals.

With only 38 minutes gone, Puskas, now in his 36th year, had already claimed three goals, and was thriving on the service of Di Stefano, himself 35 years old, Gento and Del Sol. This remarkable Hungarian remains the only player to have scored hat-tricks in two European Cup Finals. However, Benfica had pulled two back through Aguas in the 25th minute and Cavem in the 34th, with Real's goalkeeper Araquistain appearing to be at fault on both counts. At half-time the scoreline was 3-2 in Real's favour.

The astute Guttman, however, had noticed Di Stefano's influence on play, and he detailed Cavem to mark the Argentinian closely in the second half. With Puskas' main line of supply cut off, and with the ageing Madrid side tiring

and right-back Casado limping, Benfica began to dominate the game. Coluna took advantage of a mistake by Puskas, and brought Benfica level with a 25-yard strike.

Then 19-year-old Eusebio took over. Brought down in the box by a desperate Pachin, he deceived Araquistain with his penalty kick. Three minutes later, he connected with a short pass from a Coluna free kick and the ball went in the net via a defender. Towards the end, Di Stefano appealed for a penalty for a Germano obstruction, but it was turned down and the game was now out of Real's grasp. Benfica were again champions of Europe, and deservedly so.

The game can be seen as the final triumph of open, attacking football in the tournament before the dour and cynical defensive play that lay ahead.

The teams
Benfica: Costa Pereira, Mario Joao, Angelo, Cavem, Germano, Cruz, Jose Augusto, Eusebio, Aguas, Coluna, Simoes (manager: Guttman) [Aguas 25, Cavem 34, Coluna 51, Eusebio 65, 68]
Real Madrid: Araquistain, Casado, Miera, Felo, Santamaria, Pachin, Tejada, Del Sol, Di Stefano, Puskas, Gento (manager: Munoz) [Puskas 17, 23, 38]

The European Cup had by now become the most prestigious and financially rewarding football club competition in the continent. The crowds in the stadiums and those watching on television were growing dramatically in number, and there were huge rewards for winning the Cup, including the lucrative 'friendlies' which the winner could expect. The pressures on the clubs, therefore, were enormous. Terrified of elimination, many clubs were employing defensive formations, hoping to frustrate the opposition away and win at home, by the odd goal, if necessary. Adventurous football, with a few exceptions, was on the wane and tactics were increasingly based on caution and containment.

In the 1962/63 tournament, Real Madrid fell at the first hurdle. A 3-3 draw at the Bernabeu with Anderlecht featured an exceptional individual goal from the young Anderlecht striker Paul Van Himst. In Belgium, the Spaniards were defeated by a goal from Jef Jurion, and went out 4-3 on aggregate. What was now seen as a comparatively weak overall line-up nonetheless contained Portuguese champions Benfica and AC Milan, the Italian champions, both of whom were favourites to reach the Final.

Bela Guttman had left Benfica that summer to join Penarol of Uruguay, and his role as manager had been assumed by the Chilean Fernando Riera, a disciplinarian who was less enthusiastic than Guttman about the merits of attacking football. Shortly after the club's second round 6-2 defeat of Norrköping, in which Eusebio scored four, the centre-forward position went to the strong and imposing Jose Torres. The great goal scorer Aguas was soon to move to

Austria Vienna. Unfortunately for the Portuguese, centre-half Germano incurred an injury and was ruled out for the rest of the season.

In the Quarter-finals, a narrow 2-1 win over Dukla Prague in Lisbon and a 0-0 draw in Prague, with Benfica kept in the game by Costa Pereira's inspired goalkeeping, saw Benfica through to the semis. A home 3-1 result over Feyenoord, who had beaten Reims in the previous round, proved sufficient to see the club to the Final at Wembley on 22 May, the first Final to be played in Britain.

AC Milan, whose skipper and sweeper Cesare Maldini was one of only three players in the team to have played in the 1958 Final, had been joined from Sao Paulo by the aggressive Brazilian centre-forward Jose Altafini, who was to finish this year's competition as top scorer with 14 goals. Playing at inside-forward was the young Gianni Rivera, the 'Golden Boy' of Italian football with the breathtaking skills, who was to prove such an important supplier to the rampant Altafini. Alongside Rivera was the Brazilian inside-right Dino Sani and goal-scoring winger Paulo Barison.

In the preliminary round they destroyed Union Luxembourg 14-0, eight of the goals coming from Altafini, and in the first round they knocked out English champions Ipswich Town 4-2. In the Quarter-finals an 8-1 aggregate result finished off Turkey's Galatasaray, with Altafini scoring a hat-trick in the home leg. They then ended Dundee's hopes in the Semi-final with a ruthless but effective display at the San Siro. Next to come was Benfica in the Final.

Results

First Round

	1st leg	2nd leg	Agg	
AC Milan v US Luxembourg	8-0	6-0	14-0	
ASK Vorwaerts v Dukla Prague	0-3	0-1	0-4	
CDNA Sofia v Partizan Belgrade	2-1	4-1	6-2	
Dundee v Cologne	8-1	0-4	8-5	
Dynamo Bucharest v Galatasaray	1-1	0-3	1-4	
FK Austria v HJK Helsinki	5-3	2-0	7-3	
Floriana v Ipswich Town	1-4	0-10	1-14	
Frederikstad v Vasas	1-4	0-7	1-11	
Linfield v Esbjerg	1-2	0-0	1-2	
Norrköping v Partizan Tirana	2-0	1-1	3-1	
Polonia Bytom v Panathinaikos	2-1	4-1	6-2	
Real Madrid v Anderlecht	3-3	0-1	3-4	
Servette v Feyenoord	1-3	3-1	4-4	1-3(a)
Shelbourne v Sporting Lisbon	0-2	1-5	1-7	

a) Play-off in Dusseldorf. Byes: Reims, Benfica.

Second Round

AC Milan v Ipswich Town	3-0	1-2	4-2	
CDNA Sofia v Anderlecht	2-2	0-2	2-4	
Esbjerg v Dukla Prague	0-0	0-5	0-5	
Feyenoord v Vasas	1-1	2-2	3-3	1-0(b)
FK Austria v Reims	3-2	0-5	3-7	
Galatasaray v Polonia Bytom	4-1	0-1	4-2	
Norrköping v Benfica	1-1	1-5	2-6	
Sporting Lisbon v Dundee	1-0	1-4	2-4	

b) Play-off in Antwerp

Quarter-finals

Anderlecht v Dundee	1-4	1-2	2-6	
Benfica v Dukla Prague	2-1	0-0	2-1	
Galatasaray v AC Milan	1-3	0-5	1-8	
Reims v Feyenoord	0-1	1-1	1-2	

Semi-finals

AC Milan v Dundee	5-1	0-1	5-2
Feyenoord v Benfica	0-0	1-3	1-3

BRITISH CLUBS

Linfield again exited at the preliminary stage, a creditable 0-0 away draw against Esbjerg being insufficient to turn around a 1-2 home defeat.

Unlikely English representatives in the competition this year were **Ipswich Town** who, under the guidance of ex-Tottenham defender Alf Ramsey, had gained promotion from the Second Division the previous year and won the league title at their first attempt.

Essentially a journeyman side, and a mixture of youngsters and older professionals, Ipswich had reached the pinnacle of the English game through Ramsey's astute tactical understanding and management skills and the goal scoring of their forwards, England international Ray Crawford and Ted Philips. But they were novices in Europe.

Not that this was evident in the preliminary round, however, as Crawford added to his tally by putting seven goals past Floriana in Ipswich's 14-1 aggregate humiliation of the Maltese team. Coming against AC Milan in the first round, a 3-0 defeat in the San Siro and a 2-1 win at home saw them out of the competition.

Another British team playing in the European Cup for the first time was **Dundee**, the Scottish champions. New to the competition they may have been, but their performance in this year's tournament outclassed many of the more experienced sides.

Playing on the right wing was veteran Gordon Smith, who had moved from Hearts in 1961, and now became the first player to appear in the European Cup with three different clubs. In defence was centre-half Ian Ure, a tall imposing stopper, while up front were inside-forward Andy Penman and goal-scoring Scottish international centre-forward Alan Gilzean.

In the first round at home against Cologne they ran up an 8-1 victory over the top German side, Gilzean contributing a hat-trick, and held on in the second leg of an ill-tempered match to lose 4-0 and qualify for the second round. They then faced Sporting Lisbon, where a 1-0 deficit away was converted into a 4-2 win, thanks to Gilzean's second consecutive hat-trick at Dens Park.

In the Quarter-finals away to Anderlecht, who had eliminated Real Madrid, a 60-second goal from Gilzean and another later in the game contributed to a shock 4-1 victory, and they beat the Belgian champions again at home, this time 2-1.

In April Dundee contested the first leg of the Semi-final at the San Siro against AC Milan, where the Scots equalised a third-minute Italian goal before half-time, but four Milan goals in the second half settled the tie. Dundee goalkeeper Bert Slater claimed the photographers' flashbulbs had obscured his vision throughout the game, but the reality was that the Scots were over-run in the second half.

Dundee managed a 1-0 win in the second leg, Gilzean yet again finding the net, but he was sent off for retaliation on Milan defender Benitez shortly before full time.

1963 THE FINAL

Altafini brings European Cup to Italy

AC Milan (0) 2 Benfica (1) 1

Wembley Stadium, London, 22 May 1963
Attendance: 45,000
Referee: Holland (England)

The famous old stadium was less than half full as Wembley welcomed its first European Cup fixture, fittingly the Final.

AC Milan, as was increasingly the Italian fashion, had arrived in England determined not to lose, and had dropped goal-scoring winger Barison and detailed Gino Pivatelli to man-mark Benfica playmaker Coluna. Benfica were without centre-half Germano, who was still injured, but otherwise were at full strength.

The game started cagily, neither side wishing to cede an advantage, until a Torres interception in the 18th minute fed Eusebio who sped down the right, leaving left-half Giovanni Trapattoni in his wake, and shot past goalkeeper Moraio Ghezzi in off the far post.

In the second half, Milan's greater determination and purpose began to dominate Benfica's artistry. In the 58th minute, Rivera found Altafini on the edge of the crowded penalty box. The Brazilian spun round and placed a low shot to the right of Costa Pereira. Soon after, Benfica suffered another blow when Pivatelli upended Coluna, who effectively became a passenger for the rest of the game.

Twelve minutes later the game was won. A Portuguese defensive mix-up allowed Rivera to deflect the ball off a defender into the path of Altafini standing just over the centre-line. He ran half the length of the pitch, shot, the ball came back off Costa Pereira and Altafini netted the rebound for his 14th goal of the tournament. Two-one to Milan, and Italy had their first European Cup. It was to stay in Italy for the following two seasons.

The teams
AC Milan: Ghezzi, David, Trebbi, Benitez, Maldini, Trapattoni, Pivatelli, Sani, Altafini, Rivera, Mora (manager: Rocco) [Altafini 58, 70]

Benfica: Costa Pereira, Cavem, Cruz, Humberto, Raul, Coluna, Jose Augusto, Santana, Torres, Eusebio, Simoes (manager: Riera) [Eusebio 18]

José Altafini scores AC Milan's winner past Costa Pereira.

Benfica started the new campaign nervously, and then collapsed altogether. They could only draw with Distillery away in the first round, but they beat the Northern Ireland champions convincingly at home. They were eliminated in the next round by Borussia Dortmund although they had won the first leg 2-1. Without Eusebio, Germano and Costa Pereira, they were defeated 5-0 in Germany.

As well as holders AC Milan, Italy were represented by league champions Inter Milan, co-habitants of the San Siro Stadium and newcomers to the European Cup. Owned by millionaire Angelo Moratti and managed by ex-Barcelona coach Helenio Herrera, Inter were gaining an unenviable reputation as the prime exponents of the stultifying *catenaccio* system.

Although Inter possessed creative attacking talents such as Sandro Mazzola, the subtle provider Luis Suarez and tall, speedy Brazilian right-winger Jair, their sweeper Armando Picchi and full-backs Giacinto Facchetti and Tarcisio Burgnich ran a tight and solid defence. In goal was the ever-reliable Giuliano Sarti. The system was not pretty but, for a while, it was extremely effective.

Inter began with a tedious 1-0 victory over Everton, and a 4-1 win against Monaco. In the Quarter-finals they put out Partizan Belgrade and met Borussia Dortmund in the semi. A 2-2 draw in Germany, with Brungs scoring both for Borussia, was followed by a 2-0 win for Inter in Milan, Mazzola scoring just after the interval. Later, there were allegations of Inter offering inducements to the referee. However, in their first year in the Cup, Inter were through to the Final.

Real Madrid, meanwhile, were cheering romantics everywhere and putting all the sceptics to shame. They had won the Spanish league and, although Del Sol had gone to Juventus, Real thought they had Pele waiting in the wings. However, the deal with Santos broke down. Recent arrivals at the Bernabeu were the incisive winger Amancio Amaro from La Coruna and defender Zoco from Osasuna, and Puskas, Di Stefano, Santamaria and Gento were still very much in place.

In the first round they trounced Rangers 7-0, and in the next round put out Dynamo Bucharest 8-4. In the Quarter-final they met AC Milan who, under new coach Nereo Rocco, had bought Amarildo from Botafago. Without Trapattoni, and with the Italians playing for a draw, Milan unexpectedly lost 4-1 in Madrid, Di Stefano and Puskas both scoring.

Catenaccio

This was a defensive system, based on the Swiss 'bolt' formation, which involved a sweeper (or 'libero') playing behind the back four defenders. The sweeper's task was to pick up any forwards who penetrated the man-marking back four, and under Hererra and other Italian managers was a purely defensive position. There were at least three players in midfield, and one or two in attack. The idea was to absorb the pressure, make sure no goals were given away, score on the break and then settle back to protect the lead. The role of sweeper was redefined by Franz Beckenbauer in the 1970s into an attacking position.

Results

First Round	1st leg	2nd leg	Agg	
Distillery v Benfica	3-3	0-5	3-8	
Dukla Prague v Valletta	6-0	2-0	8-0	
Dundalk v FC Zurich	0-3	2-1	2-4	
Dynamo Bucharest v Carl Zeiss Jena	2-0	1-0	3-0	
Esbjerg v PSV Eindhoven	3-4	1-7	4-11	
Everton v Inter Milan	0-0	0-1	0-1	
Galatasaray v Ferencvaros	4-0	0-2	4-2	
Gornik Zabrze v FK Austria	1-0	0-1	1-1	2-1(a)
Lyn Oslo v Borussia Dortmund	2-4	1-3	3-7	
Monaco v AEK Athens	7-2	1-1	8-3	
Partizan Belgrade v Anorthosis	3-0	3-1	6-1	
Partizan Tirana v Spartak Plovdiv	1-0	1-3	2-3	
Rangers v Real Madrid	0-1	0-6	0-7	
Standard Liège v Norrköping	1-0	0-2	1-2	
Valkeakosken Haka v Jeunesse Esch	4-1	0-4	4-5	

a) = Play-off in Vienna. Bye: AC Milan

Second Round				
Benfica v Borussia Dortmund	2-1	0-5	2-6	
Dynamo Bucharest v Real Madrid	1-3	3-5	4-8	
FC Zurich v Galatasaray	2-0	0-2	2-2	2-2(b)
Gornik Zabrze v Dukla Prague	2-0	1-4	3-4	
Inter Milan v Monaco	1-0	3-1	4-1	
Jeunesse Esch v Partizan Belgrade	2-1	2-6	4-7	
Norrköping v AC Milan	1-1	2-5	3-6	
Spartak Plovdiv v PSV Eindhoven	0-1	0-0	0-1	

b) FC Zurich won on toss of coin.

Quarter-finals				
Dukla Prague v Borussia Dortmund	0-4	3-1	3-5	
Partizan Belgrade v Inter Milan	0-2	1-2	1-4	
PSV Eindhoven v FC Zurich	1-0	1-3	2-3	
Real Madrid v AC Milan	4-1	0-2	4-3	

Semi-finals				
Borussia Dortmund v Inter Milan	2-2	0-2	2-4	
FC Zurich v Real Madrid	1-2	0-6	1-8	

In the San Siro, Milan scored two without reply, but it was not enough. The Italians were all over Real, and only an excellent performance by goalkeeper Jose Vicente and desperate defending kept the tally down to two. As Real right-half Müller commented afterwards, 'Our defenders just kicked the ball anywhere'.

An easy victory over FC Zurich in the Semi-final meant that yet again Real were in the European Cup Final, this time against Herrera's Inter.

BRITISH CLUBS

Although there was no progress beyond the preliminary round for any of the British clubs, this year's European Cup provided Northern Ireland's **Distillery** with the proudest day in the club's history.

On 25 September, at home in front of 19,000 fans against mighty Benfica, Distillery scored in the first

Sandro Mazzola (in stripes) takes on Real Madrid's defence in the 1964 Final.

60 seconds. Benfica equalised, and Distillery went ahead before half-time. Eusebio made it 3-2 to Benfica but, with minutes to go, the great Tom Finney who had come out of retirement for this match, sent a through ball to Ellison who put it in the net for a famous draw. Predictably, Distillery lost heavily in the return leg, but in Ulster they talk about that game still.

Everton, under manager Harry Catterick, had won the English title by six points with forwards Alex Young and Roy Vernon finishing as the league's top scorers. The first leg tie at Goodison was against ultra-defensive Inter Milan, and the Italians came for a draw. Packing their defence, they forced a 0-0 draw, although Vernon had what appeared to be a perfectly good goal disallowed. A goal from Jair at the San Siro finished off Everton.

Rangers fared no better against Real Madrid. Puskas ended any hopes they may have had of progressing to the first round with a hat-trick in Madrid which contributed to an overall 7-0 defeat.

Alessandro (Sandro) Mazzola (1949). Son of Valentino, the captain of Italy and Torino who was killed in the 1949 Superga air crash, Mazzola began his career with Inter Milan as a striker and his goals helped Inter claim the 1963 league title. He scored two in Inter's 3-1 win over Real Madrid in the 1964 European Cup Final, as well as the opener in the club's 2-1 defeat by Celtic in 1967. Moving back to midfield later in his career, he played for his country in their victorious 1968 European Nations championship and in the 1970 World Cup Final where Italy were over-run by an exuberant Brazilian side. He earned 70 caps in his career.

THE FINAL

Defensive Inter secure Viennese victory

Inter Milan (1) 3 Real Madrid (0) 1

Prater Stadium, Vienna, 27 May 1964
Attendance: 71,000
Referee: Stoll (Austria)

Helenio Herrera had not forgotten Barcelona's defeat and his personal humiliation at the hands of Real in the 1960 Semi-final, and he was out for revenge. His team had conceded only four goals in their eight games in the tournament, and his tight, well-drilled Inter defence was to be deployed again against Real in the Final.

A Mazzola shot from 25 yards in the first half sent Inter in at the interval with a 1-0 lead. Shortly after the break, a Puskas effort beat goalkeeper Sarti but came back off the crossbar, and in the 61st minute a mistake by Real keeper Vicente let in Aurelio Milani to put Inter 2-0 ahead.

Suarez was now orchestrating the game from midfield, with his repertoire of clever flicks, accurate passes and deceptive runs and, although Felo restored Real's interest with a header from a corner, a bad attempted clearance by centre-half Santamaria allowed Mazzola to claim his second in the 76th minute. Real no longer had the stamina to make a fight of it, and the European Cup was Inter's.

Inter had become the first team to win the trophy without losing a game, and their victory was a justification of sorts for Herrera's *catenaccio* system. As if to signal the end of an era, this was Di Stefano's last game for Real, and he moved in the summer to Espanol. He had scored 49 goals in the European Cup, a record which stands to this day.

The teams
Inter Milan: Sarti, Burgnich, Facchetti, Tagnin, Guarneri, Picchi, Jair, Mazzola, Milani, Suarez, Corso (manager: Herrera) [Mazzola, 43, 76, Milani 61]
Real Madrid: Vicente, Isidro, Pachin, Müller, Santamaria, Zoco, Amancio, Felo, Di Stefano, Puskas, Gento (manager: Munoz) [Felo 70]

Inter Milan began their defence of the European Cup with an emphatic 7-0 victory over Dynamo Bucharest in Milan, Mazzola and Jair bagging two apiece. In the Quarter-final they met Rangers, and a 3-1 win at home compensated for a 1-0 defeat at Ibrox. They were drawn against another British side, Liverpool, in the semi, and a brilliant goal by Facchetti in the second leg, aided by some highly dubious refereeing decisions, enabled them to squeeze through to the Final 4-3 on aggregate, after they had suffered their first defeat in the tournament at Anfield.

Real Madrid had promoted Ramon Grosso to fill Di Stefano's boots, and they had also acquired another forward, José Martinez Sanchez, known as Pirri. Five goals from the evergreen Gento helped Real ease through against Odense, and Dukla Prague were seen off 6-2 in the second round, with four goals coming from Amancio.

But Benfica in the Quarter-final were a different proposition.

Germano had now recovered from injury, and Eusebio and Torres were scoring at will in the Portuguese league. They sailed through the first two rounds 16-3 on aggregate, Torres scoring four away against hapless Aris Bonnevoie, and met Real at the Stadium of Light in the first leg. Eusebio hit two in their 5-1 victory over the once-impregnable Spaniards, and a 2-1 defeat by Real in Madrid made no difference to the outcome.

Hungarian champions Vasas Gyor, managed by Nandor Hidegkuti, were their opponents in the Semi-final, and Benfica had little trouble in making it to the Final, a second leg 4-0 win in Lisbon, with two goals each to Eusebio and Torres underlining their superiority. The Final was to be contested between Inter and Benfica at the San Siro Stadium.

Results

First Round

	1st leg	2nd leg	Agg	
Anderlecht v Bologna	1-0	1-2	2-2	0-0(a)
Aris Bonnevoie v Benfica	1-5	1-5	2-10	
Chemie Leipzig v Vasas Gyor	0-2	2-4	2-6	
Dukla Prague v Gornik Zabrze	4-1	0-3	4-4	0-0(b)
DWS Amsterdam v Fenerbahçe	3-1	1-0	4-1	
Glentoran v Panathinaikos	2-2	2-3	4-5	
KR Reykjavik v Liverpool	0-5	1-6	1-11	
Lahden Reipas v Lyn Oslo	2-1	0-3	2-4	
Lokomotiv Sofia v Malmo	8-3	0-2	8-5	
Odense v Real Madrid	2-5	0-4	2-9	
Partizan Tirana v Cologne	0-0	0-2	0-2	
Rapid Vienna v Shamrock Rovers	3-0	2-0	5-0	
Rangers v Red Star Belgrade	3-1	2-4	5-5	3-1(c)
Sliema Wanderers v Dynamo Bucharest	0-2	0-5	0-7	
St Etienne v La Chaux-de-Fonds	2-2	1-2	3-4	

Bye: Inter Milan. a) Play-off in Barcelona. b) Play-off in Duisburg.
c) Play-off in Highbury, London.

Second Round

DWS Amsterdam v Lyn Oslo	5-0	3-1	8-1
Inter Milan v Dynamo Bucharest	6-0	1-0	7-0
La Chaux-de-Fonds v Benfica	1-1	0-5	1-6
Liverpool v Anderlecht	3-0	1-0	4-0
Panathinaikos v Cologne	1-1	1-2	2-3
Rangers v Rapid Vienna	1-0	2-0	3-0
Real Madrid v Dukla Prague	4-0	2-2	6-2
Vasas Gyor v Lokomotiv Sofia	5-3	3-4	8-7

Quarter-finals

Benfica v Real Madrid	5-1	1-2	6-3	
Cologne v Liverpool	0-0	0-0	0-0	2-2(d)
DWS Amsterdam v Vasas Gyor	1-1	0-1	1-2	
Inter Milan v Rangers	3-1	0-1	3-2	

d) Play-off in Rotterdam. Liverpool won on the toss of a coin.

Semi-finals

Liverpool v Inter Milan	3-1	0-3	3-4
Vasas Gyor v Benfica	0-1	0-4	0-5

BRITISH CLUBS

Glentoran of Northern Ireland were narrowly knocked out in the preliminary round, a 3-2 defeat by Panathinaikos in Greece being enough to put the Greek champions through after a 2-2 first-leg draw.

Rangers had a successful start to their sixth European Cup campaign against Red Star Belgrade, although it took a play-off at Highbury in November to settle the tie. Rangers won the play-off 3-1 with two goals from centre-forward Jim Forrest and one from Ralph Brand. In the first round they took a 1-0 lead to Vienna, where a further two goals from Forrest and Davie Wilson ensured their continuance in the competition. Unfortunately, their playmaker 'Slim' Jim Baxter broke a leg at the Prater Stadium, and his influence was badly missed in the Quarter-final against Inter Milan.

Inter took the first leg at the San Siro 3-1, and in the return an early seventh-minute Forrest goal raised hopes among the 80,000 crowd that an upset was possible. However, Inter simply closed ranks and held on to win.

English champions **Liverpool,** under Bill Shankly, had built a formidable side. Ron Yeats, the massive centre-half, stamped his authority on the defence, while up front wingers Peter Thompson and Ian Callaghan fed the ball to the twin international strikers Ian St John and Roger Hunt. Liverpool had signalled their championship intentions by disposing of Reykjavik 11-1 and the experienced Anderlecht 4-0 by the time they faced Cologne in the Quarter-final. However, two goal-less draws against the Germans meant a play-off in Rotterdam in March.

In front of a 48,000 crowd, St John and Hunt put the Reds 2-0 up but Cologne came back through Thielen and Lohr. The game went into extra time, but finished in stalemate yet again. Under UEFA rules, a coin was tossed, and it stuck in the mud. Tossed again, it came up red and Liverpool were through to the Semi-final.

In May, three days after winning the FA Cup, Liverpool met Inter Milan at Anfield, the English club's powerful and speedy goal-scoring forwards up against one of the world's finest defences. In the third minute Hunt scored, then Mazzola equalised, and St John and Callaghan added two more to make the score 3-1. 'We have been beaten before', said Herrera, 'but tonight we were defeated'.

In the second leg one week later at the San Siro, 77,000 deafening Inter fans, complete with firecrackers, rockets and smoke bombs, created an hysterical atmosphere, and Liverpool were 2-0 down within ten minutes, both goals being highly dubious decisions from referee Ortiz de Mendebil. In the eighth minute, an indirect free-kick from winger Mario Corso went into the net and a goal was given. Two minutes later, Piero kicked the ball out of goalkeeper Tommy Lawrence's hands, scored, and again a goal was awarded. The tie remained level on aggregate until, in the second half, a magnificent run and shot from full-back Facchetti put Inter into the Final.

Ian St John (1938). A devastatingly effective centre-forward, St John left his home club of Motherwell in 1961 to join Liverpool under Bill Shankly. He scored a hat-trick in his first game for the club, against local rivals Everton, and was his club's main goal scorer in Liverpool's two league titles, FA Cup victory and European adventures in the 1960s. For such a relatively small man, he was a fine header of the ball, and his touch and control were immaculate. He left the club in 1971 to move into coaching and management and later began a successful career in television. He appeared 21 times for Scotland.

Inter play for time in dull final

Inter Milan (1) 1 Benfica (0) 0

San Siro Stadium, Milan, 28 May 1965
Attendance: 89,000
Referee: Dienst (Switzerland)

Before this game, Benfica had formally objected to UEFA about the venue, arguing that playing the Final at home was to Inter's advantage – which, of course, it was. Indeed, they threatened to withdraw from the tournament, or send their youth team, but UEFA were unmoved. The interests of fairness were now clearly secondary to commercial considerations, and the game went ahead at the San Siro.

Played in pouring rain on a sodden pitch, and with the players finding it difficult to maintain their footing, the game was hardly a showpiece. It was decided by a shot from Jair which slithered through Costa Pereira's hands in the 42nd minute. Then, in the 60th minute, an injury to Costa Pereira led to him leaving the field, although Simoes and Germano seemed annoyed at his decision, with sweeper Germano taking over in goal. Benfica no longer needed a sweeper – they had to attack.

However, rather than taking advantage of a depleted Benfica and making a game of it, Inter closed shop and played for time. The masters of negative football had triumphed yet again in Europe.

The teams
Inter Milan: Sarti, Burgnich, Facchetti, Bedin, Guarneri, Picchi, Jair, Mazzola, Peiro, Suarez, Corso (manager: Herrera) [Jair 42]
Benfica: Costa Pereira, Cavem, Cruz, Neto, Germano, Raul, Jose Augusto, Eusebio, Torres, Coluna, Simoes (manager: Schwartz)

Ian St John (centre) on the attack for Liverpool.

Thirty-one clubs entered the competition in 1965/66, with only Wales and the Soviet Union not having a representative. This was the first year that the runners-up in a country whose championship was won by the title-holders did not automatically qualify. Only the champions were now to play in the European Cup.

As the competition began, it was clear that many of the European teams had learnt from the success of the Italian system. The carefree, five-man attacking systems of the early days were now a distant memory and, although there were players and teams capable of thrilling, creative football, more emphasis was now being placed on the importance of sound, well-organised defensive play.

However, news of this tactical development had obviously not reached Luxembourg, whose representatives Stade Dudelange were defeated 18-0 by Benfica in the preliminary round. Benfica went on to knock out Levski Sofia 5-4, but were themselves eliminated 8-3 in a thrilling Quarter-final against Manchester United.

Holders Inter were to discover that Milan's domination of the competition was about to end. Given a bye in the preliminary round, they squeezed past Dynamo Bucharest 3-2, Mazzola and Facchetti scoring in the home second leg, and more convincingly defeated Ferencváros 5-1 in the Quarter-final. The Semi-final brought the Italians against their defeated opponents in the 1964 Final, Real Madrid.

Real had shed most of the members of their great 1950s side, with only Gento, now 32 years old, still a regular in the team. Now younger, faster and fitter than the 1962 finalists, although not quite possessing the flair and élan of the Di Stefano era, Real remained one of the continent's top sides.

They gained revenge for a surprise 2-1 defeat away to two disputed goals from Feyenoord in the first round by trouncing the Dutch 5-0 at the Bernabeu, Puskas scoring four. A second-round 2-2 draw at Scottish champions Kilmarnock, where Puskas and Santamaria played their last European games for the club, was followed by a 5-1 win in Madrid. Two goals apiece from Amancio and Gento were sufficient to remove Anderlecht in the Quarter-final, and Madrid were to face Inter at the Bernabeu in the Semi-final.

Inter came to Madrid to defend, and restricted Real to a single goal, scored by Pirri. In the second leg Gento laid on a goal for Amancio, and Real were two ahead on aggregate. A gritty defensive performance and some excellent goalkeeping from Real, helped by Inter's unusually poor control and inaccurate passing, saw them through to the Final, although Facchetti pulled one back for Inter towards the end of the game.

Real's opponents in the Final were to be Partizan Belgrade who were a tough and committed side. The Yugoslavs, although considered outsiders, had players of the quality of Milutin Soskic in goal and Velibor Vasovic (who was to play for Ajax in two European Cup Finals) in defence, and Vladimir Kovacevic and Milan Galic up front.

They had progressed with wins over Nantes and Werder Bremen, and had overcome a seemingly irretrievable 4-1 defeat by Sparta Prague in the Quarter-final with a 5-0 win at home against the defensive but utterly ineffectual Czechs, a fourth-minute goal from Mustafa Hasaganic starting the Partizan fight-back. A surprise 2-1 aggregate victory over a listless Manchester United took them to the Final, the first Eastern European team to have reached this stage.

Results

First Round

	1st leg	2nd leg	Agg
17 Nentori Tirana v Kilmarnock	0-0	0-1	0-1
Apoel Nicosia v Werder Bremen	0-5	0-5	0-10
ASK Linz v Gornik Zabrze	1-3	1-2	2-5
Dynamo Bucharest v BK Odense	4-0	3-2	7-2
Djurgarden v Levski Sofia	2-1	0-6	2-7
Drumcondra v ASK Vorwaerts	1-0	0-3	1-3
Fenerbahçe v Anderlecht	0-0	1-5	1-5
Feyenoord v Real Madrid	2-1	0-5	2-6
HJK Helsinki v Manchester United	2-3	0-6	2-9
IBK Keflavik v Ferencvaros	1-4	1-9	2-13
Lausanne v Sparta Prague	0-0	0-4	0-4
Lyn Oslo v Derry City	5-3	1-5	6-8
Panathinaikos v Sliema Wanderers	4-1	0-1	4-2
Partizan Belgrade v Nantes	2-0	2-2	4-2
Stade Dudelange v Benfica	0-8	0-10	0-18

Bye: Inter Milan.

Second Round

	1st leg	2nd leg	Agg
Anderlecht v Derry City	9-0(a)		
ASK Vorwaerts v Manchester United	0-2	1-3	1-5
Dynamo Bucharest v Inter Milan	2-1	0-2	2-3
Ferencvaros v Panathinaikos	0-0	3-1	3-1
Kilmarnock v Real Madrid	2-2	1-5	3-7
Levski Sofia v Benfica	2-2	2-3	4-5
Partizan Belgrade v Werder Bremen	3-0	0-1	3-1
Sparta Prague v Gornik Zabrze	3-0	2-1	5-1

a) Anderlecht walkover. Derry withdrew after first leg.

Quarter-finals

	1st leg	2nd leg	Agg
Anderlecht v Real Madrid	1-0	2-4	3-4
Inter Milan v Ferencvaros	4-0	1-1	5-1
Manchester United v Benfica	3-2	5-1	8-3
Sparta Prague v Partizan Belgrade	4-1	0-5	4-6

Semi-finals

	1st leg	2nd leg	Agg
Real Madrid v Inter Milan	1-0	1-1	2-1
Partizan Belgrade v Manchester United	2-0	0-1	2-1

BRITISH CLUBS

In the ten years of the competition, no British club had made it to the Final. A number – Hibs, Manchester United, Spurs, Rangers, Liverpool and Dundee – had come tantalisingly close, but British footballing self-respect demanded victory at the highest level.

This was unlikely to be provided by Northern Ireland's **Derry City,** who nonetheless began well with an aggregate 8-6 win over Lyn Oslo in the preliminaries and met Anderlecht in the second round. However, UEFA and the Irish FA decided that Derry's home ground, Brandywell, was unsuitable for European competition, in spite of the fact that the first round had been played there. Derry refused to consider alternatives and, after a 9-0 away defeat, they scratched from the competition.

Kilmarnock had won the only Scottish league championship in their history, beating Hearts on goal average although Hearts had scored 28 goals more. This statistical anomaly eventually persuaded the Scottish FA to introduce goal difference.

The Ayrshire side, who have never subsequently qualified for the European Cup, began with a 1-0 win over Albania's 17 Nentori Tirana, Bertie Black scoring the winner 13 minutes from the end in the second leg at Rugby Park. In the second round they drew Real Madrid which, although a prestige fixture for Killie, did not offer much hope of progress in the tournament. And so it proved, a fighting 2-2 draw in front of 25,000 home supporters followed by an inevitable defeat at the Bernabeu, by a 5-1 margin.

A young Irishman called George Best was establishing himself as a regular in the **Manchester United** team, who won the English championship in 1964/65. United, with an attack force of Denis Law, Bobby Charlton, David Herd and Best, were developing into one of the leading European sides and, although they scrambled a 3-2 away win against HJK Helsinki, a 6-0 home win, with two from Best and three from John Connelly, saw them through to play Vorwaerts in the second round.

A 2-0 away win on a freezing day and a 3-1 victory at home, with a hat-trick for Herd, put them against Benfica in the Quarter-final. At Old Trafford in February, in front of a 65,000 crowd, United were 3-1 up in the second half until a piece of Eusebio trickery led to a Torres goal. In the return in Lisbon, where Benfica had never lost in a European competition, nervous manager Matt Busby asked his team to contain the high-scoring Portuguese. George Best, however, was clearly not listening, as he scored two within the first 12 minutes, the second a sublime solo goal past three defenders, and by full-time United had scored another three, from Connelly, half-back Crerand and Charlton, with Benfica only managing one.

Now full of confidence after this memorable display of attacking football, United met the under-rated Partizan Belgrade in the Semi-final. In the first leg in Belgrade, Best was carrying a cartilage injury and made little impact on the game. This, combined with a generally poor performance from the team, including a fluffed early opportunity from Law, saw Partizan score twice. At Old Trafford, with Best now out, Partizan stoutly defended their two-goal lead, and an own goal from keeper Soskic from a Nobby Stiles cross was not enough for United.

The club had now lost their third European Cup Semi-final and Busby and the team were beginning to wonder if they would ever reach the Final.

George Best

George Best (1946). 'Bestie' was one of the true football greats. A multi-talented attacker for Manchester United in the 1960s, his pace and acceleration, combined with his strength and dribbling ability, helped him to score and create many important goals for his club. The most memorable was his goal against Benfica in the 1968 European Cup Final in extra time, when he eased through the Benfica defence to put United ahead in injury time. That year he was also European Footballer of the Year, English Footballer of the Year and the league's top scorer. However, his indulgent and chaotic private life cut short his career at the highest level, and he eventually left United in 1974 to play for a variety of British and American clubs.

1966

THE FINAL

Real regain the European Cup

Real Madrid (0) 2 Partizan Belgrade (0) 1

Heysel Stadium, Brussels, 11 May 1966
Attendance: 46,000
Referee: Kreitlein (GFR)

Although the club was in its eighth European Cup Final, a young Real side started the game in a jittery and nervous fashion. Partizan immediately went on the attack, led by Galic and Vasovic, until captain Gento, moving in off the left wing, began to steady his midfield. Towards the end of the first half, the juggling and dribbling of Amancio and Serena were carving holes in the Partizan defence, and Ramon Grosso missed a six-yard open goal.

In the 56th minute, a cross from winger Pirmajer connected with the head of the soaring Vasovic, and the Yugoslavs were ahead. Stung by this, Real immediately went on all-out attack. Galic, Partizan's best forward, was injured in a counter-attack and played little further part in the game, and Real took advantage of the weakened opposition with

two goals within six minutes. In the 70th minute, Amancio latched onto a through pass from Grosso and shot the ball past Soskic, and in the 76th minute a swivel and left-foot shot from Serena from 25 yards proved to be the winner.

German referee Kreitlein blew the whistle one minute from time and the crowd invaded thinking the game was over. The pitch was cleared and the game restarted, and Real held on, an edgy conclusion to what was a tense but not particularly memorable Final. This was to be Real's last appearance in the Final for fifteen years, and the club was not to regain the trophy until 1998. Real's glorious reign in the European Cup was over.

The teams
Real Madrid: Araquistin, Pachin, Sanchis, Pirri, De Felipe, Zoco, Serena, Amancio, Grosso, Velazquez, Gento (manager: Muñoz) [Amancio 70, Serena 76]
Partizan Belgrade: Soskic, Jusufi, Mihajlovic, Bacejac, Rasovic, Vasovic, Bajic, Kovacevic, Hasaganic, Galic, Pirmajer (manager: Gegic) [Vasovic 56]

Inter Milan had again qualified as Italian champions, and played the first Russian team to have entered the tournament, Moscow Torpedo. In the first leg at the San Siro, Torpedo were unlucky in hitting the post twice and losing to a Voronin 63rd-minute own goal. In Moscow, a crowd of over 75,000 roared their support as Torpedo went on all-out attack, but the Russians couldn't break down the Inter defence.

Inter had two new strikers – Domenghini and Cappellini – but their defence was essentially the same as the team which had won the 1964 and 1965 tournament – Sarti in goal, the attacking full-back Facchetti and his defensive companions Burgnich and Guarneri, and Picchi the sweeper. Mazzola and Suarez were still the creative hub of the team, and Jair was on the wing, although increasingly injury-prone. And the autocratic Helenio Herrera was aiming for a third European Cup.

Drawn against Vasas, with their feared Hungarian international strikers Puskas and Farkas, Inter won the first leg at the San Siro 2-1, the winner coming from a Corso free-kick. In Budapest, two superb goals from Mazzola put Inter through to the Quarter-final where they faced, yet again, Real Madrid.

Cup holders Real had scraped through against 1860 Munich, a 1-0 defeat in Munich followed by an admirable performance at home, the goals coming from Grosso, Veloso and Pirri. At the San Siro, new striker Cappellini scored the only goal, and in the return he scored again, with an own goal from Zoco combining to eliminate Real.

Bulgarian side CSKA Sofia, who had narrowly beaten battling Linfield in the Quarter-finals, were next in the Semi-final. The Bulgarians put on an efficient defensive performance at the San Siro and held on to draw 1-1, in spite of Raikov being sent off after half an hour for fighting. In the return leg, a Facchetti goal and a Radlev equaliser sent the tie to a play-off. A significant share of the gate money enticed Sofia to Italy for the play-off, which was held in Bologna, and a Cappellini strike in the 13th minute earned Inter a place in the Final against Jock Stein's Celtic.

The ultimate clash of footballing styles – Celtic's fast, exciting attacking football against Italian caution and the defensive wall – was to take place in Lisbon on 25 May. Inter were the favourites but the uncommitted would be supporting the Scots.

Results

Preliminary Round

	1st leg	2nd leg	Agg	
Sliema Wanderers v CSKA Sofia	1-2	0-4	1-6	
Waterford v ASK Vorwaerts	1-6	0-6	1-12	

First Round

	1st leg	2nd leg	Agg	
1860 Munich v Omonia Nicosia	8-0	2-1	10-1	
Admira Vienna v Vojvodina	0-1	0-0	0-1	
Ajax v Besiktas	2-0	2-1	4-1	
Aris Bonnevoie v Linfield	3-3	1-6	4-9	
Celtic v FC Zurich	2-0	3-0	5-0	
CSKA Sofia v Olympiakos	3-1	0-1	3-2	
Esbjerg v Dukla Prague	0-2	0-4	0-6	
Gornik Zabrze v ASK Vorwaerts	2-1	1-2	3-3	3-1 (a)
Inter Milan v Moscow Torpedo	1-0	0-0	1-0	
KR Reykjavik v Nantes	2-3	2-5	4-8	
Liverpool v Petrolul Ploiesti	2-0	1-3	3-3	2-0 (b)
Malmö v Atlético Madrid	0-2	1-3	1-5	
Valkeakosken Haka v Anderlecht	1-10	0-2	1-12	
Vasas v Sporting Lisbon	5-0	2-0	7-0	

17 Nentor Tirana withdrew. Walkover for Valerengen. a) Play-off in Budapest; b) Play-off in Brussels. Bye: Real Madrid.

Second Round

	1st leg	2nd leg	Agg	
1860 Munich v Real Madrid	1-0	1-3	2-3	
Ajax v Liverpool	5-1	2-2	7-3	
CSKA Sofia v Gornik Zabrze	4-0	0-3	4-3	
Dukla Prague v Anderlecht	4-1	2-1	6-2	
Inter Milan v Vasas	2-1	2-0	4-1	
Nantes v Celtic	1-3	1-3	2-6	
Valerengen v Linfield	1-4	1-1	2-5	
Vojvodina v Atlético Madrid	3-1	0-2	3-3	3-2 (c)

c) Play-off in Madrid after extra time.

Quarter-finals

	1st leg	2nd leg	Agg	
Ajax v Dukla Prague	1-1	1-2	2-3	
Inter Milan v Real Madrid	1-0	2-0	3-0	
Linfield v CSKA Sofia	2-2	0-1	2-3	
Vojvodina v Celtic	1-0	0-2	1-2	

Semi-finals

	1st leg	2nd leg	Agg	
Celtic v Dukla Prague	3-1	0-0	3-1	
Inter Milan v CSKA Sofia	1-1	1-1	2-2	1-0 (d)

d) Play-off in Bologna.

As a Matter of Fact

The European Cup was the fifth trophy which Celtic won in 1966/67. They had already secured the Glasgow Cup, Scottish Cup, Scottish League Cup and Scottish League Championship in that remarkable season.

Billy McNeill (1940). McNeill, known as 'Caesar' for his imperious leadership qualities, was centre-half and captain of Jock Stein's great Celtic side in the 1960s and 1970s. A one-club man, he steered Celtic to the European Cup Final in 1967, scoring a rare goal and the winner against Vojvodina Novi Sad in the quarter-final at Parkhead, and became the first British foot-baller to lift the trophy in the 2-1 victory over Inter in Lisbon. He made his first appearance for Scotland in 1961, when the Scots were hammered 9-3 by England at Wembley, and achieved 29 caps. He later managed Celtic, Aston Villa and Manchester City.

Celtic in 1967. Back (l to r): O'Neill, McNeill, Craig, Gemmell, Simpson, Hughes, Murdoch, Clark. Front (l to r): Johnstone, Lennox, Wallace, Chalmers, Gallagher, McBride, Auld.

CELTIC 1966/67

Jock Stein, one of the greatest managers the game has ever produced, had assembled in Scottish champions Celtic a team which was to dominate Scottish football for the next decade: centre-half, the commanding captain Billy McNeill; the veteran 39-year-old goalkeeper Ronnie Simpson, whose career had been resurrected by Stein; Tommy Gemmell, the attacking left-back; Bertie Auld and Bobby Murdoch, the midfield schemers; Bobby Lennox, John 'Yogi' Hughes and Joe McBride, the goal scorers; and the mesmerising, tiny Jimmy 'Jinky' Johnstone, the unstoppable right-winger. Celtic were a fast, attacking and creative team who played with passion and pride, and they were soon to nail the coffin of *catenaccio*.

Celtic's first game in the European Cup was played in front of 48,000 fans at Parkhead in the first-round game against FC Zurich, managed by ex-Honvéd, Barcelona and Hungarian striker Kubala. Goals by Gemmell and McBride got the better of the Swiss in a dirty, bad-tempered match, and two more from Gemmell and one from Chalmers secured victory in Zurich, where the 41-year-old Kubala played to little effect.

Nantes were next and, in the first leg in France, Magny scored in the 14th minute for the home side. Johnstone, however, was displaying his full repertoire of wing wizardry and supplied McBride with the equaliser seven minutes later. A Murdoch pass to Lennox added another and Chalmers hit a third. The second leg also went 3-1 Celtic's way.

Stein had by now added to the squad front man Willie Wallace, bought for £40,000 from Hearts as a replacement for the injured McBride, but he was ineligible for the Quarter-final against Yugoslavia's Vojvodina. In Novi Sad in the first leg Celtic were kept at full stretch by the strong and skilful Yugoslavs, and Simpson and his back four were resolute until a mistake by Gemmell in the 69th minute allowed Stanic in to score.

Back at Parkhead Vojovodina turned in a brilliant defensive performance, allied to intelligent movement and passing, and came close to increasing their lead in the first half. In the second half, Hughes moved to the right wing and Johnstone to the left, and the pressure was on the Yugoslavs. Chalmers drew the tie level and, with nearly 70,000 fans screaming for the winner, it finally arrived in the last minute when a high corner from Johnstone was met by a glorious, unstoppable header from McNeill.

Dukla Prague, the Czech Army side, were Celtic's opponents in the Semi-final. Conquerors of Ajax in the Quarter-final, and captained by the great midfielder Josef Masopust, Dukla came to Parkhead to attack, and a fast, exciting game developed. By half time the score was 1-1, a Johnstone volley in the 27th minute cancelled out by a goal from Strunc after a defensive mix-up by Celtic. Two goals from Wallace, one a 20-yard shot from a crafty Auld free-kick, settled the leg. In Prague, an untypically dour, defensive performance from Celtic resulted in a 0-0 draw, and later Stein and his players admitted to having been embarrassed about their tactics.

No matter, though, as Celtic had now become the only British side to have reached the European Cup Final, where they were to face Helenio Herrera's Inter Milan in Lisbon.

English champions **Liverpool** were drawn against Petrolul Ploiesti of Romania in the first round. Perhaps taking advantage of the Romanians' first game under floodlights, Liverpool won 2-0, the goals scored by St John and Callaghan. In the Romanian oilfields, however, a spirited performance by the home side, with only ten men for much of the match, resulted in a 3-1 victory. Two first-half goals from St John and Thompson in the play-off in Brussels put Liverpool through to the second leg against Ajax of Amsterdam.

Under manager Rinus Michels, Ajax were a different proposition to the Ajax side eliminated from the tournament in the early stage in 1960. Although largely part-timers, they were a young but talented team, featuring the 19-year-old centre-forward Johan Cruyff. In the first leg in Amsterdam's Olympic Stadium in a fog-shrouded game, the Dutch were 4-0 up by half-time, completely over-running Liverpool, with Cruyff scoring the second. Liverpool pulled one back, but the final score was a humiliating 5-1. Curiously, Liverpool manager Bill Shankly berated his team for losing so many goals to what he claimed was a 'defensive' side.

Although Shankly was prophesying a 'landslide' of goals from Liverpool in the return game, Ajax were 2-1 up with five minutes to go, both goals coming from the precocious Cruyff, until Hunt levelled the score on the day. Liverpool were out of the tournament, and had learnt not to underestimate European opposition. Evertonian reaction to the result can be gauged by the tins of Ajax cleanser which mysteriously appeared on their Liverpool-supporting colleagues' desks the next morning.

Linfield began what was to be their most successful campaign ever. They drew 3-3 away against Luxembourg's Aris Bonnevoie, and overwhelmed Aris 6-1 in the return game. In the second round in Norway against Valerengen, they put away four goals in ten minutes and won 4-1, while the home leg resulted in a 1-1 draw in what was a poor game. Nevertheless, Linfield had qualified for the Quarter-final, the first Northern Ireland team ever to have got this far.

CSKA Sofia were the opposition, and by half time at Windsor Park, Linfield were astonishingly 2-1 up, an early strike by Romanov answered by goals from Hamilton and Shield. In the second half Romanov blasted a 25-yard equaliser to make the final score 2-2. The second leg in Sofia was decided by a Yakimov shot, but Linfield had shown themselves to be no pushover.

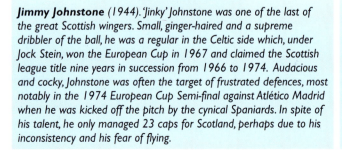

Jimmy Johnstone

Giacinto Facchetti

Jimmy Johnstone (1944). 'Jinky' Johnstone was one of the last of the great Scottish wingers. Small, ginger-haired and a supreme dribbler of the ball, he was a regular in the Celtic side which, under Jock Stein, won the European Cup in 1967 and claimed the Scottish league title nine years in succession from 1966 to 1974. Audacious and cocky, Johnstone was often the target of frustrated defences, most notably in the 1974 European Cup Semi-final against Atlético Madrid when he was kicked off the pitch by the cynical Spaniards. In spite of his talent, he only managed 23 caps for Scotland, perhaps due to his inconsistency and his fear of flying.

Giacinto Facchetti (1942). A tall, elegant, attacking defender with Inter Milan, Facchetti made the left-back position his own with the club and the Italian national side in the 1960s and 1970s. For a full-back he was an accomplished goal scorer, and his forays into attack were a hallmark of Italian football of the time. His most famous club goal was probably his brilliant and decisive winner against Liverpool in the 1965 European Cup Semi-final. He played for his country 94 times and in three World Cup finals – 1966, 1970 and 1974 – and captained Italy in the 1970 World Cup Final, where, as sweeper, he could not prevent Pele and Brazil routing Italy 4-1.

Lisbon lions maul the men from Milan

Celtic (0) 2   Inter Milan (1) 1

Stadium Of Light, Lisbon, 25 May 1967
Attendance: 45,000
Referee: Tschenscher (West Germany)

The temperature was touching the 80s as the men of Milan lined up against the Scottish champions in the Final. The heat was matched by the passionate fervour of the massed Celtic fans, who turned the majestic old Portuguese stadium into a sea of green and white, and the club's anthems rang round the ground.

The astute Jock Stein had one blanket instruction for his men – attack from the kick-off. He saw that the only way to break down Inter's famous defence was to take the game to them and unsettle them by shooting from every possible angle. Fast movement, quick passing and a relentless quest for goal were to be the keys to unlock *catenaccio*. And so it proved.

However, Inter, although missing the injured Suarez and Jair, seized the first opportunity. In the sixth minute, a suspicious over-reaction by Cappellini to a tangle with right-back Jim Craig in the Celtic box was deemed a penalty. Mazzola stepped forward and sent goalkeeper Simpson the wrong way for the opening goal. Inter now knew what they had to do – defend their advantage.

Celtic continued on the all-out attack. Jinky Johnstone pulled infield to tease and torment his marker Burgnich, while Lennox kept the pressure on Facchetti. Craig and Gemmell raided down the wings, supplying crosses for Wallace and Chalmers, while Auld and Murdoch controlled the midfield. Inter's captain and sweeper Picchi was being run ragged by the speed and determination of Celtic's onslaughts. But by half-time Celtic were still behind.

In the second half, Auld and Gemmell had both hit the bar, but in the 62nd minute a pass from Craig to Gemmell set up the left-back for a 20-yard rocket high into the corner of goalkeeper Sarti's net.

Celtic continued to press the rattled Inter defence, for whom Sarti was in inspirational form, and the keeper made an acrobatic leap to touch away a goal-bound Murdoch header. In the 83rd minute, Gemmell passed to Murdoch whose shot was going wide until it met a deliberate deflection from Chalmers, and Celtic were ahead. The final whistle blew and ecstatic Celtic fans invaded the pitch. A British team had at last won the European Cup and the trophy had left the stranglehold of the Latin nations.

Inter had been outplayed, out-thought and overwhelmed by a skilful, determined Celtic performance, and Herrera was gracious in defeat – 'We can have no complaints. Celtic deserved their victory'. Jock Stein and his 'Lisbon Lions' had shown to all of Europe that creative, attacking play could overcome even the most defensive of systems.

Inter's domination in Europe was now over, and Herrera and his stars were to leave the club in the coming months. The club has never subsequently won the Cup and has made only one further appearance in the Final. As for Stein, Bill Shankly hailed the delighted manager after the game with the words 'John, you're immortal'.

The teams

Celtic: Simpson, Craig, Gemmell, Murdoch, McNeill, Clark, Johnstone, Wallace, Chalmers, Auld, Lennox (manager: Stein) [Gemmell 62, Chalmers 83]
Inter Milan: Sarti, Burgnich, Facchetti, Bedin, Picchi, Guarneri, Domenghini, Bicicli, Mazzola, Cappellini, Corso (manager: Herrera) [Mazzola 6]

Celtic keeper Ronnie Simpson rises to stop an Inter attack in the 1967 Final.

Real Madrid opened their challenge with a first-round tie against the talented Dutchmen of Ajax, fast emerging as one of the more skilful sides in Europe. In the first leg in Amsterdam, a Cruyff goal was cancelled out by a Pirri strike. In Madrid, a stylish, counter-attacking match saw Gento put Real in front and then Groot equalise. At the end of normal time, the sides remained drawn, and in the 11th minute of extra time a wonderful Veloso goal, when he dribbled past what seemed the entire Ajax defence, settled the tie in Real's favour.

A 6-3 victory followed against the amateur Danish side Hvidovre, Gento claiming two of the goals. In the Quarter-final against Sparta Prague, a brilliant spell by Amancio, when he scored a hat-trick within ten minutes, finished off the Czechs, who beat Real 2-1 in Prague. Then, in an absorbing two-leg encounter against Manchester United in the Semi-final, a Bill Foulkes goal at the Bernabeu was enough to kill off Real's hopes.

The previous season's Finalists, Inter, failed to qualify, the Italian representatives this year being Juventus. Two tough games against

Seeding 1967/68

For the first time, the European Cup draw was 'seeded' to lessen the chances of too many of the bigger clubs going out early in the competition. In other words, the glamour clubs, with the financial muscle and large fan base, would not meet each other until the later stages. The seeding status was based on

a) the clubs which had already reached the Finals and

b) the countries which had previously supplied the Finalists.

Many observers felt that the essential romance of the competition had been damaged by this new arrangement. and that the smaller clubs were being discriminated against. However, money and expediency overrode these objections.

Olympiakos in the first round were settled 2-0 in favour of Juventus, and the next round against Rapid Bucharest was won by a single goal from Juve's star Swedish striker Roger Magnusson.

Germany's Eintracht Brunswick were the Italians' opposition in the Quarter-finals, and a surprisingly high-scoring 3-2 defeat in Germany was countered with a 1-0 victory in Turin, the goal coming from a spectacular solo effort from Magnusson. The play-off in Berne was goal-less until the last minute when Del Sol gave away a penalty and Bercellino converted the kick. The draw pitted Juventus against Benfica in the Semi-final.

Benfica, although still parading the attacking talents of Eusebio, Torres and Jose Augusto, were now an older team and more defensively-minded than in their heyday of five years before. They received a shock from minnows Glentoran in the first round, and scraped through on an away goal. In the next round they played France's St Etienne, winning 2-0 at home through Eusebio and Jose Augusto and, without Coluna and Simoes, losing 0-1 away and playing in an untypically defensive manner. The Quarter-final put them against Vasas Budapest, who had totalled 20 goals in their first two rounds. However, the Hungarians' scoring had to stop, and it did in both Budapest (0-0) and in Lisbon, where two goals for Eusebio and one for Torres eased Benfica into the Semi-final against Juventus.

In Lisbon, Eusebio and Torres were again on target, with no reply from Juventus, and in Turin, Eusebio, with his leg injured,

nonetheless fired home a 30-yard free-kick to win the tie for Benfica. The Portuguese were to meet Manchester United in the European Cup Final.

Away Goals 1967/68

UEFA decided to institute an 'away goals' rule this season, in order to encourage teams to attack more away from home. If sides were level after the two legs, the team with more goals scored away was the winner. If the number was equal, 'extra time' of 30 minutes would be played. If still equal, then a toss of a coin would decide. However, this new ruling applied only to the first two rounds – from the Quarter-final onwards, the teams would continue to a play-off.

Results

First Round

	1st leg	2nd leg	Agg
Ajax v Real Madrid	1-1	1-2	2-3
Basle v Hvidovre	1-2	3-3	4-5
Besiktas v Rapid Vienna	0-1	0-3	0-4
Celtic v Dynamo Kiev	1-2	1-1	2-3
Dundalk v Vasas	0-1	1-8	1-9
Glentoran v Benfica	1-1	0-0	1-1
Gornik Zabrze v Djurgarden	3-0	1-0	4-0
Manchester United v Hibernians Malta	4-0	0-0	4-0
Olympiakos v Juventus	0-0	0-2	0-2
Olympiakos Nicosia v Sarajevo	2-2	1-3	3-5
St Etienne v Kuopian Palloseura	2-0	3-0	5-0
Skeid Oslo v Sparta Prague	0-1	1-1	1-2
Trakia Plovdiv v Rapid Bucharest	2-0	0-3	2-3
Valur v Jeunesse Esch	1-1	3-3	4-4
Wismut Karl-Marx-Stadt v Anderlecht	1-3	1-2	2-5

Dynamo Tirana withdrew. Walkover for Eintracht Brunswick.

Second Round

Benfica v St Etienne	2-0	0-1	2-1
Dynamo Kiev v Gornik Zabrze	1-2	1-1	2-3
Hvidovre v Real Madrid	2-2	1-4	3-6
Juventus v Rapid Bucharest	1-0	0-0	1-0
Rapid Vienna v Eintracht Brunswick	1-0	0-2	1-2
Sarajevo v Manchester United	0-0	1-2	1-2
Sparta Prague v Anderlecht	3-2	3-3	6-5
Vasas v Valur	6-0	5-1	11-1

Quarter-finals

Eintracht Brunswick v Juventus	3-2	0-1	3-3	0-1(a)
Manchester United v Gornik Zabrze	2-0	0-1	2-1	
Real Madrid v Sparta Prague	3-0	1-2	4-2	
Vasas v Benfica	0-0	0-3	0-3	

a) Play-off in Berne.

Semi-finals

Benfica v Juventus	2-0	1-0	3-0
Manchester United v Real Madrid	1-0	3-3	4-3

MANCHESTER UNITED 67/68

There had been several changes to Manchester United's line-up since their last European adventure two years previously. Alex Stepney, who was to show his worth in the Final, had replaced Harry Gregg in goal; David Sadler was a young centre-forward who was adaptable enough to play in defence; left-winger John Aston was a fast and effective attacker; and 18-year-old Salford-born striker Brian Kidd had come up from the youth team. The core of the team – Charlton, Best, Crerand, Stiles and Law – remained in place, although Law carried a knee injury for much of the season and his appearances were infrequent.

Their first round home tie against part-timers Hibernians of Malta was won by a predictably easy 4-0 margin, although a crassly inept away performance, in front of the entire Maltese Manchester United Supporters Club, resulted in a disappointing 0-0 draw. Sarajevo provided the second-round opposition and United, without Stiles or Law, managed another 0-0 result in an uncompromising and vicious match in Yugoslavia. The Old Trafford return was equally unappealing. In a nasty and ill-tempered game, Aston scored in the 11th minute and then Best put United 2-0 ahead. Prljaca was sent off for scything Best and, although Delalic reduced the deficit in the 87th minute, United went through 2-1.

Poland's Gornik Zabrze, who had beaten Dynamo Kiev, the eliminators of Cup holders Celtic, were regarded as a good outside bet for the trophy. With the exciting young inside-forward Lubanski leading the attack, and marshalled by centre-back Oslizlo, they met United at Old Trafford in the Quarter-final and the teams produced an exciting and sporting contest. Their keeper Kostka was in inspired form, but he could not prevent an own goal from defender Florenski and was unsighted for Kidd's 89th minute goal.

In the away leg, Matt Busby tried unsuccessfully to use the frozen pitch and the blizzard conditions as reasons for postponing the match. A disciplined defensive performance from United, again without Law, restricted Gornik to a 1-0 victory, converted by Lubanski when the ball rebounded off a defensive wall. United were now through to the Semi-final against their old adversaries Real Madrid.

The first leg, in April at Old Trafford, was a sell-out, and an estimated 150 million watched the game on television. With Gento captaining the side, and star striker Amancio suspended, Real came to defend, and a 15-yard Best goal from an Aston cross in the 37th minute was all United could wrest from the game. United were only taking a one-goal advantage to Madrid.

In the return leg in the intimidating atmosphere of the Bernabeu, Real showed their true selves. With Law again absent, and veteran Bill Foulkes at centre-half, United were given a first-half football lesson. Pirri, from an Amancio free-kick, put Real ahead in the 32nd minute, Gento capitalised on a Shay Brennan error to make it 2-0 and, although Zico deflected in an own goal from a lob by Kidd, Amancio scored a third before half time.

A dejected and demoralised United went in at the interval, to be told by Busby, in one of his most effective and inspiring team talks, to go out in the second half and attack – 'Go out there and enjoy yourselves'. And they did. A rejuvenated team began to run at a visibly tiring Real and, in the 70th minute, Best's header was touched in by Sadler. The tie was now level on aggregate.

Five minutes later, a low Best cross found the unlikely figure of Foulkes running into the Real penalty area. A precise sidefoot from the big defender, who was being screamed at by his bench to get back into position, eluded keeper Bétancort, and United held on till the final whistle.

United were in the Final for the first time, and Benfica would be waiting for them at Wembley in May.

Manchester United with the European Cup in 1968. Back row (l to r): Bill Foulkes, John Aston, Jimmy Rimmer, Alex Stepney, Alan Gowling, David Herd. Middle (players l to r): David Sadler, Tony Dunne, Shay Brennan, Pat Crerand, George Best, Francis Burns. Front (l to r): Jimmy Ryan, Nobby Stiles, Denis Law, Bobby Charlton, Brian Kidd, John Fitzpatrick. Matt Busby sits in front with the trophy.

Bobby Charlton (1937). The most famous English player in the world, Charlton possessed all the skills of greatness. He was powerful and elegant, with an unerring ability to find colleagues with a perfect pass. His shot was explosive with either foot, and in his long career with Manchester United and England he played in attack, on the wing and in midfield. He played in three World Cup finals for England, including the country's 1966 victory, and gained a total of 106 caps. He made over 600 appearances for United and scored 199 league goals, retiring in 1972. He was European Footballer of the Year in 1966 and was knighted in 1994. He is currently on the Manchester United board.

BRITISH CLUBS

Cup holders **Celtic** were somewhat unfortunate to meet the highly-rated Dynamo Kiev in the first round. The new seeding system seemed to give as much, if not more, weight to a country's record in the competition as to the club's and, Celtic apart, Scotland's achievements in the tournament generally had been less than impressive. Celtic were also the first holders of the trophy not to have received a 'bye' in the first round.

In September, a 52,000 crowd at Parkhead saw Celtic take to the pitch against the Soviet champions. The omens were good. They had beaten Dynamo two years previously in the Cup Winners Cup, the team on the day was the same as that which beat Inter in the previous year's Final, and the same referee was officiating. However, Celtic's performance was a pale shadow of that glorious evening in Lisbon.

After only three minutes Dynamo went ahead. A sluggish Gemmell was dispossessed in the Dynamo half, the ball was swept out to Sabo who passed to Puzach and the ball was in the Celtic net. Celtic's defending was insouciant, even careless, and they were punished again in the 30th minute when a bad clearance by McNeill was seized on by Byshovets to make it 2-0.

In the second half Celtic tried to make a game of it and they were rewarded with a Lennox goal from a Chalmers pass. Auld then hit the bar with the keeper nowhere, but Dynamo held firm to finish the game 2-1 ahead.

Under the new 'away goals' rule, Celtic now had to travel to the Ukraine and beat Dynamo by at least two clear goals. Their cause in the second leg was not helped by a piece of petulance from Murdoch in the 54th minute when he threw the ball away and was sent off for a second offence. An Auld free-kick was converted by Lennox in the 60th minute, and a Hughes goal disallowed shortly afterwards, but a dramatic last-minute strike by Byshovets put Dynamo through to the next round and Celtic out of the competition.

Northern Ireland's **Glentoran** met Benfica at Windsor Park in the opening round, and surprised the Portuguese and the watching 25,000 crowd by going ahead in the tenth minute through a penalty converted by player-manager John Colrain. Eusebio provided some relief for Benfica with his 86th-minute equaliser. In Lisbon, a fighting display by Glentoran again held the famous opposition to a draw, this time 0-0, but the Irish club was eliminated under the 'away goals' rule, only the second club in the European Cup to suffer this fate.

Glory for Busby as United crush Benfica

Manchester United (1) 4   Benfica (1) 1 (after extra time)

**Wembley Stadium, London, 29 May 1968
Attendance: 92,000
Referee: Lo Bello (Italy)**

Matt Busby was now only one game away from his dream of European greatness, but his side first had to overcome one of the legendary European teams, the four-time Finalists Benfica. With over 250 million watching on TV across Europe, and a partisan crowd at Wembley, the expectations placed on United were enormous. However, they were familiar with Benfica, having beaten them 5-1 two years before in the tournament, and they fielded the same team as in the remarkable victory over Real the previous month in Madrid.

Bobby Charlton watches his shot elude Keeper José Henriqué for his second and United's fourth goal in the 1968 Final.

The game plan was obvious. Cruz would be keeping a close eye on Best, while Stiles and Foulkes would be marking danger men Eusebio and Torres respectively. Charlton and Crerand would contest the midfield with Augusto and Coluna, while Kidd and Sadler, replacing the hospitalised Law, would go for goal.

The first half was a scrappy, foul-ridden affair, with potential match-winner Best being closely marked, and tripped, by Cruz and Humberto, the latter being booked for one particularly unpleasant intervention. By half time, Sadler had missed a couple of chances but the score sheet remained blank. In the second half, Ashton's teasing, speedy runs down the left were causing serious problems for the Benfica defence and, in the 52nd minute, United's persistence paid off when a rare Charlton header from a Tony Dunne cross put United 1-0 up. Now Benfica found their second wind and went on the attack. A header in the 81st minute from the towering centre-forward Torres found Graca, and a fine shot gave Stepney no chance. Minutes later, Eusebio burst through with only Stepney to beat, but he hit the ball straight at the keeper who produced an excellent reflex save. Busby could breathe again.

The game went into extra time, with Busby coming on to the pitch to lift his tired side. 'If you pass the ball to each other you will beat them,' he said. Taking his advice to heart, United went back on to the pitch and won the game with three goals in six minutes. First, Best waltzed round two defenders, glided past the keeper Henrique and slid the ball into the empty net. Then, in the 97th minute, Kidd celebrated his 19th birthday with a headed goal from a rebound off Henrique. A minute later, Charlton effectively won the game with an emphatic right-foot curving shot from the edge of the box.

Benfica were too tired and demoralised to fight back and, at the final whistle, the score was 4-1 to United. An emotional Charlton collected the trophy and a tearful Matt Busby had finally laid the ghost of 1958. 'I am the proudest man in England tonight,' said Busby. Benfica's star was now on the wane and the club was not to reach another Final for twenty years.

The teams
Manchester United: Stepney, Brennan, Dunne, Crerand, Foulkes, Stiles, Best, Kidd, Charlton, Sadler, Ashton (manager: Busby) [Charlton 52, 98, Best 92, Kidd 97]
Benfica: José Henriqué, Adolfo, Cruz, Graca, Humberto, Jacinto, Jose Augusto, Coluna, Torres, Eusebio, Simoes (manager: Gloria) [Graca 81]

Results

First Round	1st leg	2nd leg	Agg
AEK Athens v Jeunesse Esch	3-0	2-3	5-3
Anderlecht v Glentoran	3-0	2-2	5-2
FC Zurich v AB Copenhagen	1-3	2-1	3-4
Floriana v Lahden Reipas	1-1	0-2	1-3
Malmö v AC Milan	2-1	1-4	3-5
Manchester City v Fenerbahçe	0-0	1-2	1-2
Nuremberg v Ajax	1-1	0-4	1-5
Real Madrid v Limassol	6-0	6-0	12-0
Rosenborg v Rapid Vienna	1-3	3-3	4-6
St Etienne v Celtic	2-0	0-4	2-4
Steaua Bucharest v Spartak Trnava	3-1	0-4	3-5
Valur v Benfica	0-0	1-8	1-8
Waterford v Manchester United	1-3	1-7	2-10

Carl Zeiss Jena withdrew. Walkover for Red Star Belgrade. Levski Sofia, Ferencvaros, Dynamo Kiev and Ruch Chorzow withdrew.

Second Round

	1st leg	2nd leg	Agg
AEK Athens v AB Copenhagen	0-0	2-0	2-0
Ajax v Fenerbahçe	2-0	2-0	4-0
Celtic v Red Star Belgrade	5-1	1-1	6-2
Lahden Reipas v Spartak Trnava	1-9	1-7	2-16
Manchester United v Anderlecht	3-0	1-3	4-3
Rapid Vienna v Real Madrid	1-0	1-2	2-2

Byes: AC Milan, Benfica.

Quarter-finals

	1st leg	2nd leg	Agg
AC Milan v Celtic	0-0	1-0	1-0
Ajax v Benfica	1-3	3-1	4-4 3-0(a)
Manchester United v Rapid Vienna	3-0	0-0	3-0
Spartak Trnava v AEK Athens	2-1	1-1	3-2

a) After extra time, play-off in Paris.

Semi-finals

	1st leg	2nd leg	Agg
AC Milan v Manchester United	2-0	0-1	2-1
Ajax v Spartak Trnava	3-0	0-2	3-2

Ajax of Amsterdam were developing a fluid and open system of play, in which the emphasis was on versatility and attack. Under coach Rinus Michels, they were a fit and fast side, spurred on by attacking full-backs Wim Suurbier and Theo van Duivenbode, with the defence held together by Barry Hulshoff and sweeper Velibor Vasovic, who had played for Partizan Belgrade in the 1966 Final. The attack force was led by the young Cruyff and Jaques Swart, with Swedish winger Inge Danielsson another danger in the front line.

A 5-1 first round victory over Nuremberg preceded a 4-0 defeat of Fenerbahçe, Nuninga scoring twice. A Quarter-final tie against Benfica, who had received a second-round bye, saw the Dutch surprisingly lose 3-1 in Amsterdam, courtesy of goals from Jacinto, Torres and Jose Augusto. At the Stadium of Light, Ajax hit back with two goals from Cruyff one from and Danielsson, and Ajax were 3-0 up within the first 30 minutes. Benfica were rescued by a 70th-minute strike from Torres. At the play-off in Paris, with 63,000 spectators in attendance (of which more than half were Dutch fans), a goal-less game at the end of 90 minutes was set alight in extra time when the Dutch scored three, this time Danielsson getting two and Cruyff one.

Their opponents in the Semi-final were the Czechoslovaks Spartak Trnava, who had earlier eliminated Steaua Bucharest and put 16 goals past the unfortunate Finns, Lahden Reipas. Ajax took a 3-0 home victory to Trnava and, in spite of conceding two goals to Spartak forward Kuna, they held out largely due to a stirring display of goalkeeping by Bals. They were through to the Final to play AC Milan.

Milan were virtually a different team to that which had won the Cup in 1963. However, their manager on that occasion, Nereo Rocco, had returned to the San Siro, and he had built an exceptional defensive side with a tight and effective marking system and the ability to counter-attack at speed. Only Rivera and Trapattoni remained from 1963. In goal was Fabio 'the Spider' Cudicini, in defence German international Karl-Heinz Schnellinger, while up front were the big Brazilian centre-forward Sormani, the outside-left Prati and the small, goal-scoring Swedish right-winger Kurt Hamrin.

Dismissing Malmö 5-3 in the first round, they received a bye for the second. They then eliminated in turn the two previous Cup holders Celtic and Manchester United to set themselves up for the Final in Madrid against Ajax.

BRITISH CLUBS

Glentoran entered their third tournament hoping to progress beyond the opening round for the first time. However, a 2-2 home draw with Anderlecht was not enough after their 3-0 defeat in Belgium.

Manchester City, in the European Cup for the first time, had won the English championship by two points over local rivals United. Colin Bell, Franny Lee and Mike Summerbee were the stars of the side, and the flamboyant Malcolm Allison and astute Joe Mercer the coaches. Against Turkish team Fenerbahçe, City could not capitalise on home

advantage and drew 0-0. In the second leg, a Coleman goal in the 12th minute enabled City to go off at half time 1-0 up, but they eventually went down 2-1, with the opening Turkish goal scored by Abdullah.

Celtic, beaten 2-0 in France by St Etienne in the first leg of the first round, went ahead in the opening half at Parkhead when St Etienne's Camerin fouled centre-forward McBride in the box. Gemmell coolly scored the penalty, and the floodgates opened in the second half, with Johnstone rampant and Craig, Chalmers and McBride each netting a goal.

In the next round against Red Star Belgrade at Parkhead Celtic went ahead after only three minutes, Murdoch playing a one-two with Johnstone and walloping the ball past goalkeeper Dujkovic. Red Star, however, rallied and by half time Lazarevic had scored to level the tie.

According to *The Celtic Official History*, Stein then told Johnstone, who hated flying, that, if Celtic won by four clear goals, he would not have to fly to Belgrade. The second half belonged to 'Jinky'. He scored two and made two more, for Lennox and Wallace, in an electrifying and unstoppable display of wing skills and precision passing. Without Johnstone, Celtic defended in depth in the return leg and secured a 1-1 draw, the goal coming from Wallace.

In the Quarter-final Celtic were drawn away in the first leg against AC Milan at the San Siro. The match produced record gate receipts and attracted a crowd of 64,000. Played in a blizzard, the game ended goal-less with Celtic again defending intelligently and reserve goalkeeper Fallon outstanding. Back in Glasgow, an error by McNeill in the 12th minute allowed outside-left Pierino Prati to dispossess him and run through to score. The Italians, as was their custom, pulled back into defence, and Celtic could not break them down. Celtic were out.

Manchester United, who had strengthened their attack in the summer by buying Scottish international winger Willie Morgan, easily disposed of Waterford 10-2 in the first round, Law scoring seven of them. With Best suspended in the next round against Anderlecht, Law scored two in their 3-0 victory at Old Trafford and Best's replacement Carlo Sartori opened the scoring in Belgium. Anderlecht replied with three, but United survived.

Rapid Vienna were the opposition in the Quarter-final. They had stunned a 40,000 crowd at the Bernabeu by knocking out Real Madrid on away goals, with the crowd turning on the veteran Gento who was substituted. A brilliant performance at Old Trafford by the restored Best with two goals, and another from Morgan, was followed by a non-scoring draw in Vienna, and United were through to the Semi-final against the conquerors of Celtic, AC Milan.

Denis Law celebrates yet another goal. The 'Lawman' was fast, powerful in the air and on the ground, and a prolific goal-scorer for Manchester United and Scotland.

The Invasion of Czechoslovakia

On 20 August 1968, Russian tanks rolled into Czechoslovakia to crush the liberal regime of Alexander Dubcek. As a protest against Russia's action, Celtic withdrew from their first-round tie against Ferencvaros of Hungary, one of the Warsaw Pact bloc, and other clubs, notably AC Milan who were drawn against Levski Sofia, threatened to do the same.

UEFA scrapped the original draw, and redrew the competition with western and eastern clubs separated. This created further problems, and provoked all the east European countries who had supplied troops for the invasion – Bulgaria, East Germany, Hungary, Poland and the Soviet Union – to withdraw, citing discrimination. The only exception was Czechoslovakia itself, which allowed its representative Spartak Trnava to remain in the competition.

An under-strength United, with Jimmy Rimmer in goal in place of Stepney, conceded two goals to Milan. Poor defending, particularly by Foulkes, allowed Hamrin to survive a handball protest and score in the 33rd minute, and Sormani added another in the second half. At Old Trafford, United went on the attack but could not erode Milan's lead until the 77th minute, when Best outwitted his marker Anquilletti and crossed for Charlton to find the back of the net. Shortly after, a Law deflection from a Crerand shot, which was kicked away on the line by substitute Santin, was disallowed, with Law later claiming 'it was a travesty of justice'. The Stretford End started to throw missiles onto the pitch in protest and goalkeeper Cudicini was felled by an object. The game ended 1-0 to United but Milan went through to the Final.

Karl-Heinz Schnellinger (1939). A strong, commanding and determined full-back, Schnellinger was one of the key defenders for West Germany throughout the 1960s. His club career encompassed Cologne, Mantova, Roma and Milan, and he was a crucial member of the Milan side which won the European Cup in 1969. He played in four World Cup finals – 1958, 1962, 1966 and 1970 – and he scored in the last minute of the Semi-final against Italy in 1970 to equal Boninsegna's early goal and ensure extra time, although Italy won 4-3 in that riveting game.

Kurt Hamrin (1934). Hamrin was a Swedish outside-right with a flair for goal scoring who began his Italian career with Juventus and Padua. He moved to Fiorentina and won a European Cup Winners Cup medal with the club in 1961. In 1967 he went to AC Milan and won a European Cup winner's medal in 1968. He left Milan for Napoli in 1969. He played for Sweden in the 1958 World Cup finals, scoring four goals, and achieved 32 caps, ending his international career in 1965.

Substitutes

Starting with the 1968/69 tournament, UEFA allowed teams to make up to two outfield substitutes, for any reason and at any time, during a game. Teams were also permitted to have up to five players on the bench as nominated substitutes.

1969 THE FINAL

Italian experience prevails over youthful Ajax

AC Milan (2) 4   Ajax (0) 1

Santiago Bernabeu Stadium, Madrid, 28 May 1969
Attendance: 32,000
Referee: De Mendibil (Spain)

A youthful, precocious Ajax side faced the guile and experience of Milan in the Final, and they were overcome by the Italians in a one-sided game at the Bernabeu.

Untypically, and in a tactical switch which seemed to confuse Ajax, Milan attacked from the outset. In the sixth minute they went ahead, a precise ball from captain Angelo Sormani finding the head of Prati whose looping header sailed over the Ajax goalkeeper Gert Bals. Ajax turned up the pressure but Milan increased their lead just before half time, a piece of delicate skill from Rivera setting up Prati to smash a right-foot shot into the net from the edge of the penalty area.

With Cruyff unfit and Danielsson played out of the game, Ajax were short of scoring options, although a Vasovic penalty in the 60th minute, for a debatable Lodetti foul on Keizer, raised their hopes. This goal, incidentally, meant that Vasovic became the first player to score for different clubs in the Final, his first coming for Partizan Belgrade in 1966.

Just over five minutes later, Sormani put away Milan's third with a shot from outside the area past the out-of-position keeper. In the 74th minute, a skilful chip over the Ajax defence from Rivera was headed in by Prati for his hat-trick. At the final whistle, the crowd decked out in black and red flooded onto the pitch and AC Milan had won their second European Cup. It was to be another twenty years before they did it again, but Ajax were shortly to become the masters of European football.

The teams
AC Milan: Cudicini, Anquilletti, Schnellinger, Malatrasi, Rosato, Trapattoni, Hamrin, Lodetti, Sormani, Rivera, Prati (manager: Rocco) [Prati 6, 39, 74, Sormani 66]
Ajax: Bals, Suurbier (Müller), Van Duivenbode, Vasovic, Hulshoff, Pronk, Groot (Nunninga), Swart, Cruyff, Danielsson, Keizer (manager: Michels) [Vasovic 60]

Helenio Herrera

(1917-1997). The obsessively dedicated, Argentinian-born Herrera began his managerial career in France and moved to Spain, where he coached Atlético Madrid, Valladolid and Sevilla. He took over at Barcelona in the mid-1950s, and developed a fast, attacking side based around the forwards Kubala, Kocsis and Czibor and was defeated finalist in the 1961 European Cup Final. He then moved to Inter Milan, where he developed the defensive catenaccio system which was effective enough to win him the European Cup in 1964 and 1965. After the 1967 defeat by Celtic, he managed Roma. He also took Spain to the 1962 World Cup finals.

Jock Stein

(1922-1985). One of the greatest ever Scottish managers, the blunt but visionary Stein managed Dunfermline and Hibernian in the early 1960s, moving to Celtic in 1965. He turned Celtic into one of the finest European teams, winning the European Cup in 1967, the first British club to do so, and losing Finalists in 1970. When he left the club in 1978, he had led them to ten Scottish league championship, nine Scottish Cups and six Scottish League Cups. After a brief spell at Leeds United, he took over as Scottish manager and oversaw 61 international games. He died from a heart attack immediately after the Scotland v Wales World Cup qualifier, a game which assured Scotland a place in the 1986 World Cup finals.

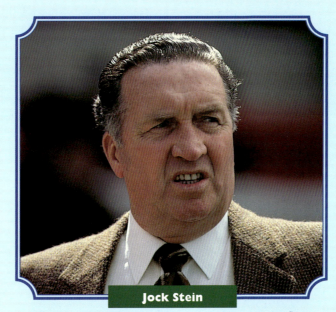

Jock Stein

Rinus Michels

Matt Busby

Marinus 'Rinus' Michels

(1928). The man credited with inventing 'total football', Michels was also something of a disciplinarian. He was a Dutch international in the 1950s and took over as Ajax coach in 1965, discovering the young Johan Cruyff. Michels' young team won the Dutch league four times and the Dutch Cup three times between 1966 and 1971. He moved to Barcelona after Ajax's 1971 European Cup victory over Panathinaikos. He became Dutch national manager and guided his side to the 1974 World Cup Final, losing 2-1 to West Germany, and he came back to lead Holland to victory in the 1988 European Championship Final.

Matt Busby

(1909-1994). Scots-born, ex-Manchester City player Busby became Manchester United manager just after World War Two. He was soon successful, winning the FA Cup in 1948. His young, talented Busby Babes team, built around Duncan Edwards, won two league titles in the mid-1950s, but was destroyed in the Munich air crash in 1958 on the way back from a European Cup tie against Red Star Belgrade. Ten years later, Busby's side, containing Bobby Charlton and George Best, became the first English team to win the European Cup and Busby received a knighthood. He resigned in 1969, but stayed on at the club as general manager and then president.

After his club's resounding defeat in the previous year's Final, manager Michels moved quickly to reinforce his Ajax side. Van Duivenbode was allowed to go to Feyenoord and was replaced by the young Ruud Krol, a star of the future for his club and country, and Vasovic took over the captaincy. A Cruyff-inspired Ajax would shortly be back in style on the European stage but, in this year's tournament, Holland were represented by the 1969 league champions, Feyenoord of Rotterdam.

Managed by Ernst Happel, a legendary defender with Rapid Vienna and Austria in the 1950s, Feyenoord were led from the midfield by Wim Van Hanegem, the masterful left-sided playmaker who would play such an important role in the Dutch national side in the 1970s. The sweeper was Rinus Israel, while in attack Ove Kindvall, the Swedish centre-forward, was ably supported by wingers Coen Moulijn and Henk Wery. Although Feyenoord lacked the fluency and élan of Ajax, they were strong and determined in defence, and fast and direct in attack.

Having destroyed KR Reykajvik 16-2 in the first round, they faced AC Milan in the next round, losing the first away leg 1-0 in the San Siro. Milan had recently acquired the Argentinian striker Nestor Combin and midfielder Domenico Fontana, and appeared

formidable, but they were still recovering from their bruising battles with Estudiantes in the World Club Championships. In Holland they were beaten 2-0, the first goal coming in the seventh minute from an error by keeper Fabio Cudicini who left alone a curving ball from Jansen which hit the inside of the bar and went in. The second was scored five minutes from the end by Van Hanegem, headed in from a cross by Moulijn, and the favourites were out.

AC Milan were not the only big club to leave the competition early. Also in the second round, Standard Liège twice defeated Real Madrid, the second leg at the Bernabeu marking Gento's last appearance in the competition; Red Star Belgrade went out on away goals to ASK Vorwaerts; Benfica were eliminated on the toss of a coin in Lisbon against Celtic; and a poor defensive performance by St Etienne at home was punished by a goal from Kazimierz Deyna, to ensure a Quarter-final place for Legia Warsaw.

In the Quarter-final, Feyenoord were drawn against ASK Vorwaerts and proceeded to the Semi-final 2-1. Legia Warsaw were next, and two goals in Holland, from Van Hanegem and Hasil, put Feyenoord through to the Final. Celtic were to provide the opposition.

Results

Preliminary Round

	1st leg	2nd leg	Agg
Turun Palloseura v KB Copenhagen	0-1	0-4	0-5

First round

	1st leg	2nd leg	Agg
AC Milan v Avenir Beggen	5-0	3-0	8-0
ASK Vorwaerts v Panathinaikos	2-0	1-1	3-1
Basle v Celtic	0-0	0-2	0-2
Bayern Munich v St Etienne	2-0	0-3	2-3
Benfica v KB Copenhagen	2-0	3-2	5-2
CSKA Sofia v Ferencvaros	2-1	1-4	3-5
Feyenoord v KR Reykjavik	12-2	4-0	16-2 (a)
FK Austria v Dynamo Kiev	1-2	1-3	2-5
Fiorentina v Osters IF	1-0	2-1	3-1
Galatasaray v Waterford	2-0	3-2	5-2
Hibernians Malta v Spartak Trnava	2-2	0-4	2-6
Leeds United v Lyn Oslo	10-0	6-0	16-0
Real Madrid v Olympiakos Nicosia	8-0	6-1	14-1
Red Star Belgrade v Linfield	8-0	4-2	12-2
Standard Liège v 17 Nentori Tirana	3-0	1-1	4-1
UT Arad v Legia Warsaw	1-2	0-8	1-10

a) Second leg played in Rotterdam.

Second Round

	1st leg	2nd leg	Agg
AC Milan v Feyenoord	1-0	0-2	1-2
ASK Vorwaerts v Red Star Belgrade	2-1	2-3	4-4
Celtic v Benfica	3-0	0-3	3-3 (a)
Dynamo Kiev v Fiorentina	1-2	0-0	1-2
Leeds United v Ferencvaros	3-0	3-0	6-0
Legia Warsaw v St Etienne	2-1	1-0	3-1
Spartak Trnava v Galatasaray	1-0	0-1	1-1 (a)
Standard Liège v Real Madrid	1-0	3-2	4-2

a) Spartak Trnava and Celtic won the coin toss.

Quarter-finals

	1st leg	2nd leg	Agg
ASK Vorwaerts v Feyenoord	1-0	0-2	1-2
Celtic v Fiorentina	3-0	0-1	3-1
Galatasaray v Legia Warsaw	1-1	0-2	1-3
Standard Liège v Leeds United	0-1	0-1	0-2

Semi-finals

	1st leg	2nd leg	Agg
Leeds United v Celtic	0-1	1-2	1-3 (b)
Legia Warsaw v Feyenoord	0-0	0-2	0-2

b) Second leg played at Hampden Park, Glasgow.

BRITISH CLUBS

Leeds United had been dragged out of Second-Division obscurity by Don Revie in the mid-1960s, and were now English champions. A tough, uncompromising side, with a defence containing four English internationals – Terry Cooper, Paul Reaney, Jack Charlton and Norman Hunter – they also possessed abundantly skilful players. In midfield were the small, tenacious captain Billy Bremner and Johnny Giles, the gifted and visionary distributor of the ball. Scottish wingers Peter Lorimer, of the thunderous shot, and the dribbling supremo Eddie Gray made up the forward line with the forwards Mick Jones and Allan 'Sniffer' Clarke, the sharpshooting striker bought in the close season from Leicester City. Revie had forged a side with enormous self-

belief and team spirit, and they expected much from their first season in the European Cup.

A 16-0 thrashing of poor Lyn Oslo preceded a meeting with Ferencváros, with the tie effectively decided in the first 30 minutes of the first leg at Elland Road, where two goals from Jones and one from the scheming Giles killed off the Hungarians' hopes. Leeds scored another three without reply in the away leg. Away to Standard Liège in the Quarter-final, a Lorimer goal from a tight angle, following a typically intricate passing move, gave them the buffer they needed in the home tie. They struggled to contain a lively and determined Liège, but a Giles penalty ten minutes from time squeezed them through to the Semi-final against

Celtic, the first-ever all-British Semi-final. Leeds had scored 24 goals and conceded none, but domestic fixture congestion was catching up with the team.

Celtic had defeated Basle 2-0 on aggregate in the first round and met Eusebio's Benfica at Parkhead in the second. A typical Tommy Gemmell 25-yard rocket put Celtic in front in the second minute. A Wallace super strike made it two just before the interval, and new signing Harry Hood headed in the third in the second half. Fortunes were reversed in Lisbon, where one each from Eusebio and Graca, followed by another, deep in injury time, from Diamantino Costa enforced

extra time. A goal-less thirty minutes resulted in the toss of a coin, the last time this would happen in the competition, to decide the Quarter-finalists. Celtic rode their luck.

Against an ultra-defensive Fiorentina at Parkhead, Celtic turned on the style. A delightful Auld strike from a Hughes header opened their account, and an own goal and a last-minute Wallace header were sufficient for the team to absorb a 1-0 defeat in the away tie in Florence.

Two Johnstone-inspired, ebullient performances by the Celts against Leeds United in the 'Battle of Britain' Semi-final in April took them to the Final at the San Siro against Feyenoord, and Jock Stein's exciting Scottish team were the clear favourites.

The Battle of Britain

On the first Wednesday after Easter, 1970, Leeds lined up at Elland Road to contest the European Cup Semi-final against Celtic. A tired Leeds, who were also chasing the League title and FA Cup, were missing centre-half Norman Hunter through injury. They faced an in-form Celtic, holders of the Scottish 'treble' and for whom Johnstone was playing the best football of his career.

To counter the Leeds midfield of Bremner and Giles, Stein cleverly deployed a 4-3-3 formation, with Auld, Murdoch and George Connelly in midfield. A mistake by Madeley allowed Connelly to latch onto a Wallace through ball to score in the second minute. Eddie Gray hit the crossbar but Celtic held on to take a 1-0 lead back to Scotland.

A huge crowd of 133,461, still the record attendance for the competition, packed Hampden Park, to where Stein had moved the fixture. In the 14th minute, Bremner cracked in a 20-yard volley past keeper Williams, and Celtic piled into attack with right-back Hay and Johnstone controlling the right wing. Two minutes into the second half, Hughes crashed in a diving header from an Auld cross to make it 2-1 overall. Leeds' goalkeeper Sprake was concussed after a clash with 'Yogi' Hughes and replaced by David Harvey and, shortly after, Celtic scored another, Murdoch converting an inch-perfect cross from the dazzling Johnstone.

Scotland had won the 'Battle of Britain' and Celtic were through to the Final for the second time.

Billy McNeill clears a Leeds United attack in the first leg at Elland Road, watched by Eddie Gray.

Tommy Gemmell crashes in Celtic's goal at the San Siro in the 1970 Final.

Dutch delight as Feyenoord sink Celtic

Feyenoord (1) 2   Celtic (1) 1 (after extra time)

San Siro Stadium, Milan, 6 May 1970
Attendance: 53,000
Referee: Lo Bello (Italy)

The horns honked, the flags flew and the rockets exploded around the San Siro as the Feyenoord supporters welcomed a Dutch side to the Final for the first time. The Dutch outnumbered and out-sang the 20,000 Scottish fans, a harbinger of what was to happen on the pitch.

An over-confident Jock Stein dropped the versatile and effective midfielder Connolly and reverted to 4-2-4, reckoning on his forwards having the beating of the underdogs Feyenoord, whose coach Happel adopted the sweeper system that had served him well in the competition to date.

In the 29th minute, a cheeky back-heeled free-kick from Murdoch was lashed in from 25 yards by Gemmell through the Dutch defensive wall, with the goalkeeper momentarily unsighted by the referee. Within three minutes, however, Feyenoord had pulled one back, when a free kick from Franz Hasil over the static Celtic defence gave sweeper and captain Rinus Israel space to plant a lobbed header over keeper Williams.

In the second half Feyenoord took over the game. The Austrian international Hasil and Van Hanegem controlled the midfield, Hasil hitting both post and bar, and the Dutch gave an exhibition of superb, one-touch football. Celtic were playing well below form, bemused by the constantly-moving inventive football of the opposition, and Feyenoord's tactics compounded a woefully ineffective performance from Celtic's normally dependable match-winner Johnstone.

However, Celtic made it to extra time, when keeper Evan Williams was Celtic's best player, at one point making an excellent double save from Kindvall and then Wery. Four minutes from the end, McNeill's misjudgement of a pass from Israel led to him handling the ball which, with the referee playing advantage, reached Kindvall in the box, and the ball was in the Celtic net. The game was over.

A lacklustre Celtic, perhaps believing their own publicity, never really got into the game, and Stein had been out-manoeuvred by Happel's deployment of what was an attacking *catenaccio* system, with sweeper Israel alternating when required between attack and defence. 'The better team's won,' said Stein.

Neither club has again reached the Final, although Feyenoord's victory was the first of four consecutive Dutch triumphs in the tournament. 'Total football' was around the corner, and Ajax were about to assert their dominance over European football.

The teams
Feyenoord: Pieters Graafland, Romeijn (Haak), Van Duivenbode, Jansen, Israel, Hasil, Wery, Laseroms, Kindvall, Van Hanegem, Moulijn (manager: Happel) [Israel 32, Kindvall 116]
Celtic: Williams, Hay, Gemmell, Murdoch, McNeill, Brogan, Johnstone, Wallace, Hughes, Auld (Connelly), Lennox (manager: Stein) [Gemmell 29]

THE 1970-71 SEASON

Feyenoord's unexpected, although deserved, victory in the previous year's competition had alerted European observers to the increasing sophistication and strength of Dutch football. Although the Dutch league was only part-time as recently as the 1950s, Holland was now producing competitive and skilful sides more than able to hold their own against the top European teams, and none more so than Ajax.

Still under the management of the authoritative Rinus Michels, and directed by the pace, vision and breathtaking ability of Johan Cruyff, Ajax were on the threshold of European mastery. As in the Final against Milan two years previously, the team was based on the defensive pairing of sweeper Vasovic and central defender Hulshoff, with Swart, centre-forward Dick Van Dijk and the clever left-winger Piet Keizer on the offensive. However, some gifted young players were emerging from the youth team, in particular the 19-year-old prodigy Johann Neeskens, who combined intelligence and adroit ball play with firmness in the tackle and a powerful shot. Also coming through were Ruud Krol, an athletic, attacking left-back, and the versatile 22-year-old midfielder, Arie Haan. The years of 'total football' were about to begin.

A first round 4-2 victory over Albania's 17 Nentori Tirana, with Cruyff missing through injury, was followed by a 5-1 result against Basle. Celtic were next in the Quarter-final, and a 3-1 aggregate win over the Scots saw Ajax in the Semi-final to face Atlético Madrid, who had eliminated the Italian champions Cagliari and Legia Warsaw in previous rounds. An untypically defensive performance in Madrid resulted in Ajax conceding a single goal to Irureta, but in Amsterdam a 76th-minute goal from right-back Suurbier and a strike apiece from Keizer and Neeskens put Ajax through to the Final.

Greek side Panathinaikos had entered the competition several times since 1960 but they had never progressed beyond the first round. Even though they were now managed by the legendary Hungarian Ferenc Puskas, the team was still regarded as something of a makeweight by the bigger clubs. However, the experienced

Total Football

'Total football', as developed by the Ajax side of the early 1970s, was a system to delight spectators and purists alike. The idea was that, rather than players each having a separate, well-defined role and position in the team, all players were to play in any and every position, if required. Improvising and reacting to the game as it developed were at the heart of the system, which demanded intelligent, gifted and fit players just as capable of switching back to defence as surging forward in attack.

Although nominally a 4-3-3 formation, total football's exponents were fast, creative and fluid, and were able to interchange roles with team-mates and adapt with ease to the changing rhythms and fluctuating fortunes on the park. The system was adapted further by the Bayern Munich team under Franz Beckenbauer in the mid-1970s.

Results

Preliminary Round	1st leg	2nd leg	Agg
Levski Spartak v FK Austria	3-1	0-3	3-4

First Round			
17 Nentori Tirana v Ajax	2-2	0-2	2-4
Atlético Madrid v FK Austria	2-0	2-1	4-1
Cagliari v St Etienne	3-0	0-1	3-1
Celtic v Kokkolan	9-0	5-0	14-0
EPA Larnaca v Borussia Moenchengladbach	0-6	0-10	0-16(a)
Everton v IBK Keflavik	6-2	3-0	9-2
Fenerbahçe v Carl Zeiss Jena	0-4	0-1	0-5
Feyenoord v UT Arad	1-1	0-0	1-1
Glentoran v Waterford	1-3	0-1	1-4
IFK Gothenburg v Legia Warsaw	0-4	1-2	1-6
Jeunesse Esch v Panathinaikos	1-2	0-5	1-7
Rosenborg v Standard Liège	0-2	0-5	0-7
Slovan Bratislava v BK Copenhagen	2-1	2-2	4-3
Spartak Moscow v Basle	3-2	1-2	4-4
Sporting Lisbon v Floriana	5-0	4-0	9-0
Ujpest Dózsa v Red Star Belgrade	2-0	0-4	2-4

a) = 1st leg played in Augsburg.

Second round			
Ajax v Basle	3-0	2-1	5-1
Borussia Moenchengladbach v Everton	1-1	1-1	2-2(b)
Cagliari v Atlético Madrid	2-1	0-3	2-4
Carl Zeiss Jena v Sporting Lisbon	2-1	2-1	4-2
Panathinaikos v Slovan Bratislava	3-0	1-2	4-2
Red Star Belgrade v UT Arad	3-0	3-1	6-1
Standard Liège v Legia Warsaw	1-0	0-2	1-2
Waterford v Celtic	0-7	2-3	2-10

b) = Everton won 4-3 on penalties.

Quarter-finals			
Ajax v Celtic	3-0	0-1	3-1
Atlético Madrid v Legia Warsaw	1-0	1-2	2-2
Carl Zeiss Jena v Red Star Belgrade	3-2	0-4	3-6
Everton v Panathinaikos	1-1	0-0	1-1

Semi-finals			
Atlético Madrid v Ajax	1-0	0-3	3-1
Red Star Belgrade v Panathinaikos	4-1	0-3	4-4

Penalties

The 1970/71 season saw an end to the lottery of tossing a coin to decide ties, and to the time and expense involved in play-offs. From this season onward, in the event of ties finishing level on aggregate after extra time and with the same number of away goals, a penalty 'shoot-out' would determine the winner.

Each team would take a penalty in turn, up to a maximum of five kicks, with the team converting the most the winner. If the scores were level after the five kicks, then the shoot-out moved into 'sudden death'– ie. the first missed penalty loses the tie, as long as the next penalty by the opposing team is converted.

defender Aristidis Kamaras, inside-forward playmaker Dimitri Domazos and the tall, languid but deadly striker Antonidas Antoniadis were players capable of upsetting more fancied opposition. In the early rounds they disposed of Jeunesse Esch 7-1 and Slovan Bratislava 4-2, seven of the goals coming from Antoniadis, who would finish the tournament as top goalscorer.

In the Quarter-final they knocked out Everton on away goals. In the Semi-final they were drawn away to Red Star Belgrade, under the coaching direction of Milan Miljanic and with the great left-winger and captain Dragan Dzajic as inspiration. Red Star were masterminded in midfield by the experienced Acimovic, and the exciting 19-year-old striker Filipovic had scored five goals in the team's wins over Ujpest Dzosa, when Red Star came back from 2-0 down, and UT Arad. A 4-1 Semi-final defeat in Belgrade appeared to have ended Panathinaikos' interest in the competition, but a marvellous fightback in Athens saw them win 3-0, two coming from Antoniadis, and proceed to the Final, again on away goals.

Johan Cruyff

BRITISH CLUBS

Celtic were continuing their relentless domination of Scottish football, and yet again were Scotland's representatives in the European Cup. Having shrugged aside Kokkolan and Waterford in the early rounds, scoring 24 and conceding 2, Celtic held Ajax at bay for most of the game in the first leg of the Quarter-final in Amsterdam until, in the 63rd minute, Neeskens found Cruyff who volleyed home, and Ajax were one up. Celtic were unable to handle Cruyff, who was in magisterial form, and Hulshoff scored a second from a free kick, awarded for a Connelly foul on Cruyff. Keizer shot in a third after some clever work from Cruyff. At Parkhead a 28th-minute goal from Johnstone was all that Celtic could manage.

Harry Catterick's **Everton** had qualified for the second time, their previous appearance being their first-round defeat by Inter Milan in 1964. The team had won the English title by a handsome nine points from Leeds United, and their success had largely been achieved through their creative midfield of Alan Ball, Howard Kendall and Colin Harvey. With bustling centre-forward Joe Royle providing the goals in concert with fellow striker Jimmy Husband and left-winger John Morrissey, they were an attractive and enterprising team.

After a 9-2 defeat of Iceland's IBK Keflavik, they faced sterner opposition in the second round in the shape of the forbidding and multi-talented Borussia Moenchengladbach, whose star players included German internationals Berti Vogts, Jupp Heynkes and midfield provider Günter Netzer. In the first leg in Germany, Vogts put Borussia ahead but the score was levelled by a 25-yard effort from Kendall. A Morrissey strike in the first minute in the home leg was equalised by Laumen, and the game went into extra time, which ended scoreless. In the penalty shoot-out at an unbearably tense Goodison Park, Royle missed the first attempt. With the score at 4-3, Laumen having missed for Borussia, the young Everton goalkeeper Rankin saved from Müller, and the German champions were out.

Ferenc Puskas' Panathinaikos travelled to Goodison for the first leg of the Semi-final and, although Everton attacked incessantly, the first goal went to the Greeks, Antoniadis taking advantage of a counter-attack. The young substitute David Johnson saved Everton with a goal in the 89th minute. In a torrid and hostile atmosphere in Athens in the return leg, neither side could manage to find the net, and Everton were eliminated on away goals.

Glentoran went out in the first round after an all-Ireland tie with Waterford.

European Cup stays in Holland

Ajax (1) 2 Panathinaikos (0) 0

Wembley Stadium, London, 2 June 1971
Attendance: 83,000
Referee: Taylor (England)

Ferenc Puskas' Panathinaikos had scraped through to the Final after winning their two previous games on away goals, and were not expected to produce a shock result against the total footballers of Ajax. And so it proved, in a generally uninspiring anticlimax to this year's tournament.

To the delight of the enthusiastic, mainly Dutch crowd, Ajax went ahead in the fifth minute. Keizer, carrying an injury, crossed from the left and Van Dijk headed into the net past a nervy Ekonomopoulos. The goalkeeper's confidence returned as the half progressed, and he made a string of fine saves from the Dutch forwards, particularly Cruyff, who were carving their way through the tall but static Greek defence. Panathinaikos tried to make a contest of it, with Domazos using his repertoire of backheels, flicks and short passes to try to lift his team from midfield, and Kamaras missed a good opportunity to equalise three minutes from half time.

At half time, Rijnders was taken ill and replaced by Horst Blankenburg, and Arie Haan came on for Swart. Ajax seemed happy to rest on their one-goal advantage in the second half, and pulled back into defence. The Greeks were afforded more space as Ajax withdrew, but could only lift high crosses into the Ajax goalmouth, which was effectively policed by keeper Stuy. The game was over in the 87th minute when a glorious run from Cruyff culminated in a pass to Haan, whose shot was deflected into the net by Kapsis.

The result was the correct one, as Ajax always had something in reserve and were the superior team on the day. Vasovic collected the European Cup after what was his last European game for Ajax. His successor as captain, Keizer, was to become familiar with the trophy in the following two years.

The teams

Ajax: Stuy, Suurbier, Neeskens, Vasovic, Rijnders (Blankenburg), Hulshoff, Swart (Haan), Van Dijk, Cruyff, Mühren, Keizer (manager: Michels) [Van Dijk 5, Haan 87]

Panathinaikos: Ekonomopoulos, Tomaras, Vlahsos, Elefterakis, Kamaras, Sourpis, Grammos, Filakouris, Antoniadis, Domazos, Kapsis (manager: Puskas)

Dick Van Dijk (10) celebrates his 5th-minute goal in the 1971 Final. Gerrie Mühren (9) shows his delight.

Barcelona had made Rinus Michels an offer he could not refuse, and his role as Ajax coach was taken over by the Romanian Stefan Kovacs.

Vasovic had left Ajax, and the German Horst Blankenburg took over his role in the centre of defence alongside Hulshoff. The Dutchmen were now at full strength for this year's tournament. Neeskens was established in midfield, linking up with Haan and Gerrie Mühren to feed the wingers Swart and Keizer and centre-forward Cruyff, and this was the line-up which dispensed with Dynamo Dresden and Marseille in the opening rounds of the 1971-72 competition. In the Quarter-final, English champions Arsenal were defeated 3-1 and in the Semi-final Benfica were waiting.

Benfica were now managed by the English ex-international forward Jimmy Hogan, whose coaching career in England included a spell at West Bromwich Albion. The seemingly ageless Eusebio was still leading the line with his prolific striking partner Artur Jorge, and they were flanked by the brilliant young Portuguese winger Nene on the right and the Angolan Jordao on the left. They progressed with wins over Innsbruck and CSKA Sofia. One-nil down after the away leg Quarter-final to Feyenoord, Benfica produced a sparkling performance in Lisbon, with Nene grabbing a hat-trick and Eusebio and Jordao scoring one apiece.

In the Semi-final in Amsterdam, a determined rearguard action by Benfica restricted the score to one goal, scored by

Roberto Boninsegna (1943). Boninsegna was a much-travelled Italian centre-forward whose career included spells at Inter Milan, Varese, Cagliari, Juventus and Verona. He played for Inter between 1969 and 1976 and scored 113 league goals for the club. He is best remembered for being felled by a soft-drink can in Moenchengladbach in a 1971/72 European Cup game. He won a UEFA Cup winner's medal with Juventus in 1977. He made his international debut in 1967 and gained 22 caps, and was in the Italian squad in the 1970 and 1974 World Cup finals.

Roberto Boninsegna

Results

Preliminary Round	1st leg	2nd leg	Agg
Valencia v US Luxembourg	3-1	1-0	4-1
First Round			
Ajax v Dynamo Dresden	2-0	0-0	2-0
Akranes v Sliema Wanderers	0-4	0-0	0-4
BK Copenhagen v Celtic	2-1	0-3	2-4
CSKA Sofia v Partisan Tirana	3-0	1-0	4-0
Cork Hibernians v Borussia Moenchengladbach	0-5	1-2	1-7
Dynamo Bucharest v Spartak Trnava	0-0	2-2	2-2
Feyenoord v Olympiakos Nicosia	8-0	9-0	17-0
Galatasaray v CSKA Moscow	1-1	0-3	1-4
Innsbruck v Benfica	0-4	1-3	1-7
Inter Milan v AEK Athens	4-1	2-3	6-4
Lahden Reipas v Grasshoppers Zurich	1-1	0-8	1-9
Marseille v Gornik Zabre	2-1	1-1	3-2
Standard Liège v Linfield	2-0	3-2	5-2
Stromsgodset v Arsenal	1-3	0-4	1-7
Ujpest Dózsa v Malmö	4-0	0-1	4-1
Valencia v Hajduk Split	0-0	1-1	1-1
Second Round			
Benfica v CSKA Sofia	2-1	0-0	2-1
Celtic v Sliema Wanderers	5-0	2-1	7-1
CSKA Moscow v Standard Liège	1-0	0-2	1-2
Dynamo Bucharest v Feyenoord	0-3	0-2	0-5
Grasshoppers Zurich v Arsenal	0-2	0-3	0-5
Inter Milan v Borussia Moenchengladbach	4-2	0-0	4-2(a)
Marseille v Ajax	1-2	1-4	2-6
Valencia v Ujpest Dózsa	0-1	1-2	1-3

a) = The first match was annulled and replayed

Quarter-finals			
Ajax v Arsenal	2-1	1-0	3-1
Feyenoord v Benfica	1-0	1-5	2-5
Inter Milan v Standard Liège	1-0	1-2	2-2
Ujpest Dózsa v Celtic	1-2	1-1	2-3
Semi-finals			
Ajax v Benfica	1-0	0-0	1-0
Inter Milan v Celtic	0-0	0-0	0-0 5-4(P)

P = (penalties)

Swart from a free-kick. In the second leg, English referee Norman Burtenshaw turned down a Benfica penalty appeal and was pelted with bottles and fruit. The game ended in a goalless draw, and Ajax were through to the Final, while Benfica were reported to UEFA and received a derisory fine.

Inter Milan had been rebuilding since their last Final appearance against Celtic in 1967, and only six members of the great 1960s team remained – full-backs, Facchetti and Burgnich; midfielders, the long-serving and rejuvenated Corso and his partner Bedin; and forwards Mazzola and the mazy dribbler Jair. The club had acquired the strong, brave centre-forward Roberto Boninsegna from Cagliari, in exchange for

Domenghini, and defensive midfielder Mario Bertini from Fiorentina. Newcomers in defence were stopper Mario Giubertoni and right-back Mario Bellugi. In their first tie against AEK Athens, a 6-4 aggregate saw Inter through, although Bertini was sent off.

Borussia Moenchengladbach met Inter in the second round in Germany, and by the 22nd minute Inter were 2-1 down. Suddenly, Inter's scorer Boninsegna was on the ground, felled by a Coca-Cola can thrown from the German crowd. He was carried off, replaced by new recruit Ghio and Inter went into free-fall. By half-time they were 4-1 down and goalkeeper Vieri was replaced by the youthful and inexperienced Ivano Bordon. Things went from bad to worse for the Italians when Jair was injured, but could not be replaced as Inter had used up their two substitutes, and then Corso was sent off for kicking the referee. A nine-man Inter succumbed 7-1 to Borussia, with a brace each from Netzer and Heynkes.

Because of the Boninsegna incident, Inter afterwards demanded that, under UEFA rules, they be awarded the match. A compromise from UEFA declared the game null and void and that a replay should be staged on a neutral ground. In the second leg in Milan, Inter were without Corso, who had received one year's suspension for his rash behaviour in the first game, but beat Borussia 4-2 with Boninsegna sufficiently recovered to get his name on the scoresheet. The replayed match in Berlin was a 0-0 draw, although Bordon saved a penalty.

In the Quarter-final at the San Siro in March, a Jair goal against Standard Liège gave Inter a 1-0 lead, and a 2-1 defeat in Liège, with Mazzola scoring for Inter, a fortnight later put the Italians through on away goals. The Semi-final tie against Celtic produced no goals, and Inter's ability to convert penalties decided the tie. The Italians were to make their fourth appearance in the European Cup Final, this time against Ajax in Rotterdam on 31 May.

BRITISH CLUBS

The emphasis **Celtic** had placed on developing their youth team was now paying dividends. The 'Quality Street Gang', as these young players had become known, was a reservoir of exciting talent. The strong, cultured full-back Danny McGrain, who was to represent his club and country for nearly twenty years, had his European blooding the previous season; the small, mercurial striker Lou Macari was making his European debut (scoring five goals in the process); George Connelly was becoming an indispensable utility player and fitting in well alongside McNeill; and brilliant young forward Kenny Dalglish was also a newcomer to the tournament. Johnstone, Murdoch, Lennox, Wallace and McNeill represented the older generation, but remained the core of the side.

Two easy eliminations of BK Copenhagen and Sliema Wanderers, 4-2 and 7-1 respectively, led Celtic to Budapest to play Ujpest Dózsa, a team in the Hungarian tradition of flowing and attractive football, who had knocked out Malmö and Valencia. A headed own goal by defender Horvath in the 19th minute was cancelled by the same player in the second half, and little Lou Macari scored the winner for Celtic. At Parkhead, a resolute Ujpest equalised on aggregate in the fifth minute, but a Connelly through-ball in the second half caught the Hungarians napping and Macari again nipped in to put Celtic into the Semi-final.

Their old sparring partners Inter Milan were waiting for them in the first leg at the San Siro, where a solid defensive display saw Celtic hold on to a 0-0 draw. In the return, Celtic, without the injured Hay and McGrain, launched waves of attacks against the Italians in front of a crowd of 75,000, but Inter's desperate defence and Lido Vieri's inspired goalkeeping prevented a goal. John 'Dixie' Deans had come on for Dalglish, took the first penalty, and skied it over the bar. All the other spot-kicks were converted, and Inter were through to the Final.

For only the second time that century, the 'double' of league and cup titles had been achieved in England, with **Arsenal** following in the footsteps of Spurs ten years earlier. A strong, well-disciplined side, the Gunners were managed by Bertie Mee and coached by Don Howe, an ex-English international with wide experience and astute tactical understanding. Up front was the attacking partnership of big John Radford and young Ray Kennedy, the latter soon to be an integral part of the Liverpool side who were to storm their way through Europe in the years to come, with Cup Final hero Charlie George also in the goal

hunt. The defence was commanded by Scotsman Frank McLintock, ably aided by Peter Storey and Peter Simpson, and Bob Wilson was dependable and agile in goal. Arsenal were on their first European Cup campaign.

Progress in the early rounds was simple enough, a 7-1 defeat of Norway's Stromsgodset Drammen followed by a 5-0 victory over Grasshoppers Zurich, Kennedy scoring in both legs. However, in the Quarter-final they were drawn against the best team in Europe, Ajax.

> **Ray Kennedy** (1951). A big, powerful forward, Ray Kennedy began his career at Arsenal in 1968 and came to prominence in Arsenal's 1969/70 Fairs Cup win, scoring in the away leg of the Final against Anderlecht. He was a member of the 1971 'double' team and transferred to Liverpool in 1974 where Bob Paisley shrewdly transformed him into a midfielder. He subsequently helped Liverpool to a variety of domestic honours and three European Cups. He moved to Swansea in 1982, and then Hartlepool. He gained 17 caps for England. Sadly, he now suffers from Parkinson's Disease.

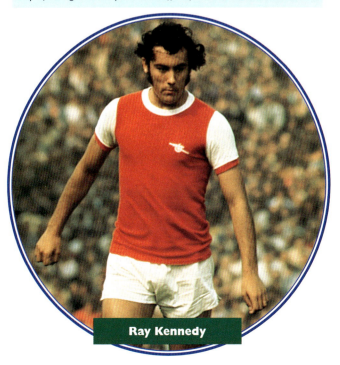

Ray Kennedy

Bob Wilson makes a vain attempt to prevent the header by George Graham (right) entering the net, watched by Arie Haan of Ajax, in the Quarter-final at Highbury.

At a packed Olympic Stadium in Amsterdam, Kennedy took advantage of a mis-timed headed back-pass from Keizer to Stuy in the 14th minute, and Arsenal went one-up. Arsenal defended stoutly, but were fortunate not to suffer more than a 2-1 defeat against an Ajax team playing with superlative ease. Although Wilson had a splendid game, and kept the marauding Dutchmen at bay for most of the match, two goals from Gerrie Mühren, one a penalty and the other a deflection off Simpson, gave the Dutch a 2-1 lead to take to Highbury.

In the second leg, Radford was suspended and his place was taken by the gifted but erratic young Scottish forward, Peter Marinello. In the first minute, a mistake by Blankenburg allowed Marinello through with only Stuy to beat, but a poor shot bounced off the keeper's leg and the ball was blasted wide by Kennedy. In the 15th minute, a badly-judged backheader from George Graham to his goalkeeper eluded Wilson, and Ajax were 3-1 ahead on aggregate. Ajax were happy to defend their lead till the final whistle.

1972

THE FINAL

Total football overcomes Italian caution

Ajax (0) 2   Inter Milan (0) 0

Feyenoord Stadium, Rotterdam, 31 May 1972
Attendance: 61,000
Referee: Helies (France)

With over 25 European countries watching on Eurovision, 'total football' met *catenaccio* in the Rotterdam stadium, home to Ajax's bitter rival, Feyenoord.

As the game began, it was clear from the lone figure of Roberto Boninsegna in attack that Inter were here to defend. However, it soon became apparent that even the most stubborn and cynical defence in Europe was unable to cope with Ajax's precise, flowing football. Ajax had won the Dutch league and cup, and were intent on gaining an historic treble.

The Dutchmen were interchanging positions, passing the ball with accuracy and flair and revelling in the occasion. Inter's resolve was weakened in the 12th minute when centre-back Giubertoni was injured and replaced by Mario Bertini, and goalkeeper Ivano Bordon, in for the injured Vieri, had to be alert. Mazzola and 19-year-old Gabriell Oriali in midfield were pressed back in an attempt to shore up the back line, who were being twisted and turned by Ajax's constant incursions

and swift movement. The Ajax full-backs, too, were getting in on the act, Suurbier sending in a stream of crosses from the right and Krol smashing a 25-yard shot against Bordon's post.

Although the game remained goal-less at half time, early in the second half the Dutch scored the goal their football deserved. In the 47th minute, Bordon and Burgnich collided trying to reach a cross from Suurbier, Bordon dropped the ball, and Cruyff turned and coolly stroked in a simple goal at the far post. Midway through the half, Inter roused themselves and Stuy did well to save from the feet of Mazzola. However, Ajax made the game safe in the 77th minute when European Footballer of the Year Cruyff soared to meet a Keizer free kick and head the ball beyond Bordon's grasp. Inter were finished and their dreary tactics had been exposed as redundant by a scintillating Ajax side.

The teams
Ajax: Stuy, Suurbier, Krol, Blankenburg, Hulshoff, Neeskens, Swart, Mühren, Cruyff, Haan, Keizer (manager: Kovacs) [Cruyff 47, 77]
Inter Milan: Bordon, Burgnich, Facchetti, Bellugi, Giubertoni (Bertini), Oriali, Jair (Pellizzaro),Bedin, Boninsegna, Mazzola, Frustalupi (manager: Invernizzi)

Weary from their exertions against Independiente in the World Club Championship in September, Ajax were fortunate to be given a bye in the first round of the tournament. They were now the undisputed champions of European football and all the top clubs were hoping to keep them at arm's length until the later stages.

Some of the more familiar names were back in the draw. Real Madrid had won the Spanish league, and Bayern Munich, the fast-emerging German side who were to take over the mantle of Ajax, were making their second appearance. Regular contestants Benfica and Celtic were also eyeing the trophy, and Juventus were making their fifth attempt at European domination. It was a strong field, but it was difficult to envisage a serious threat to Cruyff and his all-conquering Ajax.

Eclipsed in Europe in the 1960s by the two Milan teams, Juventus had spent some of the Agnelli family's lire on the world's most expensive player Pietro Anastasi, an explosive goalscorer, to assert the primacy of Turin. He lined up in attack with the 35-year-old Brazilian Jose Altafini, who still held the competition goal record of 14 in one tournament, set when he had played for AC Milan ten years previously. In goal was the great Dino Zoff, a long-serving Italian international keeper who was later to manage Juventus to European success, and in defence were Luciano Spinosi and Francesco Morini. Fabio Capello and Franco Causio were the midfield playmakers in a team boasting no less than six Italian internationals.

Juventus started badly, going down 1-0 in Marseille, but a Roberto Bettega-inspired 3-0 win at home put them through to meet Magdeburg. A Juventus goal in each leg knocked out the East Germans, and two away goals from Anastasi and Altafini against Ujpest Dózsa, conquerors of Celtic in the previous round, saw the Italians into the Semi-final on away goals. A controversial 3-1 win against Derby in Turin, after which Derby accused Juventus of cheating

Results

First Round

First Round	1st leg	2nd leg	Agg
Anderlecht v Vejle	4-2	3-0	7-2
Aris Bonnevoie v Arges Pitesti	0-2	0-4	0-6
Celtic v Rosenborg	2-1	3-1	5-2
CSKA Sofia v Panathinaikos	2-1	2-0	4-1
Derby County v Zeljeznicar Sarajevo	2-0	2-1	4-1
Galatasaray v Bayern Munich	1-1	0-6	1-7
Innsbruck v Dynamo Kiev	0-1	0-2	0-3
Magdeburg v Turun Palloseura	6-0	3-1	9-1
Malmö v Benfica	1-0	1-4	2-4
Marseille v Juventus	1-0	0-3	1-3
Real Madrid v IBK Keflavik	3-0	1-0	4-0
Sliema Wanderers v Gornik Zabrze	0-5	0-5	0-10
Ujpest Dózsa v Basle	2-0	2-3	4-3
Waterford v Omonia Nicosia	2-1	0-2	2-3

Byes: Ajax, Spartak Trnava

Second Round

Second Round	1st leg	2nd leg	Agg
Arges Pitesti v Real Madrid	2-1	1-3	3-4
Bayern Munich v Omonia Nicosia	9-0	4-0	13-0
Celtic v Ujpest Dózsa	2-1	0-3	2-4
CSKA Sofia v Ajax	1-3	0-3	1-6
Derby County v Benfica	3-0	0-0	3-0
Dynamo Kiev v Gornik Zabrze	2-0	1-2	3-2
Juventus v Magdeburg	1-0	1-0	2-0
Spartak Trnava v Anderlecht	1-0	1-0	2-0

Quarter-finals

Quarter-finals			
Ajax v Bayern Munich	4-0	1-2	5-2
Dynamo Kiev v Real Madrid	0-0	0-3	0-3
Juventus v Ujpest Dózsa	0-0	2-2	2-2
Spartak Trnava v Derby County	1-0	0-2	1-2

Semi-finals

Semi-finals			
Ajax v Real Madrid	2-1	1-0	3-1
Juventus v Derby County	3-1	0-0	3-1

and bribing the referee, allowed the Italians to defend cynically at the Baseball Ground and reach the Final for the first time.

Meanwhile, Ajax had limbered up for their attempt at a third consecutive trophy with a 6-1 demolition of CSKA Sofia, Cruyff claiming two goals, and advanced to the Quarter-finals against Bayern Munich. Bayern, based around the domineering figure of 'Der Kaiser' Franz Beckenbauer, were confirming the re-emergence of German football signalled by the country's success in the 1972 European Championship. Indeed, international interest in the game was so intense that a group of British club managers, taking a rare break from insularity, chartered a plane to observe the contest.

In the first leg in Amsterdam, Bayern had no answer to Ajax's technical and artistic superiority, nor to the individual genius of Cruyff. Although centre-forward Gerd Müller was less than fully fit, and keeper Sepp Maier had an unusually jittery game, nonetheless the Dutch were rampant.

Well into the second half Bayern absorbed the fast and fluid pressure from the Dutch. However, in the last thirty minutes, with Cruyff at his most inspirational, Haan scored twice with two more from Mühren and Cruyff, and Bayern were incapable of replying. In the return leg, Cruyff was unavailable through injury, although there was talk of a lack of harmony in the dressing room. Keizer scored in the 15th minute, and two goals from Müller could not turn the tide in Bayern's favour. Ajax were to play Real Madrid in the Semi-final.

Real, who had defeated Dynamo Kiev in the Quarter-final 3-0 at the Bernabeu, were not the team of old, and this was their first appearance in the Semi-finals for five years. In two one-sided games, Ajax won both, with Hulshoff and Krol scoring in Holland and Pirri pulling one back for Real. A Mühren strike in Madrid settled the matter, and Ajax were on their way again to the Final.

Johan Neeskens (1951). A tough and tenacious midfielder, Neeskens was at the heart of the Cruyff-inspired Holland and Ajax teams of the early 1970s. In keeping with the ethos of 'total football', he was at home in most positions and was the perfect foil for Cruyff and winger Piet Keizer in the Dutch team. He scored a second-minute penalty in the 1974 World Cup Final against West Germany after Cruyff was fouled in the box, and ended the tournament as second-highest scorer with five goals. He also played in the 1978 World Cup Final against Argentina, again picking up a loser's medal. He followed Cruyff to Barcelona in 1974 and, having won the Cup Winners Cup with Barca in 1979, he again followed Cruyff, this time to the USA. He gained 49 caps for his country.

Johan Neeskens

Johnny Rep (1951). Christened Nicolaus, Rep was a fair-haired forward who made his debut for Ajax in the 1971/72 season. He won a European Cup winner's medal in 1973, scoring the only goal against Juventus in the third of Ajax's consecutive wins in the competition. He also played for Valencia, Bastia and finished his career with St Etienne. He played for his country 42 times, and scored 12 goals, including the 30-yard rocket which killed off Scotland's hopes in the 1978 World Cup finals.

Jose Altafini (1938). Altafini was a strong Brazilian centre-forward who began his career with Palmeiras and Sao Paulo. He signed for AC Milan in 1958, having represented his country in the World Cup that year, and played for Italy in the 1962 World Cup finals. He scored 14 goals in Milan's 1963 European Cup victory, including two in the Final. He then moved to Naples and Juventus, playing in the 1973 European Cup Final, and finished his career with Swiss side Chiasso.

BRITISH CLUBS

Brian Clough and his partner Peter Taylor had taken the unfashionable Midlands club **Derby County** from the old Second Division in 1969 to the English league title in 1972, pipping Leeds and Liverpool by one point after a nail-biting climax to the season.

Clough – 'Ol' Big Head' – was an abrasive, dictatorial but inspirational figure who had assembled a squad of inexpensive, quality players radiating self-belief and exuberant *esprit de corps*. In defence were the England international centre-half Ray McFarland, the quick, stylish Colin Todd, and David Nish, the full-back for whom Clough had broken the British transfer record; Archie Gemmill, a small, quicksilver Scot and the hard-working John McGovern patrolled the midfield; while up front Kevin Hector and John O'Hare were the goal scorers, with Alan Hinton patrolling the left wing. Clough's team played fast, attacking football, and were determined to make their mark in Europe on their first attempt.

A 4-1 win over Yugoslavia's champions Zeljeznicar presented Derby with the chance to show their mettle – a second-round tie against mighty Benfica, for whom over half the team, including Adolfo, Simoes and Eusebio, were veterans of the 1968 Final. In the first leg at the Baseball Ground, Todd marked Eusebio out of the game and Derby turned in a stirring display of positive, controlled football. In the eighth minute, McFarland scored a header from a corner, and in the 39th minute Hector volleyed a left-foot shot into the net from a McFarland headed pass. Twelve minutes later, John McGovern hit a left-foot shot from 25 yards, and Derby were 3-0 ahead. In the second half Hector had two good shots saved by keeper Jose Henrique, but failed to find the net again. Benfica were

demoralised, and could not raise their game in Lisbon, where Derby managed a 0-0 draw.

In the Quarter-final a 1-0 defeat in Czechoslovakia by Spartak Trnava was overturned by two Hector goals, and they were drawn against Juventus in the Semi-final. In the San Siro, a deftly-controlled piece of juggling from Anastasi put Altafini through to score in the 29th minute, but Hector tucked a shot past Zoff two minutes later to equalise. However, two magnificent goals from Causio and Altafini made the final score 3-1 to the Italians. Unfortunately for Derby, both McFarland and Gemmill received second bookings and were suspended for the return leg.

Back in Derby, a 57th-minute penalty awarded to Derby for a Spinoni foul on Hector was sent wide by the normally reliable Hinton. Juventus indulged in some vicious tackling and the game degenerated, Roger Davies receiving his marching orders for retaliation after he had been fouled by Morini. Juventus went through to the Final.

Celtic, with the Scottish League and Cup double under their belt, cruised past Rosenborg of Trondheim 5-2, and again faced Ujpest Dózsa, whom they had defeated the previous season. At Parkhead, a Bene goal after 38 minutes put the Hungarians ahead but, in the 60th minute, a sweet pass from Connelly found Dalglish who scored. In the 75th minute, with Celtic well on top, substitute Lennox crossed to Dalglish, whose header gave Celtic a 2-1 victory. In Hungary a 15-minute spell produced three goals for Ujpest and, although a Dalglish shot hit the bar, Celtic could not score. For the first time in five seasons they had failed to reach the Quarter-final.

Juventus's Roberto Bettega (in stripes) taking on Johnny Rep in the 1973 Final.

Cruyff inspires Dutch masters

Ajax (1) 1   Juventus (0) 0

Belgrade, 30 May 1973
Attendance: 90,000
Referee: Gugulovic (Yugoslavia)

Like the Final the previous year, this encounter between Ajax and Juventus was one of exuberance against obduracy, of thrilling, attacking football against defensive parsimony.

The young forward Johnny Rep, soon to be a mainstay of the Dutch national team, was drafted in to the Ajax side as a replacement for Swart, and was the only member of the side not to have played in a Final. Indeed, for four of the team – Cruyff, Suurbier, Keizer and Hulshoff – this was their fourth Final.

On an oppressively hot and steamy night in Belgrade, Ajax did not wait long to strike. In the fourth minute, Blankenburg sent over a long high cross to the far post of the Juventus net and the blond-haired Rep rose above defender Marchetti to head past Dino Zoff. The Dutch, particularly in the first half, overwhelmed the disappointing Italians, but failed to capitalise on the number of chances they created. The teasing and prompting of Cruyff was tormenting the Juventus defence, but his team-mates could not take full advantage. A brilliant cut-back by Cruyff from the right in the 40th minute found Mühren in space in space but unable to convert the opportunity.

In the second half, Causio, Anastasi and Altafini moved forward in an attempt to get the equaliser, but Ajax enjoyed most of the possession and easily contained the Juventus counter-attacks. The supremely confident Dutchmen strolled through the half, arrogantly stroking the ball between them and displaying all their skills and artistry. When the whistle went, Ajax had become only the second team, after Real Madrid, to have won the European Cup three times in succession.

The teams
Ajax: Stuy, Suurbier, Krol, Blankenburg, Hulshoff, Neeskens, Haan, Mühren, Cruyff, Rep, Keizer (manager: Kovacs) [Rep 4]
Juventus: Zoff, Longobucco, Marchetti, Furino, Morini, Salvadore, Causio (Cuccureddu), Altafini, Anastasi, Capello, Bettega (Haller) (manager: Vycpalek)

At the beginning of this year's tournament, Rinus Michels had taken advantage of Cruyff's increasing disaffection at Ajax to lure him, after protracted negotiations, to Barcelona for £922,000, a new world-record transfer fee. With Cruyff gone, long-serving winger Swart retired after over 450 games for the club, and coach Kovacs also leaving to manage the French international team, the heart and inspiration had left Ajax, and the club was to finish the tournament in relative disarray. By the summer of 1974, new coach George Knobel, appointed to succeed Kovacs, had left, Feyenoord had won the Dutch title, and Ajax had entered into a period of European decline.

The club received a bye for the first round and, in the second round against army team CSKA Sofia, whom they had outplayed 6-1 in the previous tournament, they were beaten 2-1. Striker Jan Mulder scored in the deeply disappointing 1-0 home leg, but a goal in extra time in Bulgaria put out the Dutchmen. They would not be back in the European Cup for another four years.

Ajax were not the only top club to exit early. Juventus struggled against Dynamo Dresden and were 2-0 down after the first leg. In Turin, a 3-2 Italian victory was not enough to prevent an aggregate defeat by the East Germans. Benfica made it to the second round after a 2-0 win over Olympiakos, but Ujpest Dzosa, after a 1-1 draw in Lisbon, scored two in Hungary without reply. Bill Shankly's revamped Liverpool also reached the second round but were unlucky to meet Red Star Belgrade, who overcame the English team at Anfield in a game of sparkling, attacking football.

Bayern Munich, however, were in no mood for anything other than the trophy. The German side, who saw themselves as the natural European successors to Ajax, were playing an open, attacking game and contained players of enormous natural ability. In the hugely influential captain Franz Beckenbauer – 'Der Kaiser' – they had the man who invented the concept of the attacking sweeper, and who played a pivotal role in

Results

First Round

	1st leg	2nd leg	Agg
Atletico Madrid v Galatasaray	0-0	1-0	1-0
Basle v Fram Reykjavik	5-0	6-2	11-2
Bayern Munich v Atvidaberg	3-1	1-3	4-4 4-3(P)
Benfica v Olympiakos	1-0	1-0	2-0
Bruges v Floriana	8-0	2-0	10-0
Crusaders v Dynamo Bucharest	0-1	0-11	0-12
CSKA Sofia v Innsbruck	3-0	1-0	4-0
Dynamo Dresden v Juventus	2-0	2-3	4-3
Jeunesse Esch v Liverpool	1-1	0-2	1-3
Red Star Belgrade v Stal Mielec	2-1	1-0	3-1
Turun Palloseura v Celtic	1-6	0-3	1-9
Vejle v Nantes	2-2	1-0	3-2
Viking Stavanger v Spartak Trnava	1-2	0-1	1-3
Waterford v Ujpest Dózsa	2-3	0-3	2-6
Zarja Voroshilovgrad v Apoel Nicosia	2-0	1-0	3-0

Bye: Ajax

Second Round

Ajax v CSKA Sofia	1-0	0-2	1-2
Bayern Munich v Dynamo Dresden	4-3	3-3	7-6
Benfica v Ujpest Dózsa	1-1	0-2	1-3
Bruges v Basle	2-1	4-6	6-7
Celtic v Vejle	0-0	1-0	1-0
Dynamo Bucharest v Atletico Madrid	0-2	2-2	2-4
Red Star Belgrade v Liverpool	2-1	2-1	4-2
Spartak Trnava v Zarja Voroshilovgrad	0-0	1-0	1-0

Quarter-finals

Basle v Celtic	3-2	2-4	5-6
Bayern Munich v CSKA Sofia	4-1	1-2	5-3
Red Star Belgrade v Atletico Madrid	0-2	0-0	0-2
Spartak Trnava v Ujpest Dózsa	1-1	1-1	2-2 3-4(P)

Semi-finals

Celtic v Atletico Madrid	0-0	0-2	0-2
Ujpest Dózsa v Bayern Munich	1-1	0-3	1-4

P = (penalties)

both the Bayern and West German team; Sepp Maier was a goalkeeper of the highest quality, an expert at crosses and a dependable stopper of shots; in defence was the big, tough centre-back George Schwarzenbeck who also had the knack of scoring some important goals, and attacking left-back, the fiery, Afro-coiffed Paul Breitner, very much his own man and a maker and scorer of brilliant goals; and 'Der Bomber' Gerd Müller, a small, stocky goal scorer of genius led the attack alongside the blonde, right-winger Uli Hoeness. All six players were internationals, and played in the side which was to win the 1974 World Cup Final, appropriately against a Cruyff-led Holland.

Given Bayern's line-up, it was surprising that they struggled against Swedish side Atvidaberg in the first round. In Bayern's Munich stadium they went two up through Müller, and finished 3-1 ahead. However, towards the end of the away leg, they were 3-0 down, with two coming from forward Conny Torstensson, and only a late Hoeness strike forced extra time. The game went to penalties and Bayern inched through.

Before their next tie against Dynamo Dresden, coach Udo Lattek had acquired Bayern's tormentor Torstensson and, as there was no UEFA rule against playing for two clubs in the same tournament, Torstensson went straight into the side. After a nervous 4-3 win in Munich over the East Germans, they went two up in Dresden only to concede three. A Müller goal in the 60th minute put Bayern through.

In the Quarter-final, two goals from Torstensson helped Bayern to a 4-1 win over CSKA Sofia, and in the return Breitner was back from injury and scored a penalty. They were beaten 2-1 but were through to play Ujpest Dózsa in the Semi-final, against whom Torstensson scored another pair in a 4-1 aggregate win. Bayern Munich were the first German club in fourteen years to have reached the European Cup Final.

Atlético Madrid had received some difficult draws but had managed to overcome Galatasaray after extra time, eliminate Dynamo Bucharest 4-2, and defeat the impressive Red Star Belgrade, two goals in Yugoslavia doing the trick for the Spaniards. Unusually for what was essentially a defensive team, all their victories had come away from home.

A disgracefully cynical performance at Parkhead scraped a 0-0 draw from Celtic and two goals in Madrid put the Spanish champions into the Final for the first time.

Franz Beckenbauer (1945). 'Der Kaiser' was the fulcrum of the triple-European Cup-winning Bayern Munich side of the 1970s and the inspirational attacking sweeper for West Germany. He played in three World Cup finals – in 1966, 1970 and 1974 – leading his country to victory in the last tournament, and he captained the team which won the European Nations Championship in 1972. Twice European Footballer of the Year, he gained 103 international caps in his career. After spells with New York Cosmos and Hamburg he retired in 1984 to manage the national team, and he was in command in 1990 when Germany won the World Cup.

Beckenbauer issues instructions.

BRITISH CLUBS

Since his last appearance in the tournament in 1966/67, Bill Shankly had been busy strengthening and rebuilding his **Liverpool** team. In 1973, the Reds had won the English title by three points over Arsenal and had achieved their first European trophy, beating Borussia Moenchengladbach in the Final of the UEFA Cup.

Only Tommy Smith and Ian Callaghan remained from the 1966/67 side, with the combative Smith now captain. Ray Clemence had been bought from Scunthorpe to fill the goalkeeping position, and was embarking on a long and illustrious international career; Larry Lloyd and Alec Lindsay formed the centre of the defence, with the effervescent Emlyn Hughes and the skilful Peter Cormack controlling the midfield; in attack, the energetic Kevin Keegan and big Welshman John Toshack were piling in the goals, backed up by university graduate Steve Heighway, a tall, speedy winger and effective finisher. Liverpool were forming the nucleus of the team which was going to sweep all before it by the end of the decade.

Paired against Jeunesse Esch in the first round, they had to battle against the determined part-timers for a 1-1 draw in Luxembourg, the Liverpool goal coming from midfielder Brian Hall. An own goal and a Toshack strike saw them through at Anfield. The formidable Red Star Belgrade were the opponents in the next round. Miljan Miljanic, Red Star's cosmopolitan and multilingual manager, oversaw a side containing internationals Acimovic and Karasi in midfield, with Bogicevic sweeping up in the centre of defence. Forwards Dzajic and Lazarevic profited up front from the scheming of the midfield pair, and 18-year-old winger Vladimir Petrovic was on the fringes of the first team.

In the away leg in a freezing Belgrade, the Yugoslavs were two goals ahead late into the second half, until a goal by right-back Chris Lawler brought some hope for Liverpool. At Anfield, Red Star played some forceful attacking football, and early in the second half a Lazarevic long-range effort put them 1-0 up. Lawler levelled the game shortly after, but the tie was over for Liverpool when Jankovic converted a free-kick in the dying minutes.

Celtic brushed aside Finland's Turun Palloseura 9-1 in the first round, and a goal from Lennox settled the second-round tie against the Danish side Vejle. A more testing confrontation followed in the Quarter-final. They lost 3-2 away to Basle in the first leg, but went two up at Parkhead through Deans and Dalglish, the scorer of 43 goals for the club the previous season. The Swiss recovered to level the game, and a Callaghan shot in the 62nd minute ushered in extra time. A Steve Murray header from a Harry Hood cross settled the tie in Celtic's favour. The Semi-final drew the Scots against Juan Carlos Lorenzo's Atlético Madrid.

Lorenzo was a manager with something of a reputation for cynical, negative football. Manager of Argentina's 1966 World Cup side – described by Alf Ramsey as 'animals' – his career had been a controversial one. The first leg at Parkhead was an evening of appalling behaviour from the Spanish side. Atlético kicked, spat and fouled their way through the game, with no attempt to do anything other than secure a goal-less draw. Three of their players – the Argentinian centre-forward Ayala, Diaz and Quique – were sent off and a further six were booked in a display which shocked the 72,000 spectators and disgusted Jock Stein and his players. Jimmy Johnstone, in particular, was mercilessly hacked and bruised. The game ended 0-0 and Atlético had got what they wanted. An unseemly brawl in the tunnel at the end of the game was a depressing finale to what had occurred on the pitch.

After 'The Battle of Parkhead', UEFA delivered a surprisingly low-key rebuke to Atlético for their disgraceful antics, and imposed an equally modest fine on the club. Atlético were now in the driving seat for the next leg in Madrid. In spite of death threats against Stein and Jimmy Johnstone, and a massive police presence in the Estadio Vicente Calderon, Celtic refused to be intimidated. They went on the attack against an Atlético team who had six of their players suspended as a result of the Parkhead debacle, but could not break down the Spanish defence. A stylish and assured performance from Atlético resulted in two second-half goals from Garate and Adelardo, and Celtic were out of the tournament.

Although **Crusaders** produced a good defensive performance against Dynamo Bucharest to lose only 1-0 at Windsor Park, an eleven-goal hammering in Romania exposed yet again the deficiencies of football in Northern Ireland.

Beckenbauer and Bayern win European Cup

Bayern Munich (0) 1   Atlético Madrid (0) 1 (after extra time)

Heysel Stadium, Brussels, 15 May 1974
Attendance: 49,000
Referee: Loraux (Belgium)

REPLAY
Bayern Munich (1) 4   Atlético Madrid (0) 0

Heysel Stadium, Brussels, 17 May 1974
Attendance: 23,000
Referee: Delcourt (Belgium)

Bayern Munich had fulfilled their pre-tournament promise and the expectations aroused by their international line-up, and they were the first German team to reach the Final since Eintracht Frankfurt in 1960. Atlético had demonstrated their skill and resilience against strong European sides, and their less attractive face against Celtic. The Final appeared a well-balanced proposition.

The game was closely-fought, Atlético putting Bayern under pressure with their confident passing and stylish movement. The second half saw Bayern upping the pace and counter-attacking through Müller and Hoeness, but a stalemate after 90 minutes led to extra time. In the 113th minute a brilliant free-kick round the defensive wall from the 36-year-old midfielder Luis Aragones deceived Maier, and Atlético were ahead with seven minutes to go. In the very last seconds, Bayern defender Schwarzenbeck went on a final desperate run and unleashed a powerful, speculative shot from nearly 35 yards, and it was the unsighted Reina's turn to be beaten. The Final was now going to a replay for the first time in the history of the tournament.

Two days later, the teams lined up again with Bayern at full strength and Atlético missing their hard-working midfielder

Irureta who was suspended. A more confident Bayern moved into attack, and a long pass from Schwarzenbeck to Hoeness in the 28th minute was converted by the winger. In the second half, a tired Atlético were no match for the younger and faster Germans and, with Atlético captain and central defender Adelardo injured and substituted, it was no surprise when Bayern scored another, this time Müller volleying home a cross from Jupp Kapellmann in the 56th minute from a tight angle. Soon after, a delicately-judged lob from Müller made it three, and with eight minutes to go, Hoeness ran from the halfway line, round the helpless goalkeeper and placed the ball in the empty net.

Franz Beckenbauer, who had controlled the direction and pace of the game in an inspired performance, collected the trophy, and German football had gained its first European Cup. Bayern had shown that they were more than worthy heirs to Ajax crown as the masters of modern football. They were to confirm their status in the next two years.

The teams
Bayern Munich: Maier, Hansen, Breitner, Schwarzenbek, Beckenbauer, Roth, Torstensson (Durnberger), Zobel, Müller, Hoeness, Kapellmann (manager: Lattek) [Schwarzenbeck 120]
Atlético Madrid: Reina, Melo, Capon, Adelardo, Heredia, Eusebio, Ufarte (Becerra), Luis Aragones, Garate, Irureta, Salcedo (Alberto) (manager: Lorenzo) [Aragones 113]

(Replay) The teams
Bayern Munich: Maier, Hansen, Breitner, Schwarzenbeck, Beckenbauer, Roth, Torstensson, Zobel, Müller, Hoeness, Kapellmann (manager: Lattek) [Hoeness 28, 82, Müller 56, 70]
Atlético Madrid: Reina, Melo Capon, Adelardo (Benegas), Heredia, Eusebio, Salcedo, Luis Aragones, Garate, Alberto (Ufarte),Becerra (manager: Lorenzo)

Uli Hoeness scores his second goal in the 1974 Final.

As with 1960, this year's tournament was to be remembered chiefly for its Final, but for very different reasons.

At the draw in Zurich, officiated over by the new FIFA president Brazilian Joao Havelange, it was clear that the competition was going to be the most open for some time. The traditional big clubs – Benfica, Real Madrid, Inter Milan, Ajax, AC Milan – were absent, and there was no representative from Italy, whose champions Lazio had been banned for one year by the European Union for crowd trouble in the UEFA Cup. The fancied clubs – Bayern, Anderlecht, Leeds United, Celtic and Feyenoord – had been kept apart in the early stages by the seeding system, but other teams, such as this year's favourites Barcelona and Upjest Dózsa, were willing to stage a few upsets.

In Munich, a personality clash with Beckenbauer and the Bayern management had persuaded the single-minded Paul Breitner that his future lay elsewhere, and he left in the summer of 1974 for Real Madrid. There was dissent within the Bayern team, exacerbated by the number of games, particularly friendlies, they were forced to play in order to service their high wages, and there were concerns over the players' motivation. However, Bayern had just acquired left-winger Klaus Wunder, and Jupp Kapellmann was back to full fitness, although Müller and Hoeness were carrying recurring injuries.

Having received a bye in the first round, Bayern entertained East Germany's champions Magdeburg, holders of the European Cup Winners Cup, in the second round. In the first minute in Munich, Magdeburg scored, a Hoffman cross deflecting off right-back Hansen into the net. By half time Magdeburg had gone two up, their second coming from Sparwasser. However, in the second half the irrepressible Müller eased the pressure on the home side with two goals including a penalty for a foul on Hoeness. Wunder added another. In the return, Müller grabbed another two, and a second-half goal from Sparwasser was too late for the East Germans.

In January 1975, manager Lattek resigned. The media attention, the backbiting and the strife within the club had

Results

First Round

	1st leg	2nd leg	Agg
Celtic v Olympiakos	1-1	0-2	1-3
Feyenoord v Coleraine	7-0	4-1	11-1
Hajduk Split v IBK Keflavik	7-1	2-0	9-1
Hvidovre v Ruch Chorzow	0-0	1-2	1-2
Jeunesse Esch v Fenerbahçe	2-3	0-2	2-5
Leeds United v FC Zurich	4-1	1-2	5-3
Levski Sparta v Ujpest Dózsa	0-3	1-4	1-7
St Etienne v Sporting Lisbon	2-0	1-1	3-1
Slovan Bratislava v Anderlecht	4-2	1-3	5-5
Universitatea Craiova v Atvidaberg	2-1	1-3	3-4
Valletta v HJK Helsinki	1-0	1-4	2-4
Viking Stavanger v Ararat Erevan	0-2	2-4	2-6
Voest Linz v Barcelona	0-0	0-5	0-5

Byes: Bayern Munich, Magdeburg. Omonia Nicosia withdrew, Cork Celtic walkover.

Second Round

Anderlecht v Olympiakos	5-1	0-3	5-4
Bayern Munich v Magdeburg	3-2	2-1	5-3
Cork Celtic v Ararat Erevan	1-2	0-5	1-7
Feyenoord v Barcelona	0-0	0-3	0-3
HJK Helsinki v Atvidaberg	0-3	0-1	0-4
Hajduk Split v St Etienne	4-1	1-5	5-6
Ruch Chorzow v Fenerbahce	2-1	2-0	4-1
Ujpest Dózsa v Leeds United	1-2	0-3	1-5

Quarter-finals

Barcelona v Atvidaberg	2-0	3-0	5-0
Bayern Munich v Ararat Erevan	2-0	0-1	2-1
Leeds United v Anderlecht	3-0	1-0	4-0
Ruch Chorzow v St Etienne	3-2	0-2	3-4

Semi-finals

Leeds United v Barcelona	2-1	1-1	3-2
St Etienne v Bayern Munich	0-0	0-2	0-2

proved too much of a burden, and he was in dispute with Beckenbauer and club owner Neudecker. He was replaced by Dettmar Cramer, the American Olympic coach and an old colleague of Beckenbauer. In his first game in charge, Bayern met the Soviet side Ararat Erevan in the Quarter-final. Ararat, whose ground stood under Mount Ararat in Armenia, the site of the beaching of Noah's Ark, had achieved the Russian 'double' and were seeded and strongly fancied.

With the score 0-0 in Munich at half time, Cramer sent on an injured and strapped-up Hoeness. Crocked he may have been, but Hoeness scored in the 78th minute and Torstensson made it two. In the return Bayern lost 1-0 to the Russians, but they were safely through to the Semi-final against St Etienne.

The French side, with the brothers Herve and Patrick Revelli in attack, and the Yugoslavian goalkeeper Yvan Curkovic, the Argentinian sweeper Oswaldo Piazza, left-midfielder and playmaker Jean-Michel Larque and striker Triantafyllos, were managed by ex-player and local hero, 36-year-old Roby Herbin. The club was carrying the hopes of France, a country which had instigated the tournament but whose record in the tournament had been negligible since Reims' Final appearances nearly twenty years before. 'Les Verts' had beaten Sporting Lisbon in the opening round, and they had amazingly come back from a 4-1 defeat against Hajduk Split, the backbone of the Yugoslav national team, to win 5-1 at home. Polish champions Ruch Chorzow were defeated 4-3 in the Quarter-final.

Against Bayern in the first leg in France, St Etienne took the game to the Germans but an organised defence, with Müller playing deep, held them to a 0-0 draw. Within the first two minutes of the game in Munich, Beckenbauer slid the ball in from the corner of the six-yard box, and in the 70th minute a solo run from Durnberger put the game out of the reach of the French. Bayern Munich were in the Final where they were to play Leeds United.

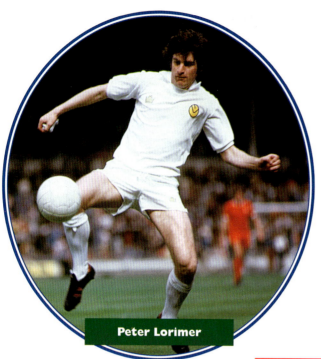

Peter Lorimer

Peter Lorimer (1946). Lorimer was a speedy right-winger famous for his blistering shot. Scots-born, he joined Leeds United in 1962 and left the club in 1979 to play in the USA. He played in the 1975 European Cup Final and had a 'goal' disallowed. He scored a club record 168 league goals in his time at Leeds, and briefly returned to the club in 1984. He represented Scotland on 21 occasions between 1970 and 1976, including the 1974 World Cup finals.

Sepp Maier (1944). With his long shorts, oversized gloves and clumsy gait, Maier looked an awkward figure. However, his international haul of 95 caps indicates that appearances can be deceptive, and he was West Germany's best and most consistent keeper in the 1970s. He spent his career with Bayern Munich, making 422 consecutive appearances for the Bavarians, and was in goal for their three European Cup victories. In particular, his Final performances in 1975 against Leeds and in 1976 against St Etienne went a long way to securing the trophy for Bayern. A relisher of the big occasion, he was also outstanding in West Germany's 2-1 win over Holland in the 1974 World Cup Final. A road accident in 1979 ended his career.

BRITISH CLUBS

In the summer of 1974 Don Revie had left **Leeds United**, to the dismay of his players, to manage the English national team. Brian Clough had endured 44 days of 'player power' from the Leeds team before accepting a no-doubt welcome pay-off from the board, and ex-England full-back Jimmy Armfield was now shouldering responsibility for team matters.

The team had remained more or less intact since their previous attempt on the trophy. Centre-half Jackie Charlton had retired and had been replaced by the tall, fair-haired Scottish stopper Gordon McQueen, a recent arrival from St Mirren. Another Scottish international, centre-forward Joe Jordan, an unselfish goal-scorer who was particularly effective in the air, had proved a more than adequate replacement for Mick Jones. But the essence of the team continued to be Bremner, Giles, Gray and Lorimer, with Hunter and Reaney providing the backbone.

A 5-3 victory over FC Zurich took the team to Hungary where, without the injured Bremner, a header from McQueen and a typical long-range goal from Lorimer overcame Ujpest Dózsa 2-1, although maverick forward Duncan Mckenzie was sent off. With Bremner back for the return at Elland Road, another McQueen header contributed to the 3-0 defeat of the Hungarians, the other two goals coming courtesy of Bremner and Welsh defender Terry Yorath.

At a foggy Elland Road in the Quarter-final, they met Anderlecht. The Belgian side, with the Dutch star winger Rob Rensenbrink and Belgium's leading player, 31-year-old striker Paul Van Himst, were admired for the elegance and quality of their football, and they had just put five goals past Olympiakos, the conquerors of Celtic.

The first time Anderlecht had played an English team in the competition was in 1956 against the Busby Babes, when they were humiliated 12-0. However, against Leeds they only found themselves on the end of a 3-0 defeat, McQueen again getting on the score sheet. In Belgium, on a sodden pitch in torrential rain, a lobbed goal from Bremner was the only score of the game, and Leeds moved on to the Semi-final to meet Barcelona.

Barcelona had won the Spanish league at a canter, and were feeding everything through the two Johans, Cruyff and Neeskens. The defence was held together by the Brazilian international Mario Marinho, with Spanish internationals

Asensi and Marcial in midfield. Carlos Rexach provided the speed and guile on the wing. In the second round they had knocked out Feyenoord, Rexach scoring a hat-trick at the Nou Camp, and in the Quarter-final they disposed of Atvidaberg 5-0, both games played in Barcelona because of the grim Swedish winter.

Within ten minutes of the first encounter at Elland Road, Giles crossed, the ball was flicked on by a Jordan header, and Bremner smacked it into the top corner of the net. Leeds continually threatened throughout the first half but Barcelona stood firm. In the 66th minute Asensi equalised from a Cruyff free-kick but, with thirteen minutes to go, an enterprising run down the right by full-back Reaney was followed by a cross and a goal from Clarke. Two-one to Leeds, but the Nou Camp awaited.

Leeds silenced the intimidating 54,000 crowd in Barcelona within seven minutes when an in-form Lorimer smashed in a right-foot rocket from a Jordan header. A stung Barcelona poured into attack, but Leeds knew all about pressure and defended manfully, with goalkeeper David Stewart, in the team for the injured Harvey, making some heroic saves. Barcelona breached the Leeds rearguard in the 70th minute when Clares headed in from central defender Gallego's free kick, but Leeds held on till the final whistle, in spite of McQueen being sent off for a silly punch at Clares.

Leeds' fighting spirit and determination had seen off a technically more gifted side, and they were through to their first European Cup Final. Barcelona, smarting from the defeat, made a scapegoat out of Rinus Michels, who left the club shortly afterwards.

David Hay, one of the heroes of Scotland's 1974 World Cup squad, had left **Celtic** to move to Chelsea, and this season was to be Billy McNeill's last. They had won the league title nine times in a row, but their period of hegemony in Scottish football was nearing its end. As something of an augury, they had an unusually poor tournament, drawing 1-1 with Olympiakos at Parkhead, with Paul Wilson scoring, and deservedly going down 0-2 in Athens. Olympiakos had won their first-ever European tie. But for Celtic a remarkable run of nine consecutive European Cup appearances was over.

Leeds fail amid disgraceful scenes

Bayern Munich (0) 2   Leeds United (0) 0

Parc des Princes, Paris, 28 May 1975
Attendance: 48,000
Referee: Kitabdjian (France)

Leeds were only the second English team to reach the Final and, for many of the older players, this was their last chance to win a European Cup medal.

Spectators were reminded of the physical side of Leeds' football as early as the fourth minute when a late tackle by Yorath resulted in Andersson being carried off. The Germans were unsettled by this, and even more so when Hoeness limped off just before half-time, forcing coach Cramer to adopt a more defensive system than he had intended.

During the first half, Leeds were dominant, with Lorimer outstanding, and only the acrobatic efforts of Sepp Maier and the tireless promptings of Beckenbauer kept Bayern in the game. Leeds had two penalty appeals turned down, firstly when Beckenbauer appeared to have handled to prevent the ball reaching Lorimer and secondly when the German captain tripped Clarke inside the box in the 38th minute. After the game, Beckenbauer admitted that the Clarke incident should have been a penalty.

In the 67th minute, with Leeds laying siege to Maier's goal, the ball came to Lorimer who volleyed it into the roof of the net. Leeds' celebrations were cut short when the referee, Marcel Kitabdjian, disallowed the goal, citing the fact that Bremner was offside and interfering with play, a decision later confirmed by television replay.

A section of the Leeds fans, fuelled by alcohol and outrage, started ripping up seats and throwing them onto the pitch, and an ugly scene developed, compounded by the provocative actions of the French riot police. The fighting continued as the game went on and intensified in the 72nd minute when a through ball from Müller, playing a surprisingly effective role in midfield, found Torstensson, who passed to Roth, who scored with a firm right-foot shot. Ten minutes later, another counter-attack took Kapellman down the right wing, and Müller out-manoeuvred Madeley to meet the cross at the near post and beat Stewart.

Leeds continued to bombard the massed Bayern defence, particularly targeting the heading ability of Jordan, but Schwarzenbeck, substitute Weiss and Zobel, who was closely marking Clarke, kept them out. The English side had virtually all the possession but could not capitalise. At the final whistle, a desolate Leeds team trudged wearily into the dressing room, aware that their last opportunity for European greatness had gone. A lucky Bayern Munich had survived a searching test by a better team and the European Cup remained in Germany.

The fighting continued after the game and throughout the night, and was the worst example of mindless hooliganism yet seen in the competition. That summer, as a final indignity for Leeds, UEFA banned the club from European competition for four years, although the period of suspension was later reduced to one year after Leeds appealed.

The teams
Leeds United: Stewart, Reaney, F. Gray, Bremner, Madeley, Hunter, Lorimer, Clarke, Jordan, Giles, Yorath (E.Gray) (manager: Armfield)
Bayern Munich: Maier, Andersson (Weiss), Durnberger, Schwarzenbeck, Beckenbauer, Zobel, Torstensson, Roth, Müller, Hoeness (Wunder), Kapellmann (manager: Cramer) [Roth 72, Müller 82]

Alan Clarke (8) contests possession of the ball in the 1975 Final.

The field for the 1975/76 tournament was far stronger than the previous season. Real Madrid and Benfica were back, and Rangers and Juventus had also returned. Last year's Cup Winners Cup medalists Dynamo Kiev were among Eastern Europe's representatives, and Borussia Moenchengladbach, the UEFA Cup winners, were one of the two German sides in the competition.

Borussia were taking over from Bayern Munich as Germany's top team. Although their star player Günter Netzer had gone to Real, the admired Udo Lattek had recently arrived as coach. In defence they had Berti Vogts, the tough little defender, later to manage his country, and Rainer Bonhof in midfield. The attack was composed of two Danish internationals, the quick and skilful Henning Jensen and little Alan Simonsen, flanked by German international Jupp Heynckes, a tough, pacy left-winger with a powerful shot. They began their campaign with a 7-2 defeat of Innsbruck, Heynckes scoring four at home, and eliminated Juventus 4-2 in the second round. The Quarter-final drew them against Real Madrid.

Under the diligent and astute leadership of Milan Miljanic, Real had secured the Spanish league and cup 'double'. He had rejuvenated Netzer's career and had moved his German

Karl-Heinz Rummenigge (1955). Originally a right-winger, Rummenigge became a striker for Bayern Munich and Inter Milan, whom he joined for £3.5 million. He scored 45 goals for West Germany in his 95 appearances between 1976 and 1986. The fair-haired forward played in the 1978 World Cup finals, scoring three goals, West Germany's triumphant 1980 European Championship, and in the 1982 and 1986 World Cup finals. He won the European Cup with Bayern in 1976 against St Etienne and was on the losing side in 1982 against Aston Villa. He was named European Footballer of the Year in 1980 and 1981, and he ended his career with Servette.

Karl-Heinz Rummenigge

Results

First Round	1st leg	2nd leg	Agg	
Benfica v Fenerbahçe	7-0	0-1	7-1	
Borussia Moenchengladbach v Innsbruck	1-1	6-1	7-2	
CSKA Sofia v Juventus	2-1	0-2	2-3	
Floriana v Hajduk Split	0-5	0-3	0-8	
Jeunesse Esch v Bayern Munich	0-5	1-3	1-8	
KB Copenhagen v St Etienne	0-2	1-3	1-5	
Linfield v PSV Eindhoven	1-2	0-8	1-10	
Malmö v Magdeburg	2-1	1-2	3-3	2-1 (P)
Olympiakos v Dynamo Kiev	2-2	0-1	2-3	
Omonia Nicosia v Akranes	2-1	0-4	2-5	
Rangers v Bohemians	4-1	1-1	5-2	
Real Madrid v Dynamo Bucharest	4-1	0-1	4-2	
Ruch Chorzow v Kuopion Palloseura	5-0	2-2	7-2	
RWD Molnebeek v Viking Stavanger	3-2	1-0	4-2	
Slovan Bratislava v Derby County	1-0	0-3	1-3	
Ujpest Dózsa v FC Zurich	4-0	1-5	5-5	

P = penalties

Second Round			
Benfica v Ujpest Dózsa	5-2	1-3	6-5
Borussia Moenchengladbach v Juventus	2-0	2-2	4-2
Derby County v Real Madrid	4-1	1-5	5-6
Dynamo Kiev v Akranes	3-0	2-0	5-0
Hajduk Split v RWD Molenbeek	4-0	3-2	7-2
Malmö v Bayern Munich	1-0	0-2	1-2
Ruch Chorzow v PSV Eindhoven	1-3	0-4	1-7
St Etienne v Rangers	2-0	2-1	4-1

Quarter-finals			
Benfica v Bayern Munich	0-0	1-5	1-5
Borussia Moenchengladbach v Real Madrid	2-2	1-1	3-3
Dynamo Kiev v St Etienne	2-0	0-3	2-3
Hajduk Split v PSV Eindhoven	2-0	0-3	2-3

Semi-finals			
Real Madrid v Bayern Munich	1-1	0-2	1-3
St Etienne v PSV Eindhoven	1-0	0-0	1-0

colleague Breitner into midfield to act as his foil. The veteran sweeper Pirri was as dependable as ever, and the equally venerable Amancio had come back from injury to rediscover his scoring form. Winger Roberto Martinez and forward Santillana supplied a youthful dimension to the attack, and Real were parading their strongest team for several years.

A 4-2 win over Dynamo Bucharest and an exciting 6-5 victory over Derby County had brought them to the Quarter-final. In Germany, Jensen and Wittkamp put Borussia two up until a Martinez header and a 61st-minute 25-yard strike from Pirri levelled the game. In Madrid, with the game attracting record crowd receipts, a 25th-minute Heynckes header sent Borussia in at half time one up. Breitner had gone off injured early in the game, and the referee had booked three Germans in the first half. In the 51st minute

Santillana headed in a cross from Amancio, and Borussia needed to score. The Germans claimed two goals in the last twenty minutes but both were disallowed and, although Borussia played the better football, Real were through. Borussia later complained to UEFA about referee bias, but to no avail. The Spaniards were to meet holders Bayern Munich in the Semi-final.

After the previous Final, Bayern had tried to buy Leeds' Joe Jordan, but the price of £330,000 was considered too high, The club needed a long-term replacement for the ageing Müller, who, when fit, was nonetheless still producing the goods. Wunder had moved to Hanover, disenchanted with the Bayern 'star system', and Hoeness and Müller were both injured for much of the early part of the tournament. However, a young, blond-haired winger, Karl-Heinz Rummenigge, was making an impression.

Bayern made an uncertain start, edging past Malmö, the surprise conquerors of Magdeburg, 2-1 in the second round, and met Benfica in the Quarter-final. Although now without Eusebio and Simoes, Benfica had given Fenerbahçe a 7-1 roasting in the first round with a hat-trick for Jardao and Nene scoring two. The strong Ujpest Dózsa suffered a 5-2 defeat in Lisbon in the next round. Back in Hungary for the return leg, Dózsa threw away a three-goal advantage to lose to a 25-yard shot from Nene.

In Lisbon, Benfica attacked and only some spectacular goalkeeping from Maier kept the score 0-0. A very different Bayern came out at Munich and, although there were no goals in the first half, Durnberger and Müller both grabbed two, with Rummenigge producing a tremendous display by scoring the third in a 5-1 win.

For a game of such promise, the Semi-final in Madrid was something of a disappointment. Without the injured Breitner, Madrid went ahead with a 7th-minute goal from Martinez and Müller equalised just on half-time. At the end of the game, a Madrid fan hit Müller who had to be helped off the pitch. In the second leg, Breitner was back but he could do nothing about Müller's two goals, and Bayern were through to the Final for the third year in succession.

St Etienne, meanwhile, had been consolidating their position as one of the most exciting and successful teams to have emerged from France since Reims in the late 1950s. Now with their squad enhanced by the tough, young midfielder Dominique Bathenay and the even younger outside-right Dominique Rocheteau, they had powered their way through the tournament.

A 5-1 victory over KB Copenhagen and an impressive 4-1 defeat of Rangers took the club to the Quarter-final against Dynamo Kiev and European Footballer of the Year Oleg Blokhin. Although the Russian season had not yet

Dominique Rocheteau

Dominique Rocheteau (1955). A long-haired French winger with exceptional pace and ability, Rocheteau began his career with St Etienne. He scored three goals in St Etienne's 1976 run in the European Cup, coming on as an 82nd-minute substitute in the final but too late to snatch victory. He then moved to Paris St-Germain and ended his career at Toulouse. He was awarded 49 caps for his country and played in the 1978, 1982 and 1986 World Cup finals.

begun, and bad weather in the Ukraine meant that their home game had to be played in the Crimea, a fine goal from Blokhin helped the Ukranians to a 2-0 victory. Back in France, St Etienne turned in a magnificent performance, with Herve Revelli scoring after half-time and Larque smashing in a free-kick to take the game to extra time. A neat pass from Patrick Revelli to Rocheteau in the 115th minute found the young forward in space, and the ball was in the net. The Semi-final tie against PSV Eindhoven, who had broken the Ajax/Feyenoord stranglehold on Dutch football, was won by another Larque free-kick early in the first leg in France, with the French holding on to a 0-0 draw in Holland. France was back in a European Cup Final.

BRITISH CLUBS

Rangers were in the tournament for the first time in eleven years, having taken the Scottish title by seven points from Hibs. Captain John Greig was the only survivor of the team that had gone out to Inter Milan in the 1964/65 Quarter-final, and Jock Wallace, a disciplinarian and fitness fanatic, was now the manager. The cool and cultured Sandy Jardine was full-back, and central defence was patrolled by the ferocious tackler Tam Forsyth and the tall, dependable Colin Jackson. The goalkeeper Peter McCloy, at 6ft 4in the tallest

keeper in Britain, often initiated attacks with his long kicking from the line, and the goals came from the 'two Dereks', Parlane and Johnstone, fed by the accurate crossing of right-winger Tommy McLean.

In the first round they put out Irish club Bohemians 5-2, and took on St Etienne in the next round in Paris. A goal each from Patrick Revelli and Dominique Bathenay saw Rangers take a two-goal deficit to Glasgow, where the French again struck twice, this time through Patrick's brother

Herve and Dominique Rocheteau. A late goal from the little inside-forward Alex MacDonald made no difference and the Gers were out of the tournament.

Brian Clough had left **Derby County** in 1973 and his place had been taken by Dave Mackay, the ex-Spurs and Derby half-back. Several of Clough's players – Gemmill, Hector, Nish and McFarland – were still at the club, and MacKay had introduced some of his own men. He had bought the elegant half-back Bruce Rioch from Aston Villa, Welsh full-back Rod Thomas from Swindon and the mercurial little striker Francis Lee from Manchester City. Joining Lee in attack was ex-Gunner Charlie George.

In the first round Derby met Slovan Bratislava, with six Czech internationals in the side, and went through 3-1, two of the goals coming from Lee at the Baseball Ground. Real Madrid were the opposition in round two. George delighted a packed home crowd with a 10th-minute volleyed goal and, when Lee was tripped by Camacho in the box five minutes later, George was again on hand to convert the penalty. Pirri got one back for Real in the 25th minute but a 25-yard drive from David Nish on half time restored Derby's lead. George claimed his hat-trick when a foul on Hector resulted in another penalty. Real would have to score at least four at the Bernabeu.

In a typically passionate night of football in Spain, Real opened the scoring through the Argentinian Martinez in the 3rd minute and Santillana put away another just after half time. When a Santillana header levelled the tie on aggregate, Derby, without the injured Rioch and suspended Lee, were on the ropes and had to absorb the ceaseless attack of Real. A George goal from a counter-attack briefly offered Derby some hope, but Pirri again levelled the tie in the 83rd minute. Another Santillana strike in extra time finished off a tired and outplayed Derby.

THE FINAL

Bayern beat spirited St Etienne

Bayern Munich (0) 1 St Etienne (0) 0

Hampden Park, Glasgow, 12 May 1976
Attendance: 55,000
Referee: Palotai (Hungary)

Sixteen years after the Real Madrid masterclass against Eintracht Frankfurt, the Final was back in Glasgow. Although not in the same league as the 7-3 thriller, it was an exciting match, with the bulk of the attacks coming from the imaginative St Etienne and the more cautious Bayern content to absorb French pressure and launch counter-attacks.

In the second minute Müller received a Durnberger pass, slipped Piazza and had the ball in the net, only for the referee to award an offside to St Etienne. TV replays showed that Müller had been onside but his acceleration had fooled the linesman. A spirited performance from the French resulted in Bathenay smacking a 20-yard left-foot shot against the bar in the 34th minute and then, five minutes later, a header from the tall Santini also came back off the woodwork. Although the French goalkeeper was also in action, saving well from Rummenigge, St Etienne were the more dangerous team. Piazza was resolute in defence, captain Larque was finding his forwards accurately from midfield and left-winger Christian Sarramagna was making life difficult for the Bayern defence.

Within twelve minutes of the second half, however, Bayern were in the lead. A push by Piazza on Müller gave away a free kick, and a tap from the unusually subdued Beckenbauer to the hard-working midfielder Roth allowed the latter time and space to beat Curkovic with a thundering right-foot shot. With Hoeness gradually coming into his game and Schwarzenbeck keeping out the St Etienne attacks, Bayern began to threaten. Although Maier was forced to scramble a save from Santini, Hoeness was unlucky to see his effort denied by Curkovic.

With eight minutes to go, a fading Sarramagna was replaced by Rocheteau and the winger was immediately in action to force a corner. With three minutes to go, a goal-line clearance from Beckenbauer prevented the equaliser, and a counter-attack from Roth forced a fine save from Curkovic. In the last minute a Patrick Revelli shot from a clever dribble and cross by Rocheteau was saved on the line by Maier.

Bayern had won the trophy for the third season running, but their inability to replace Beckenbauer and then Müller was to accelerate their decline as a major power in Europe. Bayern have never since won the trophy. It was also St Etienne's last appearance in a Final. However, in England a resurgent Liverpool were awaiting with anticipation the next tournament, and the stage was being set for English dominance of the European Cup over the next few years.

The teams
Bayern Munich:
Maier, Hansen, Horsmann, Schwarzenbeck, Beckenbauer, Roth, Kapellmann, Durnberger, Müller, Hoeness, Rummenigge
(manager: Cramer) [Roth 57]

St Etienne:
Curkovic, Janvion, Repellini, Piazza, Lopez, Bathenay, Santini, Larque, P. Revelli, H. Revelli, Sarramagna (Rocheteau) (manager: Herbin)

Franz Roth after scoring his winner.

Bayern Munich were now an ageing team and heavily dependent on Beckenbauer, Müller and Maier who were not the force they had once been. However, Bayern easily disposed of Danish champions Koge BK 7-1 in the first round, Torstensson claiming three, and in the second round it was Müller's turn to add three to a 6-2 total against Banik Ostrava.

In the Quarter-final they met Dynamo Kiev. Dynamo, who were in effect the Soviet national team, had gone through their first two legs in the tournament without giving away a goal, and had international captain Victor Kolotov and the famed striker Oleg Blokhin up front. They had demolished the respected Partizan Belgrade 5-0 in the first round, and they were seen as one of the most dangerous teams in the tournament..

In the first leg in Munich, Müller was missing through injury, but a goal by his replacement Rainer Kunkel took Bayern to the Ukraine with a 1-0 lead. In the freezing conditions, Bayern did well to hold Dynamo till late in the second half, and Maier in particular performed heroics and saved a Blokhin penalty just before half time.

With ten minutes to go, Dynamo were awarded another penalty and Burjak scored from the spot, making the tie level on aggregate. In virtually the last minute, substitute Slobodian scored, and Bayern had suffered their first European Cup defeat since 1973. Soon afterwards, Beckenbauer left to try his hand with New York Cosmos.

Borussia Moenchengladbach had won the German championship. Sweeper Uli Stielike ran the defence along with little captain Berti Vogts, and in midfield Rainer Bonhof ferried the ball to the strikers Simonsen and Jupp Heynkes. Bonhoff was to join Valencia but not until after the 1978 World Cup, as the German authorities had banned international transfers until then.

A first-round win over Austria WAC took them to Turin, where Vogts and Klinkhammer scored in a surprise 2-1 victory over Torino in the Italian club's first appearance in the tournament. The second leg in Düsseldorf, in front of 67,000 spectators, developed into a disgraceful brawl. Without their key strikers Francesco Graziani and Paolini Pulici, a desperate Torino kicked and hacked the Germans and had three players – Caporale, Zaccarell and Castellini – sent off. Borussia kept their cool to draw 0-0.

Bruges, 2-0 conquerors of Real Madrid in the second round, were next. The Belgians, now coached by Feyenoord hero Ernst Happel, were spearheaded by ex-Derby centre-forward Roger Davies and Raoul Lambert, the long-serving 'Lion of Flanders'. Bruges managed a valuable 2-2 draw in Germany, and at one stage were 2-0 up. However, they were beaten back at home by a goal eight minutes from time from 19-year-old Borussia substitute Hannes. In the Semi-final against Dynamo Kiev, Kiev won their home tie by a single goal. One each from Bonhof and Wittkamp in Germany, however, meant that Borussia would be facing Liverpool in the Final in Rome.

BRITISH CLUBS

The representatives of Northern Ireland and Scotland were both unceremoniously dumped out of the tournament in the first round.

Rangers, who had won the Scottish 'treble', could only draw 1-1 at Ibrox against FC Zurich through a Derek Parlane goal after the Swiss had gone ahead in the first minute. A 1-0 defeat in Switzerland marked the end of Rangers' European ambitions this season. **Crusaders** were Liverpool's first obstacle on the way to the Final, and seven goals from Liverpool without reply finished off the Northern Irish.

Results

First Round	1st leg	2nd leg	Agg
Akranes v Trabzonspor	1-3	2-3	3-6
Austria WAC v Borussia Moenchengladbach	1-0	0-3	1-3
Bruges v Steaua Bucharest	2-1	1-1	3-2
CSKA Sofia v St Etienne	0-0	0-1	0-1
Dundalk v PSV Eindhoven	1-1	0-6	1-7
Dynamo Dresden v Benfica	2-0	0-0	2-0
Dynamo Kiev v Partizan Belgrade	3-0	2-0	5-0
Ferencvaros v Jeunesse Esch	5-1	6-2	11-3
Koge BK v Bayern Munich	0-5	1-2	1-7
Liverpool v Crusaders	2-0	5-0	7-0
Omonia Nicosia v PAOK Salonika	0-2	1-1	1-3
Rangers v FC Zurich	1-1	0-1	1-2
Stal Mielec v Real Madrid	1-2	0-1	1-3
Sliema Wanderers v Turun Palloseura	2-1	0-1	2-2
Torino v Malmö	2-1	1-1	3-2
Viking Stavanger v Banik Ostrava	2-1	0-2	2-3

Second Round			
Banik Ostrava v Bayern Munich	2-1	0-5	2-6
Dynamo Kiev v PAOK Salonika	4-0	2-0	6-0
FC Zurich v Turun Palloseura	2-0	1-0	3-0
Ferencvaros v Dynamo Dresden	1-0	0-4	1-4
Real Madrid v Bruges	0-0	0-2	0-2
St Etienne v PSV Eindhoven	1-0	0-0	1-0
Torino v Borussia Moenchengladbach	1-2	0-0	1-2
Trabzonspor v Liverpool	1-0	0-3	1-3

Quarter-finals			
Bayern Munich v Dynamo Kiev	1-0	0-2	1-2
Borussia Moenchengladbach v Bruges	2-2	1-0	3-2
FC Zurich v Dynamo Dresden	2-1	2-3	4-4
St Etienne v Liverpool	1-0	1-3	2-3

Semi-finals			
Dynamo Kiev v Borussia Moenchengladbach	1-0	0-2	1-2
FC Zurich v Liverpool	1-3	0-3	1-6

Rainer Bonhof, Borussia's skilful midfielder.

LIVERPOOL 1976/77

In the summer of 1974 Liverpool fans had been stunned by the sudden resignation of Bill Shankly, whose side had just won the FA Cup. His successor from the Liverpool 'boot room', Bob Paisley, set to work refining and adding to the squad. Under Paisley's guidance, Liverpool were blending the techniques of European football – the emphasis on quick, accurate passing, intelligent running off the ball and the importance of retaining possession – with Liverpool's traditional direct, attacking style. He was creating a team which would reign supreme, not only in English football but also in the more demanding and sophisticated European arena.

Inheriting Ray Kennedy, Shankly's last buy for the club, Paisley shrewdly moved the big, ex-Arsenal striker into midfield to replace Peter Cormack, a switch which was to re-invigorate and prolong Kennedy's career, and to provide strength in the centre of the park. He also bought wisely. Attacking right-back Phil Neal joined from Northampton, to link up with Welshman Joey Jones, and goal-scoring midfielder Terry McDermott arrived from Newcastle. Local lad Jimmy Case was promoted from the reserves, and he was to form the passionate heart of the team along with captain and defender Emlyn Hughes and the gangling Phil Thompson. A somewhat surprising newcomer, given the strength of the team's attack, was centre-forward David Johnson, but he was to be the replacement for Keegan who, unknown to the fans, had decided leave the club at the end of the season. Toshack and Heighway remained, with Keegan, the attacking options. Clemence, Callaghan and the old warhorse Tommy Smith were also survivors from the club's last European Cup season of four years ago.

Liverpool had won the English title by one point, a goal from Kennedy against Wolves deciding the championship, and they had also again lifted the UEFA Cup, beating Bruges in the Final. In the first round of the 1976/77 tournament, Northern Ireland's Crusaders defended well at Anfield to keep the score down to 2-0, but four goals from Liverpool in the last ten minutes of the return leg took Liverpool to Trabzonspor in the second round. In a scrappy game, the Turkish team scored the only goal, but a 3-0 victory at Anfield – with goals from Heighway, Johnson and Keegan within the first eighteen minutes – secured Liverpool a Quarter-final place against last season's Finalists, St Etienne. The French had reached the last eight with 1-0 victories

over CSKA Sofia and PSV Eindhoven, both goals scored by centre-half Piazza.

At the Geoffroy Guichard Stadium, Liverpool were without an injured Keegan and Toshack was carrying an injury. However, they defended well and contained the French main threat, Rocheteau, although they conceded a goal from Bathenay in the second half.

In the return leg, Anfield witnessed a pulsatingly exciting match. Keegan, now restored to fitness, scored in the second minute with a speculative cross from the left which confused keeper Curkovic, who was to have a nervous match throughout. This spurred on St Etienne, playing without the suspended Piazza, and Clemence came under almost constant pressure from the skilful forwards. In the second half, a 30-yard shot from Bathenay put the French ahead on aggregate. Shortly after, a Kennedy goal from a Callaghan cross put Liverpool one up on the night but still behind on away goals.

Steve Heighway about to cross the ball in the 1976/77 Semi-final against FC Zurich.

With thirteen minutes to go, an injured Toshack was replaced by 'supersub' David Fairclough, a tall, ginger-haired striker who specialised in coming off the bench to score match-winning goals. In the 82nd minute, Fairclough collected the ball inside his own half, powered half the length of the pitch leaving two French defenders in his wake, and cracked the ball past the despairing Curkovic. The Kop was delirious and the pandemonium continued until the final whistle.

After such a thrilling game, the Semi-final could only have been anti-climactic, and so it was. FC Zurich, who had eliminated Rangers in the first round and beaten Dynamo Dresden on away goals in the Quarter-final, were without their Sicilian star striker Franco Cucinotta in Zurich. They succumbed to Liverpool 3-1 with two goals from Neal and one from Heighway. Two from Case and one from Keegan at Anfield meant that Liverpool had reached their first European Cup Final, and were to meet the champions of Germany, Borussia Moenchengladbach.

Steve Heighway (1947). A university economics graduate, Heighway was a fast, goal-scoring winger for Liverpool. He made his senior debut in 1970 and played in the 1971 Cup Final against Arsenal, where his extra-time goal put Liverpool briefly in front. He won two European Cup winner's medals, in 1977 and 1978, and he made two of the goals in the first game. He left Liverpool to join Minnesota Kicks in 1981. The possessor of 34 caps for Eire, he now runs Liverpool's Youth Academy.

Kop celebrates thrilling victory in Rome

Liverpool (1) 3   Borussia Moenchengladbach (0) 1

Olympic Stadium, Rome, 25 May 1977
Attendance: 52,000
Referee: Wurtz (France)

Four days before Liverpool walked out into the vast Olympic Stadium that May evening, they had been narrowly defeated by Manchester United in the FA Cup Final. However, any lingering dejection or self-doubts they may have harboured were instantly swept away by the roar that greeted the players from their massive 30,000 support in the stadium.

'The last time I was here I was in a tank', said a whimsical Bob Paisley. The manager had reverted Callaghan, dropped for Wembley, back to midfield and Tommy Smith was in for the injured Phil Thompson. Paisley was resigned to the match being Keegan's last appearance for Liverpool. Borussia were at full strength, although Heynkes and Simonsen were carrying injuries, and the 500 million watching were hoping for a classic between two of Europe's finest sides. And a classic was what they got.

Liverpool began with some marvellous, flowing football, and Borussia also twice went close through Heynckes and Bonhof. In the 27th minute, their creative movement was rewarded when Callaghan stole the ball from Bonhof and passed to Heighway whose cross was met by McDermott. A beautifully-taken low shot from McDermott, who had run into space from midfield, eluded keeper Kneib and Liverpool were ahead.

In the 51st minute, Borussia equalised. A bad back-pass from Case was swiftly intercepted by Simonssen who beat Clemence with a stunning, left-foot swerving shot. The Germans piled on the pressure and Clemence was called upon to make a world-class save from Stielike. Liverpool absorbed the Borussia onslaught and, in the 65th minute, a high cross from Heighway on the left wing found the soaring head of defender Smith, and Liverpool were 2-1 up.

Keegan and Heighway were running rings around their man-markers, international captain Vogts and Klinkhammer and, after Keegan had given Vogts the slip yet again with seven minutes to go, the German defender scythed him down in the penalty area. Referee Wurtz had no hesitation in awarding a penalty and, with Callaghan praying on the edge of the box, Phil Neal cooly converted the spot-kick.

The final whistle went, and a magnificent Liverpool had become the second English team to win the great European prize. They went on two laps of honour and saluted their ecstatic support. The Eternal City belonged to the Kop and the fans partied all night long, at one stage finding the players' hotel and throwing several of them into the swimming pool. And an elated Tommy Smith decided to postpone his retirement.

Berti Vogts fouls Kevin Keegan to give away the penalty which led to Liverpool's third goal in the 1978 Final.

The teams
Liverpool:
Clemence, Neal, Jones, Smith, R. Kennedy, Hughes, Keegan, Case, Heighway, McDermott, Callaghan
(manager: Paisley)
[McDermott 27, Smith 65, Neal 83]

Borussia Moenchengladbach:
Kneib, Vogts, Klinkhammer, Wittkamp, Bonhof, Wohlers (Hannes), Simonsen, Wimmer (Kulik), Stielike, Schaffer, Heynckes
(manager: Lattek)
[Simonsen 51]

The European Cup continued to be a hugely popular tournament across the continent, boasting average attendances of nearly 35,000 the previous season, with millions of fans following the games on TV. This year saw the return of some illustrious names – Celtic, Ajax and Juventus – and Borussia Moenchengladbach were back as champions of the Bundesliga.

Striker Henning Jensen had left Borussia to join Real Madrid and been replaced by 20-year-old fellow Scandinavian Carsten Nielsen. Stielike had also gone to Real (and been dropped from the national team for defying the no-transfer rule) while Heynckes and Simonsen continued as the threats in attack. The midfield had been strengthened with the purchase of the Yugoslav Branko Oblak.

They had beaten Vasas 4-1 in the first round, the highlight being a marvellous solo goal by Simonsen in Budapest. An 8-1 crushing of Red Star Belgrade, with three from Simonsen and some dreadful defending by the Yugoslavs, saw Borussia away to Innsbruck in the Quarter-final first leg. Innsbruck had knocked out Basle in the first round, and three first-half goals in the return leg in Salzburg had finished off Celtic in the second round.

The Austrians had Borussia in real trouble by half time and went 3-0 ahead, although Heynckes pulled one back in the 65th minute. In Germany, two goals without reply – a Bonhof

Jimmy Case

Jimmy Case (1954). Case joined Liverpool as a right-winger in 1975 but shortly after his arrival he settled into midfield. He was a combative but effective player, with a strong shot and a powerful tackle and, from 1977 to 1981, he was an essential part of the Liverpool team which won three European Cups. Playing alongside Souness, McDermott and Ray Kennedy, Case's distribution and pace was an important contribution to the much-feared unit. He moved to Brighton and Hove Albion in 1981 and his career petered out with a number of smaller clubs. He was manager of Brighton from 1995 to 1998.

Results

First Round

	1st leg	2nd leg	Agg	
Basle v Innsbruck	1-3	1-0	2-3	
Benfica v Moscow Torpedo	0-0	0-0	0-0	4-1 (P)
Celtic v Jeunesse Esch	5-0	6-1	11-1	
Dukla Prague v Nantes	1-1	0-0	1-1	
Dynamo Bucharest v Atlético Madrid	2-1	0-2	2-3	
Dynamo Dresden v Halmstad	2-0	1-2	3-2	
Floriana v Panathinaikos	1-1	0-4	1-5	
Koupio Palloseura v Bruges	0-4	2-5	2-9	
Levski Spartak v Slask Wroclaw	3-0	2-2	5-2	
Lillestrom v Ajax	2-0	0-4	2-4	
Omonia Nicosia v Juventus	0-3	0-2	0-5	
Red Star Belgrade v Sligo Rovers	3-0	3-0	6-0	
Trabzonspor v BK Copenhagen	1-0	0-2	1-2	
Vasas v Borussia Moenchengladbach	0-3	1-1	1-4	
Valur v Glentoran	1-0	0-2	1-2	

Bye: Liverpool   P = penalties

Second Round

Benfica v BK Copenhagen	1-0	1-0	2-0
Bruges v Panathinaikos	2-0	0-1	2-1
Celtic v Innsbruck	2-1	0-3	2-4
Glentoran v Juventus	0-1	0-5	0-6
Levski Spartak v Ajax	1-2	1-2	2-4
Liverpool v Dynamo Dresden	5-1	1-2	6-3
Nantes v Atlético Madrid	1-1	1-2	2-3
Red Star Belgrade v Borussia Moenchengladbach	0-3	1-5	1-8

Quarter-finals

Ajax v Juventus	1-1	1-1	2-2	0-3 (P)
Benfica v Liverpool	1-2	1-4	2-6	
Bruges v Atlético Madrid	2-0	2-3	4-3	
Innsbruck v Borussia Moenchengladbach	3-1	0-2	3-3	

P = penalties

Semi-finals

Borussia Moenchengladbach v Liverpool	2-1	0-3	2-4
Juventus v Bruges	1-0	0-2	1-2

penalty and a Heynckes header from a Bonhof cross – were enough to send Borussia to the Semi-final against Liverpool on away goals. A 3-0 defeat by Liverpool at Anfield eliminated the Germans.

Ajax were almost unrecognisable from their glorious 'total football' days. Cruyff, Neeskens, Mühren, Rep and Haan had all gone. New Yugoslavian coach Tomislav Ivic had instilled a defensive element into his team's play and Krol and Hulshoff acted as twin sweepers. In attack were Holland's top league scorer Ruud Geels and the 21-year-old winger Tscheu La Ling. Ajax recovered from a 2-0 defeat by Lillestrom in Sweden in the first round to score four in Amsterdam, and in the second round beat Levski Spartak 4-2. Lying in wait in the Quarter-final were Juventus.

UEFA Cup holders Juve were now coached by Giovanni Trapattoni and contained most of Italy's World Cup team for Argentina. In the autumn of 1976 they had exchanged Anastasi for Inter's free-scoring Roberto Boninsegna, and Capello had gone to AC Milan. In return, they had acquired forward Romeo Benetti from the Milanese club. Altafini had also gone, but Causio and Bettega remained and the young left-back Antonio Cabrini was attracting attention. In the opening rounds they had dispensed with Omonia Nicosia and Glentoran, the latter after something of a fright in Northern Ireland.

In Amsterdam, Geels and La Ling both came close to scoring and were denied by the crossbar and goalkeeper Dino Zoff. Zoff kept out the Dutch until, in the 86th minute, Pim Van Dord scored from a corner. With under a minute to play, however, Causio equalised. In the return, an early goal from Tardelli seemed to have secured the tie for Juventus but substitute La Ling pulled a goal back for Ajax with fifteen minutes to go. The game went to penalties and the experienced Zoff held his nerve to save two Dutch attempts, while Juventus slotted in three. The Italians were to face Belgian champions Bruges in the Semi-final.

Roger Davies and the 33-year-old Raoul Lambert were in net-finding form for Bruges, and the stylish midfield pairing of Rene Vandereycken and Paul Courant was the motor of the side. The young Danish winger Jan Sorensen

added flair and width to the attack. A 9-2 hammering of Koupio Palloseura and a 2-1 win over Panathinaikos qualified them for the Quarter-final against Atlético Madrid. Luis Aragones' Atlético, with sweeper Luis Pereira and striker Ruben Ayala, had eliminated Dynamo Bucharest and the fancied and skilful French side Nantes.

In the first leg in Belgium, Birger Jensen was inspired in goal for Bruges, saving a penalty from Marcial towards the end. A clever goal from Courant and a De Cubber thunderbolt gave the Belgians a 2-0 lead to take to Madrid. Although the Spanish were 2-0 up by half-time in the return, Cools and Lambert both scored after the interval. A final aggregate score of 4-3 meant that Bruges were through to the Semi-final against Juventus.

Juventus were favourites to meet Liverpool in the Final at Wembley, but in Turin had to wait until the 81st minute to beat the well-organised Bruges defence through a Bettega goal. In Belgium, a goal in the third minute from captain and right-back Alfons Bastijns rocked Juventus and, despite the constant attacks from Bettega and Benetti, the game ended level on aggregate. With five minutes to go in extra time, Vandereycken connected with a ball from Sorensen and Zoff was beaten. Bruges had become the first Belgian side to reach the European Cup Final.

LIVERPOOL 1977/78

Liverpool seamlessly adjusted to the loss of Keegan, who was looking for a new challenge with SV Hamburg. A shrewd Paisley paid Celtic £440,000 for their star forward Kenny Dalglish, an unselfish player with an unerring eye for goal, and he was the perfect replacement for Keegan. Graham Souness was acquired from Middlesbrough to add steel and creativity to the midfield, and the tall, elegant defender Alan Hansen joined from Partick Thistle. These three gifted Scottish internationals were to form the backbone of the team in the years to come.

Having received a bye in the first round, Liverpool met the East German side Dynamo Dresden at Anfield in the first leg of the second. Paisley surprised Dynamo (and the player) by picking Toshack, who had been injured for several months, and the big forward caused confusion in the Dynamo defence from the kick-off. Alan Hansen scored in the 14th minute, and Case and then Neal, from a penalty after a foul on Dalglish, contributed to a 3-0 Liverpool lead at the interval. Dynamo pulled one back through Hafner, but Case again and Kennedy in the 64th minute made the score a comfortable 5-1. The margin could well have been greater had it not been for the agility of Dynamo keeper Claus Boden.

An unusually poor and unco-ordinated performance by Liverpool in Dresden was capitalised on by the Germans, who went 2-0 ahead early in the second half. The inevitable Fairclough came on, and a fine pass from the substitute was converted by Heighway, taking advantage of poor defending. The game finished 2-1, Liverpool going through 6-3 on aggregate, and they were away to Benfica in the Quarter-final.

Two-times winners Benfica were now managed by English ex-Southampton manager John Mortimore and were unbeaten in 46 games. Captained by midfielder Toni, with Nene and Fernando Chalana in attack, the team had struggled to score in the tournament. A 0-0 aggregate draw

with Moscow Torpedo was settled by penalties in Benfica's favour, and they could only put two goals past outsiders BK Copenhagen in the second round.

In Lisbon in the pouring rain, Benfica took the lead in the 13th minute when a pass from Toni was turned in by Nene. Liverpool equalised twenty minutes later from a Case free-kick, and went 2-1 up in the 71st minute, Hughes scoring from a Dalglish pass. A Hansen foul on Pietra in the box late in the game went unpunished by the referee. At home, Liverpool were in command throughout. A deeply unconvincing display by Benfica's goalkeeper Bento helped the Reds to score four goals – from Callaghan, Dalglish, McDermott and Neal – against hapless defending, and a Nene strike did little to redress the balance.

Last season's Final opponents Borussia Moenchengladbach now stood between Liverpool and a second consecutive Final appearance. Liverpool went immediately into the attack in Germany, Hughes and Dalglish both forcing fine saves from keeper Wolfgang Kleff, and Heynckes also had two good chances early in the game. In the 28th minute, defender Wilfried Hannes scored from a corner, and Borussia, although missing their injured star striker Alan Simonsen, began to control the contest. McDermott went off to be replaced by Johnson and, in the 87th minute, the substitute headed in the equaliser from a corner. A minute later, however, a typically well-struck free-kick from Bonhof ensured a 2-1 victory for the Germans.

At Anfield, Borussia were again without Simonsen as well as influential defender Klinkhammer, and were no match for the home side. A sixth-minute headed goal from Kennedy squared the tie, after clever movement between Dalglish and Souness, playing his first full game in Europe. Liverpool went ahead before half time through Dalglish. Although Borussia applied some pressure early in the second half, the German defence was again breached in the 54th minute by Kennedy, and Case scored the third goal. An aggregate 4-2 victory sent Liverpool into the Final against Bruges.

Celtic suffered a serious blow in the summer of 1977 when Kenny Dalglish decided to move to Liverpool. Of the other players from the club's last European Cup appearance, Billy McNeill had retired and Jimmy Johnstone had moved to San José Earthquakes. Celtic were undergoing a period of reconstruction and 1977/78 was to be Jock Stein's last season as manager.

Midfielder Ronnie Glavin and forward Jim Craig were providing the goals, and the defence was marshalled by sweeper Pat Stanton and inspirational left-back Danny McGrain. Stanton, however, missed this year's European Cup games with a serious injury.

An 11-1 defeat of Jeunesse Esch, with Glavin scoring two and Craig three, preceded a 2-1 win at Parkhead against Innsbruck, Burns and Craig both getting on the scoresheet. A lacklustre display in Austria, without an injured McGrain, resulted in Celtic going down by three goals and out of the tournament.

Glentoran progressed into the second round for the first time, beating Valur 2-0 at home overturning a 1-0 defeat in Iceland. The Northern Ireland club managed to hold Juventus 1-0 at the Oval, the goal coming from Boninsegna, but succumbed 5-0 in Turin.

Kenny Dalglish (1951). 'King Kenny' was a hero at Parkhead and a superstar at Anfield. He made his Celtic debut in 1969, and soon impressed with his control and awareness, and his ability to find the net. He took in the last few years of the Stein era, winning four Scottish league titles, and moved to Liverpool in 1977 for a record transfer fee of £440,000 as replacement for Keegan. He scored the only goal in the 1978 European Cup Final against Bruges and played in two more European Cup Finals, winning both. He took over as Liverpool manager on the day of the Heysel disaster and subsequently managed Blackburn Rovers and Newcastle United. He then became director of football at Celtic. He achieved a record 102 caps for Scotland and played in the 1974, 1978 and 1982 World Cup finals.

1978 — THE FINAL

Liverpool plod to victory against boring Belgians

Liverpool (0) 1   Bruges (0) 0

Wembley Stadium, London, 10th May 1978
Attendance: 92,000
Referee: Corver (Netherlands)

This year's Final was as dull and disappointing as the previous year's had been thrilling. Bruges, perhaps daunted by the occasion and the opposition, came to defend and play for penalties. Hit by injuries, with their two most influential players Lambert and Courant sidelined, it made little sense to take risks. Liverpool were below par, and the game was a tedious affair.

Fairclough started the game in place of an unfit Heighway and Hansen replaced the injured Smith. Danish international goalkeeper Birger Jensen produced a classy and assured performance to keep out Liverpool's assaults on goal, many of which originated from Souness's intelligent probing from midfield. The game remained goal-less at half time, and a Case free-kick was the closest Liverpool had come to scoring.

In the 64th minute Heighway came on for Case and Liverpool made their breakthrough two minutes later. Souness chested down on the edge of the area and found Dalglish with a neat through pass which split the defence. Dalglish waited until Jensen advanced and he chipped delicately over the keeper to the inside of the far post. And that was that, apart from a scare towards the end of the game when a bad Hansen back-pass let in Sorenson, and Thompson had to clear the ball off the goal line.

It had been a long season for Liverpool: they had lost the League championship to Nottingham Forest and been beaten in the League Cup Final, also by Forest. As consolation, they had just become the first British club to have won the European Cup twice. However, they were not finished in Europe yet.

The teams
Liverpool: Clemence, Hughes, Neal, Thompson, R. Kennedy, Hughes, Dalglish, Case (Heighway), Fairclough, McDermott, Souness (manager: Paisley) [Dalglish 66]
Bruges: Jensen, Bastijns, Maes (Volder), Krieger, Leekens, Cools, de Cubber, Vandereycken, Simoen, Ku (Sanders), Sorensen (manager: Happel)

Kenny Dalglish lines up his chip for his goal in the 1978 Final.

Swedish side Malmö were a muscular team who played a long-ball game, and they were particularly adept at the offside trap. They had only twice before – 1960/61 and 1975/76 – progressed beyond the first round and they were unfancied this season. However, under 32-year-old English manager Bob Houghton, they had won the Swedish league title three times in the past four seasons and eight of the team had been selected for Sweden's World Cup squad.

Malmö defeated French champions Monaco 1-0 in the first round. Several of the bigger names had also been eliminated in the first round, including Juventus, Liverpool, Partizan Belgrade, Fenerbahçe and last year's Finalists Bruges. Only one team in the second round – Real Madrid – had ever reached a European Cup Final. So the possibility of a smaller club going far in the tournament was on the cards.

Malmö did well to achieve a goalless draw in the Ukraine against Dynamo Kiev in the second round, keeper Jan Moller in heroic form. A 2-0 victory at home, with second-half goals from young striker Jan-Olof Kinnvall and winger

Results

Preliminary Round

	1st leg	2nd leg	Agg	
Monaco v Steaua Bucharest	3-0	0-2	3-2	

First Round

	1st leg	2nd leg	Agg	
AEK Athens v Porto	6-1	1-4	7-5	
Bruges v Wisla Krakow	2-1	1-3	3-4	
Cologne v Akranes	4-1	1-1	5-2	
Fenerbahçe v PSV Eindhoven	2-1	1-6	3-7	
Grasshoppers Zurich v Valletta	8-0	5-3	13-3	
Juventus v Rangers	1-0	0-2	1-2	
Linfield v Lillestrom	0-0	0-1	0-1	
Malmö v Monaco	0-0	1-0	1-0	
Nottingham Forest v Liverpool	2-0	0-0	2-0	
Odense v Lokomotiv Sofia	2-2	1-2	3-4	
Omonia Nicosia v Bohemians	2-1	0-1	2-2	
Partizan Belgrade v Dynamo Dresden	2-0	0-2	2-2	4-5 (P)
Real Madrid v Progres Niedercorn	5-0	7-0	12-0	
Valkeakosken Haka v Dynamo Kiev	0-1	1-3	1-4	
Vllaznia v Austria WAC	2-0	1-4	3-4	
Zbrojovka Brno v Ujpest Dózsa	2-2	2-0	4-2	

P = penalties

Second Round

	1st leg	2nd leg	Agg
AEK Athens v Nottingham Forest	1-2	1-5	2-7
Austria WAC v Lillestrom	4-1	0-0	4-1
Bohemians v Dynamo Dresden	0-0	0-6	0-6
Dynamo Kiev v Malmö	0-0	0-2	0-2
Lokomotiv Sofia v Cologne	0-1	0-4	0-5
Rangers v PSV Eindhoven	0-0	3-2	3-2
Real Madrid v Grasshoppers Zurich	3-1	0-2	3-3
Zbrojovka Brno v Wisla Krakow	2-2	1-1	3-3

Quarter-finals

	1st leg	2nd leg	Agg
Austria WAC v Dynamo Dresden	3-1	0-1	3-2
Cologne v Rangers	1-0	1-1	2-1
Nottingham Forest v Grasshoppers Zurich	4-1	1-1	5-2
Wisla Krakow v Malmö			

Semi-finals

	1st leg	2nd leg	Agg
Austria WAC v Malmö	0-0	0-1	0-1
Nottingham Forest v Cologne	3-3	1-0	4-3

Tore Cervin, brought the Swedish side up against Polish champions Wisla Krakow, who had unexpectedly knocked out Bruges in the first round. Although 2-1 behind from the first leg, a 4-1 victory, including a hat-trick from Swedish international midfielder Anders Ljungberg, saw Malmö into the Semi-finals for the first time.

Austria WAC, Malmö's opponents in the Semi-final, had reached the final of the Cup Winners Cup the previous season. The Austrians had a fairly easy route to the semis, taking on Vllaznia Shkoder, the first Albanian side in the tournament for some years, and Norway's Lillestrom, although East Germany's Dynamo Dresden provided them with a stiffer test.

With most of Europe's footballing attention concentrated on the glamour tie of Nottingham Forest v Cologne, Malmö again achieved a goal-less draw in the away leg, and a single goal in Malmö, from a header from Tommy Hansson, took a Swedish club into the European Cup Final for the first time.

BRITISH CLUBS

Jock Wallace had departed **Rangers** and ex-captain John Greig had taken over as manager. The club had won the 'treble' for the second time within three years, and Celtic had collapsed to mid-table in the league. The team was largely the same as two seasons before, although three new forwards had joined the club since then. Davie Cooper was a highly gifted but inconsistent left-winger who had signed from Clydebank; Bobby Russell was a talented, ball-playing inside-right who rose from the junior leagues; and Gordon Smith, bought from Kilmarnock, could play in midfield, although he was also second-top goal scorer behind Derek Johnstone.

In the first round the Gers met an exhausted Juventus, over half of whose team had represented Italy in the World Cup finals in Argentina. The Italians nonetheless came away from the first leg in Turin with a 1-0 lead, scored in the ninth minute by winger Pietro Paolo Virdis playing at centre-forward in place of Boninsegna. Keeper Peter McCloy kept

Rangers in the tie with a valiant performance.

Back at Ibrox, inside-forward Alex MacDonald headed in an equaliser in the 18th minute, and Smith headed in from a free kick to make the score 2-0 for Rangers.

PSV Eindhoven were the opposition in round two. The Dutch champions were UEFA Cup holders and they fielded six players from the Holland World Cup squad. With star player Rene van der Kerkhof missing in the first leg at Ibrox, PSV defended well to travel back to Holland with a 0-0 draw. In the return, a Harry Lubse goal put PSV in front after only 34 seconds, but a MacDonald header in the 57th minute gave Rangers the lead on away goals. Three minutes later, however, Gerrie Deyckers scored for PSV. A header from Derek Johnstone restored Rangers' advantage, and PSV laid siege to Peter McCloy and his defenders in search of the winner.

With three minutes remaining, a perfectly-weighted ball from winger Tommy McClean through the PSV defence was picked up by Russell, who advanced to the edge of the penalty area and bent a fine shot around keeper Van Engelen. Rangers were through to play Cologne in the Quarter-final and PSV had suffered their first home defeat in Europe.

In Germany against Cologne, Rangers were without Johnstone, and Müller scored the only goal of the game in the 58th minute from a Flohe cross. At Ibrox, another strike by Müller was equalised by McLean but it was too late to affect the overall result. For Rangers, the European Cup remained an elusive trophy.

Linfield were yet again knocked in the first round – this time 1-0 by Norwegian part-timers Lillestrom – and the glorious season of 1966/67 was fast becoming a fading memory.

1979 — THE FINAL

Francis repays investment as Clough triumphs in Europe

Nottingham Forest (1) 1 Malmö (0) 0

Olympic Stadium, Munich, 30 May 1979
Attendance: 57,000
Referee: Linemayr (Austria)

This was the second desperately poor Final in succession, and prompted *World Soccer* magazine to ask if the European Cup was finished.

Injuries were partly to blame, and Forest were without Gemmill and O'Neill. However, Forest could replace O'Neill with £1 million man Trevor Francis, although he was playing out of position on the right wing. Malmö were missing their two key defenders – Bo Larsson and Roy Andersson – and their captain Staffan Tapper broke his toe on the eve of the game. In attack, Tore Cervin was not fully fit. Even at full strength, however, it is unlikely that they would have strayed from their game plan of deep defending, containment and reliance on the offside trap.

Throughout the first half Forest were in control but were making heavy weather of it. The breakthrough came in injury time at the end of the first half. Robertson scurried down the left, whipped past two defenders and sent in a high cross with his left foot. Francis was racing in from the other flank and, as the ball evaded the clutches of keeper Jan Moller, Francis was in the right spot to send in a header high inside the post.

In the second half, Birtles uncharacteristically missed a sitter with only the keeper to beat in the 59th minute, and two minutes later Robertson hit the post from a Francis cross. Malmö's attack was almost non-existent, and a Ljungberg free-kick towards the end was virtually their only attempt on goal.

The deeply disappointing game finished 1-0 and Peter Taylor commented, 'As a Final it was a non-event'. Nonetheless, Forest had become only the third English team to land the trophy, and it was a triumph for Clough, Taylor and their battling side.

The teams
Nottingham Forest: Shilton, Clark, McGovern, Lloyd, Burns, Francis, Bowyer, Birtles, Woodcock, Robertson (manager: Clough) [Francis 45]
Malmö: Moller, R. Andersson, Jonsson, M. Andersson, Erlandsson, Tapper (Malmberg), Ljungberg, Prytz, Kindvall, Hansson (T. Andersson), Cervin (manager: Houghton)

Trevor Francis meets John Robertson's cross to score in the 1979 Final.

NOTTINGHAM FOREST 78/79

Brian Clough and Peter Taylor had worked their magic again. The irascible duo had taken the small East Midlands club Nottingham Forest from the old Second Division in 1976/77 to the English league title the following year, seven points ahead of second-placed Liverpool, and had also won the League Cup.

Clough had joined Forest early in 1975, with Taylor joining eighteen months later, and had transformed the squad. Already at the club were attacking right-back Viv Anderson, who was soon to become England's first black international, the tubby left-winger John Robertson, and striker Tony Woodcock. Clough brought in his two lieutenants, the industrious midfielder and captain John McGovern and centre-forward John O'Hare, who had followed him on his travels from Derby to Leeds. English international goalkeeper Peter Shilton arrived from Stoke City, and two Scottish internationals – fiery central defender Kenny Burns and crafty, hardworking inside-forward Archie Gemmill – were also persuaded to the City Ground. And a 20-year-old striker, Gary Birtles, was acquired from local non-league club Long Eaton to fill the gap left by the departure of the unsettled Peter Withe to Newcastle. The Clough powers of motivation then went to work.

Clough's philosophy with Forest was to defend and counter-attack in numbers, and his first attempt to put this into practice in Europe was against an English side. An unseeded Forest were drawn against the European champions Liverpool in the first round. At the City Ground, Forest went ahead in the 26th minute when Woodcock cleverly drew Clemence and slipped the ball to Birtles to score. With three minutes to go, Forest broke from defence and the unlikely figure of left-back Colin Barrett was on hand to volley in a Woodcock header.

In the return at Anfield, Forest turned in a clinically effective defensive performance, with Shilton and Anderson outstanding, and prevented the Liverpool midfield from operating. Liverpool could not score and Forest had overcome their first major hurdle in Europe.

In round two, Forest travelled to Athens to play AEK, managed by Ferenc Puskas. Without their veteran midfielder Dimitris Domazos, AEK conceded a 9th-minute goal to McGovern and a 44th-minute strike to Birtles, both goals made by 35-year-old left-back Frank Clark. AEK scored from a controversial Tassos penalty in the second-half, but in Nottingham a 5-1 victory for Forest, with two from Birtles, sent them through to play Grasshoppers Zurich in the Quarter-final.

Young striker Claudio Sulser was in rampant form for the Swiss side, having scored five against Valletta and three in Grasshoppers' away goals victory over mighty Real Madrid in the second round. Sulser scored in the tenth minute at the City Ground, and was denied another in the 75th minute by a splendid Shilton save. However, by then Forest had virtually wrapped the game up, with goals from Birtles, Robertson and Gemmill. Big, bustling centre-half Larry Lloyd, another Clough recruit, headed the fourth in the last minute. In Zurich, a penalty from Sulser, his eleventh goal in the tournament, was equalised by Northern Ireland international midfielder Martin O'Neill.

A prestige Semi-final beckoned against Cologne. Managed by Hennes Weisweiler, Cologne had beaten Rangers 2-1 in the Quarter-final, both goals coming from their high-scoring centre-forward Dieter Müller. In goal was West German international Harald Schumacher, who was to become infamous in the 1982 World Cup for his assault on Patrick Battiston.

International midfielder Heinz Flohe was absent from the first leg in Nottingham, and an injured Burns and suspended Anderson were missing from the Forest side. On a boggy pitch, Roger Van Gool shot in off the post in the 6th minute, with Shilton shouldering the blame, and Müller made it two a few minutes later. Gemmill went off injured close to half time, Clark came on to shore up the defence, and full-back Ian Bowyer moved into midfield. A Birtles header and a shot from Bowyer had levelled the tie by the 53rd minute. A flying header from Robertson in the second half put Forest ahead. With less than ten minutes to go, substitute Yasuhiko Okudera's first touch of the ball deceived a nervy Shilton, and the game finished all square. 'Forest sunk by Japanese sub' was the predictable headline in the next day's paper.

Cologne were odds-on favourites to go through to the Final, and in the return game they piled on the pressure. With Burns and Anderson back, however, Forest withstood the onslaught. In the 65th minute, a training ground set-piece provided the decisive goal, a Robertson corner being flicked on by Lloyd and nodded in by Bowyer. Although back-in-form Shilton had to make a superb last-minute save from full-back Konopka, Forest held on to their lead.

Within two years, Forest had gone from the Second Division to the European Cup Final. And Clough's £1 million signing in February from Birmingham City, the speedy, powerful forward Trevor Francis, was eligible to play.

Nottingham Forest's Ian Bowyer heads in the winning goal in the Semi-final second leg against Cologne.

Larry Lloyd of Nottingham Forest (right) evades a Kevin Keegan tackle in the 1980 Final.

THE 1979-80 SEASON

Results

Preliminary Round	1st leg	2nd leg	Agg
Dundalk v Linfield	1-1	2-1	3-1
First Round			
Arges Pitesti v AEK Athens	3-0	0-2	3-2
Dundalk v Hibernians Malta	2-0	0-1	2-1
Dynamo Berlin v Ruch Chorzow	4-1	0-0	4-1
Hajduk Split v Trabzonspor	1-0	1-0	2-0
HJK Helsinki v Ajax	1-8	1-8	2-16
Levski Spartak v Real Madrid	0-1	0-2	0-3
Liverpool v Dynamo Tbilisi	2-1	0-3	2-4
Nottingham Forest v Osters IF	2-0	1-1	3-1
Partizan Tirana v Celtic	1-0	1-4	2-4
Porto v AC Milan	0-0	1-0	1-0
Red Boys Differdange v Omonia Nicosia	2-1	1-6	3-7
Start Kristiansand v Strasbourg	1-2	0-4	1-6
Servette v Beveren	3-1	1-1	4-2
Ujpest Dózsa v Dukla Prague	3-2	0-2	3-4
Valur v Hamburg	0-3	1-2	1-5
Vejle v Austria WAC	3-2	1-1	4-3
Second Round			
Ajax v Omonia Nicosia	10-0	0-4	10-4
Celtic v Dundalk	3-2	0-0	3-2
Dukla Prague v Strasbourg	1-0	0-2	1-2
Dynamo Berlin v Servette	2-1	2-2	4-3
Hamburg v Dynamo Tbilisi	3-1	3-2	6-3
Nottingham Forest v Arges Pitesti	2-0	2-1	4-1
Porto v Real Madrid	2-1	0-1	2-2
Vejle v Hajduk Split	0-3	2-1	2-4
Quarter-finals			
Celtic v Real Madrid	2-0	0-3	2-3
Hamburg v Hajduk Split	1-0	2-3	3-3
Nottingham Forest v Dynamo Berlin	0-1	3-1	3-2
Strasbourg v Ajax	0-0	0-4	0-4
Semi-finals			
Nottingham Forest v Ajax	2-0	0-1	2-1
Real Madrid v Hamburg	2-0	1-5	3-5

Although under coach Cor Brom Ajax had won the Dutch league and cup, just before the tournament began he was replaced by Leo Beenhakker, coach of the Ajax youth team. Ajax had sold the previous season's 36-goal striker, Englishman Ray Clarke, to Bruges and filled the centre-forward position with Henning Jensen from Real Madrid. Ruud Geels had departed to Anderlecht but right-winger La Ling and young winger Simon Tahamata remained, along with sweeper Ruud Krol. In midfield, the Danish internationals Soren Lerby and Frank Arnesen dictated play.

In the first three games of the competition, against HJK Helsinki and Omonia Nicosia, Ajax scored a record 26 goals with Lerby netting five against the Cypriots in the home game. The Quarter-final set them against French club Strasbourg. Strasbourg's manager Gilbert Gress had added to his small squad the Swiss midfielder Michel Decastel and leading French league goal-scorer, the Argentinian Carlos Bianchi. In goal was Dominique Dropsy. In the second round they eliminated a strong Dukla Prague side, the winner coming from Decastel in injury time.

In Strasbourg, a commanding performance kept the tie goal-less,

and in Amsterdam Ajax had an easy 4-0 victory. However, an away defeat by Nottingham Forest in the Quarter-final, and a magnificent Peter Shilton in Amsterdam denied Ajax the opportunity to reach the Final for the fifth time.

Real Madrid had signed young Englishman Laurie Cunningham, a fast and skilful forward with a wicked shot, and paired him up front with Santillana. With Angel and Stielike in midfield, and Pirri still the sweeper, coach Vujadin Boskov was confident about his chances in the tournament. In the second round Real met FC Porto who had surprisingly beaten AC Milan in the San Siro through a free-kick in the 60th minute from the Brazilian Duda. With Rivera retired and sweeper Baresi ill, Milan were unable to cope with the fast Portuguese team.

In the first leg in Lisbon, with Pirri injured, Real were two down at half time to striker Gomes, the second goal a dubious penalty. In the 50th minute, Stielike found Cunningham and the striker secured a vital away goal. In front of a full house in Madrid, Cunningham had a perfectly good first-half goal disallowed. He gained his revenge in the 72nd minute by sending in a cross which was converted by Gregorio Benito to put Real through on away goals to meet Celtic in the Quarter-final.

Against Celtic, a headed goal with four minutes to go in the second leg from Juanita, back from suspension, decided the tie 3-2 in Real's favour, and SV Hamburg were next for the Spaniards.

One of Germany's oldest clubs, Hamburg had won the league title for the first time in twenty years. The strong, attacking international full back Manni Kaltz and Dietmar Jacobs were pillars of the defence, and Kevin Keegan and captain Felix Magath provided the midfield creativity. In attack, the powerful Horst Hrubesch and Willi Reimann scored the goals. Keegan had a bad start to his career in Germany, with personal difficulties compounded by an eight-week suspension for punching an opponent. When he returned, however, Günter Netzer and 'the silent man', coach Branko Zebec, were in charge, and Keegan settled down.

Three goals from Hrubesch saw off Valur in the first round, and Dynamo Tbilisi, who had knocked out Liverpool, were next. A match-winning performance by Kaltz put Hamburg into the second leg 3-1 up, and in Russia a fine Keegan goal contributed to a 3-2 win for the Germans. In the first leg of the Quarter-final in Hamburg against Hajduk Split, the Yugoslavs defended well and it took a suspicious Hrubesch collision with the Split keeper to create space for Reimann to score. In Split, Hrubesch scored within two minutes, equalised by Zlatko Vujovic twenty minutes later. A minute later the Hamburg keeper Kargus saved a penalty and then the young full-back Holger Hieronymus put the Germans 3-1 ahead on aggregate. Although Split scored two more, Hamburg went through to the Semi-final on away goals.

The Final was to be held in Madrid and Real wanted to be there. They started in top gear at the Bernabeu in the first leg, having two goals disallowed in the first seven minutes against a defensive Hamburg. In total control, Madrid scored twice in the second half, with Santillana firstly taking advantage of a defensive mix-up and then getting a second after intelligent movement from Stielike.

A very different Hamburg awaited the Spaniards in Germany. Hamburg were two up after seventeen minutes, through a disputed Kaltz penalty and a Hrubesch header, although Real scored in the 30th minute from a clever Cunningham lob. A Hrubesch header just before half time and, in the last minute, a Caspar Memering close range finish made the score 5-1, and Hamburg were to meet Nottingham Forest in the Final.

BRITISH CLUBS

Billy McNeill, the heroic captain of the 1967 'Lisbon Lions', was appointed manager of **Celtic** in May 1978 to succeed Jock Stein. He acted straight away to strengthen his young team in which Danny McGrain and Roddy McDonald were still the centre of defence, with Roy Aitken in midfield, while centre-forward George McLuskey, winger Johnny Doyle and an ageing Bobby Lennox supplied the firepower.

In September 1978 McNeill broke the Scottish transfer fee record when he paid Kilmarnock £120,000 for their lively right-winger Davie Provan. A week later Provan was followed to Celtic Park by Murdo Mcleod, a goalscoring young midfielder from Dumbarton. McNeill's judgement and leadership abilities were rewarded within his first year at the club. By the end of the season, Celtic had won the Scottish league, beating Rangers 4-2 at Celtic Park to secure the title in Celtic's last game of the season, and they were back in the European Cup.

Celtic travelled to the Stalinist seclusion of Albania to play Partizan Tirana in the first round and, hampered by zealous bureaucracy and an extremely hot evening, they lost 1-0 to an Agim Murati goal. Back in Glasgow, Tirana went two-up on aggregate, thanks to an athletic headed own goal by right-back Alan Sneddon. Provan then took over and was instrumental in Celtic scoring four goals by half-time, with two headers from Aitken and one each from McDonald and Vic Davidson.

Celtic suffered a real scare in their second-round home leg against Irish part-timers Dundalk. McDonald headed them in front in the fourth minute, and a McLuskey 20-yarder made it two in the 32nd minute. An immediate reply from Dundalk's Cathal Muchlan was countered by a Burns goal one minute later. A lovely chip from Mick Lawlor finished off the scoring, and Celtic scraped through 3-2. A 0-0 draw in Ireland in front of a record crowd of 22,000 was enough to progress to the Quarter-final.

Their opponents were to be one of the legends of European football, Real Madrid. Celtic had played the Spanish masters before, but never in competition, and the expectation in Scotland was intense as the teams kicked off in the first leg at Celtic Park. Real Madrid, without an injured Pirri, dominated the first half, and shots from Cunningham and the little right-winger Juanito went close. However, the second half belonged to Celtic. In the 52nd minute, right-back Alan Sneddon turned in a cross which was dropped by keeper Garcia Ramon, and the ball was rammed home by McLuskey. In the 75th minute, Sneddon again sent in a far post cross, which was headed in by Doyle. A delighted Celtic finished the game 2-0 up, although manager McNeill cautioned against complacency.

He was right to do so. In Madrid, McLuskey missed a sitter in the fifth minute and hit the bar a few minutes later, but Madrid took control. A Cunningham corner was smashed in by Santillana just on half time. In the 56th minute, an inch-perfect pass from De Bosque to Cunningham was crossed by the English winger and rammed home by Steilike. In the 86th minute, Juanito supplied the coup de grace with a header from a cross by midfielder Angel. Celtic had played well, but they were out.

Emlyn Hughes had left **Liverpool** to go to Wolves, but otherwise the squad had changed little from the previous year. For their first-round home leg against a skilful and under-rated Dynamo Tbilisi, Hansen and Kennedy were both injured, and 21-year-old Soviet Player of the Year, Ramas Shengelia, missed two chances in the first twenty minutes. Johnson put Liverpool in front in the 20th minute, but sweeper Chivadze put through Shengelia in the 33rd minute to score past Celemence. A Case free-kick just on half time gave Liverpool a 2-1 advantage to take to Georgia.

A student demonstration at four in the morning in Liverpool's hotel in Tbilisil was bad preparation for the next day's game. The home side went on the attack, and Clemence was called upon to make three important saves. Liverpool were outclassed by the mobile and tricky

Georgians, and a goal each from Gutsaev and Shengelia, along with an 80th-minute penalty from Chivadze, eliminated Liverpool from the European Cup.

Linfield drew 1-1 away against Dundalk, and looked to be in a good position to reach the second round for the first time since 1967. However, their game in the Republic took place only two days after the murder of Lord Mountbatten, and serious crowd trouble erupted. UEFA ordered the second leg to be played in Holland, and Linfield were knocked out 3-1 on aggregate.

NOTTINGHAM FOREST 79/80

Forest had finished the league season in second place eight points behind Liverpool, but they had won the League Cup. Gemmill had left in the summer for Birmingham City, and Frank Gray, an attacking and adventurous left-back, had joined from Leeds United. For contractual reasons, Trevor Francis remained in America at the start of the season and missed rounds one and two in the tournament.

Drawn against Sweden's Osters in the first round, Forest scored two without reply through Ian Bowyer at the City Ground. In the away leg, a Woodcock header from young winger Gary Mills' cross cancelled out Mats Nordgren's 53rd minute strike for Osters. Arges Pitesti were the second-round opposition and a four-minute spell early in the first half saw Forest go two up through Woodcock and Birtles. They took the lead to Romania and another two goals – from Bowyer in the fifth minute and a Birtles far-post tap-in in the 23rd – ensured comfortable progress to the Quarter-final against East Germany's Dynamo Berlin in March.

Woodcock had left for Cologne in November and Clough was in need of a striking partner for Gary Birtles. In December he paid Queens Park Rangers £200,000 for Stan Bowles, a mercurial, gifted but inconsistent player who had never quite hit the heights his talent demanded. Bowles took the field along with Francis at the City Ground in the first leg and a well-organised Dynamo defence contained Forest well. In the 63rd minute, a speedy counter-attack by Dynamo

was finished off by the strong centre-forward Hans-Jurgen Riediger, and Forest had suffered their first European defeat. Worryingly, Burns received his second yellow card of the tournament and was suspended for the return.

The clubs met again in Berlin three days after Forest had lost the league Cup Final to Wolves, where a collision between Shilton and Needham presented Andy Gray with the only goal. Dynamo went immediately on the attack but Francis, playing centre-forward, was in inspired form. He scored from a Needham pass in the 15th minute and bagged another off the underside of the bar twenty minutes later. In the 38th minute Robertson was tripped in the box, took the penalty and scored. Although Terletzky converted a penalty early in the second half, Forest went through to the Semi-final against Ajax with a deserved 3-2 aggregate victory.

In the home leg, Francis was again unstoppable. An Ajax defensive mistake in the 33rd minute presented him with the ball in the box, and he fired it in the Dutch net. On the hour, a cross from Francis was unnecessarily handled in the area by the Ajax defender Cees Zwamborn, and Robertson netted the penalty.

In Amsterdam, a 65,000 capacity crowd watched Ajax surge forward from the kick-off. Playing with Bonsink instead of the dropped Tahamata, they continually tested the Forest defence for whom Burns and Lloyd were outstanding, and Shilton had to make two magnificent saves in the second half. Shilton was beaten, however, in the 67th minute by a Soren Lerby far post header from a cross by Jensen, and that remained the only goal of the game.

Forest were to meet Hamburg in the Final in Madrid.

Peter Shilton (1949). The tall, commanding Shilton took over the England goalkeeping position from Gordon Banks in 1971 and, by the time he retired from international duty in 1990, he had amassed 125 caps. He joined Stoke City from Leicester in 1974, and in 1977 moved to Brian Clough's Nottingham Forest where he won two European Cups. He kept goal for England in the 1982, 1986 (where he was famously deceived by Maradona's 'hand of God') and 1990 World Cup Finals. He left Forest for Derby in 1987 and became player-manager of Plymouth Argyle in 1992. He made his 1000th English appearance in 1996 playing for Leyton Orient.

Brian Clough (1935). The eccentric and outspoken Clough twice took the unfashionable Nottingham Forest to European greatness. An ex-striker for Middlesbrough and Sunderland, he and his partner Peter Taylor (right) had previously managed Hartlepool and Derby County, whom they led to the 1972 English league title, and Clough had an unhappy 44 days in charge at Leeds. At Forest, whom he joined in 1975, his motivational powers and his tactical understanding formed a side which won the European Cup in 1979 and 1980. He was unable to repeat the feat, however, and Forest have never since qualified for the tournament. He retired in 1993.

Battling Forest deny Hamburg

Nottingham Forest (1) 1   Hamburg (0) 0

Santiago Bernabeu Stadium, Madrid, 28 May 1980
Attendance: 50,000
Referee: Garrido (Portugal)

The famous home of Real Madrid, which had seen so many titanic contests in the European Cup, was less than half full as the 25th European Cup Final kicked off. Perhaps it was because the match was live on Spanish TV, or because the two sides had not caught the interest of the Madrid fans. Whatever the reason, the stay-aways missed an enthralling game of contrasting styles.

Trevor Francis had torn an Achilles tendon and was out, and Shilton played the game helped by pain-killing injections for a calf injury. The temperamental Bowles was also not available, having walked out of the club in a fit of pique. As the game unfolded, therefore, it was no surprise to see Gary Birtles alone in attack in front of a packed five-man midfield designed to smother the lively Hamburg forwards.

As expected, Hamburg immediately went on the offensive, with full-backs Kaltz and Memering marauding down the wings and Keegan being closely shadowed by his marker Burns, who also found time to foul Milewski in the first minute. Forest's plan was to frustrate the Germans and score on the break, and in the 19th minute the tactic worked brilliantly.

On the counter-attack, Robertson cut in from the left wing, exchanged a one-two with Birtles and, ignoring the screams from Clough and Taylor to get back in defence, let rip from the edge of the box. The ball beat keeper Kargus,

hit the inside of the far post and went into the net. The next minute, Reimann had an offside 'goal' disallowed and in the 32nd minute Shilton magnificently tipped away a fierce shot from Milewski.

In the second half, Hamburg brought on an unfit Hrubesch, and Keegan, having a rather disappointing game, dropped deep into midfield. Hamburg battered away at Forest but Burns and Shilton were outstanding and managed to scramble away efforts from Keegan and full-back Peter Nogly. In the 75th minute another Nogly shot, this time from nearly thirty yards, was expertly turned away by man-of-the-match Shilton. Within the last few minutes, a weary Birtles could have scored a second had it not been for a desperate saving tackle from Kaltz.

At the final whistle, the Forest players collapsed into each others' arms in a mixture of relief, joy and complete exhaustion. Their performance had not been a pretty one, but they had demonstrated remarkable teamwork and determination, and had worn down a technically better side. As Cloughie said, 'It was one of the best ninety minutes we have ever had. Absolutely marvellous'. And the European Cup remained in Nottingham.

The teams
Nottingham Forest: Shilton, Anderson, Lloyd, Burns, Gray (Gunn), O'Neill, McGovern, Bowyer, Mills (O'Hare), Robertson, Birtles (manager: Clough) [Robertson 19]

Hamburg: Kargus, Jakobs, Buljan, Nogly, Kaltz, Hieronymous (Hrubesch), Magath, Memering, Milewski, Keegan, Reimann (manager: Zebec)

John Robertson (far right, dark shirt) watches his 20-yard shot beat Hamburg keeper Kargus for the winning goal in the 1980 Final.

Bayern Munich had adjusted to the loss of Beckenbauer and Müller to the North American Soccer League, and to the retirement of Sepp Maier due to injuries sustained in a car crash. Schwarzenbeck was also about to retire through injury, but Bayern had won the Bundesliga title for the first time in six years and were back in the European Cup they had dominated in the mid-1970s. Paul Breitner had returned from Real Madrid via Eintracht Braunschweig and had moved into midfield where he had an excellent season, and Karl-Heinz Rummenigge's 26 goals had helped Bayern to the title. The club was drawn against Olympiakos in the first round.

The Greek champions had a lively Swedish striker, Thomas Ahlstroem, alongside regular centre-forward Mike Galakos, and had beaten Aris Salonika in a play-off to take the title. However, they provided little competition to the Germans, who won 4-2 in Athens, with Rummenigge and Dieter Hoeness, brother of Uli, adding one each to the 3-0 winning scoreline in Munich.

A weak Ajax could not handle them either in the second round. Although the Amsterdam side had gained a new striker, Piet Hamberg from Servette, Ruud Krol had finally left to join Vancouver Whitecaps and been replaced by the Dane Steen Ziegler. They were further weakened by the transfer of Simon Tahamata to Standard Liège. After a 5-1 crushing in Munich, with two goals apiece from Rummenigge and Hoeness, Ajax could only manage a 2-1 win in the return.

However, a brilliant performance by Liverpool in the second leg of the Semi-final, and an away goal by Ray Kennedy, ended Bayern's interest in the tournament.

Real Madrid were again dominating Spanish football and had won the league and cup 'double'. Pirri had left the club to join Puebla in Mexico, but their pivotal midfield man Stielike had signed a three-year contract, and Cunningham, Juanito and Santillana continued to plunder defences in attack. There had been no major summer signings at the Bernabeu. After surviving a testing tie in Ireland in the first round, they knocked out Limerick 7-2.

Results

Preliminary Round	1st leg	2nd leg	Agg
Honved v Valletta	8-0	3-0	11-0
First Round			
Aberdeen v Austria Vienna	1-0	0-0	1-0
Bruges v Basle	0-1	1-4	1-5
CSKA Sofia v Nottingham Forest	1-0	1-0	2-0
Dynamo Berlin v Apoel Nicosia	3-0	1-2	4-2
Dynamo Tirana v Ajax	0-2	0-1	0-3
Halmstad v Esbjerg	0-0	2-3	2-3
IBV v Banik Ostrava	1-1	0-1	1-2
Inter Milan v Universitatea Craiova	2-0	1-1	3-1
Jeunesse Esch v Spartak Moscow	0-5	0-4	0-9
Limerick v Real Madrid	1-2	1-5	2-7
Linfield v Nantes	0-1	0-2	0-3
Olympiakos v Bayern Munich	2-4	0-3	2-7
Oulu Palloseura v Liverpool	1-1	1-10	2-11
Sporting Lisbon v Honved	0-2	0-1	0-3
Trabzonspor v Szombierki Bytom	2-1	0-3	2-4
Viking Stavanger v Red Star Belgrade	2-3	1-4	3-7
Second Round			
Aberdeen v Liverpool	0-1	0-4	0-5
Banik Ostrava v Dynamo Berlin	0-0	1-1	1-1
Basle v Red Star Belgrade	1-0	0-2	1-2
Bayern Munich v Ajax	5-1	1-2	6-3
CSKA Sofia v Szombierki Bytom	4-0	1-0	5-0
Nantes v Inter Milan	1-2	1-1	2-3
Real Madrid v Honved	1-0	2-0	3-0
Spartak Moscow v Esbjerg	3-0	0-2	3-2
Quarter-finals			
Bayern Munich v Banik Ostrava	2-0	4-2	6-2
Inter Milan v Red Star Belgrade	1-1	1-0	2-1
Liverpool v CSKA Sofia	5-1	1-0	6-1
Spartak Moscow v Real Madrid	0-0	0-2	0-2
Semi-finals			
Liverpool v Bayern Munich	0-0	1-1	1-1
Real Madrid v Inter Milan	2-0	0-1	2-1

Hungarian champions Honvéd, the famous old club of Puskas and Kocsis whose last appearance in the tournament had been in 1956/57, met Real in the second round. A 3-0 aggregate win took the Spaniards to the Quarter-final to play Spartak Moscow, who had narrowly beaten Denmark's Esbjerg in the previous round. Spartak were coached by Soviet team manager Konstantin Beskov and included six internationals in their side. However, Real held them to a goal-less draw in Moscow and won 2-0 in Madrid. Real were to face Inter in the Semi-final.

Inter had won the league and led the pack throughout the season. Manager Eugenio Bersellini had bought the attacking Austrian midfield player Herbert Prohaska for £425,000 from FK Austria to supply his star goal scorer, international Sandro Altobelli. The strong defence included internationals such as keeper Ivano Bordon, Giuseppe Baresi and Gabriele Oriali. Altobelli scored twice in the first leg in Milan against Romania's Universtitatea Craiova, and that was enough to take Inter through to play Nantes in the second round.

A tight 3-2 win over the French side, Altobelli again claiming two, took Inter to the Quarter-final against Red Star Belgrade, 'double' winners in Yugoslavia. A draw in Milan gave Red Star a crucial away goal, but Inter held on to win 1-0 in Belgrade where the midfield influence of Prohaska helped steady his side's nerves in front of a highly partisan crowd.

In the first leg of the Semi-final at the Bernabeu, goals from Santillana and Juanito gave Real a cushion for the return. In Milan, where the importance of the game generated record Italian crowd receipts, Stielike brilliantly led Real's rear guard defence, and defender Jose Camacho adroitly controlled the midfield manoeuverings of Prohaska. Inter could only manage one goal, from Graziano Bini, and the frustrated Italian fans bombarded the Real players with missiles after the final whistle.

Real Madrid were back in the Final for the first time in fifteen years.

LIVERPOOL 1980/81

Liverpool had beaten Manchester United to the league title by two points, and the squad had changed little from the previous European tournament. Towards the end of the 1979/80 season, Paisley had been persuaded to part with £300,000 for an 18-year-old Fourth Division striker, Ian Rush, who was to achieve much in the years to come, and he also acquired Ronnie Whelan from the League of Ireland. From the youth team came the small, tricky inside-forward Sammy Lee, and left-back Alan Kennedy, who was to stamp his name on this year's competition, replaced Joey Jones. The spine of the team remained the attacking duo of Johnson and Dalglish, the inspiration of the side, with McDermott and Souness in midfield, and defenders Thompson and Hansen in front of keeper Clemence.

The Finnish outsiders Oulu Palloseura were making their first appearance in Europe and managed to hold Liverpool to a 1-1 draw at their small ground in the first round, McDermott scoring for the Reds in the 15th minute. However at Anfield, the outclassed Scandinavians were swamped 10-1, Souness claiming a hat-trick and McDermott scoring twice.

Scottish champions Aberdeen lined up against Liverpool in the second leg at Pittodrie and went down 1-0 to a fifth-minute McDermott goal. At Anfield, the Dons were trounced 4-0 by the Liverpool scoring machine, centre-half Miller opening the floodgates with an own goal. CSKA Sofia, who had eliminated Nottingham Forest in the first round, were the opposition in the Quarter-final, and in the first leg at Anfield another magnificent Souness hat-trick underpinned a 5-1 win. A 1-0 victory in Bulgaria drew them against Bayern Munich in the Semi-final.

In Liverpool, Souness was injured and an uninspiring game resulted in a 0-0 draw. The Germans were confident of victory in Munich in the second leg. Forced by injury to field two reserves – Richard Money and Colin Irwin – Liverpool nonetheless had Souness back. Bayern appeared confused by the team changes and, when another reserve, Howard Gayle, came on in place of the injured Dalglish, they could not match the speed and aggression of the Liverpool attack. Seven minutes from the end of the game, Ray Kennedy scored and, although Rummenigge equalised four minutes later, Liverpool had won through to the Final on away goals.

Liverpool's Sammy Lee (white shirt) in the Semi-final second leg against Bayern Munich.

The years of European success were coming to an end for **Nottingham Forest**. Drawn away against the Bulgarian army team, CSKA Sofia, Forest returned home 1-0 down to a goal by Yonchev. However, their famed ability to bounce back from defeat deserted them at the City Ground, and they meekly conceded a Kerimov strike to go out 2-0 in the first round.

The following season Peter Taylor walked out of the club after an acrimonious split with Clough. Forest went into decline, and they have never again appeared in the European Cup.

Aberdeen were the team to watch in Scotland. The Dons had won the title by one point from Celtic, their first league title for 25 years, and manager Alex Ferguson was building on the hard work of previous manager Billy McNeill to turn them into a formidable side. The defensive pairing of Willie Miller and Alex McLeish steadied the side, with fiery little Gordon Strachan adding bite and intelligence to the midfield. Drew Jarvie and Mark McGhee were the twin strikers now that Steve Archibald had left the club for Spurs.

Austria Vienna were the visitors to Pittodrie in the first leg of the first round, and Mark McGhee's 31st-minute goal was the difference between the sides at the finish. A sound defensive performance by Aberdeen in Vienna allowed them to hang on to a 0-0 draw and meet Liverpool in the second round. A 5-0 aggregate defeat by Liverpool was a fair reflection on the difference between the sides.

Linfield could not score against France's highly regarded Nantes, and went out 3-0 in the first round.

Bob Paisley

Bob Paisley (1919 - 1996). The quiet, modest, Durham-born Bob Paisley emerged from the Liverpool 'boot room' as successor to Bill Shankly to become the most successful manager the English game has known. He joined the club as a player in 1939 and remained at Liverpool as a physiotherapist after his playing career. He assumed control in 1974 and was responsible for buying Kenny Dalglish, Graeme Souness and Alan Hansen, the backbone of the side. By the time he retired in 1983 his team had won six English league titles, three League Cups, the UEFA Cup in 1976 and, of course, three European Cups in 1977, 1978 and 1981. He was awarded the MBE in 1977.

Alan Kennedy

Alan Kennedy (1957). Left-back Kennedy spent six years with Newcastle and moved to Liverpool in 1978 for £300,000. He scored the winning goal in the 1981 European Cup Final and his penalty in the shoot-out brought the trophy back to Liverpool in 1984. He moved to Sunderland in 1985. He played for England 22 times.

Unlucky Limerick stun Real

Real Madrid had an apparently simple tie against Ireland's Limerick in the first round. However, it was very nearly the biggest shock in the history of the tournament. Limerick, under new manager Eoin Hand, played the first leg in Dublin, had an offside 'goal' disallowed in the first minute and were 1-0 up at half time. Outplaying a dreadful Real defence, a skilful and determined Limerick were running the game and were unlucky to lose a goal to Juanito in the 70th minute. When Pineda scrambled the ball into the net with four minutes to go, the sighs of relief could be heard from Spain. A 5-1 Real win in Madrid restored the status quo.

Real Madrid's Laurie Cunningham (white shirt) attempts to squeeze past Graeme Souness (left) and Phil Neal in the 1981 Final.

Paisley creates history as Reds beat Real

Liverpool (0) 1   Real Madrid (0) 0

Parc des Princes, Paris, 27 May 1981
Attendance: 48,000
Referee: Palotai (Hungary)

For the first time in several years, the 1981 Final promised much. The two experienced teams were well-matched, the discipline and efficiency of Liverpool contrasting with the flair and style of Real, and the 48,000 crowd in Paris were anticipating a closely-fought and exciting match.

Madrid's coach Vujadin Boskov, however, had selection problems. First-choice keeper Mariano Reman was injured and his place went to the young Agustin, and inexperienced Rafael Garcia Cortes came in to the team in place of midfielder Ricardo Gallego, another injury victim. Cunningham was fit but hadn't played for six months, and Boskov elected to play the Englishman rather than the more experienced and dependable Pineda. Liverpool could count on their normal line-up.

Madrid began defensively, Camacho closely marking Souness and Garcia Cortes shadowing Dalglish, and the game turned physical. In the 29th minute Ray Kennedy was booked for a foul on Agustin and tempers became raised in the Madrid box. The quicksilver Juanito was displaying his range of skills, but playmaker Stielike was hustled off his stride by Sammy Lee's constant attentions and Cunningham was running around to little effect. Honours were about even at half time.

Liverpool began to control the game in the second half, although skipper Camacho was clear on goal in the 50th minute only to scoop over the bar. Liverpool continued to press forward against Madrid's tiring defence and, as an indication of Real's tactics, it was not until the 73rd minute that the Spaniards forced a corner. Five minutes later Santillana shot into Liverpool's side netting from another Juanito cross, but the decisive goal came in the 82nd minute. A Ray Kennedy throw-in on the left wing was chested down by an advancing Alan Kennedy. The left-back evaded an ineffective tackle from Garcia Cortes and drove an angled shot from the edge of the six-yard box over Agustin and into the far corner.

Now Real had eight minutes in which to score and it was their turn to push forward. Liverpool, however, almost scored another on the counter-attack when Souness had a shot brilliantly saved by Agustin. The Hungarian referee blew his whistle and Liverpool had won their third European Cup.

A professional and consistent performance from Liverpool justified their victory, although the game fell some way short of expectations. Boskov later complained that Liverpool's style was 'programmed and machine-like' and Paisley confessed that 'we have in the past achieved the same result with a better performance'. However, he had just become the only manager in the history of the tournament to have won the European Cup three times.

The teams
Liverpool: Clemence, Neal, A. Kennedy, R. Kennedy, Thompson, Hansen, Dalglish (Case), Lee, Johnson, McDermott, Souness (manager: Paisley) [A. Kennedy 82]
Real Madrid: Agustin, Garcia Cortes (Pineda), Camacho, Angel, Sabido, Garcia Navajas, Juanito, Del Bosque, Santillana, Stielike, Cunningham (manager: Boskov)

Belgian champions Royal Sporting Club Anderlecht were used to European success, having won the Cup Winners Cup twice and been runner-up once between 1976 and 1978. They remain the only Belgian team to have won a major European trophy. They had taken the Belgian league title by eleven points, with Danish striker Kenneth Brylle scoring 22 league goals. Dutchman Arie Haan had gone to Standard Liège and Benny Nielsen to St Etienne, but Iceland's Petur Petursson had arrived from Feyenoord to keep the goals flowing.

Against Poland's Widzew Lódz, whose talisman Zbigniew Boniek was soon to join Juventus, an impressive 4-1 victory for Anderlecht in Poland gave Lódz too much of a mountain to climb in the return leg. An even more praiseworthy 4-2 aggregate win over perennial European under-achievers Juventus, with Anderlecht holding on for a 1-1 draw in the return leg in Turin, was followed by two 2-1 victories over Red Star Belgrade. In the Semi-final, Aston Villa took a 1-0 first-leg lead to Belgium and Anderlecht could not find the net.

Beaten Semi-finalists last season, Bayern Munich, continued to benefit from the presence of Paul Breitner in midfield and the prolific goal scoring of Europe's Footballer of the Year, Karl-Heinz Rummenigge, who was Bundesliga top scorer with 29 goals. In the first round against defensive-minded Swedish side Osters IF, Bayern ran up a 6-0 win, with three for Rummenigge and two for Dieter Hoeness. They were paired with Benfica in the second round.

Benfica were coached by Lajos Baroti and had won their first league title for four years. Humberto Coelho was centre-half and captain, with the black-glove-wearing Joao Alves in midfield and Nene and Chalana in attack. Their domestic resurgence was not repeated in Europe, however, as Bayern swamped the Portuguese 4-1 at the Stadium of Light with Breitner claiming a hat-trick. Universitatea Craiova, 'double' winners in Rumania with five internationals in the squad, were next to be eliminated by the Germans. A 2-0 victory in Rumania was a sufficient margin for Bayern to reach the Semi-finals and contest a place in the Final with CSKA Sofia.

The Bulgarian side, which formed the backbone of the national team, had reached the Quarter-final last season. Their opponents in the first leg – Real Sociedad – had won the Spanish league for the first time, and boasted Spanish

Gordon Cowans

Gordon Cowans (1958).
A small, slight midfielder with excellent ball skills, Cowans was one of the most skilful players in Aston Villa's history. He made his debut for Villa in 1976 at the age of 17 and he became a regular shortly after. He played in every Villa game in 1981/82, including their triumphant European Cup run, and again in 1982/83. Equally adept with either foot, his accurate passing created many goals for Gary Shaw, Tony Morley and Peter Withe. He missed the 1983/84 season with a broken leg, and he was transferred to Bari in Serie A in 1985. He returned to Villa in 1988 and joined Blackburn for £250,000 in 1991. He returned to Villa for a short spell in 1993. He gained ten caps for England.

Results

Preliminary Round	1st leg	2nd leg	Agg
St Etienne v Dynamo Berlin	1-1	0-2	1-3

First Round	1st leg	2nd leg	Agg
Aston Villa v Valur	5-0	2-0	7-0
Austria Vienna v Partizan Tirana	3-1	0-1	3-2
Benfica v Omonia Nicosia	3-0	1-0	4-0
Celtic v Juventus	1-0	0-2	1-2
CSKA Sofia v Real Sociedad	1-0	0-0	1-0
Dynamo Berlin v FC Zurich	2-0	1-3	3-3
Dynamo Kiev v Trabzonspor	1-0	1-1	2-1
Ferencvaros v Banik Ostrava	3-2	0-3	3-5
Hibernians Malta v Red Star Belgrade	1-2	1-8	2-10
IK Start v AZ Alkmaar	1-3	0-1	1-4
KB Copenhagen v Athlone Town	1-1	2-2	3-3
Osters IF v Bayern Munich	0-1	0-5	0-6
Oulu Palloseura v Liverpool	0-1	0-7	0-8
Progres Niedercorn v Glentoran	1-1	0-4	1-5
Universitatea Craiova v Olympiakos	3-0	0-2	3-2
Widzew Lodz v Anderlecht	1-4	1-2	2-6

Second Round	1st leg	2nd leg	Agg
Anderlecht v Juventus	3-1	1-1	4-2
Austria Vienna v Dynamo Kiev	0-1	1-1	1-2
AZ Alkmaar v Liverpool	2-2	2-3	4-5
Banik Ostrava v Red Star Belgrade	3-1	0-3	3-4
Benfica v Bayern Munich	0-0	1-4	1-4
CSKA Sofia v Glentoran	2-0	1-2	3-2
Dynamo Berlin v Aston Villa	1-2	1-0	2-2
KB Copenhagen v Universitatea Craiova	1-0	1-4	2-4

Quarter-finals	1st leg	2nd leg	Agg
Anderlecht v Red Star Belgrade	2-1	2-1	4-2
Dynamo Kiev v Aston Villa	0-0	0-2	0-2
Liverpool v CSKA Sofia	1-0	0-2	1-2
Universitatea Craiova v Bayern Munich	0-2	1-1	1-3

Semi-finals	1st leg	2nd leg	Agg
Aston Villa v Anderlecht	1-0	0-0	1-0
CSKA Sofia v Bayern Munich	4-3	0-4	4-7

internationals Jesus Zamora in midfield and Jesus Satrustegui in attack. A 1-0 victory in Bulgaria, scored by Yonchev in the last minute, put CSKA through to the next round against Glentoran. A narrow 3-2 win over the brave Northern Ireland side set up a Quarter-final tie against Cup-holders Liverpool, and an extra-time goal in Sofia decided the tie in CSKA's favour.

Within seventeen minutes of the first leg kick-off in Bulgaria, Bayern found themselves 3-0 down, but their famed resilience allowed them to battle back to a 4-3 defeat. However, in Munich CSKA were destroyed 4-0 by two Rummenigge goals and two more from Breitner. Bayern had got through to the Final for the fourth time, and were to face English newcomers Aston Villa.

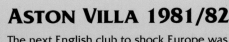

ASTON VILLA 1981/82

The next English club to shock Europe was Aston Villa. Villa were the first English club to win the 'double', admittedly in the 1890s, and they had won the league title for the first time in 71 years. A blend of youthful flair and experience, Villa played attractive attacking football, while the stern work ethic of manager Ron Saunders ensured that they were also aware of the virtues of sound defending.

In midfield, the small, left-footed Gordon Cowans crafted and created the chances for speedy left-winger and goalscorer Tony Morley and young forward Gary Shaw, while the big ex-Newcastle centre-forward Peter Withe bustled and harried on the ground and in the air. Captain and midfield general Dennis Mortimer patrolled the centre of the park and behind him the Scottish centre-half Allan Evans organised the defence, backed up by full-backs Kenny Swain and Gary Williams. The experienced Jimmy Rimmer kept goal.

A 7-0 defeat of Valur kicked off Villa's first European Cup campaign, two coming from Shaw in a freezing Iceland. In the second round away to Dynamo Berlin, who had knocked out fancied St Etienne in the preliminary round, a fourth-minute header from Shaw found Morley twelve yards from goal and he volleyed home. In the 50th minute the dangerous striker Hans-Jürgen Riediger headed in an equaliser and, with five minutes to go, a brilliant run by Morley ended with the winger beating keeper Rudweilet. In the return at Villa Park, Frank Terletzki scored in the 15th minute, and a superb save from Rimmer near the end denied Riediger. Villa went through on away goals to face Dynamo Kiev.

The first leg of the Quarter-final was moved from Kiev to the Crimea because of poor weather conditions, and Villa turned in a fine defensive display to thwart the Russian champions and the dazzling wing play of Oleg Blokhin. Blokhin hit the post in the first half and Shaw did the same in the second, but the game ended goalless. Back in Birmingham, a fifth-minute one-two between Morley and Shaw put Villa in front through Shaw, but the expected Kiev onslaught did not materialise. Defender Ken McNaught made matters safe on half-time with a header from a Cowans corner.

In February Saunders surprisingly announced his resignation as manager and was replaced as 'caretaker' by Tony Barton. Barton moved swiftly to gain the trust of his players and retain the rhythm of the team, as the Semi-final was approaching against Anderlecht, a team packed with internationals. Anderlecht came to Villa Park to defend and demonstrate their mastery of the offside trap, but a clever ball from Cowans in the 35th minute found Morley on the counter-attack and his shot went in the net off the inside of the post. Rimmer pulled off a vital save from Frank Vercauteren towards the end of the game, and Villa went to Brussels 1-0 ahead.

At the Parc Astrid, trouble erupted on the terraces from the beginning of the game, mainly involving Villa fans. The referee had to stop play for seven minutes and the Villa players appealed to the supporters to calm down. Riot police moved in and the game was played in an unpleasant and hostile atmosphere, but Villa battled to produce an excellent defensive performance and prevented an Anderlecht equaliser. Villa were fined £14,500 by UEFA for their part in the disturbances.

For the second time in three years a first-time English entrant in the competition was through to the Final of the European Cup.

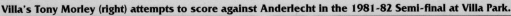

Villa's Tony Morley (right) attempts to score against Anderlecht in the 1981-82 Semi-final at Villa Park.

Celtic had triumphed in the Scottish league, largely due to the goal-scoring exploits of their two finishers, young Charlie Nicholas, who had come through the youth side, and Frank McGarvey, who had been brought back from Liverpool for £275,000. The pair finished the season with 50 goals between them. Forwards Davie Provan and George McCluskey were also adding their quota, while Tommy Burns, Roy Aitken and Murdo Mcleod were carving out the chances for Billy McNeill's team. Irishman Pat Bonner had taken over in goal from Peter Latchford, and captain Danny McGrain provided class and confidence in defence.

A tough draw brought Juventus to Celtic Park in the first round. The Italians had replaced Franco Causio with Domenico Marrochino, and had paid Arsenal £600,000 in 1980 for the visionary, left-sided midfielder Liam Brady. Hard man Claudio Gentile and Antonio Cabrini were the full-backs, with Gaetano Scirea sweeping the ball forward from defence to Roberto Bettega and Pietro Paulo Verdis. The difficulty of scoring in Serie A can be evidenced by Brady's position as the club's leading netfinder the previous season with eight goals. In spite of the quality of their players, Juventus had a poor record in Europe and never seemed to last the pace in the major tournaments.

In the first leg in Glasgow before a 60,000 crowd, and with Juventus fielding five of the Italian national team, there was no score at half time. In the 67th minute, a shot from Mcleod spun off Scirea, and Zoff in the Italian goal was helpless to prevent it looping over his head and into the net. A fortnight later in Turin, Virdis scored in the 28th minute, catching the Celtic defence flat-footed, and twelve minutes later Bettega added another. Celtic could not reply and were out. Yet again, Celtic's poor away record in Europe had eliminated them from a tournament.

In the summer of 1981 Ray Clemence had joined Spurs for £300,000, and his place in the **Liverpool** goal was taken by the athletic, if eccentric, Zimbabwean Bruce Grobbelaar, who was to become a folk hero with the Kop. Other new arrivals were the elegant defender-cum-midfielder Mark Lawrenson from Brighton and winger Craig Johnston from Middlesbrough. The pace, anticipation and goalscoring prowess of Ian Rush had given the Reds a new weapon, and he was linking cleverly with Dalglish and Johnson in attack.

A sense of apprehension must have settled on Finland's Ouiu Palloseura when they discovered they were again to be shooting practice for Liverpool in the first round. In Finland, a late Dalglish strike was all that separated the teams, but seven more went past the unfortunate Oulu in the return leg.

Dutch champions AZ Alkmaar had won the 'double' and had beaten Ajax to the title by 12 points. They lined up against Liverpool in the second round first leg in Alkmar, and a goal apiece from Johnson and Lee enabled Liverpool to take a 2-2 draw back to Anfield. In the return, an exciting tie was again level at 2-2 until a late goal by Hansen ensured Liverpool's progress to the Quarter-final against CSKA Sofia.

Although CSKA had suffered a 5-0 hammering at Anfield the previous season, they escaped in the first leg with a 1-0 defeat, the goal being scored by Whelan. In the away leg, some erratic keeping by Grobbelaar and a sending-off for Lawrenson allowed Bulgarian international winger Mladenov to score twice, the winner coming in extra time. The champions had failed to retain the European Cup.

Glentoran had a soft draw against Luxembourg's Progres Niedercorn in the first round, and a 4-0 home victory followed a 1-1 result away. Taking a 2-0 deficit back from Bulgaria to the Oval in the second round, Glentoran scored twice, through Cleary and Manley, but were edged out 3-2 by CSKA Sofia.

> ***Peter Withe*** *(1951). A big, bustling centre-forward, and good in the air, Withe played for several clubs, including Birmingham, Nottingham Forest and Newcastle. He played in every one of Aston Villa's European Cup games in 1981/82, and is best known for scoring the winner against Bayern Munich to secure Villa's only European Cup trophy. He played 11 times for England and ended his career at Hartlepool.*

An injured Jimmy Rimmer makes way for substitute keeper Nigel Spink (16) in the 1982 Final.

Peter Withe puts Aston Villa ahead from close range in the 1982 Final.

Villa delight as Withe strikes home

Aston Villa (0) 1   Bayern Munich (0) 0

Feyenoord Stadium, Rotterdam, 26 May 1982
Attendance: 46,000
Referee: Konrath (France)

Villa's intelligent passing football and unselfish teamwork had brought them to the Final against Bayern, for whom skipper Rummenigge and Hoeness were in top scoring form. Indeed, Hoeness finished the tournament as highest scorer with seven goals. Bayern, with their team of internationals and their long experience in Europe, started as favourites but Villa were on a roll and determined to make it five European Cups in a row for an English side.

Villa started brightly, Withe and Evans going close in the opening minutes. However, in the ninth minute, keeper Rimmer had to retire with a cricked neck and was replaced by 23-year-old Nigel Spink, making only his second full appearance in the first team. And he did not disappoint. Although Villa were dominating the game, with Evans sitting closely on Rummenigge, Bayern were dangerous on the attack and Spink had to pull off two fine saves from Durnberger and Rummenigge.

In the second half, the momentum swung Bayern's way and Villa came under sustained pressure. Durnberger and Augenthaler went close, and full-back Swain was in the right position to clear off the line from another Augenthaler header which had beaten Spink.

In the 67th minute, Shaw turned Dremmler and passed to Morley on the wing. With his marker stranded, Morley cleverly deceived centre-back Weiner and sent in a low cross which found Withe on the edge of the six-yard box. With the ball bobbling on the uneven surface, Withe stuck out his foot and toed it past keeper Müller, off the inside of the post and into the net.

Encouraged by their lead, Villa went back on the attack and Morley had a 20-yard shot well saved by Müller. At the other end, Hoeness had an offside 'goal' disallowed, and that was the tired Germans' last chance. An ecstatic team saluted their jubilant supporters at the final whistle, and English domination in Europe had been maintained.

Villa have never again reached the Final, but their spirited performances against some of the finest teams in Europe assures them of a prominent place in the history of the tournament.

The teams
Aston Villa: Rimmer (Spink), Swain, Williams, Evans, McNaught, Mortimer, Bremner, Shaw, Withe, Cowans, Morley (manager: Barton) [Withe 67]
Bayern Munich: Müller, Dremmler, Horsmann, Durnberger, Augenthaler, Weiner, Kraus (Niedermayer), Breitner, Hoeness, Mathy (Guttler), Rummenigge (manager: Csernai)

Real Sociedad had won the Spanish league, and were regarded as a solid but effective defensively-minded side. The imperious keeper Luis Arconada kept the defence in order, while midfield general Zamoro supplied forwards Lopez Ufarte and Uralde.

Real narrowly defeated Iceland's Vikingur in the first round, and two own goals by Celtic in Spain in the second round contributed to the Scots' downfall. The Quarter-final found Real facing in-form Sporting Lisbon, who had scored three goals in Portugal against Dynamo Zagreb and had eliminated CSKA Sofia on away goals. In Lisbon, a last-minute goal from striker Manuel Fernandes gave the Portuguese a 1-0 advantage, but a 68th-minute strike by Bakero in San Sebastian put Real through to the Semi-final against Hamburg.

Hamburg were without Keegan, who had returned to British football, but Kaltz and Magath were still the pillars of the team and midfielders Jimmy Hartwig and Wolfgang Roth pulled the strings. The Danish forward Lars Bastrup teamed up in attack with Hrubesch. In the opening rounds they had dispensed with tough opposition – Dynamo Berlin and Olympiakos – and were looking ominous.

A Quarter-final tie against Dynamo Kiev was won 3-0 in the Ukraine by Hamburg through a hat-trick from Bastrup, his first goal scored within the opening five minutes. Kiev scored two in Hamburg from Bessonov and Yevtushenk, but went out 4-2 on aggregate.

A composed Hamburg opened the scoring in the Semi-final first leg in Spain, Rolff heading in a Hartwig cross in the 58th minute, and defender Gajate levelled in the 74th minute from a cross by Lopez Ufarte. In Germany, the game was goal-less for the first 75 minutes, until defender Jakobs headed in a Kaltz corner. Diego equalised for Real four minutes later, but the tie was settled when young forward Thomas Von Heesen pounced on a loose ball to send a shot past Arconada. Hamburg were in the Final.

Liam Brady had moved to Sampdoria, but Juventus were able to field French midfield star and spot-kick expert Michel Platini alongside Zbigniew Boniek. Roberto Bettega, playing his last season for the club, was partnered by the Italian international centre-forward Paolo Rossi, recently returned to football from a two-year betting and bribes suspension.

A fighting performance by Denmark's Hvidovre in Turin could not prevent an aggregate defeat by Juventus in the first round, and a two-goal defeat of Standard Liège in Turin put Juventus into the Quarter-final to play Aston Villa. Juventus were too good for the English Cup-holders in both legs, and the Italians reached the Semi-final to play Poland's Widzew Lódz. An efficient Lódz side had beaten Rapid Vienna in a thrilling 5-3 victory in Vienna to win 6-5 on aggregate in the second leg, and had eliminated Liverpool in the Quarter-final.

Juventus dominated the first leg in Turin, Marco Tardelli putting them ahead after seven minutes and Bettega getting another in the 59th minute. In Lódz, a Platini pass set up a Rossi goal in the 33rd minute, and shortly after half time Krzysztof Surlit equalised. Scirea deflected the ball into his own net with ten minutes to go, but Platini made things safe for Juventus from a penalty three minutes later after Boniek had been brought down in the box.

Two of the biggest teams in Europe were to meet in the Final in Athens on 25 May.

Zbigniew Boniek

Results

Preliminary Round	1st leg	2nd leg	Agg
Dynamo Bucharest v Valerengen	3-1	1-2	4-3

First Round			
17 Nentori Tirana v Linfield	1-0	1-2	2-2
Avenir Beggen v Rapid Vienna	0-5	0-8	0-13
Aston Villa v Besiktas	3-1	0-0	3-1
Celtic v Ajax	2-2	2-1	4-3
Dundalk v Liverpool	1-4	0-1	1-5
Dynamo Berlin v Hamburg	1-1	0-2	1-3
Dynamo Bucharest v Dukla Prague	2-0	1-2	3-2
Dynamo Zagreb v Sporting Lisbon	1-0	0-3	1-3
Grasshoppers Zurich v Dynamo Kiev	0-1	0-3	0-4
Hibernians Malta v Widzew Lodz	1-4	1-3	2-7
Hvidovre v Juventus	1-4	3-3	4-7
Monaco v CSKA Sofia	0-0	0-2	0-2
Olympiakos v Osters IF	2-0	0-1	2-1
Omonia Nicosia v HJK Helsinki	2-0	0-3	2-3
Standard Liège v Vasas Gyor	5-0	0-3	5-3
Vikingur v Real Sociedad	0-1	2-3	2-4

Second Round			
CSKA Sofia v Sporting Lisbon	2-2	0-0	2-2
Dynamo Bucharest v Aston Villa	0-2	2-4	2-6
Dynamo Kiev v 17 Nentori Tirana (a)			
Hamburg v Olympiakos	1-0	4-0	5-0
HJK Helsinki v Liverpool	1-0	0-5	1-5
Rapid Vienna v Widzew Lodz	2-1	3-5	5-6
Real Sociedad v Celtic	2-0	1-2	3-2
Standard Liège v Juventus	1-1	0-2	1-3

a) Dynamo Kiev walkover, 17 Nentori Tirana withdrew.

Quarter-finals			
Aston Villa v Juventus	1-2	1-3	2-5
Dynamo Kiev v Hamburg	0-3	2-1	2-4
Sporting Lisbon v Real Sociedad	1-0	0-2	1-2
Widzew Lodz v Liverpool	2-0	2-3	4-3

Semi-finals			
Juventus v Widzew Lodz	2-0	2-2	4-2
Real Sociedad v Hamburg	1-1	1-2	2-3

Zbigniew Boniek (1956). One of the greatest footballers in Polish history, and possessor of eighty international caps, Boniek began his senior career with Widzew Lodz and scored two goals for his country in the 1978 World Cup finals. Four years later, his hat-trick eliminated Belgium from the tournament in the second round, and Poland finished in third place. His goal-scoring feats alerted Juventus whose transfer offer of £1.1 million was a Polish record. He scored the winning goal for Juve in the 1984 Cup Winners Cup 2-1 defeat of Porto, and he also played in two European Cup Finals, against Hamburg in 1983 and in the ill-fated game at the Heysel in 1985. He finished his career with Roma.

BRITISH CLUBS

Liverpool had fought off a challenge by Ipswich to win the English league. In the first round they easily negotiated their way past Ireland's Dundalk, winning 5-1, and travelled to Finland in the second round to play HJK Helsinki. HJK came to Anfield for the second leg carrying a 1-0 advantage, but five goals without reply, two from Alan Kennedy, finished off the Finns.

In Poland for the Quarter-final against Widzew Lódz, Liverpool were content with a 0-0 scoreline at half time. Shortly after the interval, however, Grobbelaar fumbled a comparatively simple cross and Tlokinski slotted home. In the 80th minute Wraga scored another, with Grobbelaar again at fault. At Anfield, Neal put Liverpool ahead in the 14th minute but a Tlokinski penalty 20 minutes later and a goal from Smolarek in the second half decided the tie. A 70th-minute strike from Rush and a last-second goal from new striker David Hodgson were too little and too late to keep Liverpool in the tournament.

Aston Villa had struggled in the league but were in the competition as Cup holders. They began their defence against Turkish champions Besiktas in a deserted Villa Park. UEFA had ordered the club to play their first European game behind closed doors as punishment for the trouble in Belgium last season. With Alan Evans injured, Withe, Morley and Mortimer had put Villa 3-0 ahead after only 30 minutes, and Besiktas could only score once. In a hostile atmosphere in Istanbul, Villa defended well to emerge with a 0-0 draw, and went through to meet Dynamo Bucharest in Romania..

The Romanians were a strong side and had already knocked out Dukla Prague. Villa, however, were unfazed by their reputation and by the huge local support, and gave a demonstration of positive, controlled football, with Shaw netting from a Withe header and Shaw scoring again in the second half from a Morley cross. In the return at Villa Park, Shaw scored a hat-trick and substitute Mark Walters slotted in a fourth. A resurgent Juventus were to be the opposition in the Quarter-final.

Juventus began the first leg in Birmingham in style, Paolo Rossi heading in the first goal within the first minute from a Cabrini cross, before the ball had been touched by a Villa player. Cowans headed in the equaliser in the 53rd minute, but Boniek smartly converted a pass from Platini towards the end. In Turin, a damp 70,000 crowd saw Platini beat Spink in the 13th minute, and fifteen minutes later Tardelli sent a well-placed header past the keeper. Platini made it three in the second half and, although Withe beat Zoff in the 81st minute, Villa were out.

A young Paul McStay had made his debut for **Celtic** at the start of the 1983/83 season, and in the years to come the midfielder would secure his place in the pantheon of Celtic greats. Nicholas was injured for much of the previous season, but was now back to fitness and form. Ajax,

Paolo Rossi

Paolo Rossi (1956). Rossi's career was short but eventful. Dropped by Juventus as a boy, he moved to Vincenza and scored three goals in the 1978 World Cup finals. Perugia then paid £3.5 million for the young striker, who was promptly banned for two years for alleged involvement in match-fixing. Rescued by Juventus during his suspension, he came back immediately after the ban to score six goals in the 1982 World Cup finals, including a brilliant hat-trick against Brazil in the Quarter-final, to win the Cup for Italy. He was named European Footballer of the year in 1982. He played for Juventus in the 1983 and 1985 European Cup Finals, and injuries forced him to retire in 1986. He made 48 international appearances for Italy during his roller-coaster career.

rejuvenated by the return of Cruyff from Barcelona, travelled to Celtic Park in the first round, and a marvellous game followed. Within thirty minutes, four goals had been scored, the first in the fourth minute from Olsen. A penalty from Nicholas, after a foul on Burns, levelled matters. Then Lerby put Ajax in front and a typically opportunistic strike from McGarvey made the score 2-2. The crowd applauded the teams off the pitch at the final whistle.

In Amsterdam, a wonder goal from Nicholas opened Celtic's account. Waltzing past two defenders, he played a one-two with McGarvey and perfectly timed his chip over the keeper. In the second half, Vanenburg equalised, but McCluskey ensured Celtic's progress in the tournament with an 88th-minute goal.

In San Sebastian against Real Sociedad in the second round, the game appeared to be heading for a goalless draw, until deflections from Reid and Aitken in the last fifteen minutes handed a 2-0 win to Real. In the return, McGarvey nearly scored in the first fifteen seconds, Arconada scrambling the ball past the upright. However, a Uralde header from a Ufarte cross in the 25th minute eluded Bonner, and Real retreated into defence. Two goals from Murdo McLeod made no difference to the overall result.

Linfield again fell at the first hurdle, losing on away goals to Nentori Tirana.

Roberto Bettega (1950). Bettega was an excellent finisher for Juventus in the 1970s. Strong in the air, and two-footed, he came up through the Juve youth system and made his debut in 1970 in the first team. Known as 'Bobby-gol' for his predatory scoring ability, he scored 178 goals in his Juventus career. He received the first of his 42 Italian caps in 1975 and he represented his country in the 1978 World Cup finals, although he missed the 1982 tournament due to an injury sustained in a 1981 European Cup game against Anderlecht. He retired after the 1983 European Cup Final and is now vice-president of Juventus.

Juve lose out to determined Germans

Hamburg (1) 1   Juventus (0) 0

Olympic Stadium, Athens, 25 May 1983
Attendance: 75,000
Referee: Rainea (Romania)

For the first time in six years, there was no English representative in the Final, Liverpool and Aston Villa having failed to progress beyond the Quarter-final stage.

Before the game, held for the first time at the Olympic Stadium in Athens, Juventus were seen as clear favourites. Agnelli had spent heavily, particularly on Platini and Boniek, in order to win the European Cup, a trophy the Italian giant had never won. As well as their two foreign stars, Juventus played six of the Italian World Cup-winning team – Zoff, Gentile, Cabrini, Scirea, Tardelli and Rossi – and were expected to demonstrate their superiority over a dogged but essentially workmanlike Hamburg.

In players such as Kaltz, Magath and centre-forward Hrubesch, however, Hamburg had strong, determined and skilful internationals of their own, and the tactical brain of manager Ernst Happel organised and directed the side. Midfield influence Jimmy Hartwig was suspended, but Wolfgang Rolff was available, as were Bastrup and young Milewski to support the big centre-forward. Hamburg were also keen to avenge their country's defeat by Italy in the 1982 World Cup Final.

As the game began, Hamburg immediately took the initiative. Cabrini was marking Bastrup and Brio was sticking closely to Hubresch, but Milewski on the left and Groh on the right were running at the Italians. Within eight minutes, Hamburg were ahead, a run and a clever curling shot from Magath fooling the 41-year-old keeper Zoff. Playing with skill and confidence, Hamburg imposed their will on an increasingly disorganised Juventus. Although German keeper Stein was called on to make a couple of important saves, the Italians were unable to out-think the Hamburg midfield, brilliantly led by captain Magath.

Rossi, having a bad game and a poor season generally, was substituted in the 54th minute and replaced by Marocchino, and Platini, top scorer in the Italian league, was unimpressive. Bettega, playing his last game before moving to Torino, was also well below par. Boniek was the most effective Juventus player, but his runs too often came to nothing.

At the final whistle, the score had stayed at 1-0, and the Germans had deserved their victory. Juventus, however, had played poorly and believed their own pre-match publicity. Underestimating Hamburg had proved to be a mistake.

The teams
Hamburg: Stein, Kaltz, Wehmeyer, Jakobs, Hieronymus, Rolff, Milewski, Groh, Hrubesch, Magath, Bastrup (Van Heesen) (manager: Happel) [Magath 8]
Juventus: Zoff, Gentile, Cabrini, Bonini, Brio, Scirea, Bettega, Tardelli, Rossi (Marocchino), Platini, Boniek (manager: Trapattoni)

Dino Zoff can only watch as Magath's well-struck shot enters the net in the 8th minute in the 1983 Final.

Italian club Roma had won the championship for only the second time in their history, under manager Nils Liedholm, a member of the famous AC Milan Swedish forward line of the 1950s.

In the summer of 1980, Roma had bought the 28-year-old Brazilian international midfielder Paolo Roberto Falcao, whose brilliance had guided Roma to the title. Fellow Brazilian international Toninho Cerezo, with 67 caps, had joined Falcao in the midfield, and Roberto Pruzzo and Francesco Graziani plundered upfront, with Bruno Conti, one of the stars of the 1982 World Cup, launching the raids from the right wing. The defence was secured by 21-year-old Ubaldo Righetti and full back Sebastiano Nela, with Franco Tancredi keeping goal.

A 3-0 home win against IFK Gothenburg saw them safely through to the second round against CSKA Sofia. Two 1-0 victories over the Bulgarians, the goals coming from Falcao and Graziano, drew Roma against Dynamo Berlin, who were in the middle of their midwinter break. In Rome, goals from Graziani, Pruzzo and Cerezo, gave them a 3-0 advantage. In Sofia, Roma scored first through right-back Emilio Oddi, but two Dynamo goals in the last fifteen minutes provided some consolation for the Bulgarians. A 2-0 defeat away to Scotland's Dundee United in the Semi-final gave Roma a scare, but a 3-0 win in Italy put Roma into their first and only European Cup Final.

The surprise result of the first round had been the elimination of Ajax by Olympiakos. Following a 0-0 result in Holland, the game went into extra time in Athens, when striker Nikos Anastopoulos scored twice. Olympiakos then faced Benfica in the second round.

Results

First Round

	1st leg	2nd leg	Agg
Ajax v Olympiakos	0-0	0-2	0-2
Athlone Town v Standard Liège	2-3	2-8	4-11
Benfica v Linfield	3-0	3-2	6-2
CSKA Sofia v Omonia Nicosia	3-0	1-4	4-4
Dynamo Berlin v Jeunesse Esch	4-1	2-0	6-1
Dynamo Minsk v Grasshoppers Zurich	1-0	2-2	3-2
Fenerbahce v Bohemians Prague	0-1	0-4	0-5
Hamburg v Vllaznia (a)			
Hamrun Spartans v Dundee United	0-3	0-3	0-6
Kuusysi Lahti v Dynamo Bucharest	0-1	0-3	0-4
Lech Poznan v Athletic Bilbao	2-0	0-4	2-4
Odense v Liverpool	0-1	0-5	0-6
Partizan Belgrade v Viking Stavanger	5-1	0-0	5-1
Rapid Vienna v Nantes	3-0	1-3	4-3
Roma v IFK Gothenburg	3-0	1-2	4-2
Vasas Gyor v Vikingur	2-1	2-0	4-1

a) Hamburg walkover, Vllaznia withdrew.

Second Round

Bohemians Prague v Rapid Vienna	2-1	0-1	2-2
CSKA Sofia v Roma	0-1	0-1	0-2
Dynamo Berlin v Partizan Belgrade	2-0	0-1	2-1
Dynamo Bucharest v Hamburg	3-0	2-3	5-3
Liverpool v Athletic Bilbao	0-0	1-0	1-0
Olympiakos v Benfica	1-0	0-3	1-3
Standard Liège v Dundee United	0-0	0-4	0-4
Vasas Gyor v Dynamo Minsk	3-6	1-3	4-9

Quarter-finals

Dynamo Minsk v Dynamo Bucharest	1-1	0-1	1-2
Liverpool v Benfica	1-0	4-1	5-1
Rapid Vienna v Dundee United	2-1	0-1	2-2
Roma v Dynamo Berlin	3-0	1-2	4-2

Semi-finals

Dundee United v Roma	2-0	0-3	2-3
Liverpool v Dynamo Bucharest	1-0	2-1	3-1

Benfica had a new manager – 34-year-old Sven-Goran Eriksson – and the veterans Nene, Chalana and keeper and captain Bento remained the heart of the side. In Athens, Anastopoulos scored the only goal, while in Lisbon an early strike by centre-forward Zoran Filipovic equalised the tie. A 28th-minute goal from Diamantino and another near the end from substitute Manniche took Benfica to the Quarter-final at Anfield, where an Ian Rush goal proved the difference between the sides. A thumping 4-1 defeat by Liverpool in Lisbon exposed the difference in class between the teams.

Romania's Dynamo Bucharest had easily beaten Finland's Kuusysi 4-0 but the second round against Cup-holders Hamburg proved rather more problematic. Hrubesch had left Hamburg to join Standard Liège and Schatzschneider was his replacement. A surprise 3-0 victory by Dynamo in Romania was levelled in Hamburg within the first 60 minutes, defender Jakobs scoring two. In a sensational ending, with five minutes to go, Dynamo substitute Talnar scored, and in the 89th minute Multescu clinched the tie for Dynamo.

Their opponents in the Quarter-final were Soviet champions Dynamo Minsk, a fast, attacking team from Byelorussia. In the first leg played in Tbilisi, a seventh-minute goal from the home side remained the difference between the teams until an 88th-minute equaliser from Bucharest right-back Rednic. In Romania, an early goal from Bucharest midfielder Augustin settled the tie, and Liverpool were next in the Semi-final.

In a tough, unpleasant game at Anfield, Liverpool won 1-0, and two Ian Rush goals in Bucharest put Liverpool into the Final to play Roma.

BRITISH CLUBS

Jim McLean's **Dundee United** had won the Scottish league title for the first time in the club's history. They won their last six games to beat Celtic, who led the race throughout, by one point, and were making their debut in the European Cup.

In defence, Richard Gough was an energetic, attacking back who teamed up well with stylish centre-half Paul Hegarty and the fast, left-sided Maurice Malpas; Eamonn Bannon and David Narey, scorer of a memorable goal for Scotland against Brazil in the 1982 World Cup finals, ran the midfield; and Ralph Milne, Davie Dodds, a bustling, traditional centre-forward, and Derek Stark piled in the goals. They were a tricky, attacking side who had reached the Quarter-finals of the previous two UEFA Cups, knocking out such eminent teams as Borussia Moenchengladbach, PSV Eindhoven and Werder Bremen.

After an easy 6-0 aggregate win over Hamrun Spartans, champions of Malta, United met Standard Liège in the second round. Hrubesch had joined Liège from Hamburg but midfield leader Arie Haan had left. Simon Tahamata had moved to the centre striker position and had scored 20 goals the previous season, but no-one could find the net at Tannadice in the first leg. It was a different story, however, in Liège, where Milne had put United 2-0 up by half time. Hegarty in the 51st minute and Dodds in the 68th completed the rout of the Belgian champions.

In the Quarter-final United travelled to Austria to play Rapid Vienna, and they were ahead to a Dodds 30th-minute goal until the last fifteen minutes, when Vienna scored twice. Back in Scotland, another early Dodds strike was enough for United to progress on away goals to the Semi-final against the wealthy Italian plutocrats Roma. It had been ten years since a Scottish club, Celtic, had reached the Semi-final, and 21 years since United's next-door rival, Dundee, had done the same.

Roma were without an injured Falcao, and United made a blistering start. Roma did well to keep the game goal-less until, just after half time, Dodds scored past keeper Tancredi from a Gough cross. Stark unleashed an unstoppable 25-yard rocket in the 60th minute, and United were taking a 2-0 lead to the Eternal City.

Derided by the Italian press after their poor showing in Scotland, Roma had a point to prove in Rome. With Falcao back, the Italians turned on the style and flair. Conti had an offside 'goal' disallowed early on, and Milne should have scored shortly afterwards. However, there was only going to be one winner. Pruzzo scored a header from a Conti cross in the 23rd minute and claimed another just before the interval. Early in the second half Pruzzo was brought down by United keeper McAlpine, and Roma captain Agostino Di Bartolomei converted to win the tie. Roma's president Dino Viola was later found guilty of attempting to bribe the referee, and was banned for four years. That game marked Dundee United's last appearance in the European Cup.

Linfield never really had much chance against Benfica in the first round, losing 3-0 in Lisbon. However, they achieved respectability back home, going down by the odd goal in five.

LIVERPOOL 1983/84

Bob Paisley, the most successful manager in British history, retired after Liverpool had lifted the 1983 league title, and the affable Joe Fagan, a member of the 'boot room', took over. Fagan interfered little with the team, but bought 24-year-old striker Michael Robinson from Brighton for £200,000 and Scottish defender Gary Gillespie from Coventry for £320,000. He also promoted Scottish full-back Steve Nicol into the first-team squad. Meanwhile, the opportunistic Ian Rush had developed into a goal-scoring sensation. He had scored 32 league goals the previous season, and his ability to find the net was to be critical in Liverpool's progress through the competition.

A first round 6-0 demolition of Denmark's Odense, Dalglish scoring three, put Liverpool in competition with Athletic Bilbao in round two. After a goal-less draw at Anfield, a Rush second-half goal in Spain was enough to ensure progress to the quarter final against Benfica. The Portugese contrived to leave Anfield only one goal down, again to Rush, but a confident and assured Liverpool took Benfica apart in Lisbon. Whelan opened the scoring in the ninth minute and Johnson added one more before half time. Nene pulled one back in the 74th minute, but goals from Rush and another strike from Whelan made the final score 4-1.

The strong and intimidating Romanian side Dynamo Bucharest were Liverpool's last barrier to the Final in Rome.

At Anfield, a tough, nasty game saw four Dynamo players booked in an evening of kicking and punching. A Sammy Lee header from an Alan Kennedy cross in the 25th minute was the only goal, although Augustin nearly equalised when his shot beat Grobbelaar but came back off the post.

The return leg in the pouring rain in Romania was just as brutal. Ian Rush continued his European Cup scoring prowess in the 11th minute when he converted a pass from Souness, and left-winger Costel Oraz equalised from a 39th-minute free-kick. Towards the end of the match, as a dejected Dynamo saw the game slipping away from them, Rush sealed the victory.

Liverpool were through to yet another European Cup Final, their fourth in eight years.

Graeme Souness

Graeme Souness (1953). Souness was a tough, uncompromising midfielder, with vision, precise passing ability and a powerful shot, and he was the mainstay of the Liverpool side which dominated Europe in the late 1970s and early 1980s. His dominant personality inspired Liverpool to three European Cup victories in his time at the club. He moved to Sampdoria in 1984 and two years later to Rangers as player-manager where, in a controversial stay of four years, he became the first Gers manager to sign a Catholic player, Mo Johnston. He gained 54 Scottish caps and played in the 1978, 1982 and 1986 World Cup finals. He left to manage Liverpool in 1991 and later oversaw the fortunes of Galatasaray, Southampton and Benfica.

Liverpool keeper Grobbelaar clutches the ball from the feet of Falcao in the 1984 Final.

Kennedy does it again as Reds retain Cup

Liverpool (1) 1 Roma (1) 1 (after extra time)
(Liverpool won 4-2 on penalties)

Olympic Stadium, Rome, 30 May 1984
Attendance: 70,000
Referee: Frederiksson (Sweden)

Roma were on their home ground and the noise from the Italian crowd was overwhelming as the game kicked off. Liverpool were back in the stadium where they had won their first European Cup, but this time the Kop was drowned out by the cacophony of sound, klaxons and whistles from the Roma fans.

In the 15th minute, what the Italians claimed as a foul by Whelan on keeper Tancredi allowed the ball to drop at the feet of Neal, and Liverpool were 1-0 ahead. Seconds later, a Souness effort was in the net but was judged offside. The game ebbed and flowed through the half and in the 38th minute the score was level, centre-forward Pruzzo heading the ball over a helpless Grobbelaar from a cross by Conti.

Roma went on the offensive in the second half, and Liverpool attacked on the break, but neither side could score. Grobbelaar, having an excellent game, made a dramatic save from the restrained Falcao, and Tancredi did likewise from Dalglish, who was also having a quiet match. Nicol was taken on for a tiring Johnston in the 72nd minute but could not affect the scoreline.

The game went into extra time, with Robinson substituted for Dalglish and Strukely on for Cerezo, but at the end of the thirty minutes the score remained level and the game went to penalties at the goal in front of the Roma fans. Nicol shot over the bar, and skipper Di Bartolomei converted. Neal was next and scored but Conti, clearly unnerved by the wobbling leg antics of Grobbelaar, missed. Souness, Righetti and Rush were all successful but a visibly nervous Graziani saw his attempt hit the top of the crossbar and go over. It was now down to Alan Kennedy, who took a few steps backwards and placed his shot inside the post past Tancredi. Kennedy had again scored the winning goal in a European Cup Final, and Liverpool had won more European Cups than anyone except Real Madrid.

After the match, some of the Italian fans attacked the Scousers with knives and iron bars, and trouble continued throughout the night. The repercussions of this would be felt in next year's Final in a horrific culmination to Liverpool's dominance of European football.

The teams

Liverpool: Grobbelaar, Neal, Kennedy, Lawrenson, Whelan, Hansen, Dalglish (Robinson), Lee, Rush, Johnston (Nicol), Souness (manager: Fagan) [Neal 15]
Roma: Tancredi, Nappi, Bonetti, Righetti, Nela, Falcao, Di Bartolomei, Cerezo (Strukely), Conti, Pruzzo (Chierico), Graziani [Pruzzo 38]
Penalty shoot-out: Nicol misses, 0-0; Di Bartolomei, 0-1; Neal, 1-1; Conti misses, 1-1; Souness, 2-1; Righetti, 2-2; Rush, 3-2; Graziani misses, 3-2; Kennedy, 4-2

French champions Bordeaux, in the European Cup for the first time, were fielding four of the players from the Platini-inspired French victory in the European Nations Cup that summer. The elegant Jean Tigana and the industrious Alain Giresse in midfield, tough defender Patrick Battiston and the big forward Bernard Lacombe had all played their parts in the triumph. The club had enticed the left-winger Fernando Chalana from Benfica for £1 million, although he was injured for much of the campaign, and Dieter Müller partnered Lacombe up front. Their famed sweeper Marius Tresor had retired.

The first round threw up a tough draw against Spain's Athletic Bilbao. Andoni Zubizarreta, who was to become Spain's most capped player, kept goal for Bilbao, and he was assisted in defence by Andoni Goicoechea, known as the 'butcher of Bilbao' for his shocking foul on Maradona the previous season. Sarabia was the threat up front. Bordeaux won 3-2 in France, the goals coming from Müller, Battiston and Lacombe, and in Bilbao a 0-0 result was marred by the crowd throwing missiles at the referee, who had disallowed two Bilbao 'goals'.

A first-half Müller goal in Bordeaux and an extra-time winner from Lacombe in Romania put out Dynamo Bucharest in the second round, and they met Soviet champions Dnepr, a tough well-knit side, in the Quarter-final. Bordeaux had all the play and should have had a hatful, but had to be content with a 1-1 draw. Lacombe scored in the tenth minute, but he and Müller could not take advantage of Tigana's and Giresse's domination of the midfield. In the Ukraine, a travel-weary Bordeaux equalised an Alexander Lysenko goal through Thierry Tusseau with fifteen minutes to go. Extra time could not resolve the impasse, and the game went to penalties. Litvichenko missed for the Ukrainians, and the tie was won by a conversion by Chalana, back from injury. Juventus were to be the Semi-final opposition.

Gentile had left for Fiorentina, but otherwise the Juventus line-up was little different from the previous competition. Platini had been voted World Footballer of the Year, and was Serie A top scorer with 20 goals. Three goals each from Rossi and Platini had easily overcome Finland's Ilves in the first round, and a 4-2 second round away win against Grasshoppers Zurich took the Italians through to the Quarter-final against Sparta Prague. The tough international midfielder Marco Tardelli opened Juventus' account in the 35th minute, and two more from Rossi and Massimo Briaschi allowed Juve the luxury of losing by one goal in a wet Prague and progressing to the Semi-final, although a spirited opening half from Sparta gave Juventus a nervous 45 minutes.

In Turin, Platini made two goals – for Boniek and Massimo Briaschi – and scored the third himself past Bordeaux keeper Dropsy, with no reply from the French. In Bordeaux, the home side attacked ferociously, and had a defensive Juventus reeling. Müller headed them in front in the 24th minute, and a glorious Battiston strike made it 2-0 with ten minutes to go. A brilliant save by Juventus' Luciano Bodini from a Tigana shot prevented extra time, and a relieved Juventus could contemplate their place in the Final.

A young Panathinaikos side had surprisingly disposed of Feyenoord, now with Dutch star Johnny Rep and young midfielder Ruud Gullit, in the first round, and had scraped through against Linfield in the second. A brutal 1-0 away result against Sweden's IFK Gothenburg in the Quarter-final, with two players sent off and seven booked, was followed by a bruising 2-2 draw in Athens. In the Semi-final the Greeks met Liverpool, whose magnificent 4-0 victory at Anfield gave Panathinaikos too much to do in the return. Liverpool were to meet Juventus in the Final.

Results

First Round

	1st leg	2nd leg	Agg	
Aberdeen v Dynamo Berlin	2-1	1-2	3-3	4-5 (P)
Akranes v Beveren	2-2	0-5	2-7	
Avenir Beggen v IFK Gothenburg	0-8	0-9	0-17	
Bordeaux v Athletic Bilbao	3-2	0-0	3-2	
Dynamo Bucharest v Omonia Nicosia	4-1	1-2	5-3	
Feyenoord v Panathinaikos	0-0	1-2	1-2	
FK Austria v Valletta	4-0	4-0	8-0	
Grasshoppers Zurich v Honved	3-1	1-2	4-3	
Ilves v Juventus	0-4	1-2	1-6	
Labinoti v Lyngby	0-3	0-3	0-6	
Lech Poznan v Liverpool	0-1	0-4	0-5	
Levski Spartak v Stuttgart	1-1	2-2	3-3	
Linfield v Shamrock Rovers	0-0	1-1	1-1	
Red Star Belgrade v Benfica	3-2	0-2	3-4	
Trabzonspor v Dnepr Dnepropetrovsk	1-0	0-3	1-3	
Valerengen v Sparta Prague	3-3	0-2	3-5	

P = penalties

Second Round

Bordeaux v Dynamo Bucharest	1-0	1-1	2-1	
Dynamo Berlin v FK Austria	3-3	1-2	4-5	
IFK Gothenburg v Beveren	1-0	1-2	2-2	
Juventus v Grasshoppers Zurich	2-0	4-2	6-2	
Levski Spartak v Dnepr Dnepropetrovsk	3-1	0-2	3-3	
Liverpool v Benfica	3-1	0-1	3-2	
Panathinaikos v Linfield	2-1	3-3	5-4	
Sparta Prague v Lyngby	0-0	2-1	2-1	

Quarter-finals

Bordeaux v Dnepr Dnepropetrovsk	1-1	1-1	2-2	5-3 (P)
FK Austria v Liverpool	1-1	1-4	2-5	
IFK Gothenburg v Panathinaikos	0-1	2-2	2-3	
Juventus v Sparta Prague	3-0	0-1	3-1	

P = penalties

Semi-finals

Juventus v Bordeaux	3-0	0-2	3-2
Liverpool v Panathinaikos	4-0	1-0	5-0

LIVERPOOL 1984/85

Having won the league and League Cup for the third year in succession, Liverpool were dominant in the English game. Their main creative influence, Graeme Souness, had succumbed to the lure of the lire and had joined Sampdoria in the summer. Fagan had acted quickly to fill the midfield gap by buying from Ipswich Town the Scottish international John Wark, a strong, combative player who could burst through to score vital goals. Defender Jan Molby arrived from Ajax, and Paul Walsh, a talented striker was prised from Luton Town for £900,000.

In Poland against Lech Poznan in the first round, Wark scored the only goal. At Anfield, Fagan's foray into the transfer market was vindicated when Wark scored a hat-trick and Walsh claimed a fourth for a 5-0 aggregate win to set up a second round tie against Benfica.

Benfica were in a transitional period. Their coach Eriksson had gone to run Roma, and had been replaced by Hungarian Pal Csernai. Midfielder Glenn Stromberg had moved to Atalanta, centre-forward Filipovic was now with Boavista, Bordeaux had claimed star winger Chalana, and Humberto Coehlo had retired through injury. Nene was on his last season, but the tall Danish striker Michael Manniche had been recruited by the Lisbon club.

At Anfield, Rush was irrepressible and scored a hat-trick, with Diamantino securing an away goal. An implacable Liverpool performance in Liverpool saw the Portugese go ahead through a fifth-minute Manniche penalty and the score remained 1-0. Dalglish was sent off just on half time, and was ineligible for the Quarter-final against FK Austria.

Prohaska had returned to Austria from Roma, and FK also had three potential matchwinners in attack – Hungarian Tibor Nyilasi, the powerful but erratic Gerd Steinkogler and the young Toni Polster. In Austria, an early individual goal from Polster prompted an attacking spell from FK, although Liverpool could have scored before half time through Whelan. A Nicol goal in the 85th minute secured a draw. At Anfield, Walsh was in for Dalglish and he scored with a diving header in the 16th minute. Twenty minutes later Nicol made it two, and just after half time centre-back Obermayer deflected a Whelan shot into his own net. Walsh volleyed another in the 56th minute, and a Prohaska free-kick made it 4-1. Liverpool were now one game away from another Final.

Panathinaikos had been somewhat fortunate to have reached this stage of the competition, and their performance in the first leg at Anfield reflected this. Left-back Kennedy was absent but Dalglish was back, and Liverpool swept into the attack. Greek keeper Laftsis had a dreadful game and was responsible for the first goal from Wark. Rush added two in two minutes just after half time, and Irish right-back Jim Beglin made it 4-0 with four minutes to go, with a header from a Dalglish free-kick.

In Athens, Liverpool defended well against the attacking Greek side. Grobbelaar had to look smart on a couple of occasions but the scoreline was 0-0 after an hour. In the 60th minute, a pass from Whelan found Lawrenson on the break, and the defender shot past Laftsis from the edge of the six-yard box. Although Panathinaikos continued the onslaught, Liverpool stood firm, and were through to their fifth European Cup Final in eight years.

The opposition was to be Juventus at the Heysel Stadium in Brussels, and the game was already being described as the 'dream final'. In the event, the 'nightmare final' would be a more appropriate description.

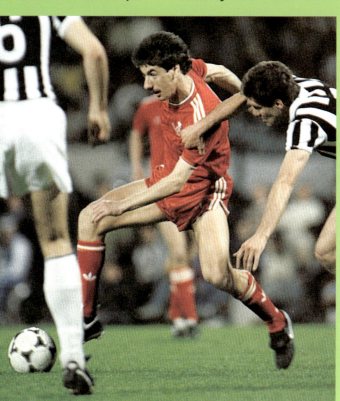

Liverpool's scoring machine Ian Rush sets off for goal, attended by Juventus defenders.

BRITISH CLUBS

Gordon Strachan had departed for Manchester United and Mark McGhee was now playing for Hamburg in the Bundesliga, but **Aberdeen** had won the Scottish league by an impressive seven points from Celtic and had also picked up the Scottish Cup. McLeish and Miller remained as the central defensive pairing, with young Stewart McKimmie as right-back, Neale Cooper in midfield and Eric Black, John Hewitt and Neil Simpson in attack. The erratic but occasionally inspired Scottish international keeper Jim Leighton was the last line of defence.

They had a difficult draw in the shape of Dynamo Berlin in the first round. Dynamo had won the East German league six times in a row, and had the league's top scorer, 22-year-old Rainer Ernst, as centre-forward. Eighteen-year-old Andreas Thom was the left-wing prodigy. Sweeper Norbert Trieloff and stopper Rainer Troppa provided the solidity at the back, and Dynamo were a fast, fit, man-marking team.

Two goals by Eric Black at Pittodrie encouraged the Dons, but midfielder Schultz pulled a goal back in the

82nd minute. In Berlin, Thom gave Dynamo the lead shortly after half-time, but Angus equalised twenty minutes later. Ernst gave Dynamo the lead on the night in the 85th minute and the game went into extra time. Neither defence could be breached, and the match went to penalties, which Dynamo won 5-4. Dynamo were to go out in the next round at the hands of FK Austria.

Linfield went through to the second round on away goals against cross-border neighbours Shamrock Rovers, and travelled to Greece to take on Panathinaikos. They scored first, through Totten, but ended the game 2-1 down, not a bad result to take back to Northern Ireland. In the return, they were an astonishing 3-0 ahead within thirty minutes, with two from forward McGaughey. Panathinaikos rallied, however, and scored three of their own before the final whistle. A brave effort by Linfield was not enough to defeat the experienced Greek side.

1984 1985
92

Michel Platini (1955). An idol in France and Turin, Platini was France's most complete footballer ever. He was a technically superb midfielder and a deadly accurate goal scorer from spot-kicks and in open play. He left St Etienne in 1982 to join Juventus and remained with the Italian club until his retirement in 1987, scoring the winning goal in the 1985 European Cup Final. In 1984, he captained France, for whom he gained 72 caps, to the European Championships, scoring nine goals in the tournament, and was the inspiration behind France's third place in the 1986 World Cup finals. Three times European Footballer of the Year, he became French national coach and was created a Knight of the Legion d'Honneur by a grateful government.

The Heysel Disaster

The blackest episode in the history of the European Cup was on 29 May 1985 at the Heysel Stadium in Brussels, just before the Final between Liverpool and Juventus. A large group of so-called Liverpool fans, many drunk and armed with impromptu weapons, charged a group of Juventus supporters. A wall collapsed under the weight of the fleeing Italians and, by the end of the day, 39 people had been crushed to death and 400 injured.

How was the disaster allowed to happen? Many felt before the game that the old, crumbling stadium was the wrong venue for such a prestigious match, and that the ground was not safe. For instance, terrace Z, where the Italians were crushed, had no means of exit. Ticket control and segregation were virtually non-existent. The Juventus supporters easily obtained tickets for terrace Z – ostensibly a neutral section of the stadium – right next to the Liverpool supporters in terraces X and Y. Policing and security were hopeless, with many supporters crawling under the fence to get in, and there were no searches for weapons or alcohol. The police were still reportedly mounting baton charges as people lay dying beneath them. Indeed, the general organisation was disgraceful, with the inefficiency of the Belgian authorities clearly exposed by the disaster.

At the stadium, many of the spectators and players were unaware of the full extent of the tragedy, although the millions watching on television knew exactly what had happened. The decision was taken to proceed with the match, in order to allow the emergency services to function and to pre-empt the possibility of further rioting, and the game began nearly one and a half hours after its scheduled kick-off.

This mindless, horrific violence marked the end of English clubs' participation in the tournament for six years, an appalled UEFA viewing the Liverpool fans' behaviour as the final act in the sorry saga of English hooliganism in the continent. The FA immediately banned all English clubs from European football for one year, but UEFA made the ban indefinite. Liverpool were to receive an extra three-year ban, to be served when English clubs were allowed back into the competition.

The emergency services attempt to clear up in the aftermath of the Heysel disaster.

Massimo Briaschi out-jumps Liverpool's John Wark in the 1985 Final.

Juventus victory overshadowed as 39 die in Heysel disaster

Juventus (0) 1 Liverpool (0) 0

Heysel Stadium, Brussels, 29 May 1985
Attendance: 50,000
Referee: Daina (Switzerland)

After the horrifying events which preceded the game, Liverpool kicked off in what was already seen as a devalued match. The Juventus players, in particular, were unhappy about playing the game in the circumstances, but were persuaded that going ahead was the only sensible option.

Within only two minutes, an injured Lawrenson had to come off to be replaced by Gary Gillepsie. Liverpool, however, had started at a fast tempo, and Juventus keeper Tacconi was soon in action with good saves from Wark, Walsh and Whelan. Then a shot from Cabrini was brilliantly saved by Grobbelaar, and just before half-time the Liverpool keeper had again to be alert to keep out Boniek.

Liverpool began the second half with Johnston on for an injured Walsh. In the 56th minute, Juventus scored the crucial goal. Platini started the move with a precise long

pass to Boniek, who ran on between Gillespie and Hansen only to be brought down. The Liverpool players heatedly protested that the foul had occurred outside the box, but referee Daina gave the penalty. Up stepped Platini, and the dead-ball expert sent the ball past Grobbelaar.

Tacconi was soon being tested again by the lively Liverpool attack, and with fifteen minutes to go, Bonini brought down Whelan in the penalty box but surprisingly no penalty was given. Although Liverpool forced a succession of corners, they could not turn them into goals. Juventus – 'La Vecchia Signora' – had finally won the European Cup after nearly thirty years of under-achievement.

The teams
Juventus: Tacconi, Favero, Cabrini, Brio, Scirea, Bonini, Platini, Tardelli, Briaschi (Prandelli), Rossi (Vignola), Boniek (manager: Trapattoni) [Platini 56]
Liverpool: Grobbelaar, Neal, Beglin, Lawrenson (Gillespie), Hansen, Nicol, Dalglish, Whelan, Wark, Rush, Walsh (Johnston) (manager: Fagan)

Barcelona's Steve Archibald (right) in the Quarter-final against Juventus.

THE *1985-86* SEASON

English manager Terry Venables had steered his Barcelona side to their first Spanish title in eleven years. The Catalans had finished ten points ahead of Atlético Madrid, thanks in no small measure to Scotsman Steve Archibald's seventeen goals, the wing play of Julio Carrasco and the midfield leadership of the controversial and single-minded Bernd Schuster. Chairman Jose Luis Nunez had achieved his goal in Spain – now his sights turned to the European Cup.

The team were 2-1 up, through Amarila and Clos, after their journey to Prague in the first round to play the Jan Berger-inspired Sparta, and they conceded a goal in the Nou Camp. However, away goals matched them against Portugal's Porto in the second round. The powerful shooting of Porto's Fernando Gomes – 39 goals in 30 games – had secured Europe's Golden Boot for the striker, and he was teaming well with the young star winger Paulo Futre. Barca took a 2-0 lead to Porto, but a two-goal burst in three minutes from midfielder Jaury levelled the tie. Archibald put the Spaniards ahead in the 77th minute, and a late equaliser from Jaury for his hat-trick could not prevent Barcelona going through to the Quarter-final, again on away goals.

The tie of the tournament was next, against Cup-holders Juventus. The Italians had a summer clear-out, with Boniek going to Roma, Tardelli to Inter and the disappointing Rossi to Milan, but they had brought the brilliant young Dane Michael Laudrup, midfielder Lionello Manfredonia and the tall striker Aldo Serena. Platini continued to run the game from midfield, and Scirea swept up with authority. They were without a suspended Serena in the Nou Camp, and Schuster was missing for Barcelona. Juventus did well to keep the score down to 1-0,

Steve Archibald (1956). An intelligent, quick striker, Archibald played for Aberdeen before moving to Tottenham Hotspur in 1980. He moved to Barcelona for £1.5 million in 1984 and helped the club to the UEFA Cup that year. He was a beaten Finalist in the 1986 European Cup. He made 22 appearances for Scotland, including the 1982 and 1986 World Cup finals, He finished his career with a variety of smaller clubs and moved into management.

Results

First Round

	1st leg	2nd leg	Agg
Akranes v Aberdeen	1-3	1-4	2-7
Bordeaux v Fenerbahçe	2-3	0-0	2-3
Dynamo Berlin v FK Austria	0-2	1-2	1-4
Gornik Zabrze V Bayern Munich	1-2	1-4	2-6
Honved v Shamrock Rovers	2-0	3-1	5-1
IFK Gothenburg v Trakia Plovdiv	3-2	2-1	5-3
Jeunesse Esch v Juventus	0-5	1-4	1-9
Kuusysi Lahti v Sarajevo	2-1	2-1	4-2
Linfield v Servette	2-2	1-2	3-4
Porto v Ajax	2-0	0-0	2-0
Rabat Ajax v Omonia Nicosia	0-5	0-5	0-10
Sparta Prague v Barcelona	1-2	1-0	2-2
Vejle v Steaua Bucharest	1-1	1-4	2-5
Verona v PAOK Salonika	3-1	2-1	5-2
Zenit Leningrad v Valerengen	2-0	2-0	4-0

Bye: Anderlecht

Second Round

Anderlecht v Omonia	1-0	3-1	4-1
Barcelona v Porto	2-0	1-3	3-3
Bayern Munich v FK Austria	4-2	3-3	7-5
Honved v Steaua Bucharest	1-0	1-4	2-4
IFK Gothenburg v Fenerbahçe	4-0	1-2	5-2
Servette v Aberdeen	0-0	0-1	0-1
Verona v Juventus	0-0	0-2	0-2
Zenit Leningrad v Kuusysi Lahti	2-1	1-3	3-4

Quarter-finals

Aberdeen v IFK Gothenburg	2-2	0-0	2-2
Barcelona v Juventus	1-0	1-1	2-1
Bayern Munich v Anderlecht	2-1	0-2	2-3
Steaua Bucharest v Kuusysi Lahti	0-0	1-0	1-0

Semi-finals

Anderlecht v Steaua Bucharest	1-0	0-3	1-3	
IFK Gothenburg v Barcelona	3-0	0-3	3-3	4-5 (P)

P = penalties

the goal coming from a 25-yarder from attacking full-back Julio Alberto in the 82nd minute. In Turin, Archibald converted a Victor cross in the 30th minute and, although Juventus had several chances, they could only break through the Spanish defence when a neat interplay between Laudrup and Platini opened a gap for the Frenchman in the 44th minute. Barcelona were through 2-1 on aggregate to meet IFK Gothenburg in the Semi-final.

IFK's striker Mats Gren had gone to Grasshoppers, but the reliable forward Torbjorn Nilsson was still with the club. The strong Swedish side had eliminated Bulgaria's Trakia Plovdiv, Fenerbahçe and Aberdeen, with Nilsson turning in five goals in their campaign, and he scored another two in their shock 3-0 win over Barca in the first leg in Sweden when IFK's speed and organisation surprised Barcelona. Revenge was sweet at the Nou Camp when Picchi Alonso, deputising for the injured Archibald, netted a hat-trick for a 3-0 aggregate draw after extra time. In the penalty shoot-out, keeper Urruti saved an IFK penalty, converted another, and Barca were through to the Final.

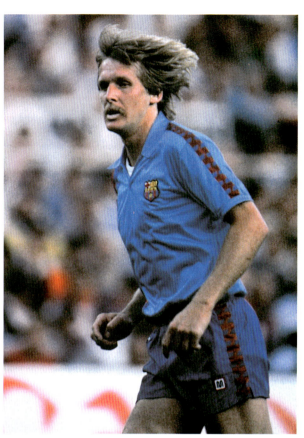

Barcelona's enigmatic and talented German playmaker, Bernd Schuster.

midfield, with playmakers Tudorel Stoica and Ladislau Boloni. The tall striker Marius Lacatus lurked in the attack with his partner Victor Piturca. Steaua had beaten Alan Simonsen's Vejle and Hungary's Honvéd to reach the Quarter-final against Kuusysi, the first Finnish team to have reached this stage in the tournament.

Piturca scored within the last five minutes of the second leg in Finland, in front of a record 30,000 crowd, to spare the Romanians' blushes and squeeze into the Semi-final against Anderlecht with a 1-0 win.

Anderlecht were an exciting, talented but inconsistent team. Captain Frankie Vercauteren led a midfield of Morton Olson and the gifted young prodigy Enzo Scifo, while Vandenbergh was the main threat in attack. They had eliminated Bayern Munich 3-2 in the Quarter-final, and a superb goal from Scifo in the first leg against Steaua gave them the advantage. In Bucharest, however, the Romanians were two up by half time, through Piturca and Gavril Balint, and Piturca swept in a Lacatus cross in the 72nd minute to win the tie on aggregate 3-1.

Steaua were in the Final, only the second Eastern European team to reach the last stage in the history of the tournament.

Steaua Bucharest, Romania's army side, was the personal fiefdom of Nicu Ceausescu, son of the Romanian dictator. Steaua had a strong defence, marshalled by the 21-year-old Miodrag Belodedici, and an international

BRITISH CLUBS

Alex Ferguson's **Aberdeen** side continued to call the shots in Scotland and had repeated their seven-point lead over Celtic in the league.

A 7-2 aggregate win over Iceland's Akranes in the first round secured their passage to meet Switzerland's Servette in the second. Servette had beaten **Linfield**, who had again produced a brave performance at home but went out 3-4. A 0-0 away result was sufficient for a McDougall goal in the 22nd minute at Pittodrie to get the Dons into the Quarter-final against IFK Gothenburg.

At Pittodrie, Leighton was out injured and his place was taken by Brian Gunn. In the 15th minute, a cross from left-winger Peter Weir found Willie Miller and Miller shot in the opener. Just before half time Tord Holmgren equalised for the Swedes. With ten minutes to go, a long ball from Gunn found John Hewitt in space and Aberdeen were 2-1 up. However, in the last minute of the game, Ekstrom took advantage of some poor defending to claim another valuable away goal. In Gothenburg, Leighton was back and his performance kept the score respectable. IFK came close several times, but the game ended goalless and Aberdeen were out on away goals. As manager Alex Ferguson conceded, 'IFK deserved it'.

Bulgaria compete

Bulgaria's Trakia Plovdiv were making their first appearance in the European Cup. The leaders and the runners-up in the Bulgarian league – CSKA Sofia and Levski Spartak – had been disbanded by the Bulgarian Communist Party for a punch-up in the country's cup final, and third-placed Trakia qualified by default. They were eliminated by IFK Gothenburg in the first round.

Barca beaten by unfancied Steaua

Steaua Bucharest 0 (0)   Barcelona 0 (0) (after extra time)
(Steaua won 2-0 on penalties)

Sanchez Pizjuan Stadium, Seville, 7 May 1986
Attendance: 50,000
Referee: Vautrot (France)

With only a few hundred Steaua supporters in the stadium in the old Spanish city of Seville, the crowd was almost entirely Catalan and they were expecting Terry Venables' Barcelona to collect the club's first European Cup. In the eyes of most observers, Steaua were complete underdogs, and the game was to signal the coronation of Barcelona as the new football kings of Europe.

The game began at a frenzied pace, with referee Vautrot handing out three Spanish and one Romanian yellow cards, but gradually things settled down. Barcelona had the better of the first half, but Balint and Balan were running the midfield for Steaua and, although Schuster went close with a header on the half hour, the game was goal-less at half time.

In the second half, Steaua began to take control, with sweeper Miodrag Belodedici majestically marshalling his defence, and Majearu and Boloni put two clear chances wide. With fifteen minutes left, Barcelona keeper Urruti had to dive to save another fierce shot from Boloni, and two minutes later Archibald headed over the crossbar. Venables substituted a clearly unfit Schuster with five minutes to go, and the sulky German stormed off the pitch without a glance at the dugout.

The game moved into extra time, and the stalemate continued for the next thirty minutes with Barcelona on the back foot and the Rumanians unable to convert any of their attacks into goals. Alonso, the Semi-final hat-trick hero, came on for Archibald and Radu came on for Piturca, but the game drifted into penalties.

The first four penalties were all saved, but Lacatus and Balint converted their efforts while Barcelona's next two attempts were magnificently held by Steaua keeper Ducadam. The completely unexpected had occurred and Steaua Bucharest were the champions, the first Eastern European side to lift the trophy.

Venables described the result as 'the biggest disappointment I have had as a manager' and he was to leave the club in September, while Steaua manager Emerich Jenei jubilantly explained his victory: 'Barcelona are a fine team but we knew what we had to do – and we did it'. However, as a spectacle the game fell somewhat short of expectation.

The teams
Steaua Bucharest: Ducadam, Iovan, Belodedici, Bumbescu, Barbulescu, Balan (Iordanescu), Balint, Boloni, Majearu, Lacatus, Piturca (Radu) (manager: Jenei)
Barcelona: Urruti, Gerardo, Migueli, Alesanco, Julio Alberto, Victor, Marcos, Schuster (Moratalla), Pedraza, Carrasco, Archibald (Pichi Alonso) (manager: Venables)

Penalty shoot-out
Majearu misses, 0-0; Alesanco misses, 0-0; Boloni misses, 0-0; Pedraza misses, 0-0; Lacatus, 1-0; Alonso misses, 1-0; Balint, 2-0; Marcos misses, 2-0

Steaua Bucharest keeper Ducadam saves the first of Barcelona's penalties – taken by Alesanco – in the 1986 Final.

Coach Leo Beenhakker had built the strongest Real Madrid side for many years. The exciting multinational strike force of Mexican Hugo Sanchez, Argentinian World Cup winner Jorge Valdano and Spain's own Emilio Butragueno were the goal scorers. Defenders Sanchis, Jose Camacho and the cool midfielder Ricardo Gallego kept order at the back.

Young Boys Berne were decisively outplayed at the Bernabeu in the first round, and the second-round draw produced the clash of the tournament, Real against Juventus. In Spain, Juventus defended with panache against an inventive, attacking Real, who took advantage of the absence of Scirea and of Camacho's shackling of Platini to score through Butragueno in the 20th minute. Juve keeper Tacconi made a string of excellent saves, and the score stayed at 1-0. The return game in Turin was equally absorbing. A wave of Juventus attacks resulted in a ninth-minute goal for Juventus, right-back Antonio Cabrini finishing off a cross from Mauro. Tacconi was again in action against the feared Real forwards, but kept them out with some fine keeping. Extra time came and went, and a penalty shoot-out decided the tie in Real's favour, with Manfredo and Favero failing to score for the Italians.

In a freezing Belgrade in the quarter final, Red Star were three up by half time, and added a fourth through Jankovic, but two from Sanchez gave Real some hope for the return. In Spain, an early strike from Butragueno and a second-half header from Manuel Sanchis put Real through on away goals to play Bayern Munich in the Semi-final.

World Cup star Lothar Matthäus and East Germany's Norbert Nachtweih ran Bayern's midfield, with captain Klaus Augenthaler acting as sweeper. In attack were Michael Rummenigge and Reinhold Mathy, with an ageing Dieter Hoeness still making a contribution. Two goals from Mathy in Holland eliminated a Gullit-less PSV Eindhoven in the first round and a 3-1 victory over a sprightly FK Austria took Bayern into the Quarter-

Results

First Round

First Round	1st leg	2nd leg	Agg	
Anderlecht v Gornik Zabrze	2-0	1-1	3-1	
Apoel Nicosia v HJK Helsinki	1-0	2-3	3-3	
Avenir Beggen v FK Austria	0-3	0-3	0-6	
Beroe Stara Zagora v Dynamo Kiev	1-1	0-2	1-3	
Besiktas v Dynamo Tirana	2-0	1-0	3-0	
Brondby v Honved	4-1	2-2	6-3	
Juventus v Valur	7-0	4-0	11-0	
Orgryte v Dynamo Berlin	2-3	1-4	3-7	
Paris St Germain v Vitkovice	2-2	0-1	2-3	
Porto v Rabat Ajax	9-0	1-0	10-0	
PSV Eindhoven v Bayern Munich	0-2	0-0	0-2	
Red Star Belgrade v Panathinaikos	3-0	1-2	4-2	
Rosenborg v Linfield	1-0	1-1	2-1	
Shamrock Rovers v Celtic	0-1	0-2	0-3	
Young Boys Berne v Real Madrid	1-0	0-5	1-5	

Bye: Steaua Bucharest.

Second Round

Second Round	1st leg	2nd leg	Agg	
Anderlecht v Steaua Bucharest	3-0	0-1	3-1	
Bayern Munich v FK Austria	2-0	1-1	3-1	
Besiktas v Apoel Nicosia (a)				
Brondby v Dynamo Berlin	2-1	1-1	3-2	
Celtic v Dynamo Kiev	1-1	1-3	2-4	
Real Madrid v Juventus	1-0	0-1	1-1	3-1(P)
Rosenborg v Red Star Belgrade	0-3	1-4	1-7	
Vitkovice v Porto	1-0	0-3	1-3	

Besiktas walkover, Apoel Nicosia failed to appear.

Quarter-finals

Quarter-finals	1st leg	2nd leg	Agg
Bayern Munich v Anderlecht	5-0	2-2	7-2
Besiktas v Dynamo Kiev	0-5	0-2	0-7
Porto v Brondby	1-0	1-1	2-1
Red Star Belgrade v Real Madrid	4-2	0-2	4-4

Semi-finals

Semi-finals	1st leg	2nd leg	Agg
Bayern Munich v Real Madrid	4-1	0-1	4-2
Porto v Dynamo Kiev	2-1	2-1	4-2

P = penalties

Bayern captain and sweeper Klaus Augenthaler, here playing for West Germany.

final to play Anderlecht. Without Matthäus and Augenthaler in Munich, Bayern nonetheless humbled the Belgians 5-0 with two goals in the last four minutes from Hoeness and winger Roland Wolfarth. The largely meaningless return game ended 2-2, and for the second year running Bayern had knocked the Belgian side out of the tournament.

In a bad-tempered and unpleasant Semi-final in Munich, Bayern were three ahead in the first forty minutes through Augenthaler, Wohlfarth and a disputed Matthäus penalty, but Butragueno scrambled a goal for Real in the 44th minute. Juanito was sent off for a vicious attack on Matthäus, and Mino was also red-carded in the 74th minute. Matthäus made it 4-1 with another penalty. In Madrid, crowd trouble delayed the start but Real roared into action and scored through the evergreen Santillana in the 27th minute. The Bayern defence kept Real at bay and, although Augenthaler was sent off for a foul on Sanchez, keeper Jean-Marie Pfaff and stopper Norbert Eder prevented Real from adding to their tally. The ugly crowd scenes continued throughout the match, and Real were reported to UEFA. Bayern were back in the Final.

Dynamo Kiev had developed into one of the most exciting and powerful teams in Europe. The Ukraine outfit, which virtually doubled as the national side, starred winger Ivan Belanov and the 34-year-old Oleg Blokhin, both European Footballers of the Year, and the midfield general Vassily Rats. In defence, captain and left-back Anatoli Demianenko and Sergei Baltacha were the rock of this smooth-passing, cultured team.

A 3-1 victory over Stara Zagora, a 3-1 Blokhin-inspired win over Celtic in the Ukraine and a Quarter-final thrashing of Turkey's Besiktas, with Blokhin and Vadim Yevtushenko both claiming hat-tricks, put the Ukranians into the Semi-final against Portugal's Porto.

Paulo Futre (centre) holds off the attentions of Lothar Matthäus (left) and Norbert Nachtweih (5) in the 1987 Final.

Porto were benefiting from the striking abilities of Gomes and the young Futre, and they had been joined by the skilful Algerian winger Rabah Madjer. Porto had dispensed with Malta's Rabat Ajax and Vitkovice, surprise first-round conquerors of Paris St-Germain, and had squeezed past Roy Hodgson's impressive Brondby side with a goal from Brazilian forward Juary in the Quarter-final.

In the first leg of the Semi-final in Oporto, an 85,000 crowd saw Porto on the attack against a resilient Kiev defence. Early in the second half, a Futre individual goal put Oporto in front, and forward Andre converted a penalty soon after. Yakovenko pulled a goal back for Kiev towards the end. In Kiev, Porto unsettled the Soviet champions with two goals in the first eleven minutes, both created by Futre and scored by Brazilian Celso from a fourth-minute free-kick and from a Gomes header. Almost immediately, young Alexei Mikhailichenko replied for Kiev, but thereafter the Porto defence stood firm to win the tie 4-2 on aggregate and take the Portuguese to their first European Cup Final.

Paulo Futre (1966). Portuguese-born forward Futre began his career with Sporting Lisbon and made his international debut at the age of 17. He joined Porto in time to help them to two Portugese league titles in 1985 and 1986, and played in their European Cup Final victory over Bayern Munich in 1987. Shortly after, he went to Atlético Madrid where he remained until 1993 when he joined Benfica and then Marseille. He then moved to Italy's Reggiana for £8 million, and finished his career with AC Milan and West Ham.

BRITISH CLUBS

Celtic were back in Europe after a three-year absence, having won the Scottish league on goal difference from Hearts. Since their last appearance in the competition, Charlie Nicholas had moved to Arsenal and manager Billy McNeill was running Aston Villa. Ex-player Davie Hay was the new boss, and he had signed the speedy, prolific centre-forward Mo Johnston from Watford in 1984. Young forward Brian 'Choccy' McClair was also rattling in the goals alongside ex-Aberdeen striker Mark McGhee, signed from Hamburg. Pat Bonner had made the keeper's position his own and the elegant McGrain was still appearing for the club, although he was to leave at the end of the season. Paul McStay was the main man in the centre of the pitch.

Celtic travelled to Ireland in the first leg of the first round to play Shamrock Rovers. Celtic were surprised by the quality and directness of the Shamrock forwards, and Bonner had to be at his best to prevent them scoring in the first half. A Murdo McLeod goal from the edge of the box, however, gave Celtic a valuable away win. In Glasgow,

Johnston scrambled in a rebound from an Alan McInally shot, and he scored again from a header with twenty minutes to go.

Celtic were drawn against Cup Winners Cup holders Dynamo Kiev in the second round and were given little chance against the classy Ukranians. In Glasgow, Kiev were without Oleg Blokhin but opened the scoring in the 17th minute through Yevtushenko. A battling Celtic performance prevented Kiev from going further ahead, and with ten minutes to go Johnston steered the ball past keeper Viktor Chanov.

One-one was not the most encouraging result to take to a cold and hostile Ukraine and, with Blokhin playing, things looked ominous for the Scots. An early Blokhin goal from a retaken free-kick seemed to set the tone for the match but, with Celtic producing another creditable fighting display, Mark McGhee equalised early in the second half. However, with twenty minutes to go Pavel Yakovenko restored Kiev's lead and Yevtushenko wrapped up.

Stylish Porto take Cup back to Portugal

Porto (0) 2   Bayern Munich (1) 1

Prater Stadium, Vienna, 27 May 1987
Attendance: 62,000
Referee: Ponnet (Belgium)

Porto had reached their first European Cup Final and were up against an experienced and fancied Bayern side. Both teams had selection problems – winger Roland Wohlfarth and sweeper Klaus Augenthaler were out for Bayern, and Porto's centre-back Lima Pereira and centre-forward Fernando Gomes were both broken leg victims.

The game started off at a fast attacking pace, with both sides going for the vital first goal. Both goals came under assault in the first 25 minutes, with a free-kick from Matthäus being well saved by keeper Mlynarczyk . However, a bizarre decision by controversial referee Ponnet in the 24th minute contributed to Bayern taking the lead. Magalhaes was surprisingly and illegally ordered back from a Bayern throw-in and, as he retreated, the ball was deflected off his head to Ludwig Kogl in the Porto goalmouth, who headed it into the net. The pressure continued from Bayern, Rummenigge connecting with a Matthäus pass and narrowly missing, and the first half ended with a 25-yard shot from Brazilian centre-back Celso over the Bayern bar.

The second half saw Bayern defending their lead and Porto on the attack. The fast and powerful raiding of Futre and Madjer was spreading disarray in Bayern's defence, and midfielder Sousa was stamping his authority in the centre of the park. Juary had come on for midfielder Quim after the interval, and it was the Brazilian striker who created the equaliser in the 77th minute when his short pass to Madjer was cheekily backheeled by the Algerian past keeper Pfaff. Two minutes later, Porto went ahead, with a Madjer cross from the left wing to the waiting Jaury, who made no mistake with a powerful shot.

Bayern brought on attacker Lunde for midfielder Flick, but Porto were now in command and stayed that way until the final whistle. Outgoing Bayern boss Udo Lattek admitted to disappointment with several of his players' performances but was generous in his praise for the Portuguese: 'Porto played very well, they are technically outstanding'. And the European Cup was back in Portuguese hands after a twenty-five year absence.

The teams
FC Porto: Mlynarczyk, Joao Pinto, Eduardo Luis, Celso, Ignacio (Frasco), Quim (Juary), Magalhaes, Madjer, Sousa, Andre, Futre (manager: Jorge) [Madjer 77, Juary 79]
Bayern Munich: Pfaff, Winklhofer, Nachtweih, Eder, Pflügler, Flick (Lunde), Brehme, Hoeness, Matthäus, Kogl, Rummenigge (manager: Lattek) [Kogl 24]

Rabah Madjer backheels Porto's first goal in the 1987 Final.

With Brazilian centre-back Jose Mozer and Fonseca in defence, and Rui Aguas and Diamantino in attack, Benfica were well-equipped to go far in this year's tournament. In the first round against Partizan Tirana, four Albanians were sent off and the second leg was awarded to Benfica. A goal from veteran Adelino Nunes gave the Portugese an aggregate 1-0 victory over Denmark's Aarhus in the second round, and they faced Anderlecht in the Quarter-final.

Anderlecht had lost Scifo to Inter and Vercauteren had gone to Nantes, and the Belgians were now relying on the goal-scoring of young Luc Nilis. Swedish forward Mats Magnusson had joined Benfica in August, and he headed home the first goal in Lisbon, which was closely followed by a strike from Brazilian midfielder Chiquino. In Belgium, a stout Benfica defence resisted Anderlecht's furious attacks and conceded only one goal, a free-kick from Arnor Gudjohnsen. A 2-1 win drew them against Steaua Bucharest in the Semi-final.

Steaua had won the Rumanian 'double', and their attack of Lacatus, Balint and Piturca was buttressed by captain Stoica and the brilliant midfielder Gheorghe Hagi. However, two first-half headed goals from Rui Aguas, son of the Benfica captain in 1961, in the second leg in Lisbon, following a goal-less draw in Bucharest, put Benfica into the Final.

Real Madrid were continuing to set the pace in Spanish football. With their high-scoring strike force of Butragueno and Sanchez, and the midfield trio of Milan Jankovic, Gallego and Michel, they were seen as favourites for the competition. By some quirk in the seeding system, they were paired in the first round with Napoli, champions of Italy. Argentinian superstar and local hero Diego Maradona led the Italians, and they had a devastating attacking line-up of their own, featuring Brazilian Careca and Bruno Giordano.

Behind closed doors at the Bernabeu, the consequence of the previous season's crowd trouble in the game against Bayern, an eerie, ill-tempered game saw Real score early on through a Michel penalty and extend their lead with 15 minutes to go, Fernando de Napoli putting the ball through his own net. Napoli right-back Giovanni Francini scored first in Naples, and Butragueno equalised just before half time from a pass by Sanchez. Real effectively kept check on Maradona and his tricky forwards, and a 1-1 draw took the Spaniards through to play Porto in the second round.

Paulo Futre had left the Portuguese Cup-holders, but the goals continued to flow from Gomes and the Algerian Madjer. In Spain, a Madjer header put Porto ahead after 60 minutes, but with under ten minutes to go Sanchez equalised and Real went further ahead in the last minute with a Manuel Sanchis header. An Antonio Sousa free-kick levelled the tie in Portugal, but an inspired Real half-time substitution of Paco Llorente for Solana turned the game, and the young winger made two goals for Michel without reply from Porto. Bayern Munich were the opponents in the Quarter-final.

The first leg in Germany produced an exciting game of fluctuating fortunes. Bayern went two ahead by half time, through Pfluger and Eder, and Wohlfarth made it three in the 50th minute. Madrid refused to admit defeat, and with two minutes to go a Bayern defensive error allowed Butragueno to score. On the

Emilio Butragueno

Emilio Butragueno. Nicknamed 'the Vulture', Butragueno was a sharpshooting goalscorer for Real Madrid and Spain. He holds the all-time Spanish goal record with 26 goals in 69 appearances for his country. He won UEFA Cup winners medals in 1985 and 1986, and his goals helped Real to claim the Spanish league title five times in succession between 1986 and 1990. He scored in his international debut in 1984 in Spain's 3-0 win over Wales, and he was second-top scorer in the 1986 World Cup finals with five goals, including four in one game against Denmark.

Results

First Round

	1st leg	2nd leg	Agg
Aarhus v Jeunesse Esch	4-1	0-1	4-2
Bayern Munich v CSKA Sofia	4-0	1-0	5-0
Benfica v Partizan Tirana	4-0 (a)		
Bordeaux v Dynamo Berlin	2-0	2-0	4-0
Dynamo Kiev v Rangers	1-0	0-2	1-2
Fram Reykjavik v Sparta Prague	0-2	0-8	0-10
Lillestrom v Linfield	1-1	4-2	5-3
Malmö v Anderlecht	0-1	1-1	1-2
Neuchatel v Kuusysi Lahti	5-0	1-2	6-2
Olympiakos v Gornik Zabrze	1-1	1-2	2-3
PSV Eindhoven v Galatasaray	3-0	0-2	3-2
Porto v Vardar Skopje	3-0	3-0	6-0
Rapid Vienna v Hamrun Spartans	6-0	1-0	7-0
Real Madrid v Napoli	2-0	1-1	3-1
Shamrock Rovers v Omonia Nicosia	0-1	0-0	0-1
Steaua Bucharest v MTK Budapest	4-0	0-2	4-2

a) Benfica walkover, Partizan expelled by UEFA.

Second Round

Aarhus v Benfica	0-0	0-1	0-1
Lillestrom v Bordeaux	0-0	0-1	0-1
Neuchatel v Bayern Munich	2-1	0-2	2-3
Rangers v Gornik Zabrze	3-1	1-1	4-2
Rapid Vienna v PSV Eindhoven	1-2	0-2	1-4
Real Madrid v Porto	2-1	2-1	4-2
Sparta Prague v Anderlecht	1-2	0-1	1-3
Steaua Bucharest v Omonia Nicosia	3-1	2-0	5-1

Quarter-finals

Bayern Munich v Real Madrid	3-2	0-2	3-4
Benfica v Anderlecht	2-0	0-1	2-1
Bordeaux v PSV Eindhoven	1-1	0-0	1-1
Steaua Bucharest v Rangers	2-0	1-2	3-2

Semi-finals

Real Madrid v PSV Eindhoven	1-1	0-0	1-1
Steaua Bucharest v Benfica	0-0	0-2	0-2

stroke of full time, Sanchez pounced on a free-kick, and it was 3-2. In Madrid, 20-foot-high crowd barriers and a massive security presence indicated the authorities' nervousness about a repeat of the previous year's trouble. Jankovic fired Real ahead in the 27th minute, and four minutes from half time a Michel shot put Real two ahead. New boy Mark Hughes, on loan from Barcelona, fluffed a couple of chances for Bayern, but the Germans could not break down Real's defence.

PSV Eindhoven were by some way Holland's top team, and they were to play Real in the Semi-final. The high-spending Dutchmen, bankrolled by the Philips electronics group, had lost Ruud Gullit to Milan, but they had acquired Soren Lerby from Monaco who teamed up in midfield with Frank Arnesen and Willy Van der Kerkhof. Ronald Koeman was a central defender with a powerful shot, and big Wim Kieft and Hans Gillhaus were the strikers. All-powerful domestically, they had impressively eliminated Galatasary and Rapid Vienna, and two tight games against Bordeaux ended in PSV's favour on away goals.

In the first leg in Madrid, an early penalty from Sanchez put the Spaniards ahead but twelve minutes later midfielder Edward Linskens replied for PSV. A jittery Real found it difficult to cope with PSV's speed and movement, but the score ended 1-1. Without Koeman, but with keeper Hans Van Breukelen in fine form, PSV held Real 0-0 in the return and went through on away goals. PSV had drawn their last four games in the tournament, but were now in the Final.

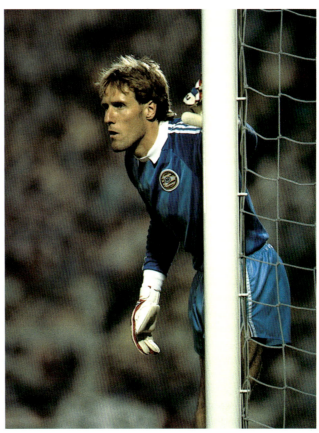

PSV keeper Hans Van Breukelen concentrates on the action.

BRITISH CLUBS

Graeme Souness had taken over as player-manager of **Rangers** at the beginning of the previous season and steered the club to its first championship in nine years. His policy of buying English players, thereby offering them the lure of European football, had been validated, and the likes of keeper Chris Woods and defenders Terry Butcher and Graham Roberts were joined in the summer by Trevor Francis and Spurs centre-forward Mark Falco. They were soon to be joined by midfielder Ray 'Butch' Wilkins from Paris St-Germain, who would take part in this season's European campaign.

The team was, however, not entirely Sassenach-dominated, with striker Ally McCoist, inside-left Ian Durrant, attacking midfielder Ian Ferguson and winger Davie Cooper among the Scottish representatives. The arrival of Scottish international defender Richard Gough from Spurs later in the tournament was to give Souness more defensive options.

The formidable Dynamo Kiev were Rangers' first test in the competition. In the Ukraine, in front of 100,000 spectators, Kiev were without the injured Belanov and Rangers survived a torrid, attacking first half. They had a couple of chances in the second half, but a Mikhailichenko penalty 20 minutes from time put Kiev ahead.

At Ibrox, Belanov was back but was replaced by Yevtushenko early in the game. Rangers were robust in attack, and Falco scored from a McCoist pass in the 24th minute. Five minutes after the interval, Falco returned the favour and McCoist made it two. After a stirring performance from Rangers, they ran out 2-0 winners and were drawn against Poland's Gornik Zabrze in the next round.

By half time in the first leg at Ibrox the Gers were three in front, McCoist giving them the lead in the sixth minute and Durrant and Falco adding another two. Rangers were well on top, but Urban scored early in the second half to give Gornik an away goal. In Gornik, McCoist again opened the scoring with a penalty after he had been tripped in the box and although Gornik levelled the game in the second half, a defensive Rangers held on to the draw and moved into to the Quarter-final.

In Romania against the Steaua Bucharest of Hagi and Lacatus, Rangers were under-strength and went one down to a Piturca shot in the second minute. Keeper Chris Woods kept Rangers in the game with a series of top-class saves, but he could not prevent Stefan Iovan scoring from a Hagi pass in the second half. Trailing by two goals at Ibrox, Rangers went further behind in the third minute when Lacatus skillfully finished off a Stoica pass. Gough headed in an equaliser in the 16th minute and McCoist converted a penalty on the half hour after Durrant had been fouled, but Rangers could not find a way through the Steaua defence and were eliminated.

Linfield travelled to Norway in the first round to take on Lillestrom, and a Stephen Baxter goal fifteen minutes from time gave them a useful 1-1 draw to take back to Northern Ireland. In Belfast, two goals in the last ten minutes from the Norwegians gave them a 5-3 victory in the tie, and the game was scarred by crowd trouble with missiles being thrown at the Lillestrom keeper. Linfield were again out of the competition in the first round.

Ronald Koeman (1963). Koeman was an attacking centre-back with a ferocious shot. He moved from Ajax to PSV Eindhoven in 1986 and won a European Cup winner's medal against Benfica in 1988. Transferred to Barcelona in 1989, he gained a second winner's medal in 1992, scoring the only goal in the game against Sampdoria. He was a member of the 1988 Dutch side which won the European Championships and also played in the 1990 and 1994 World Cup finals. He finished his career with Feyenoord, whom he joined in 1995, and retired in 1997.

Partizan banned

Albania's Partizan Tirana were thrown out of the competition by UEFA and banned for four years as a result of their players' behaviour in the first-round first leg game against Benfica in Lisbon. No less than four Tirana players were sent off by the Spanish referee Perez, and the game went into ten minutes of overtime.

Rangers pitch tactics

Before the home return leg of their first-round game against Dynamo Kiev, Rangers incensed the Ukranians by trimming the width of the pitch to the legal minimum. Kiev had trained on the pitch the previous evening before Rangers had gone to work on the white lines. This piece of gamemanship seems to have worked, as Rangers won 2-0 and progressed to the Quarter-final.

1988 — THE FINAL

PSV shoot down Eagles in tactical stalemate

PSV Eindhoven (0) 0   Benfica (0) 0   (after extra time)
(PSV won 6-5 on penalties)

Neckar Stadium, Stuttgart, 25 May 1988
Attendance: 70,000
Referee: Agnolin (Italy)

PSV were expected to win this Final. Four of the side – keeper Van Breukelen, Van Aerle, Koeman and Vanenburg – were in the Dutch team which were to win the European Championship with such style and flair that summer. Although midfielder Frank Arnesen was absent from the line-up with a broken leg, Soren Lerby and Vanenburg were playing, as were forwards Kieft and Gillhaus, and the Benfica defence was a shaky one.

Benfica winger and skipper Diamantino had torn his knee ligaments and was replaced by Han Sheu, whose job was to cut off the lines of communication between PSV's midfield and attack, and Magnusson and Aguas were to provide the firepower for the Portugese side.

For the first hour, the game was negative and boring and something of a cynical stalemate. Indeed, no shot was on target until eight minutes from half time, when a Vanenburg shot forced Benfica keeper Almeida Silvino into a diving save. Shortly after the interval, Aguas limped off with a strained hamstring and was replaced by Brazilian midfielder Valdo. Slowly, PSV began to rouse themselves and started moving forward in numbers,

forcing corners and putting pressure on defenders Mozer and Alvaro.

Vanenburg and Gillhaus both tested Silvino, stopper Ivan Nielsen missed an open goal in the 74th minute with a shot from the edge of the six-yard box, and Koeman had a free kick saved by Silvino in the last minute of normal time. The contest continued through a dreary extra time period, with the ineffective Magnusson and the equally off-form Gillhaus both being replaced, and the game went to penalties.

All the penalties were converted until, with the score 6-5, Van Breukelen dived to save left-back Veloso's soft effort, and PSV had won the European Cup.

As a spectacle, the game was tedious but tactically the organised Dutch side outplayed Benfica. PSV coach Gus Hiddink stated after the match that 'this is a team of players which compares with that of the 1970s', although most of the spectators would rather have been watching the great players of that decade.

Van Breukelen dives to save Veloso's penalty and win the Cup for PSV in the 1988 Final.

The teams
PSV Eindhoven: Van Breukelen, Gerets, Van Aerle, Koeman, Nielsen, Heintze, Vanenburg, Linskens, Lerby, Kieft, Gillhaus (Janssen) (manager: Hiddink)
Benfica: Silvino, Veloso, Dito, Mozer, Alvaro, Elzo, Sheu, Chiquinho, Pacheco, Rui Aguas (Valdo), Magnusson (Hajry) (manager: Toni)
Penalty shoot-out
Koeman, 1-0; Elzo, 1-1; Kieft, 2-1; Dito, 2-2; Nielsen, 3-2; Hajry, 3-3; Vanenburg, 4-3; Pacheco, 4-4; Lerby, 5-4; Mozer, 5-5; Jansson, 6-5; Veloso missed, 6-5

Media magnate Silvio Berlusconi had bought AC Milan in 1986 and immediately set about rebuilding the famous old club, which had fallen on hard times. His millions paid off the club's debts and brought the multi-talented, dreadlocked Ruud Gullit from PSV Eindhoven to Milan in 1987, with the brilliant centre-forward Marco Van Basten following shortly after from Ajax. The powerful midfielder Frank Rijkaard joined the following summer. The three Dutchmen were the core of the exciting Holland side which had won the European Championship in 1988.

Also in that exceptional Milan team were attacking sweeper Franco Baresi and defenders Mauro Tassotti, Alessandro Costacurta and the young Paolo Maldini. The stylish Roberto Donadoni was the playmaker in midfield.

Berlusconi had hired the little-known coach Arrigo Sacchi from Second Division Parma, and Sacchi instilled in his team the virtues of attacking, pressing football, with the emphasis on speed, skill and possession. Milan had won the Italian league in Sacchi's first season and the club was back in the European Cup for the first time in almost a decade.

Results

First Round

	1st leg	2nd leg	Agg	
Bruges v Brondby	1-0	1-2	2-2	
Dundalk v Red Star Belgrade	0-5	0-3	0-8	
Dynamo Berlin v Werder Bremen	3-0	0-5	3-5	
Gornik Zabrze v Jeunesse Esch	3-0	4-1	7-1	
Hamrun Spartans v 17 Nentori Tirana	2-1	0-2	2-3	
Honved v Celtic	1-0	0-4	1-4	
Larissa v Neuchatel	2-1	1-2	3-3	0-3 (P)
Pezoporikos v IFK Gothenburg	1-2	1-5	2-7	
Porto v HJK Helsinki	3-0	0-2	3-2	
Rapid Vienna v Galatasaray	2-1	0-2	2-3	
Real Madrid v Moss	3-0	1-0	4-0	
Sparta Prague v Steaua Bucharest	1-5	2-2	3-7	
Spartak Moscow v Glentoran	2-0	1-1	3-1	
Valur v Monaco	1-0	0-2	1-2	
Vitosha v AC Milan	0-2	2-5	2-7	

Bye: PSV Eindhoven   P = penalties

Second Round

	1st leg	2nd leg	Agg	
17 Nentori Tirana v IFK Gothenburg	0-3	0-1	0-4	
AC Milan v Red Star Belgrade	1-1	1-1	2-2	4-2 (P)
Bruges v Monaco	1-0	1-6	2-6	
Celtic v Werder Bremen	0-1	0-0	0-1	
Gornik Zabrze v Real Madrid	0-1	2-3	2-4	
Neuchatel v Galatasaray	3-0	0-5	3-5	
PSV Eindhoven v Porto	5-0	0-2	5-2	
Steaua Bucharest v Spartak Moscow	3-0	2-1	5-1	

P = penalties

Quarter-finals

	1st leg	2nd leg	Agg
IFK Gothenburg v Steaua Bucharest	1-0	1-5	2-5
Monaco v Galatasaray	0-1	1-1	1-2
PSV Eindhoven v Real Madrid	1-1	1-2	2-3
Werder Bremen v AC Milan	0-0	0-1	0-1

Semi-finals

	1st leg	2nd leg	Agg
Steaua Bucharest v Galatasaray	4-0	1-1	5-1
Real Madrid v AC Milan	1-1	0-5	1-6

Disposing of Bulgaria's Vitosha in the first round, Van Basten scoring four in the home leg, Milan next took on Red Star Belgrade. A 1-1 draw in Italy, the goals scored by Red Star skipper and playmaker Dragan Stojkovic and veteran Milan forward Pietro Paolo Virdis, was followed by a vicious 1-1 draw away, and the tie went Milan's way on penalties. They met Germany's Werder Bremen in the Quarter-final. Werder had overcome a shock 3-0 defeat by Dynamo Berlin with a 5-0 home result, and striker Karl-Heinz Riedle was on form. The first leg in Bremen produced no goals, and a controversial 32nd-minute penalty from Van Basten squeezed Milan through at home. The glittering talents of Real Madrid, now with the individualistic Bernd Schuster in midfield, awaited Milan in the Semi-final.

Real had eliminated Gornik Zabrze and the resurgent and well-funded Cup holders PSV Eindhoven on their way to the semis. Gus Huddink, who had added to his expensive PSV squad with the acquisition of Brazilian striker Romario for £3 million from Vasco da Gama, had dumped out Porto in the

Frank Rijkaard

Marco Van Basten (1964). The complete centre-forward, Van Basten was the finest striker in the world in the 1980s. Fast, powerful in the air and on the ground, and a deadly finisher, he took over Cruyff's mantle at Ajax. He moved to AC Milan in 1987 for £1.5 million where, playing alongside Gullit and Rijkaard, he claimed two European Cup winners medals. He was capped 58 times for Holland and played in the side which thrillingly won the 1988 European Championships, and he scored one of the greatest-ever goals – a 20-yard volley – in the Final against the USSR. He was three times European Footballer of the Year and was forced into retirement through injury in 1995.

Frank Rijkaard (1962). A world-class midfielder and central defender, Rijkaard was one of the unforgettable Milan and Holland Dutch triumvirate, the others being Gullit and Van Basten, which conquered Europe in the late 1980s. He started with Ajax in 1979, and in 1987 had a brief spell with Sporting Lisbon before joining Milan later that year, where he picked up two European Cup winner's medals. He returned to Ajax in 1993 and, in his final game, he helped Ajax to victory over Milan in the European Cup Final in 1995, laying on the winning goal for Kluivert. He has 73 international caps and is currently manager of Holland.

Marco Van Basten

second round. Real drew 1-1 in Holland, Butragueno's 44th-minute goal cancelled out eight minutes later by a Romario header. In Spain, with Butragueno dropped, Sanchez opened the scoring with a penalty late in the game, but Romario again equalised in the 85th minute. A Vasquez strike halfway through extra time eliminated the Dutchmen.

In the Semi-final, with 95,000 spectators in the Bernabeu, and perhaps 500 million watching on television, Hugo Sanchez opened the scoring in the 40th minute from a cross by Schuster, and Van Basten headed in off keeper Buyo's back in the 78th minute to level the score. In the return at the San Siro, Milan were simply majestic. Their pace and movement destroyed a sluggish Real, and the game finished 5-0, the goals coming from midfielder Carlo Ancelotti, Rijkaard, Gullit, Van Basten and Donadoni. Who was going to live with Milan in the Final?

Managed by Jupp Derwall, Turkey's Galatasaray, with 39-league-goal star striker and European Golden Boot winner Tantu Colak, had knocked out Rapid Vienna and Neuchatel, and they played French champions Monaco in the Quarter-final. Monaco coach Arsène Wenger had bought two English players – striker Mark Hateley and

midfield provider Glenn Hoddle – and Hateley played alongside the Liberian forward George Weah, the African Footballer of the Year. In France, a Colak diving header and a strong defensive performance gave the Turks a surprise victory over Wenger's team. In the return in Cologne, played there because of previous crowd trouble in Istanbul, Galatasaray held on to a 1-1 draw to play Steaua Bucharest in the Semi-final.

Hagi and Lacatus had each scored three in Steaua's first-round defeat of Sparta Prague, and a 5-1 win over Spartak Moscow put the Romanians into the Quarter-final. One down after their first leg visit to Sweden to play IFK Gothenburg, they destroyed the Swedes in Bucharest, with Lacatus supplying a hat-trick.

Steaua went ahead through an eighth-minute own goal against Galatasaray in Romania, and Hagi added another in the 40th minute from the spot. Galatasaray had a goal disallowed but two goals in three minutes from Piturca and Balint midway through the second half gave Steaua a four goal lead to take to the second leg. A 1-1 draw, with young Ilie Dumitrescu heading in a Hagi cross, meant that Steaua were in the Final for the second time in four years.

BRITISH CLUBS

Although **Celtic** started the new Scottish season badly, they had won the league by a convincing margin over Rangers and were back in the European Cup. Several of the team had left since 1986/87 – Johnston had gone to Nantes, McClair to Manchester United, McLeod to Borussia Dortmund, and McInally to Aston Villa. Manager McNeill, however, had acquired the young striker Andy Walker, midfielder Billy Stark and centre-forward Frank McAvennie. Mick McCarthy and Derek Whyte, and Scotland's Player of the Year Paul McStay provided the midfield leadership.

The first-round draw produced a trip to Hungary to play Honvéd. Defeated by a single goal, Celtic more than

compensated at Celtic Park, where goals from Stark, Walker, McAvennie and substitute McGhee put them through 4-1 on aggregate to meet Werder Bremen. In the home leg, Karlheinz Riedle hit a post and McAvennie was unlucky in seeing a shot touched over by the German keeper, but a 57th-minute shot from midfielder Wolter left keeper Bonner stranded. A tedious defensive display from Werder in Germany kept the scoreline goalless, and Celtic were out.

Glentoran did well to limit Spartak Moscow to a 1-1 draw in Northern Ireland, but they had conceded two goals within a minute in Moscow, and they were eliminated.

Ruud Gullit watches his shot enter the Steaua Bucharest net in the 1989 Final.

Magnificent Milan sweep aside Steaua

AC Milan (3) 4 Steaua Bucharest (0) 0

Nou Camp, Barcelona, 24 May 1989
Attendance: 97,000
Referee: Tritschler (West Germany)

AC Milan confirmed their position as Europe's top club side with an emphatic and thrilling victory over Steaua in a Nou Camp stadium lit by smoke bombs and deafened by the red and black Milan supporters.

Arguably the finest display of football in a Final since 1960, Milan's movement, passing game and pressing tactics swept aside a curiously quiescent Steaua. Sacchi had set out an attacking formation, moving Rijkaard into midfield, his place in defence taken by Costacurta, and Maldini and Tassotti were to attack down the wings. Donadoni and Ancelotti were to control the midfield. And it all went exactly to plan.

Although Steaua started the game positively, with Lacatus and Hagi causing early problems in the Milan defence, they were soon reeling under the constant Milan attacks, with Van Basten and the magnificent Gullit at the heart of the action. Within 18 minutes Milan were ahead. Steaua keeper Lung was obstructed by his defender

Bumbescu when going for a Van Basten shot, and Gullit took advantage of the confusion to tap the ball into the net.

In the 26th minute, Van Basten rose to head in a high cross from Tassotti. Then, twelve minutes later in a piece of wonderful skill, Gullit received a diagonal pass from Donadoni at waist level, spun round and volleyed past Lung, who had no chance with the shot. Steaua were now dead and buried.

Van Basten picked up a pass from Rijkaard one minute into the second half and scored Milan's fourth, which gave him the tournament's top scorer award with ten goals. Milan eased off, and ended the game 4-0 winners. Although more had been expected of the subdued Romanians, Milan mightily deserved their victory and they were about to become the dominant force in European football over the next few years.

The teams
AC Milan: G. Galli, Tassotti, Costacurta (F. Galli), Baresi, Maldini, Colombo, Rijkaard, Ancelotti, Donadoni, Gullit (Virdis), Van Basten (manager: Sacchi) [Gullit 18, 38, Van Basten 26, 46]
Steaua Bucharest: Lung, Iovan, Petrescu, Bumbescu, Ungureanu, Hagi, Stoica, Minea, Rotariu (Balaci), Lacatus, Piturca (manager: Iordanescu)

The flamboyant Bernard Tapie, president of Olympique Marseille, had spent heavily on players to bring the club the French 'double'. The small, versatile, 26-year-old striker Jean-Pierre Papin, bought from Bruges, had been France's top scorer in the previous two years; English forward Chris Waddle had arrived for a British record fee of £4.5 million; and the impressive line-up also included Uruguyan Enzo Francescoli, Manuel Amoros, the Brazilian defender Jose Carlos Mozer and Jean Tigana. Under coach Gerard Gili, Marseille were a tough, attacking side and were expected to go far in this year's tournament.

Easing past Brondby and AEK Athens in the opening rounds, they met CSKA Sofia in the Quarter-final. CSKA were resigned to losing their outstanding goalscorer Hristo Stoichkov to Barcelona at the end of the season and, in Sofia, both Stoichkov and Papin narrowly missed chances. Substitute Philippe Thys scored the important away goal for Marseille with five minutes to go. In the return, the French romped home with goals from Waddle, Papin and young midfielder Frank Sauzee, and drew Benfica in the Semi-final.

The Portuguese side had Sweden's Jonas Thern in midfield and Brazilians Ricardo and Aldair in defence, while Mats Magnusson and another Brazilian, Valdo, were the goal scorers. Benfica had reached the Semi-final by brushing aside Derry City 6-1 and humbling once-mighty Honvéd 9-0. In Lisbon against Soviet champions Dnepr, a ninth-minute Magnusson penalty gave Benfica the lead and only the goalkeeping of Dnepr keeper and captain Gorodov kept the score 1-0. A spirited second-half fight-back by the Soviets could not achieve an away goal, and in the Ukraine two counter-attacking goals from Adesvaldo Jose de Loma within five minutes gave Dnepr little chance of winning the tie. Brazilian defender Ricardo tied it up for Benfica near the end.

In the Semi-final in Marseille, Lima unexpectedly put Benfica ahead early in the game, but Sauzee and Papin, from a Waddle pass on half time, gave the French a 2-1 lead to take to Lisbon. An 80,000 crowd in the Stadium of Light saw Marseille dourly defending their lead and Benfica unable to make any headway, until an apparently handled goal from Vata Garcia with eight minutes to go gave the Portuguese a controversial aggregate lead. Benfica were in the Final.

The second round had thrown up a potentially thrilling clash – Cup holders AC Milan, without Gullit who was nursing a long-term injury, against John Toshack's star-studded Real Madrid. At the San Siro, Real were

Results

First Round

	1st leg	2nd leg	Agg
AC Milan v HJK Helsinki	4-0	1-0	5-0
Derry City v Benfica	1-2	0-4	1-6
Dynamo Dresden v AEK Athens	1-0	3-5	4-5
Honved v Vojvodina	1-0	1-2	2-2
Linfield v Dnepr Dnepropetrovsk	1-2	0-1	1-3
Malmö v Inter Milan	1-0	1-1	2-1
Marseille v Brondby	3-0	1-1	4-1
PSV Eindhoven v Lucerne	3-0	2-0	5-0
Rangers v Bayern Munich	1-3	0-0	1-3
Rosenborg v Mechelen	0-0	0-5	0-5
Ruch Chorzow v CSKA Sofaia	1-1	1-5	2-6
Sliema Wanderers v 17 Nentori Tirana	1-0	0-5	1-5
Sparta Prague v Fenerbahçe	3-1	2-1	5-2
Spora Luxembourg v Real Madrid	0-3	0-6	0-9
Steaua Bucharest v Fram Reykjavik	4-0	1-0	5-0
Tirol v Omonia Nicosia	6-0	3-2	9-2

Second Round

AC Milan v Real Madrid	2-0	0-1	2-1
Bayern Munich v 17 Nentori Tirana	3-0	3-1	6-1
Dnepr Dnepropetrovsk v Tirol	2-0	2-2	4-2
Honved v Benfica	0-2	0-7	0-9
Malmö v Mechelen	0-0	1-4	1-4
Marseille v AEK Athens	2-0	1-1	3-1
Sparta Prague v CSKA Sofia	2-2	0-3	2-5
Steaua Bucharest v PSV Eindhoven	1-0	1-5	2-5

Quarter-finals

Bayern Munich v PSV Eindhoven	2-1	1-0	3-1
Benfica v Dnepr Dnepropetrovsk	1-0	3-0	4-0
CSKA Sofia v Marseille	0-1	1-3	1-4
Mechelen v AC Milan	0-0	0-2	0-2

Semi-finals

AC Milan v Bayern Munich	1-0	1-2	2-2
Marseille v Benfica	2-1	0-1	2-2

Benfica's Magnusson shields the ball in the 1990 Final.

without Butragueno and were 2-0 down within the first 13 minutes. A neatly-directed header by Rijkaard from an inch-perfect Van Basten cross opened the scoring. Then a goal from Van Basten, when he was pulled down by keeper Buyo just outside the area but a penalty was given by the referee, left Real unable to reply. At the Bernabeu, an ugly and physical game saw seven yellow cards and Manuel Sanchis sent off. Van Basten was repeatedly kicked and fouled by a cynical Real, but a Butragueno 44th-minute goal was not enough to keep Real in the competition.

Milan's Quarter-final opponents, Belgian champions Mechelen, were a defensive side with Philippe Albert and Leo Clijsters the commanding centre-backs. International midfielder Erwin Koeman acted as provider to his fellow Dutchman John Bosman, and the team had eliminated Roy Hodgson's Malmö in the second round. In the Heysel Stadium – the first European club game there since the 1985 disaster – Mechelen had all the play but could not get past keeper Galli. In Italy, Donadoni and Clijters were both red-carded, and Milan had to wait until extra time to score through Van Basten and substitute Marco Simone and progress to the Semi-final against Bayern Munich.

With internationals Jürgen Kohler and Stefan Reuter in defence, alongside sweeper Augenthaler, Bayern were a strong, uncompromising side. Up front Scottish forward Alan McInally had been brought in to complement Wohlfarth and Strunz. Bayern had beaten Rangers at Ibrox and Nentori Tirana 6-1 to reach the Quarter-final stage against PSV Eindhoven. Struggling

Inter crash out to Swedes

The shock of this year's competition was the first round elimination of Inter Milan by Malmö in September. Inter – with the three German internationals Matthäus, Brehme and Klinsmann – were beaten in Malmö 1-0 by Englishman Roy Hodgson's side, Hakan Lindman's header putting the Swedes in the lead. At the San Siro, a header from Leif Enqvist in the 80th minute made the final score 1-1, and the Italian champions were out.

domestically, PSV had nonetheless overturned a 1-0 Steaua Bucharest lead in the second round with a 5-1 thrashing of the Romanians in Holland, Romario scoring a hat-trick.

A 2-1 Bayern lead from the first leg in Munich remained the difference between the sides until the 89th minute in Eindhoven, when Augenthaler scored for the Germans from a free-kick.

In the Semi-final against AC Milan, a late Van Basten penalty for Milan, missing Gullit and Ancelotti and the suspended Donadoni, gave them a 1-0 win at the San Siro. In a wet Munich, Strunz pulled back a goal in the 60th minute, and the game went into extra time. Substitute Borgonovo lobbed Bayern keeper Aumann in the 100th minute, and a McInally goal in the 107th minute was not sufficient to keep Bayern in the competition. Milan would play Benfica in the Final.

BRITISH CLUBS

Glentoran did well to limit Spartak Moscow to a 1-1 draw in Northern Ireland, but they had conceded two goals within a minute in Moscow, and they were eliminated.

The fast, raiding winger Mark Walters had joined **Rangers** from Aston Villa, and he played in attack alongside the club's first Catholic player, Mo Johnston, supported by McCoist and Hateley.

The £10 million team took on Bayern Munich in the first round. Bayern, fielding seven internationals, were top of the Bundesliga while Rangers were injury-hit, and McCoist suspended. They were also struggling at the bottom of the Scottish Premier League. In the first game at Ibrox, Rangers turned in a feeble performance. Although Walters scored first with a penalty for a foul on Johnston, three minutes later a cross from Stefan Reuter was misheaded by Scott Nisbet to Kogl who lashed in an accurate, left-foot shot. Immediately after the interval Thon was clumsily fouled by Gary Stevens, and the German converted the penalty. In the 62nd minute, centre-half Klaus Augenthaler advanced into midfield and his shot from fully 35 yards made the score 3-1. 'It was a lesson for us', said manager Souness.

In the return, with the Israeli Bonni Ginzburg deputising for injured keeper Chris Woods, Rangers faced an almost impossible challenge. A soporific, boring game ensued, with Bayern simply holding on to the ball in their own defence. The Germans made no attempt to attack and played for a goal-less draw. However, had Terry Butcher shot when clear through in the first minute, rather than pass to an offside Johnston, the game may have been different. Both teams were booed and whistled off the pitch at the end, and Rangers were out.

Paolo Maldini

Ruud Gullit (1962). The tall Gullit was a graceful, goal-scoring midfielder with pace, intelligence and vision. After spells at Feyenoord and PSV Eindhoven, he moved to AC Milan in 1987 for a world record £6.5 million and inspired the club to two European Cup victories. He left Milan in 1994 to join Sampdoria and then Chelsea in 1995, where he subsequently became manager, followed by a brief period as manager of Newcastle. He gained 65 caps for Holland, but a dispute with manager Dick Advocaat meant that he missed the 1994 World Cup finals. He was voted European Footballer of the Year in 1987, and was twice World Footballer of the Year.

Paolo Maldini (1968). Son of AC Milan's captain and erstwhile Italian manager Cesare Maldini, Paolo has carved out his own name in football as probaby the best defender in the world. An attacking left-back with Milan since 1985, Maldini has won most of the honours available to him in club football and, with over 100 Italian caps, is on course to become his country's most capped player ever. His versatility, speed and decisive tackling ability have been one of the cornerstones of Milan's success in recent years.

Rijkaard retains European Cup for Milan

AC Milan (0) 1 Benfica (0) 0

Prater Stadium, Vienna, 23 May 1990
Attendance: 57,000
Referee: Kohl (Austria)

Ruud Gullit had played his first game of the season the previous week and, although he had confessed to being 'only 70 per cent fit', the Dutchman played in attack alongside Marco Van Basten against the strong Benfica side. Magnusson, scorer of 33 goals in the Portugese league, and Valdo were their counterparts for Benfica. The newly-refurbished Prater Stadium was the venue for the much anticipated clash.

The game was a tactical battle, with Milan making full use of their expertise in the offside trap and the long pass-back to keeper Galli, a different team from the exuberant side of last year's Final. Benfica had most of the attack, in particular the impressive Brazilian Valdo whose running with the ball and skilful passing and turning kept Costacurta and Ancelotti on their back feet. Milan, however, were still dangerous. In the 39th minute, Gullit found Tassotti and the full-back's cross was met by Van Basten, whose shot was well saved by keeper Silvino.

Four minutes into the second half, Van Basten passed to Gullit with only the keeper to beat but Gullit's snatched shot was stopped by Silvino. It was then Benfica's turn to go close, when a 25-yard shot from Valdo beat keeper Giovanni Galli but went just wide of the post. In the 62nd minute, Costacurta picked up a ball from Filippo Galli and fed Van Basten, whose pass through the Benfica defence was met by Rijkaard who smashed the ball into the net wide of the keeper. 1-0 to Milan. Benfica brought on forward Vata Garcia to replace midfielder Vitor Paneira, but the Portuguese side had left it too late. Gullit could have added another in the 78th minute but elected to hit a good chance well over the bar and, although Jose Carlos nearly caught out keeper Galli with ten minutes to go, Milan held on till the final whistle.

The skill of Van Basten, the midfield power of Frank Rijkaard and the tireless defence of Costacurta, Baresi and Maldini had ensured that Milan's name was on the trophy for the second year in succession. Unlucky Benfica, who had provided strong and determined competition to the Italians, had now suffered their fifth defeat in seven European Cup Finals.

The teams
AC Milan: G. Galli, Tassotti, Costacurta, Baresi, Maldini, Colombo (F. Galli), Rijkaard, Ancelotti (Massaro), Evani, Gullit, Van Basten (manager: Sacchi) [Rijkaard 62]
Benfica: Silvino, Jose Carlos, Aldair, Ricardo, Samuel, Vitor Paneira (Vata Garcia), Valdo, Thern, Hernani, Magnusson, Pachedo (Cesar Brito) (manager: Eriksson)

Frank Rijkaard (right) about to score his winning goal in the 1990 Final.

Red Star Belgrade were one of the most talented and attractive attacking sides in European football. Dominant in Yugoslavia, and respected throughout the continent, Red Star could field players who were the envy of top European clubs. In defence, sweeper Miodrag Belodedic had defected from Romania after leading his club Steaua Bucharest to victory in the 1986 Final; dazzling 21-year-old playmaker Robert Prosinecki had taken over the mantle of Dragan Stujkovic who had gone to Marseille; midfielder Dejan Savicevic was a focus of interest for Spanish and Italian clubs; and forward Darko Pancev was top scorer in the league and for his country. They played as a unit with flair and panache, and were certainly capable of reaching the Final.

A 5-2 aggregate win over Grasshoppers Zurich in the first round and a glittering performance against Rangers in

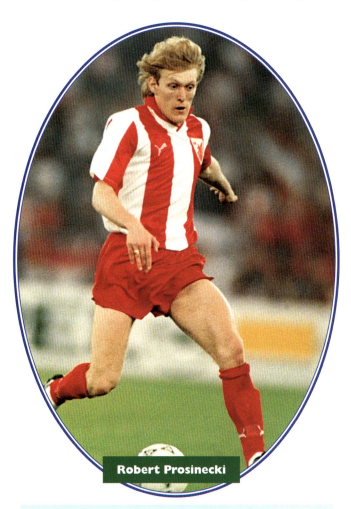

Robert Prosinecki

Robert Prosinecki (1969). Fair-haired, West German-born Croatian playmaker and striker Prosinecki was an influential member of the Red Star Belgrade team which won the European Cup in 1991, beating Marseille on penalties. He joined Real Madrid shortly afterward and then stayed in Spain with Barcelona and Seville, although his period in Spain was dogged by injuries. He gained a total of 34 caps for Yugoslavia and Croatia, and his talents spurred an exciting Croatia side to third place in the 1998 World Cup finals in France. He is currently back in Croatia playing for Croatia Zagreb.

Results

First Round

	Ist leg	2nd leg	Agg
Akureyri v CSKA Sofia	1-0	0-3	1-3
Apoel Nicosia v Bayern Munich	2-3	0-4	2-7
Dynamo Bucharest v St Patrick's Athletic	4-0	1-1	5-1
Lech Poznan v Panathinaikos	3-0	2-1	5-1
Lillestrom v Bruges	1-1	0-2	1-3
Malmö v Besiktas	3-2	2-2	5-4
Marseille v Dynamo Tirana	5-1	0-0	5-1
Napoli v Ujpest Dozsa	3-0	2-0	5-0
OB Odense v Real Madrid	1-4	0-6	1-10
Porto v Portadown	5-0	8-1	13-1
Red Star Belgrade v Grasshoppers Zurich	1-1	4-1	5-2
Sparta Prague v Spartak Moscow	0-2	0-2	0-4
Tirol v Kuusysi Lahti	5-0	2-1	7-1
US Luxembourg v Dynamo Dresden	1-3	0-3	1-6
Valletta v Rangers	0-4	0-6	0-10

Bye: AC Milan

Second Round

AC Milan v Bruges	0-0	1-0	1-0
Bayern Munich v CSKA Sofia	4-0	3-0	7-0
Dynamo Bucharest v Porto	0-0	0-4	0-4
Dynamo Dresden v Malmö	1-1	1-1	1-1 (P)
Lech Poznan v Marseille	3-2	1-6	4-8
Napoli v Spartak Moscow	0-0	0-0	0-0 (P)
Real Madrid v Tirol	9-1	2-2	11-3
Red Star Belgrade v Rangers	3-0	1-1	4-1

P = penalties

Quarter-finals

AC Milan v Marseille	1-1	0-1	1-2
Bayern Munich v Porto	1-1	2-0	3-1
Red Star Belgrade v Dynamo Dresden	3-0	3-0	6-0 (a)
Spartak Moscow v Real Madrid	0-0	3-1	3-1

a) Game abandoned due to crowd trouble. Red Star were awarded the match.

Semi-finals

Bayern Munich v Red Star Belgrade	1-2	2-2	3-4
Spartak Moscow v Marseille	1-3	1-2	1-5

Belgrade put Red Star into the quarter-final, where they met Dynamo Dresden. A Prosinecki free kick in the 21st minute and a goal from striker Dragisa Binic made the score 2-0 at half time. Savicevic added a third in the second half. In Dresden, with Red Star 2-1 ahead through Savicevic and Pancev, crowd rioting forced the abandonment of the game in the 78th minute and the tie was awarded 3-0 to Red Star. Bayern Munich awaited in the semi-final.

The Bavarian club had bought the fast, creative winger Brian Laudrup for £2 million and paired him up front with Wohlfarth. Stefan Effenberg had arrived from Gladbach, and the tough young midfielder lined up alongside Thern and Struntz, with Jürgen Kohler and Stefan Reuter helping out the veteran Augenthaler in defence. A first-round 7-2 win over Cyprus's Apoel, Mihajlovic scoring three, saw

CSKA Sofia visit Munich in the second round. The Bulgarians were no match for Bayern and, with Reuter stealing the show and scoring two goals, were on the wrong end of a 4-0 defeat. CSKA could not score in the second leg either, but Wohlfarth, Effenberg and McInally made the aggregate score a comprehensive 7-0.

Against Porto in the quarter-final in Munich, Augenthaler was sent off early in the game and a ten-man Bayern held on for a 1-1 draw. A goal each from young full-back Christian Ziege and Manfred Bender in Portugal put Bayern through 2-0.

Red Star grabbed the initiative in Munich in the semi-final when, with the score 1-1, Savicevic pounced on a ball from Prosinecki in the 70th minute to accelerate past Jürgen Kohler and score. A dramatic game followed in Belgrade, with Sinisa Mihajlovic opening the scoring with a free kick. A bad mistake by the Red Star keeper in the 63rd minute allowed Augenthaler to score from a free kick, and four minutes later Bender made it 2-1. In the very last minute, a cross from Mihajlovic was turned into his own net by skipper Augenthaler, and Red Star were in the Final.

In September the popular young manager of Marseille, Gili, resigned and, surprisingly, his role was taken over by Franz Beckenbauer on a £1.6 million contract. With the raiding and finishing skills of Waddle, the Ghanaian forward Abedi Pele and Papin now augmented by the flair of Stojkovic and the unpredictable Eric Cantona, Marseille were the leading side in French football. Papin scored a hat-trick in the first-round home leg against Dynamo Tirana and, in the second round, a 3-2 away defeat by Lech Poznan was rescued in France by a 6-1 hammering of the Poles, with midfielder Philippe Vercruysse collecting three goals. In December, Beckenbauer was moved upstairs and 67-year-old Raymond Goethals was appointed coach. Three months later they met AC Milan in the quarter-final.

Milan were in some disarray, with Gullit off form and Van Basten locked in dispute with Sacchi over tactics. Due to the absence of the suspended Ajax, Milan received a bye in the first round and played Bruges in the second round. A defensive display by the Belgians at the San Siro kept the score 0-0, and in Belgium a goal from midfielder Angelo Carbone in the 46th minute put Milan through. However, a retaliatory elbow by Van Basten on his tough marker Pascal Plovie led to a four-match ban for the striker.

In a packed San Siro, the match generating a record £2.5 million receipts, Milan were without Van Basten and an injured Baresi, but went ahead through Gullit in the 16th minute. A Papin goal ten minutes later from a Waddle pass levelled the game and, though the French deserved another, the score remained 1-1. In the return, a sweet volley from Waddle in the 74th minute had

A young Stefan Effenberg directs play in the game between England and Germany in September 1991. He reached the semi-final in 1991 with Bayern, for whom he was to appear again in the 1999 Final.

Marseille ahead on aggregate. When the floodlights partially failed near full time, the Milan team cynically walked off the pitch and refused to return when the lights were restored, clearly hoping for a replay. The referee was not impressed and the tie was awarded to Marseille. Berlusconi apologised for his team's behaviour the next day, but it was to be Marseille who were to meet Spartak Moscow in the semi-final.

Spartak, controlled from midfield by the perceptive young Igor Shalimov, had knocked out Sparta Prague in the first round, and drew Maradona's Napoli in the second. An unsettled and increasingly unpopular Maradona had scored two in the first round against Ujpest Dózsa to help his side go through 5-0 on aggregate. After two goal-less draws, the tie was settled 5-3 on penalties in front of 100,000 in Moscow.

In a freezing quarter-final in Moscow, Real Madrid did well to escape with a 0-0 draw. Although Butragueno opened the scoring at the Bernabeu, goals from winger Dmitri Radchenko and one from forward Valeri Shmarov provided the shock elimination of the round and the departure of Real caretaker coach Alfredo Di Stefano. Although Radchenko had been technically ineligible for the games, Real had left it too late to complain to UEFA.

In front of a 95,000 crowd in Moscow, and with Waddle at his buccaneering best, Marseille went two ahead in just over half an hour with a left-foot shot from Pele closely followed by a Papin goal, both set up by Waddle. Igor Shalimov opened Spartak's account in the second half, but Vercruysse headed in a third with two minutes to go. In France, with Waddle and Pele unstoppable, Marseille scored through Pele and centre-back Basile Boli and, although Spartak converted a penalty, Marseille won through to the Final 5-2 on aggregate.

Jean-Pierre Papin (1963). Wiry French striker Papin began his career with Valenciennes and Bruges before moving to captain Marseille, where he was French league top scorer for four consecutive seasons between 1989 and 1992. He joined AC Milan's foreign legion in 1992, and came on as a substitute in Milan's European Cup Final defeat by Marseille, with whom he also had a Final loser's medal against Red Star Belgrade in 1991. He played 54 times for his country, scoring 30 goals, and was European Footballer of the Year in 1991. He endeed his career at Bayern Munich.

Rangers had won the Scottish title by seven points from Aberdeen, and opened their European account against Valetta. In their first round game in Malta, McCoist and Johnston both scored twice in their 4-0 victory, and at Ibrox Rangers scored another six without reply, Johnston claiming a hat-trick.

However, in their second round tie against eventual Cup winners Red Star Belgrade they were up against an entirely different class of opposition. In Belgrade, the pressure on the Scottish side told as early as the eighth minute when defender John Brown nudged a Dusko Radinovic corner past keeper Chris Woods into his own net. Prosinecki added a second in the 65th minute with a swerving free kick, and Pancev made it 3-0 ten minutes later. Back at Ibrox, Pancev scored first early in the second half and Rangers gained a consolation through McCoist with fifteen minutes to go, but the Glasgow club were out of the tournament 4-1 on aggregate.

Northern Ireland's **Portadown** were given a footballing lesson by Porto, losing 5-0 in Portugal and 8-1 at home.

1991

THE FINAL

Red Star win by playing for penalties

Red Star Belgrade 0 (0) Marseille 0 (0) (after extra time)
(Red Star won 5-3 on penalties)

San Nicola Stadium, Bari, 29 May 1991
Attendance: 60,000
Referee: Lanese (Italy)

The futuristic new stadium in the south of Italy played host to a deeply disappointing Final as two of Europe's finest sides cast aside their attacking principles to grind out a tedious goal-less draw.

Red Star, in particular, played with only one striker, the young Darko Pancev, and deployed a defensive midfield of Prosinecki, Savicevic and Binic, with sweeper Belodedic positioned well behind the back four and Najdoski also lying deep. Marseille began with Papin and Waddle up front, but these two creative forwards struggled to make an impact on Red Star's defensive line-up.

Although in the first 15 minutes both teams showed some attacking promise, the game soon developed into a dull and sterile deadlock, with Marseille content to fall back on the offside trap. In the 11th minute, an unmarked Papin drilled a shot across the goal, and a minute later Binic on the counter-attack shot just wide of the post. Although Savicevic and Prosinecki produced the odd flash of inspiration, by half-time the game had become a tactical stalemate.

In the second half, Marseille took the attack to a dogged defence but could not make their dominance pay with a goal. In the 75th minute, 'supersub' Vercruysse came on for Fournier and his free kick was headed wide by Waddle. With six minutes to go, a Prosinecki free kick beat the Marseille wall but went narrowly wide of the post and, in the last minute of normal time, Waddle again headed wide from a long cross by Vercruysse. Extra time produced only one incident of note, when Pele missed with a header from a Waddle chip, and a penalty shoot-out was to decide the winner.

Manuel Amoros' strike, Marseille's first penalty, was saved by keeper Stevan Stojanovic and all the other kicks were converted. Pancev, a solitary figure throughout the game, scored the fifth and winning penalty and a Yugoslavian team had won the European Cup for the first time. After the game, Red Star admitted to playing for penalties from the outset.

Tapie was to rebuild his side, which would reach the Final again in two years time, where controversy awaited.

The teams
Red Star Belgrade: Stojanovic, Belodedic, Najdoski, Sabanadzovic, Jugovic, Marovic, Mihailjlovic, Binic, Savicevic (Stosic), Prosinecki, Pancev (manager: Petrovic)
Marseille: Olmeta, Amoros, Boli, Mozer, Di Meco (Stojkovic), Fournier (Vercruysse), Germain, Casoni, Pele, Papin, Waddle (manager: Goethals)
The penalty shoot-out
Prosinecki, 1-0; Amoros misses, 1-0; Binic, 2-0; Casoni, 2-1; Belodedic, 3-1; Papin, 3-2; Mihailjlovic, 4-2; Mozer, 4-3; Pancev, 5-3

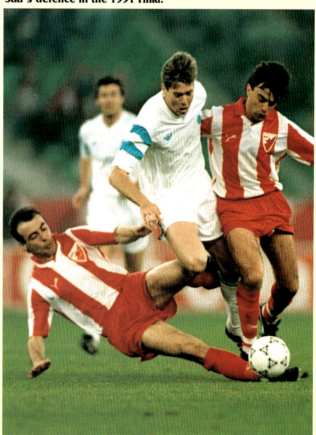
Chris Waddle (white shirt, centre) tries to break through Red Star's defence in the 1991 Final.

From the old port of Genoa, Sampdoria were this year's Italian representatives. Coached by the vastly experienced Yugoslav Vujadin Boskov, and captained by the elegant centre-forward Roberto Mancini, they had won the Italian league. In midfield were two Brazilians, the 37- year-old veteran *libero* Cerezo and Silas, and a Yugoslav, Srecko Katanec, while an international attack force of Gianluca Vialli, Mancini and Attilio Lombardo brought in the goals.

Sampdoria's league form was poor but they began well in Europe. Lombardo scored twice in their first-leg home game against Rosenborg, and Vialli and Mancini added two more in Norway to ensure progress to the next round against Honvéd. Although beaten 2-1 in Hungary, an early goal from Lombardo in Genoa and two more from Vialli booked their passage to the league stage.

Barcelona coach Johan Cruyff had paid CSKA Sofia £2 million in 1990 for striker Hristo Stoichkov, and the Bulgarian's outstanding performances for the club had more than paid off the transfer fee. Stoichkov lined up in attack with Artor Beguiristain, Julio Salinas and Denmark's highly-rated Michael Laudrup, with a midfield containing young local boy Jose Guardiola and Jose Maria Bakero. Spanish international keeper Andoni Zubizarreta, Miguel Nadal and free-kick specialist, centre-back Ronald Koeman, were the defensive bedrock.

A 3-0 first round home win against Hansa Rostock, Laudrup claiming two, allowed the team to survive a surprise 1-0 away defeat. Against German champions Kaiserslautern, who were in the competition for the first time, they won 2-0 in Spain, both coming from Aitor Beguirstain. In the away leg they were three goals down to the determined German side, until Bakero in the last minute headed in a Koeman free-kick, and they were through to the next round on away goals.

With a front line of Brazilian Marques Isaias, Rui Aguas and Sergei Yuran, Benfica were a fast, attacking side. Yuran scored five in their 10-0 aggregate first-round tie against Hamrun Spartans, and in the second round they met Arsenal, the first English club back in the competition since the 1985 ban. A sparkling extra-time performance in the away leg at Highbury put them through 4-2 on aggregate.

Prosinecki had left last year's champions Red Star Belgrade but Savicevic, Mihajlovic and Pancev remained, with Vladimir Jugovic an arrival from the youth team. Thirteen goals in the first two rounds against easy

opponents Portadown and Appollon secured a place in the new league for the Yugoslavs.

Panathinaikos, with their outstanding centre-forward Dimitris Saravakos, suffered a scare in their first round tie against Iceland's Fram Reykjavik, when they could not capitalise on a 2-2 away draw in the home leg. They squeezed through on away goals. In the second round, by half time in Sweden IFK Gothenburg had cancelled out a first leg 2-0 Panathinaikos advantage. However, Saravakos rescued the game for the Greeks with a 60th-minute individual goal and a penalty twenty minutes later, and Panathinaikos were through.

Belgian champions Anderlecht had the young star forward Luc Nilis alongside proven goal scorer Johnny Bosman, and Nilis was to prove the hero in the first round. In a tough home tie against Grasshoppers Zurich, Anderlecht could only achieve a 1-1 draw with midfielder Marc Degryse scoring, but in Zurich an inspired Nilis scored a hat-trick to set the Belgians up against PSV Eindhoven. In Holland, the star-studded PSV could make no headway against Anderlecht and took a 0-0 draw to Belgium. In the tenth minute, Degryse struck again, and Danny Boffin made the tie safe for Anderlecht with a minute to go.

Ex-Czechoslovakian national captain Zdenek Nehoda was now boss of Sparta Prague, a team depleted by the loss of twelve players to Western clubs during the past year. A 1-0 home win over Rangers was overhauled by the Glasgow club at Ibrox, until an extra-time own goal handed the tie to the Czechs on away goals. In the second round against the millionaires of Marseille, Waddle and Papin put the French 3-0 ahead, but two penalties from Petr Vrabec and Roman Kukleta gave Sparta two valuable away goals. In Prague, a Sparta-dominated game saw the fancied French side beaten 2-1, and Sparta qualified for the league.

As with Sparta, Dynamo Kiev had lost several of their star players to Western clubs. In the first round, they put four past HJK Helsinki without reply, and met Brondby in the next round. In the Ukraine, a 77th-minute penalty from Igor Salenko saved them from a 1-0 defeat. In Denmark, Pavel Yakovenko punished an early defensive error, and Kiev held on to win 2-1 on aggregate.

League Qualifiers: Anderlecht, Barcelona, Benfica, Dynamo Kiev, Panathinaikos, Red Star Belgrade, Sampdoria, Sparta Prague.

The New Format 1991/92

For this year's tournament, UEFA decided to experiment with a league system. There were to be the normal first and second round home-and-away knock-out matches, but the third round was to consist of two mini leagues of four clubs each. The clubs were to play each other home and away – a total of six games each – and the winners of each league would meet in the Final.

Although the powerful chairmen of the wealthy clubs – particularly Silvio Berlusconi (AC Milan), Bernard Tapie (Marseille) and Ramon Mendoza (Real Madrid) – had been advocating a league format for some years, this new arrangement was not exactly what they had in mind. Their conception was that the league system would replace the opening rounds, thereby ensuring that the big clubs would not be eliminated by some upstart in the early stages, with a knock-out competition beginning at the quarter-finals.

The new system was, of course, all about maximising the earnings of the super-rich clubs, and it was somewhat ironic that the introduction of the leagues coincided with the banning of AC Milan from European competition as a result of their players' petulant abandonment of last season's match against Marseille. Nor had Real Madrid qualified this year. Other 'big' clubs who did not progress to the leagues this season were Marseille, PSV Eindhoven, Rangers and Arsenal.

GROUP A

Anderlecht, Panathinaikos, Red Star Belgrade, Sampdoria

The first games were on 27 November and 11/12 December. Anderlecht could only draw 0-0 with Panathinaikos at home, and Sampdoria went top with a 2-0 defeat of Red Star, with goals from Mancini and Vialli. In December, Panathinaikos drew 0-0 again, this time against Sampdoria, while Red Star took the lead in the group with a 3-2 win over Anderlecht, Darko Pancev scoring the winner in the 88th minute.

After the winter break, the league recommenced in March. Red Star remained on top after their 2-0 away victory over Panathinaikos, Pancev scoring twice in the last 20 minutes. A thrilling game between Anderlecht and Sampdoria ended 3-2 to the Belgians. Vialli opened the scoring and Degryse equalised in the 53rd minute. Vialli again put Sampdoria in front, but three minutes later a bad back pass by Mannini was picked up by Nilis and the score was 2-2. With two minutes to go, Nilis scored the winner.

Later in the month, two goals from Lambardo and Mancini within two minutes in the first half gave Sampdoria a 2-0 victory over Anderlecht, while a Mihaljovic penalty in the 53rd minute was the difference between Red Star and Panathinaikos. In April, the Panathinaikos and Anderlecht return match produced another goalless draw, and Sampdoria went top of the group with a 3-1 win over Red Star. Mihaljovic scored first, but a Katanec strike and a Vasilijevic own goal put Sampdoria ahead by half time. Mancini made sure of victory in the 76th minute. Sampdoria needed only one point from their home game against Panathinaikos to reach the Final.

In the event, they could have lost and still gone through, as Red Star were beaten 3-2 in Belgium by Anderlecht. Bosman put Anderlecht 2-1 up just before half time and, although Cula equalised in the 82nd minute, Degryse scored the winner two minutes later. The Sampdoria game ended 1-1, and the Italians were in the European Cup Final.

Sampdoria 2	Red Star Belgrade 0
Anderlecht 0	Panathinaikos 0
Panathinaikos 0	Sampdoria 0
Red Star Belgrade 3	Anderlecht 2
Panathinaikos 0	Red Star Belgrade 2
Anderlecht 3	Sampdoria 2
Sampdoria 2	Anderlecht 0
Red Star Belgrade 1	Panathinaikos 0
Panathinaikos 0	Anderlecht 0
Red Star Belgrade 1	Sampdoria 3
Anderlecht 3	Red Star Belgrade 2
Sampdoria 1	Panathinaikos 1

	P	W	D	L	F	A	Pts
Sampdoria	6	3	2	1	10	5	8
Red Star Belgrade	6	3	0	3	9	10	6
Anderlecht	6	2	2	2	8	9	6
Panathinaikos	6	0	4	2	1	4	4

GROUP B

Barcelona, Benfica, Dynamo Kiev, Sparta Prague

In Spain, Barcelona were down to ten men within twenty minutes after Guillermo Amor was sent off, but they beat Sparta Prague 3-2 with goals from Amor, Laudrup and Bakero. A Salenko goal in the Ukraine gave Kiev victory over Benfica. In December, Benfica were held to a goalless draw in Lisbon by Barcelona, while Sparta overcame Kiev 2-1.

In a snowstorm in the Ukraine in early March, Barcelona and Kiev produced a fast and furious game, with Stoichkov in magnificent form. His speed, passing and movement stretched the Kiev defence and he opened the scoring with a 20-yard, left-foot rocket in the 33rd minute. Substitute Julio Salinas doubled the scoreline 30 minutes later with his first touch of the game from a sweet pass from Guardiola. Benfica and Sparta played out a 1-1 draw in Lisbon, with defender Jiri Novotny's 31st-minute goal equalised by a Pacheco penalty just after the interval. Later in the month, two goals from Stoichkov and one from Salinas defeated Kiev 3-0, while Sparta and Benfica scored one each in Prague.

In April, Cesar Brito and Yurian both scored twice in Benfica's 5-0 hammering of Kiev in Portugal, while a Horst Siegl goal was the difference between Sparta and Barcelona. This defeat left Barcelona needing one point from their last game, against Benfica at the Nou Camp, to win the group.

One hundred and fifteen thousand fans watched a stuttering, nervous performance by the Spanish champions. Stoichkov latched on to a Ze Carlos miskick to beat the keeper in the 12th minute, and crossed from the by-line for Bakero to score twelve minutes later. Although playing with an extra defender, Barcelona let in Cesar Brito to score for Benfica in the 28th minute, and they then settled down in defence. The game ended 2-1, and Barcelona were to meet Sampdoria in the Final. Although Kiev beat Sparta with a late Salenko goal in the other match, played before a crowd of only 3,000, the result was academic.

Barcelona 3	Sparta Prague 2
Dynamo Kiev 1	Benfica 0
Sparta Prague 2	Dynamo Kiev 1
Benfica 0	Barcelona 0
Dynamo Kiev 0	Barcelona 2
Benfica 1	Sparta Prague 1
Sparta Prague 1	Benfica 1
Barcelona 3	Dynamo Kiev 0
Sparta Prague 1	Barcelona 0
Benfica 5	Dynamo Kiev 0
Dynamo Kiev 1	Sparta Prague 0
Barcelona 2	Benfica 1

	P	W	D	L	F	A	Pts
Barcelona	6	4	1	1	10	4	9
Sparta Prague	6	2	2	2	7	7	6
Benfica	6	1	3	2	8	5	5
Dynamo Kiev	6	2	0	4	3	12	4

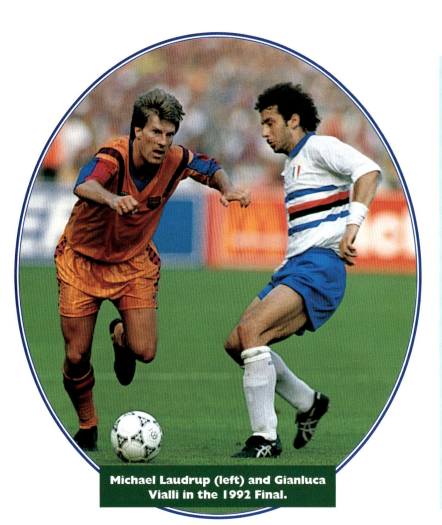

Michael Laudrup (left) and Gianluca Vialli in the 1992 Final.

Michael Laudrup (1964). Denmark's most capped outfield player with 104 international appearances, elegant midfielder Laudrup began his career with Brondby and went to Juventus in 1984. In 1989, he moved to Barcelona and his perceptive passing and attacking skills helped Barca to their first European Cup victory in 1992 and to four consecutive Spanish league titles. He then transferred to Real Madrid and, in 1996, to Japanese side Vissel Kobe. He played in the 1986, 1990 and 1998 World Cup finals, although he missed out on Denmark's 1992 European Championship triumph after a dispute with the Danish coach.

Gianluca Vialli (1964). Vialli is one of the top strikers in the history of Italian football. He moved from Cremonese to Sampdoria in 1984, striking up a lethal partnership with Roberto Mancini. After Sampdoria lost to Barcelona in the 1992 European Cup Final, he transferred to Juventus for a world record £12 million and captained the club to victory in the 1996 European Cup Final, beating Ajax on penalties. That year he joined Chelsea and, after the departure of Ruud Gullit, he was appointed manager of the club. In 1998 he guided Chelsea to victory over Stuttgart in the European Cup Winners Cup Final. He made 59 appearances for Italy.

BRITISH CLUBS

Towards the end of the previous season, Graham Souness had left **Rangers** to take over as manager of Liverpool and had been replaced by his assistant Walter Smith. The club still had a large complement of English players, including new arrival Mark Hateley, who had scored the two goals against Aberdeen which ensured the league title came to Ibrox and who had established a prolific goal-scoring partnership with Ally McCoist. Centre-back Oleg Kuznetsov had arrived from Dynamo Kiev and Alexi Mikhailichenko had been recruited from Sampdoria for £2 million. Rangers were a cosmopolitan team of internationals but they had yet to prove themselves in Europe's premier competition.

Drawn against Sparta Prague in the first round, they went down 1-0 in Prague to an early Nemec goal. At Ibrox, a 48th-minute goal from midfielder Stuart McCall took the tie into extra time. McCall scored again early in the first period, but an own goal from Rangers' Scott Nisbet meant that Prague qualified for the next round on away goals and Rangers were again eliminated at an early stage.

Arsenal approached their first European tournament for nine years with justifiable confidence. They had won the league by seven points over Liverpool, and manager George Graham's side was strong, skilful and well-organised. The defence – Lee Dixon, Tony Adams, Steve Bould and Nigel Winterburn – was the tightest in the country. The forwards, particularly the tall striker Alan Smith, Kevin Campbell and Paul Merson, were adept at converting the chances created by midfielders Michael Thomas, Paul Davis and David Rocastle. Swedish winger Anders Limpar provided the pace and crosses, and frequently found his way onto the scoresheet.

FK Austria came to Highbury in the first round and were humbled by the rampant Gunners. Stand-in centre-back Andy Linighan scored first, and at half time the score was 1-0. However, within 16 minutes in the second half marksman Smith scored four goals and Limpar sealed a fine Arsenal display with another goal ten minutes from time. Arsenal lost the return 1-0 to a Stoger penalty, but were to meet Benfica in round two.

In the Stadium of Light, an early strike from the Brazilian forward Isaias was countered by a well-taken Campbell goal, and the score remained 1-1, potentially a good result for Arsenal. Back at Highbury, a 20th-minute goal from utility defender Colin Pates was equalised by a 25-yard volley by Isaias and the aggregate score remained 2-2 at the end of normal time. In extra time, Benfica began to take advantage of a tiring Arsenal defence, and Vasili Kulkov put the Portuguese side ahead in the 100th minute. A superb piece of skill ten minutes later from Isaias caught the Arsenal defence flat, and the score was an irretrievable 3-1 to Benfica.

Portadown had the bad luck to draw Red Star Belgrade in the first round, and an 8-0 aggregate defeat was about the best the Northern Irish side could have hoped for.

Koeman strikes for Barca's first European Cup

Barcelona (0) 1   Sampdoria (0) 0

Wembley Stadium, London, 20 May 1992
Attendance: 70,000
Referee: Schmidhüber (Germany)

Barcelona, for all the club's reputation and charisma, had never won the European Cup, and Sampdoria at Wembley were the final obstacle to Barca's 30-year quest for the trophy. Sampdoria were about to lose Vialli to Juventus, coach Boskov to Roma and Cerezo to retirement, and they hoped to crown their European achievements this year before the team disintegrated. In front of a passionate, mainly Catalan 70,000 crowd, the teams took to the field.

Barcelona kicked off, in an unfamiliar orange strip, and immediately attacked, with Sampdoria happy to stay in defence. Cerezo was subduing little Bakero, and Pari and Mannini were staying close to Laudrup and Stoichkov. In the 22nd minute, Vialli and Mancini organised a counter-attack, with Pagliuca saving nimbly from Lombardo and, a minute later, a Stoichkov header brought out the best from Pagliuca. Sampdoria were playing a physical game, with Mannini earning a yellow card for up-ending Laudrup. The first half ended with neither side scoring.

The pace of the game increased in the second half and Sampdoria moved on the offensive. Vialli untypically missed two good chances, hitting over the bar and then wide, and at the other end a beautiful drive from Stoichkov beat Pagliuca but smashed back off the post. As the game neared the end, both sides became frustrated and a bad tackle on Cerezo by Bakero produced a brief skirmish. Mancini should have done better with his free kick with six minutes to go, and Barcelona substitute Goicoechea had his shot saved in the 86th minute. At the end of normal time, there was still no score.

In extra time, Renato Buso came on for Vialli to run at a tired-looking Barcelona, although the best chance in the first period fell to Stoichkov whose shot was well saved by the impressive Pagliuca. In the 110th minute, Barcelona won a controversial free kick just outside the penalty area when the referee penalised a seemingly legitimate challenge by substitute Invernezzi on Eusebio. Spot-kick expert Koeman stepped up and, receiving a short pass from Bakero, unleashed an unstoppable, ferocious rocket of a shot high into the net beyond Pagliuca. There was time for just two more Stoichkov efforts until the whistle blew and Barcelona were champions.

The delighted Barcelona players pulled on their traditional maroon and blue shirts to receive the trophy. The club had finally broken their European hoodoo after so many years of disappointment and failure. Cruyff, who had now won the competition as player and manager, commented, 'It's been a great night because it's been such a long time coming', while a euphoric Koeman added, 'That was the most important goal of my life'.

The teams
Barcelona: Zubizeretta, Ferrer, Nando, Koeman, Juan Carlos Moreno, Eusebio, Guardiola (Alexanco), Bakero, Laudrup, Salinas (Goicoechea), Stoichkov (manager: Cruyff) [Koeman 110]
Sampdoria: Pagliuca, Mannini, Lanna, Vierchowod, Katanec, Lombardo, Pari, Cerezo, Bonetti (Invernizzi), Mancini, Vialli (Buso) (manager: Boskov)

Ronald Koeman's rocket shot flies into Sampdoria's net for Barcelona's winning goal in the 1992 Final.

Jean-Pierre Papin had joined the exodus to AC Milan and Chris Waddle had gone back home to England, but Marseilles had strength in depth. The arrival from Roma of German international striker Rudi Voller to partner Alen Boksic and Pele was some compensation for the loss of the two star forwards. Midfield anchormen Didier Deschamps and Frank Sauzee combined with central defenders Basile Boli and Marcel Desailly to frustrate the opposition, and 72-year-old coach Raymond Goethals was back in charge again to provide the tactical experience. After an 8-0 routing of Northern Ireland's Glentoran, Croatian winger Boksic scored the two goals in Marseille against Dynamo Bucharest which took the club into the league stage.

AC Milan were, by common consent, virtually unbeatable. Berlusconi had dug deep and had acquired not only Papin but also, for a world record fee of £13 million, Torino forward Gianluigi Lentini, a transaction which provoked rioting in Turin by the faithful. The hugely-expensive, multi-national team was bolstered by the arrival of Dejan Savicevic from Red Star and Fernando De Napoli from Naples. Already in place were the three Dutchmen – Gullit, Van Basten and Rijkaard – with Croatia's Zvonimir Boban also vying for inclusion. Although coach Fabio Capello had permutations which were the envy of all European managers, UEFA's 'three foreigners' rule meant that some of the finest players in world football sat unhappily on the bench. However, Capello's side had won the Italian league without losing a single game and were favourites to become European champions again this year. Olympia Ljubliana were brushed aside 7-0 in the first round. A 5-0 aggregate win over Slovan Bratislava, who had earlier eliminated Hungary's Ferencvaros, ensured Milan's appearance in the third round.

Holland's PSV Eindhoven had won their sixth league title in seven years. Veteran keeper Hans Van Breukelen and Adri Van Tiggelen oversaw the defence, now without retired full-back Eric Gerets, and Romanian Gica Popescu was the midfield provider. Vim Kieft and Romario scored the goals. The petulant and erratic Brazilian demonstrated his value to an often exasperated PSV management by scoring a hat-trick against AEK Athens in Holland to put PSV into the league round.

CSKA Moscow, the Russian army team, were to prove the surprise of the tournament. Like many of the other formerly Eastern bloc clubs, several of their top players had moved to Western Europe. However, with Dimitri Kharin in goal, the versatile and attacking defender Sergei Kolotvkin, and forwards Oleg Sergeyev and Dimitri Karsakov, CSKA were well equipped to hold their own in the competition. In the first round they defeated Iceland's Vikingur 5-2 and faced Barcelona in the second.

A late goal from Amor had saved Barcelona embarrassment at home in the first-round first leg against modest Viking Stavanger, and they could only scramble a 0-0 draw in Norway. CSKA held Barca 1-1 in the first leg in Moscow, but were two down, to Nadal and Beguiristain, within half an hour at the Nou Camp. However, a spirited rally from CSKA halfway through the game produced goals from Yevgeni Bushmanov, Denis Masharin and Karsakov, and Barcelona crashed out of the competition. Against all the odds, CSKA progressed to the league section.

Bruges were now without a retired Ceuleman, but eased past Israel's Maccabi Tel Aviv 4-0 in the first round, the goals coming from Staelens and Verheyen. FK Austria proved tougher opposition, but Bruges survived a 3-1 defeat in Austria to go through on away goals.

Although IFK Gothenburg were making a bad start to their domestic season, the midfield influence of Stefan Rehn, the goalkeeping of multi-capped Thomas Ravelli and the goals of striker Johnny Ekstrom had won the club the Swedish 'double'. An early goal from Eskelinen in the return leg against Turkey's Besiktas in the first round was enough to put the Swedes through to meet Poland's Lech Poznan. IFK took a 1-0 lead to Poland and scored a further three – from Ekstrom and strikers Mikael Nillsen and Hakan Mild – without reply to reach the group stage.

Rangers did well to beat Lyngby 3-0 in the first round, and they asserted the temporary primacy of Scottish football over the English variety with a fine away win at Elland Road which put the Glasgow club into the group stage. The eighth club to qualify were Portuguese champions Porto, who had a relatively easy passage with a 9-1 hammering of US Luxembourg and a clinical demolition of Switzerland's Sion, winning the tie 6-2 on aggregate.

League Qualifiers: Bruges, CSKA Moscow, IFK Gothenburg, Marseille, AC Milan, Porto, PSV and Rangers.

Champions League 1992/93

For this year's league, the rules had changed slightly. Instead of using overall goal difference in the event of a tie between the top two clubs in each league, as was the case last year, the winner was to be selected on the basis of the results between the two tied sides. So, high scores against the other two clubs would make no difference to the final placings unless the top two team's scores against each other were equal.

Bernard Tapie, millionaire businessman and owner of Marseille.

GROUP A

Bruges, CSKA Moscow, Marseilles, Rangers

Rangers began their league campaign with a 2-2 home draw against Marseilles, coming back from 2-0 down, and Bruges' Daniel Amokachi scored and inspired his team to a 1-0 win over poverty-stricken CSKA Moscow. In December, Rangers played CSKA in Germany and escaped with a 1-0 victory over a determined Russian side. Marseille, without Voller and Boli, entertained Bruges and were three up within the first 26 minutes. Frank Sauzee scored a penalty in the fourth minute, and Alen Boksic netted two more to make the final score 3-0.

In March in Belgium, a makeshift Rangers side produced a gritty and memorable performance to draw 1-1, while in Marseille CSKA scored through a brilliant individual goal from winger Iishat Faizulin in the 58th minute and Pele equalised with twenty minutes to go to make the score 1-1. Two weeks later, Rangers met Bruges again at Ibrox and a goalkeeping error allowed the Scots to come away with a 2-1 victory. The same evening a rampant Marseille put six past CSKA with Sauzee claiming a hat-trick.

In April, with the winner of the game poised to go through to the Final, Marseille faced Rangers in France, but an exceptional goal from Ian Durrant gave Rangers a deserved draw and meant that the Group A Finalist would not be known until the last game. Bruges and CSKA, meanwhile, both out of contention, played in Germany where an 18th-minute goal from Sergeyev was countered with two from Bruges, Schaessens and Verheyen doing the damage.

The league was down to the wire in the last games in April. Marseille took on Bruges in Belgium, where the home side had not lost a European game for four years, with the French knowing that a win would get them to the Final. Even if Rangers also won, Marseille would still go through as they had a better record because of their two away goals at Ibrox. Bruges were determined to make a fight of it, partly because of their antipathy to Marseille's coach Goethals and his reluctance when Belgian national coach to pick Bruges players. However, they were lacking the influential Frankie Van der Elst, and Boksic scored the crucial goal bending a shot around keeper Verlinden to put Marseille into the Final. Rangers, with striker Ally McCoist completely off form, could only manage a draw against a young CSKA side at Ibrox.

Bruges 1		CSKA 0	
Rangers 2		Marseille 2	
CSKA 0		Rangers 1	
Marseille 3		Bruges 0	
Bruges 1		Rangers 1	
CSKA 1		Marseille 1	
Marseille 6		CSKA 0	
Rangers 2		Bruges 1	
Marseille 1		Rangers 1	
CSKA 1		Bruges 2	
Bruges 0		Marseille 1	
Rangers 0		CSKA 0	

	P	W	D	l	F	A	Pts
Marseille	6	3	3	0	14	4	9
Rangers	6	2	4	0	7	5	8
Bruges	6	2	1	3	5	8	5
CSKA Moscow	6	0	2	4	2	11	2

GROUP B

IFK Gothenburg, AC Milan, Porto, PSV Eindhoven

AC Milan began the round-robin in devastating form. In November against IFK, they played with skill and panache, beating the Swedes 4-0 in Milan. All four came from the European Footballer of the Year, Marco Van Basten, including a marvellous overhead volley from the edge of the penalty box. Porto drew 2-2 with PSV in Portugal, Romario scoring twice for the Dutch club.

The next month saw another sparkling performance from Milan, this time against PSV. Rijkaard opened the scoring in the 19th minute and Simone added another in the second half. A brilliant Romario goal in the 66th minute made no difference to the outcome, and Milan maintained a 100% record in the tournament. The same night, a late strike from Peter Eriksson gave IFK a 1-0 win over Porto.

In the spring, Papin from a Simone cross sealed a 1-0 win for Milan away against Porto, while two goals from Ekstrom and one from Nilsson were IFK's response to Arthur Numan's opening goal for PSV. Later in March, Eranio scored the only goal of the game for Milan in Portugal, and IFK scored another three against the disappointing Dutchmen, now propping up the foot of the table with one point.

Milan continued their winning streak in April with a 1-0 away defeat of IFK. Although domestically off form, they were simply too classy for the Swedes and, even without the injured Van Basten, suspended Baresi, Albertini and Eranio and dropped Gullit and Papin, they progressed with a left-foot volley from Daniele Massaro in the 71st minute. The same evening in Holland a 77th-minute penalty from Jose Carlos gave Porto victory over PSV.

With Milan now through to the Final, and still carrying a 100% record for the tournament, a largely meaningless 2-0 win at the San Siro against PSV confirmed PSV's place as bottom club with one point, and Porto achieved some respectability with a 2-0 victory in Portugal over IFK.

Milan 4		IFK Gothenburg 0	
Porto 2		PSV 2	
IFK 1		Porto 0	
PSV 1		Milan 2	
PSV 1		IFK 3	
Porto 0		Milan 1	
IFK 3		PSV 0	
Milan 1		Porto 0	
IFK 0		Milan 1	
PSV 0		Porto 1	
Milan 2		PSV 0	
Porto 2		IFK 0	

	P	W	D	l	F	A	Pts
Milan	6	6	0	0	11	1	12
IFK	6	3	0	3	7	8	6
Porto	6	2	1	3	5	5	5
PSV	6	0	1	5	4	13	1

Marseille keeper Fabien Barthez plucks the ball from the feet of AC Milan's Jean-Pierre Papin during the 1993 Final.

BRITISH CLUBS

Under the managership of the deadpan, tactically astute Howard Wilkinson, **Leeds United** had won their first English league title for eighteen years. Inspired by their fiery Scottish midfield captain, Gordon Strachan, and by the enigmatic mastery of Frenchman Eric Cantona, they had beaten Alex Ferguson's re-emergent Manchester United by four points. Another Scottish midfielder, Gary McAllister, provided the class and polish and he was ably complemented by Yorkshire midfielder David Batty, a tough, defensive battler. The tall, instinctive striker Lee Chapman and the speedy Rod Wallace played up front.

In the first round, they travelled to Stuttgart to play the German champions. New signing David Rocastle really should have scored in the first half, and the game was goalless until the 63rd minute when Fritz Walter put Stuttgart ahead. Shortly after, a misdirected pass from Eric Cantona let Walter in for another, and in the 82nd minute, Andreas Buck made it 3-0 in the Germans' favour. The tie now seemed out of Leeds' grasp.

At Elland Road in the return leg, Leeds displayed all the skill and determination which had marked their progress to the title, but four late goals – from midfielder Gary Speed, McAllister, Cantona and Chapman – could not cancel out the effect of Buck's 34th-minute goal for Stuttgart, and Stuttgart went through on away goals. However, it was pointed out after the game that the Germans had mistakenly and inadvertently fielded four 'foreign' players instead of the maximum of three.

Amid much controversy, Leeds were awarded the game 3-0, and so a replay was necessary. The two sides faced each other again at the Nou Camp in front of a tiny crowd of 7,000, and a goal apiece from Strachan and substitute Carl Shutt put Leeds through to the second round 2-1 to meet Scottish champions Rangers.

Rangers had won the Scottish Cup and the league by nine points, and were unassailable in Scotland. The prodigious goalscoring of Mark Hateley and Ally McCoist, and the midfield pairing of Stuart McCall and Ian Durrant, were important factors in the Glasgow club's success. The authority of keeper Andy Goram and the dominating figure of centre-half and captain Richard Gough kept the team tight and confident in defence. They had beaten Danish side Lyngby 2-0 at Ibrox, with goals from Hateley and Dutch winger Peter Huistra, and 1-0 in Denmark, and they awaited Leeds at Ibrox for the first leg.

Leeds opened the scoring with a beautifully-taken McAllister volley within the first minute but, in the 21st minute, Leeds keeper John Lukic appeared dazzled by the floodlights and punched the ball into his own net from a high cross. Fifteen minutes later, McCoist fired Rangers ahead, and the score stayed at 2-1. At Elland Road, Hateley scored another well-executed volley early in the game and in the 59th minute a diving header from McCoist put the Scots 2-0 up. A clever Cantona strike five minutes from time was too late to save the Yorkshire side, and Rangers progressed to the league stage.

RANGERS 1992/93

Rangers opened their challenge against Marseille in the pouring rain at Ibrox on 25 November. The French side dominated the game, displaying superior skill, possession and technique, and with just over ten minutes to go were two goals ahead. A left-wing cross from Voller to Boksic was snapped up by the Croatian, and an error by Rangers defender Pressley presented Voller with a simple chance. However, Mikhailichenko, having an otherwise poor game, crossed from the left in the 70th minute and young substitute Gary McSwegan nodded past keeper Barthez with his first touch of the game. Three minutes later, Hateley completed an unexpected but spirited Rangers fight-back with a header from a Durrant cross.

In December, Rangers travelled to Bochum in Germany to play CSKA, a 'home' game for the Russians because of the wintry conditions in Moscow. Keeper Dimitri Kharin had left, amid acrimony, to join Chelsea and was replaced by Guteyev. For the first 30 minutes CSKA were technically the superior side, even although a mistake by Guteyev allowed Ian Ferguson to score in the 13th minute. In the second half Rangers took over the game and, although Karsakov and Sergeyev were outstanding, CSKA could not find their way through the Rangers defence.

The league resumed in March with Rangers away to Bruges. The Belgians were missing Stephan Van der Heyden and international defender Pascal Plovie, and deployed a five-man midfield against the Scots, for whom Stuart McCall was inspiring. Just before the interval, a mishit clearance from Mikhailichenko allowed Tomasz Dziubinski in to score. In the second half Rangers fought back and were rewarded when McCall found Peter Huistra in space in the 74th minute. The Dutch winger made no mistake with his shot.

Later in the month, Bruges visited Ibrox. Van der Heyden was in the Belgian side and Rangers had Richard Gough back from injury. In the 39th minute, Gary Stevens played a through ball to Durrant whose shot evaded keeper Dany Verlinden to put Rangers one up, but Hateley was sent off just before the interval for raising an arm to an opponent. Shortly after half time Lorenzo Staelens equalised, but a 71st-minute speculative, deflected cross from right-back Scott Nisbet deceived Verlinden. The game ended 2-1 to Rangers.

Three weeks later, Rangers were in the south of France for a crucial tie against Marseille. Whichever side won would qualify for the Final. Early in the game, 33-year-old Rudi Voller capitalised on a bad error by David Robertson to find Frank Sauzee on the edge of the box, and Sauzee's right-foot volley sped past Andy Goram. Shortly after, McCoist spurned a golden opportunity to even the score. However, a glorious right-foot volley by Ian Durrant in the 52nd minute levelled the game, and the score remained 1-1 until the final whistle.

Everything now depended on the last two games. If both teams won, Marseille would qualify thanks to their superior away-goal tally against Rangers. Rangers could only try to win at home to CSKA and hope that Marseille slipped up against Bruges in Belgium. At Ibrox, without the suspended Hateley, Rangers went on the offensive against a young, inexperienced CSKA side. However, striker Ally McCoist, with 52 domestic goals to his credit in the season, failed to convert several easy chances in the first half, and new keeper Plotnikov added to Rangers' frustration with a series of fine saves. As news came through that Alen Boksic had scored for Marseille, Rangers' play became more frantic but they could not dent the Russian defence.

Rangers' brave attempt to reach the European Cup Final had collapsed at the final hurdle.

Ally McCoist (blue shirt, centre) fires home Rangers' winner in the second-round, first-leg game against Leeds at Ibrox.

Match-fixing scandal rocks football

After the Final, in a scandal which rocked European football, the allegations of match-fixing details came under investigation by the French police and UEFA. Marseille representatives had allegedly paid three players from French club Valenciennes to 'take it easy' in a league game just before the Final, and the resulting 1-0 victory gave them the league title. In September Marseille were banned from European football just a few days before they were due to play AEK Athens and their place was taken by Monaco. UEFA's president Lennart Johansson stated that the decision was taken 'to protect the integrity of our competitions'. The French Football Association also relegated Marseille to the Second Division. Jean-Jacques Eydelie was banned for life, a ban subsequently rescinded, for his part in the affair, while club chairman Bernard Tapie eventually ended up in prison.

Didier Deschamps (1968). Famously derided by Eric Cantona as a 'water carrier', tough little midfielder Deschamps played for Nantes from 1985 to 1989, and he won two European Cup winner's medals with Marseille in 1993 and Juventus in 1996. He was also on the losing side on two Finals, in 1997 and 1998. He is currently playing for Chelsea, with whom he won the European Cup Winners Cup in 1998. He has been capped over 90 times by France, making his international debut in 1989 against Yugoslavia, and he was captain of the French team which won the World Cup in 1998.

1993

THE FINAL

Boli brings Cup to Tapie

Marseille (1) 1 AC Milan (0) 0

Olympic Stadium, Munich, 26 May 1993
Attendance: 72,000
Referee: Rothlisberger (Switzerland)

The two multi-millionaire moguls of European football – Silvio Berlusconi and Bernard Tapie – took their seats in Munich's Olympic Stadium as their massively talented and expensively-assembled teams began the 1993 Final.

Marseille, captained by Didier Deschamps, lined up amid rumours of match-fixing, details of which were to be publicly revealed in the coming weeks. Capello preferred Massaro to Papin as striking partner for Van Basten, starting only his third game of the year due to ankle injury. Rijkaard was in the team, although he had shaken his colleagues that morning with his statement that he would shortly be leaving the club. Ruud Gullit was not even on the bench. Favourites Milan's league form had recently dipped but they had won all their ten games on the way to the Final and, with Parma having won the Cup Winners Cup and Juventus the UEFA Cup, were seeking to secure an Italian 'treble' in Europe.

A first half-hour dominated by Milan saw Massaro squander two early chances, one from Donadoni and another from the injured Van Basten who was lying deep to create space for his fellow forwards. Gradually, however, Marseille began to make their presence felt, and Sauzee and Deschamps were cutting off the balls to the dangerous Milan forwards and causing the Italians problems in midfield. A Voller shot came off keeper Sebastiano Rossi's legs and a Boksic effort went narrowly over the bar. In the 43rd minute, defender Basile Boli came upfield for an Abedi Pele corner and, as the ball came over, Boli soared above the Milan defence to send a powerful header past Rossi into the Milan net.

After the interval, Van Basten missed a simple chance in the 48th minute when he fluffed a left-foot shot from eight yards out. Six minutes later Papin came on for a disappointing Donadoni and shot just wide of Barthez's post in the 77th minute. In the 83rd minute Massaro just failed to reach a Van Basten cross, and three minutes later an obviously unhappy Van Basten was replaced by Eranio. Milan's substitutions,

however, were too late to influence the course of the game which had been cleverly masterminded by Raymond Goethals and, at the final whistle, Marseilles had become the first French team ever to win the European Cup.

An embarrassed Berlusconi reached again for his cheque book. Milan would be back next season, and in style.

The teams
Marseille: Barthez, Angloma (Durand), Boli, Desailly, Pele, Eydelie, Sauzee, Deschamps, Di Meco, Boksic, Voller (Thomas) (manager: Goethals) [Boli 43]
AC Milan: Rossi, Tassotti, Costacurta, Baresi, Maldini, Donadoni (Papin), Rijkaard, Albertini, Lentini, Van Basten (Eranio), Massaro (manager: Capello)

Boli (white shirt) rises above the Milan defence to head the goal.

Gullit and Rijkaard left AC Milan in the summer, and Van Basten's career was effectively over due to injury, but Berlusconi had again dug deep to acquire midfielder Brian Laudrup from Fiorentina and Romanian striker Florin Raducioiu from Brescia. The team was strengthened by the arrival of Christian Panucci for £7 million from Genoa and Marcel Desailly from Marseille. This now meant that Milan had seven foreigners in the squad, a situation described as 'mad' by the unhappy and under-used Savicevic. However, Capello's belief in the rotation system was to be vindicated this year. An uneasy 1-0 win over Swiss side FC Aarau was followed by a 7-0 dispatching of FC Copenhagen, Papin scoring three, and Milan were in the league.

Barcelona had offloaded a disappointing Richard Witschge to Bordeaux, but had brought in 27-year-old Romario from PSV for £3 million. The prolific striker Stoichkov had scored the goal against Real Sociedad which had given Barcelona their third consecutive league title. In the first round, a surprising 3-1 defeat away by Dynamo Kiev was overturned in the Nou Camp 4-1. Then FK Austria, who had scraped through against Rosenborg, suffered a 3-0 defeat in Spain while Stoichkov added two more in the return leg to give Barcelona a 5-1 victory and entry to the group stage.

Monaco's intelligent and respected manager Arsène Wenger had bought Enzo Scifo from Torino to add to the striking power of Youri Djorkaeff, Ipkeba, and the German international forward Jürgen Klinsmann. Entering the tournament at the last minute because of the expulsion of Marseille, they knocked out AEK Athens 2-1 in the first round. Two goals each at home from Ipkeba and Klinsmann put paid to Steaua Bucharest in the next round.

Werder Bremen had beaten Bayern Munich by one point to win the German league. Otto Rehhagel's team was an international one, with Austrian midfield playmaker Andy Herzog, Norwegian *libero* Rune Bratseth and New Zealand centre-forward Wynton Rufer creating the chances. Midfielder Mario Basler had joined in the summer from Hertha Berlin. A 6-3 aggregate win over Dynamo Minsk, Byelorussia's first entrant into the competition, drew

Romario

Werder against Bulgaria's Levski Sofia, eliminators of Rangers, in the second round. Werder were lucky to come away from Sofia with a 2-2 draw but a 73rd-minute goal from Basler in Bremen ensured their presence in the league.

Starting the tournament without the injured Marc Degryse, but with Nilis and Bosman in scoring form, Anderlecht were hardly troubled by Finland's HJK Helsinki in a 6-0 aggregate win in the opening round. A 74th-minute goal from Nilis gave them a 1-0 away win against Sparta Prague, and two more from Nilis at home contributed to a 4-2 win and a 5-2 aggregate.

An 8-0 away win had given Galatasaray the Turkish title on goal difference. Hakan Sukur had signed a new contract and linked up with Kubilay Turkyilmax in attack. Underdogs in the competition, they struggled against Cork City in the first round, but came away with a 3-1 aggregate victory. At Old Trafford in the second round, a poor Manchester United performance resulted in a 3-3 draw, and a goal-less draw in Istanbul put them into the league stage on away goals.

Spartak Moscow manager Oleg Romantsev was resigned to his best players moving westwards, but his 19-year-old top scorer Vladimir Beschastnykh and playmakers Victor Onopko and Igor Lediakhov were to remain with the club for the competition. They crushed Latvia's Skonto Riga 9-0 in the first round, and a 5-1 defeat of Lech Poznan, with two goals apiece for Onopko and Nikolai Pisarev, rendered the second leg a formality.

The eighth club to reach the group stage was Portugal's FC Porto, now managed by ex-Benfica coach Tomislav Ivic. A 2-0 defeat of lowly Maltese side Floriana matched them against powerful Feyenoord in the second round. A last-minute goal from Domingos Oliveira gave them a 1-0 victory in Portugal, and an excellent defensive display by Porto in Holland produced a goal-less draw.

Romario (da Souza Faria) *(1966).*
Temperamental and controversial Brazilian striker Romario joined PSV Eindhoven from Vasco De Gama in 1989 and scored some memorable and important goals in his total of 125 for the Dutch club. He was transferred to Barcelona in 1993 for £3 million and played in Barca's 1994 European Cup Final defeat by AC Milan. He gained 62 caps for Brazil, and his five goals in the 1994 World Cup finals, including the only goal in the semi-final against Sweden, helped Brazil to lift the trophy. After the tournament, he had a spell at Valencia and returned home to play for Flamengo and Vasco Da Gama.

League Qualifiers: AC Milan, Anderlecht, Barcelona, Galatasaray, Monaco, Porto, Spartak Moscow, Werder Bremen

Barcelona, Galatasaray, Monaco, Spartak Moscow

On 24 November Barcelona travelled, with some trepidation, to Galatasary for their opening game. Fined by Cruyff for their defeat the previous Saturday by bottom-placed Lerida, the players were greeted with 'No Exit' placards, an extremely hostile crowd and 2,500 police officers on duty at the Ali Sam Yen Stadium. The Turks, beaten at home only once in the last ten years of European competition, managed to hold Barca to a 0-0 draw.

The same evening in France, Monaco put four past Spartak Moscow, with Klinsmann and Ikpeba scoring in the first half, Igor Pisarev giving Spartak some hope in the 49th minute, and a Djorkaeff penalty and a last-minute goal by Lilian Thuram emphasising Monaco's superiority.

Two weeks later, Barcelona took on Monaco at the Nou Camp, and two first-half goals by Beguiristain underlined the Spanish side's dominance. Koeman could even afford to miss an 89th-minute penalty, a rare experience for such a master of the spot kick. In a grim battle in Moscow, Spartak had Victor Onopko and Ramiz Mamedov sent off and Galatasaray had a 20-minute spell against nine men but could still not score. Galatasaray defender Reinhardt Stumpf then also received his marching orders, and the game finished goal-less.

In early March, Barcelona met Spartak in freezing temperatures in Moscow, and Stoichkov and Romario put Barca two ahead with 25 minutes to go. However, a fightback led by Spartak captain Igor Lediakov saw Rodianov capitalise on his captain's neat flick to score in the 77th minute, and Valery Karpin sealed the draw with two minutes to go. In Monaco, Galatasaray had their striker Turkyilmaz injured and Stumpf suspended, and fell to goals from Scifo, Djorkaeff and Klinsmann. The victory put Monaco on top of the table on goal difference from Barcelona.

Their next two games, however, saw Barcelona assume the league leadership. They crushed 5-1 Spartak at the Nou Camp and, though Spartak went ahead through an early Karpin goal, a Stoichkov equaliser in the 34th minute and four more – from Amor, Koeman (twice) and Romario in the last 15 minutes – ended the semi-final hopes of the Russians. Then a home 3-0 victory over Galatasaray, provided by Amor, Koeman and Eusebio, gave Barca eight points from five games and qualification for the semi-finals.

Meanwhile, in Istanbul two second-half goals from Scifo and Gnako had also finished off Galatasaray's hopes of qualifying and ensured that Monaco went through with Barcelona to the semi-finals.

In the sixth and final league meetings, a crowd of only 11,000 watched Galatasaray succumb at home 2-1 to Spartak in a meaningless encounter. In Monaco, a well-weighted pass from Guardiola put Stoichkov through to score in the 14th minute, and give Barcelona a three-point lead in the group.

Monaco 4		Spartak 1	
Galatasaray 0		Barcelona 0	
Barcelona 2		Monaco 0	
Spartak 0		Galatasaray 0	
Monaco 3		Galatasaray 0	
Spartak 2		Barcelona 2	
Barcelona 5		Spartak 1	
Galatasaray 0		Monaco 2	
Barcelona 3		Galatasaray 0	
Spartak 0		Monaco 0	
Monaco 0		Barcelona 1	
Galatasaray 1		Spartak 2	

	P	W	D	L	F	A	Pts
Barcelona	6	4	2	0	13	3	10
Monaco	6	3	1	2	9	4	7
Spartak Moscow	6	1	3	2	6	12	5
Galatasaray	6	0	2	4	1	10	2

Dejan Savicevic

Dejan Savicevic (1966). The creative, skilful Yugoslavian midfielder Savicevic played in the Red Star Belgrade side which won the European Cup in 1991. He transferred to AC Milan for £4 million in 1992 where his assured touch and dribbling talents earned him the nickname of 'the genius'. He was man of the match in the 4-0 crushing of Barcelona in the 1994 European Cup Final, where he scored a magnificent goal and picked up his second European Cup medal. He left Milan to return to Red Star in 1998, and is currently on contract to Rapid Vienna. He has been capped 52 times for Yugoslavia.

Another Change of Format

The preliminary, first and second rounds were to remain as before for this year's tournament, as were the two leagues of four. However, in a change from the previous year, the top two clubs in each league were to progress to one-off semi-final games with the winners moving on to contest the Final.

AC Milan, Anderlecht, Porto, Werder Bremen

On a snow-covered Anderlecht pitch in November, Milan faced their Belgian opponents who were still without the injured striker Marc Degryse. Milan had most of the chances but could not score, and the game could have gone Anderlecht's way in the second half had not midfielder Johan Walem's shot hit the post. That evening, Porto took on Werder Bremen in Portugal and Domingos Oliveiria, Rui Jorge and Jose Carlos gave Porto a 3-0 lead with only eight minutes to go. However, the resilient Germans scored twice through Hobsch and Rufer, and Porto were relieved to collect the three points.

Werder continued with their knack of coming from behind two weeks later against Anderlecht in a rain-soaked Bremen. A rocket from centre-half Albert in the 16th minute and two in close succession from Danny Boffin had the visitors protecting a seemingly unassailable lead with 25 minutes to go. However, in an astonishing turnaround, Werder scored five times, through Rufer (twice), Bratseth, Hobsch and Marco Bode, and the tie finished 5-3. In Milan, lax defending by Porto allowed AC to score three through Raducioiu, full-back Panucci and Massaro, and go to the top of the league.

With play resuming in the spring, Milan met Werder at the San Siro and dropped the unproductive Papin, replacing him as third foreigner with Savicevic. Maldini's strike shortly after the interval was equalised by Marco Basler, and Savicevic justified his selection with the 68th-minute winner.

New Porto manager Bobby Robson had replaced Ivic and was turning the team into an attacking, free-scoring unit, revolving around the Bulgarian striker Emil Kostadinov. In his first European Cup appearance with the club, he travelled to Belgium where Anderlecht, without their creative Swedish midfielder Per Zetterburg, contained a lively performance from Porto. Against the run of play, Luc Nils scored the only goal in the 88th minute to move Anderlecht from bottom to second place in the table.

Two weeks later, Porto had their revenge against the Belgians when they won 2-0 in Portugal, through Drulovic and a last-minute goal from Carlos Secretario. At the end of March, a 5-0 away humbling of Werder virtually assured them of semi-final status.

Milan, meanwhile, had not been making quite the impact on the league as had been expected and had to be satisfied with a 1-1 away draw with Werder, a 74th-minute shot from Savicevic saving the point, and a nondescript match in Milan against Anderlecht ended 0-0. The Italians, however, had done enough to qualify and with one game to go, were leading the table with seven points.

In the final game in mid-April against Porto, Milan again achieved a goal-less score but striker Angelo Carbone was sent off in the 64th minute, and Maldini received a second booking rendering him ineligible for the semi-final. Porto's point guaranteed their appearance in the semi-finals. Anderlecht assured themselves of bottom place by losing 2-1 at home to Werder.

Anderlecht 0		Milan 0	
Porto 3		Werder 2	
Milan 3		Porto 0	
Werder 5		Anderlecht 3	
Anderlecht 1		Porto 0	
Milan 2		Werder 1	
Porto 2		Anderlecht 0	
Werder 1		Milan 1	
Milan 0		Anderlecht 0	
Werder 0		Porto 5	
Porto 0		Milan 0	
Anderlecht 1		Werder 2	

	P	W	D	L	F	A	Pts
Milan	6	2	4	0	6	2	8
Porto	6	3	1	2	10	6	7
Bremen	6	2	1	3	11	15	5
Anderlecht	6	1	2	3	5	9	4

SEMI FINALS

UEFA had decided that the winners from Group A would play the second-placed in Group B, and vice versa. The Group winners would host the semi-finals. One game each would decide the Finalists and, if level after 90 minutes, extra time would follow and then penalties.

Barcelona entertained Porto in the Nou Camp in front of just under 95,000 spectators. Only a few minutes into the game Stoichkov profited from a Sergi pass and Barcelona were 1-0 up. With Guardiola making continual runs from the back, and Sergi and Romario creating openings and chances, the Porto defence were crumbling in the face of Barca's fast-moving play. In the 34th minute, Stoichkov scored another. In the 61st minute Porto captain Joao Pinto was sent off for a second bookable offence and ten minutes later Koeman burst through to score a third. The game finished 3-0.

A Desailly header from a Boban cross gave Milan the lead against Monaco in the San Siro in the 14th minute. However, Costacurta was sent off five minutes before half time for a foul on Klinsmann. Their numerical disadvantage seemed only to

Fabio Capello, once a forward for Milan, became club manager after Sacchi's departure and took the club to the 1994 and 1995 European Cup Finals.

spur on Milan. Albertini scored with a long-range shot in the 48th minute, and Massaro produced a superb volley from a Panucci pass in the 66th minute to make the final score 3-0. Costacurta's sending-off and Baresi's booking, his third of the tournament, meant that these hugely influential defenders, the backbone of the Milan side, would miss the Final.

The two greatest club sides in Europe were to produce a classic Final in Athens' Olympic Stadium on 18 May.

Champions League

In December, UEFA announced yet another revised format for the following year's competition. The holders and the seven top seeded clubs in UEFA's complicated ranking system would progress to four league groups each containing four clubs. The eight other clubs in the groups would come from preliminary round ties between clubs ranked 8th to 23rd. Everyone else would go into the UEFA Cup. In future, none of the top sides would risk the humiliation and financial loss of being eliminated early by an outsider.

Dynamo Tbilisi

Dynamo Tbilisi were kicked out of the tournament after allegedly attempting to bribe the referee and linesmen with a $45,000 payment before the game against Linfield in Georgia in the preliminary round. Although they lost 3-2 on aggregate, Linfield went through to the first round proper and met FC Copenhagen, who had won the Danish league in their first year of existence. An unexpected 3-0 victory for Linfield in Northern Ireland was overturned 4-0 after extra time in Denmark.

BRITISH CLUBS

Rangers, with big Duncan Ferguson now in the attack, met Bulgarian champions Levski Sofia in the first round at Ibrox. With the resolute Stuart McCall back from injury in midfield, Rangers were on top in the first half but had only a 46th-minute goal from defender Dave McPherson to show for their dominance. Ferguson chipped to the head of Hateley in the 68th minute and Rangers were 2-0 ahead. Then the Rangers defence went to sleep. Borimorov took advantage of a defensive slip-up to head in with ten minutes to go and, although Hateley headed in another a minute later, the Gers defence allowed Todorov space to aim his header past keeper Maxwell.

A 50,000 crowd saw an intriguing contest in the second leg. Rangers patiently tried to probe for gaps in the Levski defence while the Bulgarians were looking for quick counter-attacks. A cute turn and shot by veteran forward Sirakov in the 36th minute put Levski ahead, and a 43rd-minute Durrant header off the post and then the keeper kept Rangers in the lead on aggregate. After the interval, Maxwell did well to save from Sirakov and Todorov, and Rangers pulled back into defence. However, in the 90th minute a spectacular 30-yard shot from the persistent Todorov smashed into the underside of the bar and went in the net. Levski had qualified for the next round on away goals, and Rangers rued their defensive lapses at Ibrox.

Back in the European Cup for the first time in 24 years, Alex Ferguson's young **Manchester United** side featured the maverick Eric Cantona as playmaker, while the tough abrasive midfield pairing of Paul Ince and Roy Keane provided the front runners Ryan Giggs and Welshman Mark Hughes. The colossal figure of Peter Schmeichel guarded the goals. In the first leg away against Honvéd, two goals from Keane and one from Cantona gave United a 3-2 win to take back to Old Trafford. In a scrappy game in Manchester, United ran out 2-1 winners thanks to two second-half headed goals from centre-back Steve Bruce.

Galatasaray came to Old Trafford in the next round, and the Turkish side played some sensational football. Their speedy movement and swift counter-attacks unsettled a sluggish United, who nonetheless went two-up within the first 13 minutes. In the second minute, a Hughes shot deflected off a defender into the net and then centre-forward Hakan Sukur scored an own goal. Undeterred, Galatasaray pulled one back two minutes later with a 25-yard shot from Arif and equalised when a Tugay pass was converted by Kubilay in the 32nd minute. Midway through the second half, an Arif shot hit the post and Kubilay scored from the rebound. Cantona's strike from a Giggs cross with nine minutes to go brought some relief to Old Trafford.

In Istanbul's Ali Sami Yen stadium, an inferior United struggled against a disciplined Galatasaray defence, and Tugay was again outstanding in midfield. Bruce, Paul Parker and Ince were booked for silly fouls and the petulant Cantona missed a sitter in the 58th minute. United could not score and Galatasaray deservedly went through to the group stage on away goals.

Eric sees red

Not for the first time, Eric Cantona's temper got the better of the Frenchman in Manchester United's second round game against Galatasaray in Istanbul. In the 77th minute, angry that defender Bulent was faking an injury, he ran onto the perimeter track and kicked the ball out of the reserve keeper's hands, apparently elbowing him in the ribs. He was ushered away from the protesting Turkish players by a lenient referee.

Then, after the game, Cantona protested that he had been hit on the head by a riot policeman in the tunnel. When the referee arrived, Cantona's explicitly expressed views on the official's handling of the game earned him a red card.

THE FINAL

Rampant Milan crush Catalans

AC Milan (2) 4 Barcelona (0) 0

Olympic Stadium, Athens, 18 May 1994
Attendance: 57,000
Referee: Don (England)

In a thrilling Final which defied all expectations, AC Milan roared into attack from the kick-off and humbled the 'total footballers' of Barcelona. The general view prior to the game was that Capello would use his team's strength and defensive organisation to close down Barcelona's free-running, attacking football. Indeed, Cruyff had stated that the match 'could determine the tactical direction of the game for the next few years'. However, this result was not what he had in mind.

Even without the suspended Costacurta and Baresi, and with Eranio injured, Milan's non-stop raiding, speed and superb technique quickly reduced Barcelona to a shadow of the team which had comprehensively outplayed Porto in the semi-final. An unco-ordinated and edgy Barca defence, with playmaker Guardiola and midfield partner Bakero dominated by Albertini and Desailly, could not handle Milan's marauding forwards. The dangerous pairing of Romario and Stoichkov was well policed by the veteran Filippo Galli, in for Costacurta, and Panucci, while Donadoni played the role of midfield supplier to perfection.

In front of 30,000 of their fans, Milan kicked off and Panucci had a headed 'goal' disallowed for offside in the ninth minute . Although Romario forced a save from keeper Rossi a minute later, the first goal came inevitably from Milan, Savicevic beating Nadal on the right and sending in a low cross to the far post for Massaro to score in the 22nd minute.

Just on half time, Donadoni on the left wing cut the ball back from the byline to Massaro who volleyed in past keeper Rossi for his second goal. In the 47th minute, the outstanding Savicevic pushed Sergi, a foul which went unpunished by referee Philip Don, and found space to send in a delightful 20-yard angled lob over Zubizarreta to put Milan three up. In the 58th minute, Desailly made it four from a through ball from Albertini. The game was effectively over, but Savicevic twice hit the post before the final whistle.

Barcelona had not played badly but Milan were, quite simply, awesome. Savicevic, previously regarded by Capello as something of a luxury, was deservedly man of the match, and the other players all contributed to their full potential. As Capello said, 'My team played an extraordinary match which demonstrated an enormous will to win'. Cruyff could only agree: 'Milan deserved to win'. And a jubilant Berlusconi collected his third European Cup.

The teams
AC Milan: Rossi, Tassotti, Galli, Maldini (Nova), Panucci, Boban, Albertini, Desailly, Donadoni, Savicevic, Massaro (manager: Capello) [Massaro 22, 45, Savicevic 47, Desailly 58]
Barcelona: Zubizarreta, Ferrer, Koeman, Nadal, Beguiristain (Eusebio), Bakero, Guardiola, Amor, Sergi (Quique), Stoichkov, Romario (manager: Cruyff)

Daniele Massaro (white shirt, on ground) converts Savicevic's cross for Milan's first goal in the 1994 Final.

THE 1994-95 SEASON

The new Champions League format began this season with places reserved in the four groups for last year's winner, AC Milan, and the top seven seeded European sides – Barcelona, Manchester United, Spartak Moscow, Bayern Munich, Benfica, Anderlecht and Ajax. The other eight came from a two-leg preliminary round played in August, where the only surprise eliminations were Rangers, beaten 3-0 by AEK Athens; Legia Warsaw, humbled 5-0 by Croatia's Hajduk Split; and Sparta Prague going down 2-1 to IFK Gothenburg.

GROUP A

Barcelona, Galatasaray, IFK Gothenburg, Manchester United

Johan Cruyff's Barcelona had sold Zubizarreta and Salinas, but they had signed Romanian midfielder Gheorghe Hagi from Brescia. They began with a 2-1 win over Galatasaray at the Nou Camp. In the other game, Manchester United beat IFK 4-2 at Old Trafford. Two weeks later, United secured a 0-0 draw in Istanbul while, in Gothenburg, Stoichkov opened the scoring for Barca in the tenth minute. Surprisingly, IFK came back to win 2-1, the second being a last-minute strike from the precocious and much sought-after young forward Jesper Blomqvist.

A goal from Magnus Erlingmark gave IFK victory over Galatasaray in Gothenburg the following month, and IFK went to the top of the league, where they were to remain until the conclusion of the group. United drew 2-2 at Old Trafford with Barcelona, and were trounced 4-0 at the Nou Camp, while an 86th-minute goal from Magnus Erlingmark gave IFK a 1-0 victory over Galatasaray.

In December, a 3-1 IFK win over United gave IFK the league title with a game in hand, while two late goals from Hakan and Arif cancelled out a Romario strike and ensured a 2-1 Galatasaray win over Barcelona in Istanbul. Although United put four past Galatasaray in the final game at Old Trafford, a Bakero header and a fine display by keeper Carlos Busquets secured a 1-1 draw against IFK, and Barcelona qualified on goal difference ahead of United.

Barcelona 2	Galatasaray 1
United 4	IFK 2
Galatasaray 0	United 0
IFK 2	Barcelona 1
IFK 1	Galatasaray 0
United 2	Barcelona 2
Barcelona 4	United 0
Galatasaray 0	IFK 1
Galatasaray 2	Barcelona 1
IFK 3	United 1
Barcelona 1	IFK 1
United 4	Galatasaray 0

	P	W	D	L	F	A	Pts
IFK	6	4	1	1	10	7	9
Barcelona	6	2	2	2	11	8	6
Manchester United	6	2	2	2	11	11	6
Galatasaray	6	1	1	4	3	9	3

GROUP B

Bayern Munich, Dynamo Kiev, Paris St-Germain, Spartak Moscow

Manager Luis Fernandez had created a strong, organised side in Paris St-Germain. George Weah and David Ginola led the forward line, stylishly assisted by Valdo and Le Guen in midfield. The French champions beat Giovanni Trapattoni's Bayern Munich 2-0 in Paris in their first match and came back from 1-0 down to defeat Moscow Spartak in Russia in their second. Meanwhile Dynamo Kiev, with their star striker Victor Leonenko, had their first meeting with Spartak since the dissolution of the Russian League in 1991, and won 3-2 in front of 90,000 fans in the Ukraine with Leonenko scoring twice and the other coming from Rebrov. An early goal from Mehmet Scholl gave Bayern a 1-0 win over Kiev in the next game.

In October, a 76th-minute Weah strike proved conclusive in PSG's 2-1 away win in the Ukraine, while a last-minute goal from Marcus Babbel scrambled Bayern a 1-1 draw with Spartak in Moscow. It was Weah again who made sure of two points for the French with a 1-0 win in Paris against Kiev, while on the same evening Bayern could only draw 2-2 at home with Spartak. Weah yet again scored the only goal against Bayern in Paris in the 81st minute, and Kiev went down 1-0 to Spartak.

In the final games, Bayern had Papin back from injury, and he scored twice as Bayern answered a Shevchenko opening goal for Dynamo in Kiev with a 4-1 win to qualify for the quarter-final. PSG also qualified, with a 100% record, as they routed Spartak in Paris. Weah scored twice, with Ginola and Brazilian midfielder Rai providing the other two.

Kiev 3	Spartak 2
PSG 2	Bayern 0
Bayern 1	Kiev 0
Spartak 1	PSG 2
Kiev 1	PSG 2
Spartak 1	Bayern 1
Bayern 2	Spartak 2
PSG 1	Kiev 0
Bayern 0	PSG 1
Spartak 1	Kiev 0
Kiev 1	Bayern 4
PSG 4	Spartak 1

	P	W	D	L	F	A	Pts
PSG	6	6	0	0	12	3	12
Bayern Munich	6	2	2	2	8	7	6
Spartak Moscow	6	1	2	3	8	12	4
Dynamo Kiev	6	1	0	5	5	11	2

GROUP C

Anderlecht, Benfica, Hajduk Split, Steaua Bucharest

Benfica had won their 30th Portugese league title, and long-haired Argentinian forward Claudio Caniggia was piling in the goals. Although they could only draw 0-0 with unseeded Hajduk Split in Croatia in the first game, Caniggia scored twice in their second game in Lisbon against Anderlecht, who had also ground out a goal-less draw with Steaua Bucharest. A goal from creative midfielder Aliosha Asanovic gave Hajduk a 1-0 win over Steaua the same evening.

A Caniggia penalty and a Joao Pinto goal gave Benfica a 2-1 win over Steaua in October, while Hajduk achieved a 2-1 victory over Anderlecht in Split and received a £10,000 UEFA fine for time-wasting. Helder equalised for Benfica in Bucharest in November for a 1-1 draw, and injury-hit Anderlecht could not break down a tough Hajduk defence in Belgium where the score ended 0-0. Later in the month, Benfica and Hajduk met in Lisbon, where a draw would be enough for both of them to qualify. Goals from Brazilian forward Isaias and Joao Pinto gave Benfica a 2-1 result, but Hajduk, having suffered their first group defeat, qualified anyway as Steaua and Anderlecht could only draw.

On the last match day, a goal from Silva Edilson preserved Benfica's unbeaten record in a 1-1 draw with Anderlecht, and Hajduk were defeated 4-1 at home by Steaua, the Romanian club's goals coming from Adrian Ilie (2), Lacatus and midfielder Constantin Galca.

Anderlecht 0	Steaua 0
Hajduk 0	Benfica 0
Benfica 3	Anderlecht 1
Steaua 0	Hajduk 1
Benfica 2	Steaua 1
Hajduk 2	Anderlecht 1
Anderlecht 0	Hajduk 0
Steaua 1	Benfica 1
Benfica 2	Hajduk 1
Steaua 1	Anderlecht 1
Anderlecht 1	Benfica 1
Hajduk 1	Steaua 4

	P	W	D	L	F	A	Pts
Benfica	6	3	3	0	9	5	9
Hajduk Split	6	2	2	2	5	7	6
Steaua Bucharest	6	1	3	2	7	6	5
Anderlecht	6	0	4	2	4	7	4

GROUP D

AC Milan, AEK Athens, Ajax, Salzburg

European champions AC Milan had bought back Ruud Gullit from Sampdoria but had sold Papin to Bayern and Laudrup to Rangers. They started the league badly, losing to goals from Ronald De Boer and Jari Litmanen in a 2-0 defeat by Ajax in Holland. Louis Van Gaal's Ajax was a young, skilful side featuring Litmanen, teenage striker Patrick Kluivert, winger Marc Overmars and midfielders Clarence Seedorf and Edgar Davids, and were amongst this year's favourites. The other two clubs in the group – Salzburg, in the tournament for the first time, and AEK Athens – drew 0-0 in their opening game. In Milan's next game – a 3-0 defeat of Salzburg – Austrian keeper Otto Konrad was struck on the head by a bottle thrown by a fan. UEFA subsequently fined Milan two points and ordered them to play their next two home games over 300 kilometres from Milan.

Goals from Litmanen and Kluivert gave Ajax a 2-1 away victory over AEK, but the Dutch could only draw 0-0 in Austria while the scoreline was also goal-less between Milan and AEK in Athens. In November, two goals from right-back Christian Panucci secured a 2-1 win for Milan against AEK, and a late goal from Litmanen saved a point for Ajax at home to Salzburg. At the end of the month, Milan, playing in their 'home' ground of Trieste, went down 2-0 to Ajax, the goals coming from Litmanen in the second minute and an own goal from sweeper Baresi in the second half. Salzburg kept up their challenge with a 3-1 away win over AEK.

In their sixth and final game, Milan had to beat Salzburg away to qualify, which they did through a 26th-minute strike from Daniele Massaro. Ajax, meanwhile had already qualified and confirmed their quality with a 2-0 home win over AEK.

Ajax 2	Milan 0
Salzburg 0	AEK 0
AEK 1	Ajax 2
Milan 3	Salzburg 0
AEK 0	Milan 0
Salzburg 0	Ajax 0
Ajax 1	Salzburg 1
Milan 2	AEK 1
AEK 1	Salzburg 3
Milan 0	Ajax 2
Ajax 2	AEK 0
Salzburg 0	Milan 1

	P	W	D	L	F	A	Pts
Ajax	6	4	2	0	9	2	10
AC Milan	6	3	1	2	6	5	5*
Salzburg	6	1	3	2	4	6	5
AEK Athens	6	0	2	4	3	9	2

* Milan had two points deducted for crowd trouble

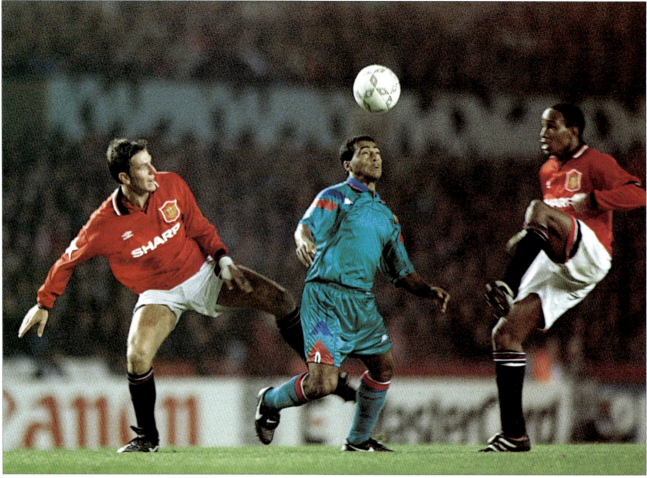

Barcelona's Romario (centre) controls the ball at Old Trafford during the 2-2 draw in Group A, flanked by Paul Ince (right) and Lee Sharpe.

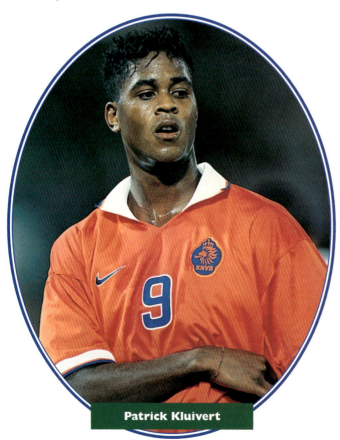

Patrick Kluivert

Zvonomir Boban *(1968). One of Croatia's most popular footballers and captain of his country, Boban led Croatia to third place in the 1998 World Cup finals, beating West Germany in the play-off. A powerful midfielder for Dynamo Zagreb, Boban joined Bari and then Milan, for whom he played in their 1994 European Cup triumph. He is still with the Italian club and he has won four league titles and two Italian Supercups with the 'rossoneri'. He has 50 caps for Croatia, as well as three for Yugoslavia, and he has scored 12 goals for Croatia.*

Patrick Kluivert *(1976). Another graduate from the famed Ajax youth team, Kluivert is a young striker of enormous potential. He gained two league titles with Ajax and scored the only goal in the Dutch club's European Cup Final victory over AC Milan while still only 18. He moved to Milan in 1996 and then to Barcelona where, with Rivaldo and Figo, he is at the centre of Louis Van Gaal's attack. In France 1998, Kluivert scored the equaliser with three minutes to go in the semi-final against Brazil to send the game into extra time, although Holland lost on penalties. Only 24 years old, he already has over 40 caps.*

AC Milan v Benfica

Benfica's Belgian keeper Michel Preud'homme made a series of magnificent saves in the first leg at the San Siro, but Marco Simone eventually broke the deadlock in the 63rd minute, tucking away a header from Marcel Desailly. Simone made it a 2-0 victory twelve minutes later when he deftly controlled and converted a cross from Panucci. In a dour display, Milan held on to draw 0-0 in Lisbon and proceed to the semis 2-0 on aggregate.

Semi-finalist: AC Milan (2-0 aggregate)

Hajduk Split v Ajax

In the first leg in Croatia, a solid defensive performance by Ajax against underdogs Hajduk resulted in a goal-less draw. In Amsterdam, A 39th-minute headed goal by lanky young Nigerian forward Nwankwo Kanu opened the scoring for Ajax in the 34th minute, and Frank de Boer added two more, including an expertly-taken free kick, in the second half to give Ajax a 3-0 aggregate win.

Semi-finalist: Ajax (3-0 aggregate)

Bayern Munich v IFK Gothenburg

Without Papin, Sutter and Matthaus, Bayern struggled to score against a well-organised IFK defence in Munich. The Germans had several chances but had to settle for a 0-0 draw. In Gothenburg, in an action-packed last 25 minutes, Alexander Zickler and then Christian Nerlinger put Bayern 2-0 ahead. With Bayern keeper Sven Scheuer having been sent off in the 20th minute, IFK finally capitalised by scoring through substitute Mats Lilienburg in the 79th minute, and an injury-time strike from Mikael Martinsson produced a draw on the night, but Bayern went through on away goals.

Semi-finalist: Bayern Munich (2-2 aggregate)

Barcelona v Paris St-Germain

A mistake from Paris keeper Bernard Lama, when he turned in an Igor Korneyev cross into his own net, gave Barcelona a 1-0 48th-minute lead in Spain. However, a George Weah header from a Valdo cross six minutes later made the final score level at 1-1. In Paris, Bakero struck first just after half time for Barcelona but a Rai goal and an 83rd-minute shot from Guerin gave the game and the tie to Paris, 3-2 on aggregate.

Semi-finalist: Paris St-Germain (3-2 aggregate)

Bayern Munich v Ajax

Injury-hit Bayern nonetheless held visiting Ajax 0-0 in Munich in the first leg. It was all Ajax in the first half, with Seedorf, Finidi Gaorge and Kanu going close. In the second half, however, Bayern rallied and Ajax keeper Edwin Van der Saar was obliged to make agile saves from Mehmet Scholl and Alain Sutter.

In Amsterdam, however, Ajax turned on the style. Litmanen headed in the first goal in the 11th minute and, although Marcel Witeczek headed in a Scholl cross to equalise, a wonderful 20-yard shot from Finidi George put Ajax 2-1 up. Just on half time, a volley from Ronald de Boer made it three and, moments into the second half, Litmanen again pounced with a left-foot shot for Ajax's fourth. Scholl scored for Bayern from a 76th-minute penalty after Ajax captain Danny Blind was adjudged to have handled in the box, but little winger Marc Overmars sealed a memorable night for Ajax with a right-foot shot two minutes from the end.

Finalist: Ajax (5-2 aggregate)

Paris St-Germain v AC Milan

In Paris, Milan summoned up all their defensive talents, with Baresi, Panucci and Maldini countering the pace and movement of Ginola, Weah and Rai in the Paris attack. Gradually, Milan started moving forward, with the elegant Savicevic at the centre of their efforts, releasing Simone and Maldini to go close. Although Ginola hit the bar, Milan were increasingly in control and, in injury time, a Savicevic-inspired move ended in Zvonimir Boban, scoring the winner at the near post.

With both clubs out of the reckoning for their respective league titles, the second leg was critical for their European futures next season, and they produced an enthralling match, watched by 80,000 in the frenzied atmosphere of the San Siro. With Maldini and Baresi again in imperious form, the Paris forwards were denied the space to play as they could. Savicevic and Boban controlled midfield from the start, and it was no surprise when, in the 21st minute, Savicevic controlled a long pass from Albertini in the box and shot past Lama into the far corner. In the 67th minute, the game was over. The imposing Marcel Desailly won the ball from Daniel Bravo, strode up the pitch and passed to Savicevic, whose well-placed shot again evaded keeper Lama. The European Cup holders AC Milan were back in the Final 3-0 on aggregate.

Finalist: AC Milan (3-0 aggregate)

Kluivert stuns Milan as Ajax become kings of Europe

Ajax (0) 1 AC Milan (0) 0

Ernst Happel Stadium, Vienna, 24 May 1995
Attendance: 50,000
Referee: Craiunescu (Romania)

In what used to be known as the Prater Stadium, and was now named after one of the greatest of all Austrian footballers, Fabio Capello's experienced, multinational Milan side faced the young and extravagantly gifted Dutchmen of Ajax.

Although Luis Van Gaal's Ajax had beaten Milan twice in the earlier stages of the Champions League, Milan had not conceded a goal in their last five European matches and the Italians started the game as favourites. Although missing the injured playmaker Savicevic, replaced by Daniele Massaro, Milan's defensively organised, containing and swift counter-attacking game was seen as a danger to the exciting young players of Ajax, and one which they might struggle to overcome. In the event, the game was an enthralling contrast of styles.

As the game began, the maturity and teamwork of the Milan defence gradually made itself felt, with Desailly, Baresi and Maldini disrupting the attacking movements of Litmanen, Overmars and George. Although the first threat to goal came from Ajax – Frank De Boer heading over an Edgar Davids corner – Milan increasingly dominated the first half with their close-passing play and perceptive movement. Desailly's shot in the 41st minute was deflected into the arms of Van der Saar and a 45th-minute instinctive volley from the boot of Simone, supplied by a cross from the dangerous Donadoni, was gratefully saved by the Ajax keeper.

After the interval Clarence Seedorf, making little impression on the game, was substituted by Kanu, whose runs and speed began to unsettle the Italian defence. Milan continued to counter-attack, however, and a superb ball in the 62nd minute from Albertini to Massaro was turned just wide by the striker. With 25 minutes to go, Van Gaal substituted 18-year-old striking sensation Patrick Kluivert for a disappointing Litmanen, but Milan kept up the attack.

With ten minutes to go, Simone and Kanu each had good chances, but the winner came in the 85th minute. Kluivert fed Davids on the left and Davids' return ball went to Rijkaard on the edge of the box. Rijkaard found Kluivert who slotted the ball past Milan keeper Rossi, and Ajax were 1-0 up. At the age of 18 years and 327 days, Kluivert became the youngest-ever European Cup Final scorer. Capello's substitutions of Lentini for Boban and Eranio for Massaro were too late to change the score, and Ajax had regained the European Cup after a 22-year wait.

Ajax's commitment to its youth policy had triumphed over Berlusconi's millions and, although Milan had played well enough to deserve at least extra time, many neutrals felt that the flair, exuberance and spirit of adventure displayed by Ajax that season had been appropriately rewarded.

The teams
Ajax: Van der Saar, Reiziger, Blind, Rijkaard, F. De Boer, Seedorf (Kanu), George, Davids, R. De Boer, Litmanen (Kluivert), Overmars (manager: Van Gaal) [Kluivert 85]
AC Milan: Rossi, Panucci, Maldini, Albertini, Costacurta, Baresi, Donadoni, Desailly, Massaro (Eranio), Boban (Lentini), Simone (manager: Capello)

Patrick Kluivert scores Ajax's goal in the 1995 Final.

The top eight seeds this season were Nantes, Porto, Spartak Moscow, Blackburn Rovers, Juventus, Borussia Dortmund, Ajax and Real Madrid. In the preliminary rounds, the main upset was the 2-1 elimination of Anderlecht by Hungary's Ferencváros, matched by Legia Warsaw's defeat of last season's quarter-finalists IFK Gothenburg. Rosenborg of Norway struggled away against Turkey's Besiktas but qualified 4-3, while a 1-1 draw in Croatia was enough for Panathinaikos to defeat Hajduk Split. Rangers also made heavy weather of their away tie against Famagusta, and a goal at Ibrox was the eventual difference between the teams.

GROUP A

Dynamo Kiev (Aalborg), Nantes, Panathinaikos, Porto

Panathinaikos had accumulated a record 83 points to win the Greek league and possessed in Polish centre-forward Krysztof Warzycha the league's top scorer. They met Dynamo Kiev in their first game. The Ukranians won 1-0 but it subsequently emerged that Kiev had attempted to bribe Spanish referee Nieto before the game. UEFA kicked them out of the tournament and gave their place to Denmark's oldest club Aalborg whom Kiev had eliminated in the preliminary round. Nantes played out a 0-0 draw with Bobby Robson's Porto side.

On match-day two, a brace from Warzycha helped Panathinaikos to a 3-1 home win over Nantes, while Porto put two past Aalborg without reply. The next round saw Nantes cruise to a 3-1 victory over Aalborg in France, while a 40th-minute goal from Dimitrios Markos gave Panathinaikos a narrow away win over Porto. Before the next set of games, Aalborg replayed their first match against Panathinaikos and top scorer Erik Bo Andersen scored first in a 2-1 win over the Greeks.

In November, goals from Laurent Guyot and Nicolas Quedec against Aalborg, after the Danish defender Torben Boye was red-carded, gave the French leadership of the group on goal difference over Panathinaikos, who could only draw 0-0 with Porto at home. In the fifth round of games, Panathinaikos went top with a home win over Aalborg while two goals from Pedros gave Nantes a 2-2 away point at Porto.

In the last games in December, in order to qualify Porto had to beat Aalborg and hope that Nantes beat Panathinaikos. Two goals from Brazilian Emerson were not enough to beat the Danes, and Nantes and Panathinaikos shared a 0-0 draw in France.

Nantes 0	Porto 0
Dynamo Kiev 1	Panathinaikos 0 (match void)
Panathinaikos 3	Nantes 1
Porto 2	Aalborg 0
Porto 0	Panathinaikos 1
Nantes 3	Aalborg 1
Aalborg 2	Panathinaikos 1 (replay of match 1)
Panathinaikos 0	Porto 0
Aalborg 0	Nantes 2
Porto 2	Nantes 2
Panathinaikos 2	Aalborg 0
Nantes 0	Panathinaikos 0
Aalborg 2	Porto 2

	P	W	D	L	F	A	Pts
Panathinaikos	6	3	2	1	7	3	11
Nantes	6	2	3	1	8	6	6
Porto	6	1	4	1	6	5	6
Aalborg	6	1	1	4	5	12	4

GROUP B

Blackburn Rovers, Legia Warsaw, Spartak Moscow, Rosenborg

Spartak had brought back their former players Sergei Yuran and Vasily Kulkov back from Porto, and Yuran scored the only goal in their away victory over English champions Blackburn in their first game. In Poland, midfield playmaker Leszek Pisz contributed two goals to Legia's 3-1 home win over Rosenborg. Later in the month in Moscow, a goal for Yuran was the difference between Spartak and Legia in a 2-1 home win, while Blackburn again stumbled, this time to a 2-1 defeat by Rosenborg in Norway.

In October, top Legia striker Jerzy Podbrozny's 25th-minute goal in Warsaw virtually finished off Blackburn's aspirations, while in Norway against Spartak Rosenborg were 2-0 up by half time, through Harald Bratbakk and Karl-Petter Loken. However, a magnificent second-half fight-back by Spartak saw the Russians score four goals, the last two coming from midfielder Valeri Kechinov. On the fourth match-day, Blackburn at last gained a point against Legia in a 0-0 draw, and Spartak again scored four against Rosenborg, this time at home. Spartak were now unbeaten in the league and certain of qualifying, while the battle for second place was between Legia and Rosenborg. In November, Spartak widened the gap with a 3-0 home crushing of hapless Blackburn and Rosenborg closed in on Legia with an emphatic 4-0 victory.

On the final day, Blackburn finally achieved some respectability with a 4-1 home win over Rosenborg and ended the Norwegians' hopes of qualifying. Legia lost 1-0 at home to Spartak, but Rosenborg's defeat meant that the Polish side qualified anyway. Spartak moved into the quarter-finals with an impressive 100% record in the group.

Legia 3	Rosenborg 1
Blackburn 0	Spartak 1
Spartak 2	Legia 1
Rosenborg 2	Blackburn 1
Legia 1	Blackburn 0
Rosenborg 2	Spartak 4
Blackburn 0	Legia 0
Spartak 4	Rosenborg 1
Rosenborg 4	Legia 0
Spartak 3	Blackburn 0
Legia 0	Spartak 1
Blackburn 4	Rosenborg 1

	P	W	D	L	F	A	Pts
Spartak Moscow	6	6	0	0	15	4	18
Legia Warsaw	6	2	1	3	5	8	7
Rosenborg	6	2	0	4	11	16	6
Blackburn Rovers	6	1	1	4	5	8	4

Borussia Dortmund, Juventus, Rangers, Steaua Bucharest

Under coach Marcello Lippi, Juventus were the top side in Italy. Even though 'the divine ponytail' Roberto Baggio had left to join AC Milan, Juve had a sparkling forward line of Alessandro Del Piero, Gianluca Vialli and Fabrizio Ravanelli. With their international midfield of Vladimir Jugovic, Didier Deschamps and Paulo Sousa, and a defence with Sergio Porrini and Moreno Torricelli outstanding, it is clear to see why Juventus were the hot favourites for the competition.

They were, however, in the most difficult group of all, particularly with Borussia Dortmund lying in wait. Dortmund had a strong ex-Juve contingent – including midfielder Andreas Möller, Brazilian centre-back Julio Cesar and defender Jürgen Kohler – and the team was masterminded by *libero* Matthias Sammer. Karlheinz Riedle and Ruben Sosa played upfront. Rangers and Steaua Bucharest were no push-overs, either, the latter relying on the goal-scoring talents of the ageing Lacatus and the young Adrian Ilie.

Although Möller scored in the first minute in the game between the two favourites in Germany, the match eventually went 3-1 Juve's way, while Steaua picked up three points against Rangers in Romania. Rangers gained their first point in a 2-2 draw with Borussia at Ibrox a fortnight later, and Juventus scored three goals in 15 minutes – through right midfielder Angelo Di Livio, Del Piero and Ravanelli – either side of half time to beat Steaua in Turin. On the third match-day, Juve destroyed Rangers 4-1 in Turin and a solitary goal from young midfielder Lars Ricken gave Borussia victory over Steaua.

Rangers were again crushed by Juventus on the fourth match-day, this time by 4-0 at Ibrox, while Borussia and Steaua ground out a goal-less draw in Bucharest. Juventus had by now qualified, and Rangers were trailing with an embarrassing one point. On the penultimate match-day, Juventus were surprisingly beaten at home 2-1 by Borussia, a last-minute Del Piero goal giving the Italians some consolation, and Rangers held Steaua 1-1 at Ibrox. On the final day, Borussia, now certain of qualifying as group runners-up, finished their campaign with a 2-2 draw in Glasgow. Juventus sent several of their reserves to Bucharest and drew 0-0 with Steaua.

Steaua 1	Rangers 0
Borussia 1	Juventus 3
Juventus 3	Steaua 0
Rangers 2	Borussia 2
Borussia 1	Steaua 0
Juventus 4	Rangers 1
Steaua 0	Borussia 0
Rangers 0	Juventus 4
Rangers 1	Steaua 1
Juventus 1	Borussia 2
Steaua 0	Juventus 0
Borussia 2	Rangers 2

	P	W	D	L	F	A	Pts
Juventus	6	4	1	1	15	4	13
Borussia Dortmund	6	2	3	1	8	8	9
Steaua Bucharest	6	1	3	2	2	5	6
Rangers	6	0	3	3	6	14	3

Ajax, Ferencváros, Grasshoppers Zurich, Real Madrid

With Ferencváros and Grasshoppers the make-weights, Group D was between Ajax and Real Madrid. The European Cup holders had bought Brazilian defender Marcio Santos to replace Rijkaard, and Seedorf had moved on, but otherwise the team was essentially that which had beaten Milan last May. With a 36-game unbeaten run in the Dutch league, they were formidable opponents for Real. Jorge Valdano's team had been considerably strengthened by the arrival of Michael Laudrup from Barcelona and the emergence of the brilliant 18-year-old striker Raul to partner the Chilean Ivan Zamorano in attack. Captain Manuel Sanchis and Fernando Hierro held the team together at the back, with Laudrup complemented in midfield by Argentinian Fernando Redondo and the tricky Luis Enrique.

In their first encounter in Amsterdam, Ajax, without captain Blind and Kluivert, turned on a masterful display but could only manage one goal, through Overmars in the 14th minute. The Spanish were outclassed and Overmars almost scored again with a magnificent volley in the 29th minute. Ferencvaros won 3-0 in Zurich, with Grasshoppers' Swedish defender Mats Gren sent off in the 33rd minute. Later in the month in Hungary, Ajax were again unstoppable, Litmanen scoring a hat-trick in their 5-1 demolition of Ferencváros, while two goals from Zamarano gave Real a 2-0 victory over Grasshoppers at the Bernabeu. On the third match-day, Ajax, with two goals from Kluivert and one from Finidi George, finished off Grasshoppers, and Real went on the rampage in Madrid against Ferencvaros. Their 6-1 victory included a hat-trick for Raul and two for Zamarano.

Although Grasshoppers held Ajax 0-0 in early November, the Dutch had already qualified. A 74th-minute equaliser by Raul gave Real a point in Hungary with a 1-1 draw. On the fifth match-day, Ajax travelled to Madrid, and yet again magnificently outplayed the Spaniards. Although they won only 2-0 – a George pass to Litmanen in the 65th minute supplying the first and Kluivert scoring the second ten minutes later – they had two more disallowed and also hit the post twice. A late equalising penalty from Nyilas kept Ferencváros' hopes alive in their 3-3 draw against Grasshoppers.

However, a 4-0 defeat by Ajax in the final game, with two from Litmanen within four minutes, eliminated Ferencváros, and Real made sure of their qualification with a 2-0 away win over Grasshoppers, Raul and Michel doing the damage.

Ajax 1	Real 0
Grasshoppers 0	Ferencvaros 3
Ferencvaros 1	Ajax 5
Real 2	Grasshoppers 0
Ajax 3	Grasshoppers 0
Real 6	Ferencvaros 1
Grasshoppers 0	Ajax 0
Ferencvaros 1	Real 1
Real 0	Ajax 2
Ferencvaros 3	Grasshoppers 3
Ajax 4	Ferencvaros 0
Grasshoppers 0	Real 2

	P	W	D	L	F	A	Pts
Ajax	6	5	1	0	15	1	16
Real Madrid	6	3	1	2	11	5	10
Ferencvaros	6	1	2	3	9	19	5
Grasshoppers	6	0	2	4	3	13	2

Juventus' Alessandro Del Piero (right) on the attack against Ajax in the 1996 Final.

The Bosman Ruling

In December 1995, the Belgian footballer Jean-Marc Bosman won a ruling in the European Court of Justice against his club Liège which was to have profound implications for all European clubs. The court decided that the existing transfer regulations contravened the law which governed the free movement of workers between member states of the European Union. It also ruled unlawful UEFA's restrictions on the number of foreign players which clubs could field in European competitions. From now on, nationality became irrelevant in the European Cup. In March 2000, Chelsea played eleven foreigners against Lazio in the competition.

BLACKBURN ROVERS 95/96

Millionaire Jack Walker had funded Blackburn Rovers to the club's first English league championship in over eighty years. Coach Ray Harford had a strong squad, including England international strikers Chris Sutton and Alan Shearer – the 'SAS' – and a defence containing Scottish centre-half Colin Hendry, uncompromising midfielder David Batty, left-back Graeme Le Saux and keeper Tim Flowers, internationals all.

For all their international experience, their naivety at European club level was ruthlessly exploited by a superb Spartak Moscow at Ewood Park in the first game. The game started promisingly enough for the Lancashire side with keeper Stanislav Cherchesov saving from Shearer and Mike Newell. Gradually, however, Spartak's superior sophistication and technique took over the midfield and it was no surprise when Valeri Shmarov set Sergei Yuran on a run in the 40th minute which ended with Yuran lobbing Flowers from the edge of the box. Blackburn pushed forward but the Spartak defence were impregnable, and the game ended 1-0.

Things did not improve for Blackburn in Norway against the part-timers of Rosenborg. The fast-moving Rosenborg attack soon had Blackburn's back four in disarray and, in the 29th minute, an unmarked Karl-Petter Loken slotted in at the far post. Winger Ivar Jakobsen missed a penalty just on half time, and Trond Soltvedt and Roar Strand narrowly missed. In the 63rd minute, Newell equalised from a Shearer header and Blackburn, spurred on by substitute Stuart Ripley, fought for the winner. However, with four minutes to go, defender Stale Stensaas made it 2-1 to the Norwegians, and Blackburn remained without a point.

It went from bad to worse when they visited Legia Warsaw in game three. Another inept defensive performance and lack of imagination in midfield allowed Legia to dominate, and the Poles went ahead in the 25th minute through a Jerzy Podbrozny header cleverly created by Cezari Kucharski. Although Blackburn pressed forward in the second half, they could not score the vital goal. In the return game against Legia at Ewood Park, Blackburn attacked with spirit and gusto, but again they could not make the all-important breakthrough. The game finished 0-0, and Blackburn had failed to qualify with two games to play.

In Moscow for game five, a petulant and unprofessional Blackburn were well beaten by Spartak 3-0 with goals from Dimitri Alenichev, Yuri Nikiforov and Ramiz Memedov. An on-field punch-up between teammates Le Saux and Batty, a row between Tim Sherwood and Hendry, and Hendry's sending-off in the 75th minute were hardly the best advertisements for the English game. Spartak qualified as group winners.

At last, in the final home game against Rosenborg, Blackburn demonstrated why they had won the league title. Shearer scored from a penalty in the 16th minute, and an exhilarating hat-trick within nine minutes from Newell had Blackburn 4-1 ahead before half time, with Stefan Iversen netting for Rosenborg. However, too little too late it most certainly was, and Blackburn exited from the Champions League with four points and very little European credibility.

RANGERS 1995/96

With his strike force of Hateley and McCoist, and the midfield talents of Laudrup and Paul Gascoigne, manager Walter Smith had good reason to feel confident about progressing in the tournament. Gough in defence and the ball-winning McCall in midfield provided the steel to the team, and the squad had strength in depth.

A Gordon Durie goal at Ibrox against Famagusta in the preliminary round proved to be decisive. The return, against a tough and determined side, ended 0-0 but demonstrated to Rangers the quality of even the most unfancied European opposition.

In their first Group C match away against Steaua, Rangers immediately came under pressure but, steadied by Gough and the trickery of Gascoigne, the game was goal-less at half time. In the second half, keeper Andy Goram pulled off two superb saves but, when defender Alan McLaren was sent off, the Romanians seized the advantage and Steaua defender Daniel Prodan volleyed home the winner with eight minutes to go.

In the second game, at Ibrox against Borussia Dortmund, with McCall back from injury, Rangers went on the attack, but fell to a counter-attack in the 18th minute when striker Heiko Herrlich headed home an inch-perfect cross from Stefan Reuter. In the 62nd minute, a free kick from Gascoigne, in inspirational form, found Gough who headed over keeper Klos. Seven minutes later, Martin Kree put Borussia 2-1 ahead with another header but, in the 72nd minute, Ian Ferguson deflected in a Gascoigne shot, to make the final score 2-2.

An embarrassing display of Juventus superiority followed in Turin. Run ragged within the first ten minutes by an exuberant Juventus, Rangers were three down by the 23rd minute through Ravanelli, Conte and Del Piero, the last with a stunning 30-yard shot. Missing midfield generals Gascoigne and Laudrup, Rangers tried to regroup, but the vision and

movement of Juventus were irresistible. Ravanelli made it four in the 74th minute. A Gough goal three minutes later was scant consolation for the travelling Rangers support.

Juventus were again the opposition in the fourth game at Ibrox, and the Italian football lesson continued. Although Rangers looked more dangerous than in Turin, they were once more overwhelmed by the skill and industry of the visitors. The mesmerising Del Piero scored the first in the 16th minute from a Gordan Petric error and, although the arrival of Ian Durrant sparked a brief resurgence from the home team, Juventus continued in command. Goram was replaced by Billy Thomson at half time, but Thomson could do nothing about Morreno Torricelli's 65th-minute run and shot, nor could he prevent substitutes Ravanelli and Giancarlo Marocchi's goals in the last two minutes. One point in four games was hardly the stuff of champions.

Back at Ibrox for the fifth game, Rangers withstood an early wave of attacks from Steaua until a typical piece of genius in the 32nd minute from Gascoigne, when he ran half the length of the pitch before placing a low shot past keeper Bogdan Stelea, gave them the lead and a chance of qualification. A reinvigorated Rangers stepped up the pressure and David Robertson and then Gascoigne again with a header nearly added to the scoreline. However, a counter-attack by Steaua in the 55th minute produced an Ilie equaliser, and Rangers were out. Their elimination was confirmed when Juventus crashed at home to Borussia.

In the final game in Germany, a pass from Charlie Miller found Laudrup in the 10th minute and Rangers were ahead. Six minutes later, a misplaced header from Gough was powerfully converted by Andy Möller, and immediately after the interval Riedle made it 2-1 to Borussia. Gascoigne received a second yellow card for arguing with the referee, after having already been booked for a foul on Möller, and was sent off and automatically suspended for the start of the following year's tournament. But ten-man Rangers salvaged a creditable point when Durie swept home a McCall pass with six minutes to go.

Alessandro Del Piero (1974). Del Piero is the golden boy of Italian football. He began his career at Padova and joined Juventus, where he remains, in 1993. Described earlier in his career as 'the new Roberto Baggio', he is a left-sided attacking player with marvellous skill and touch. He is also an expert at spot-kicks and possesses a devastating shot, as was evidenced in his hat-trick against Monaco in the 1997/98 European Cup semi-final. That season he scored 21 goals in Serie A. The following season he was absent for long stretches due to injury. He has collected three Serie A league titles with Juventus and been capped more than 30 times by Italy.

Edgar Davids (1973). Nicknamed 'pitbull' owing to his small, stocky frame and his tenacious tackling, Davids is also a skilful midfielder and distributor of the ball. He came up through the Ajax junior team and made his first team debut in 1991 at the age of 18. He moved to AC Milan in the sumer of 1996, having won three Dutch league titles and the European Cup with Ajax, and to Juventus in December 1997. He has over 30 international caps for Holland, although he was dropped from Euro 96 after a row with coach Gus Hiddink. His last-minute winner against Yugoslavia in France 1998 scraped Holland into the quarter-finals of the World Cup.

Edgar Davids

Real Madrid v Juventus

With their recent poor league form, a transfer demand from Zamorano and the sacking of coach Valdano, Real were in turmoil. However, at the Bernabeu in the first leg they managed to beat Juventus through a 20th-minute goal from Raul. At the Stadio Delle Alpi, Juventus levelled the aggregate score with a Del Piero free kick after 16 minutes. Michelle Padovano, playing instead of the suspended Ravanelli, made it 2-1 overall early in the second half, and tempers rose on both sides. Firstly, Real's Alkorta was red-carded and then Juventus's Torricelli was also sent off, and eight players were booked. But Juventus held on.

Semi-finalist: Juventus (2-1 aggregate)

Borussia Dortmund v Ajax

Without Litmanen and Overmars, yet another superb performance from Ajax in Dortmund put the Dutchmen in the driving seat for the second leg. A one-two with Kluiverts, and Edgar Davids had put Ajax ahead with a stunning goal in the eighth minute. The Dutch were playing marvellous, fluid football, and scored again in the 83rd minute when man-of-the-match Davids this time supplied Kluivert who made no mistake from fifteen yards, shooting low past keeper Stefan Klos. The frustrated Borussia had Sammer sent off in the 65th minute for fouling the young substitute Kiki Musampa. In Amsterdam, Musampa's 75th-minute goal finally finished off Borussia.

Semi-finalist: Ajax (3-0 aggregate)

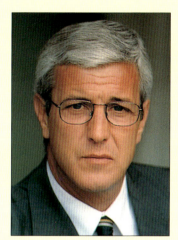

Marcello Lippi, Juventus coach from 1994-98, who took the 'Zebras' to three European Cup Finals, winning one.

Legia Warsaw v Panathinaikos

The two unfancied teams in the last eight met in their first leg in Warsaw where a crowd of only 12,000 saw a dull 0-0 draw. In Athens, the Greek champions swamped Legia 3-0, two coming from 31-year-old striker Warzycha and the other from the Argentinian Juan Jose Borelli.

Semi-finalist: Panathinaikos (3-0 aggregate)

Nantes v Spartak Moscow

Since the League stage, Spartak had lost not only their coach Romantsev, gone to run the Russian side, but also key players Onopko, Yuran, Kulkov and keeper Cherchesov. In France, strikers Japhet N'Doram and Nicolas Ouedec gave Nantes a 2-0 first leg lead. However, in Moscow, Spartak's sweeper and captain Yuri Nikiforov scored twice within six minutes in the first half to tie the score on aggregate. In the 62nd minute Ouedec scored the critical away goal for Nantes, and followed it up with another with five minutes to go, smashing a left-foot shot into the Spartak net.

Semi-finalist: Nantes (4-2 aggregate)

Ajax v Panathinaikos

Thousands of fans greeted the Panathinaikos team at Athens airport when they flew back from Amsterdam after their unexpected but deserved 1-0 away win over Ajax. The defeat ended Ajax's 19-game unbeaten run in the competition. An 87th-minute strike from Krzystof Warzycha, supplied by Georgis Donis, supplied the goal. In the return at the Olympic Stadium, Ajax restored the status quo. In front of nearly 75,000 Greeks, Ajax scored through Litmanen in the fourth minute and, in an impressive and controlled performance, dominated proceedings. Without Kluivert, but with the tenacious Edgar Davids outstanding in midfield, the Dutch had to wait until near the end to score their second, Litmanen converting a Kanu cross in the 77th minute. Substitute Nordin Wooter scored a third for the Dutchmen in the 86th minute. Young defender Michael Reiziger, however, received his second yellow card of the tournament, and would miss the Final.

Finalist: Ajax (3-1 aggregate)

Juventus v Nantes

English referee Dermot Gallagher made himself no French friends in Turin in the first leg when he sent off Nantes midfielder Bruno Carotti just before half time and disallowed a Nantes goal for offside. Within three minutes of the restart Juventus took advantage with a goal from Gianluca Vialli, his first goal in this season's tournament. Nantes, missing Japhet N'Doram and Claude Makelele, went further behind in the 66th minute through a Vladimir Jugovic goal. In Nantes, Vialli effectively killed off the home side's hopes with a 17th-minute goal but Eric Decroix equalised on half time. Vialli set up another for Juventus in the 50th minute, his pass turned in by the substitute Paulo Sousa, but a determined fightback by the French saw them score two more in the last 20 minutes, through the restored N'Doram and Frank Renou. Nantes won 3-2 on the night but were eliminated 4-3 on aggregate.

Finalist: Juventus (4-3 aggregate)

Jari Litmanen (centre, left) scores the equaliser, his ninth goal of the tournament, to equalise for Ajax in the 1996 Final.

Penalties decide thrilling final

Juventus (1) 1   Ajax (1) 1 (after extra time)
(Juventus won 4-2 on penalties)

Olympic Stadium, Rome, 22 May 1996
Attendance: 70,000
Referee: Vega (Spain)

On a warm evening in Rome, Ajax and Juventus faced each other in the European Cup Final for the first time in 23 years. Their previous meeting, in Belgrade in 1973, had been settled in favour of the Dutchmen by a Johnny Rep goal, and Juventus's only success in the competition had been at the Heysel Stadium in 1985, a win darkened by tragedy. With their three-pronged attack of Vialli, Ravanelli and Del Piero, the Italians felt they had the capability to bring home the trophy to Turin. Although missing the injured Overmars, Ajax were equally confident about retaining the trophy and consolidating their position as the best club side in the world.

Juventus started off playing with pace and commitment, although Del Piero and Ravanelli spurned chances in the early stages. In the 12th minute, a moment of confusion between Frank De Boer and keeper Van der Saar allowed the ball to bounce in space in the Ajax box. Ravanelli was on to the opportunity in a split second, leaping in between the two Dutchmen and sliding the ball from what looked like an impossible angle into the net. One-nil to Juve. The game see-sawed on, shots from Musampa and Blind matched by attempts from Del Piero and Deschamps.

In the 41st minute, a foul by Vierchowod on Kanu was punished by a free kick. Frank De Boer sent the ball curving into the Juventus goalmouth, and Peruzzi could only push it out to the waiting Litmanen who turned and sent it into the Italian net to score his ninth goal of the tournament.

Ajax began the second half with Kluivert on for Musampa, and soon after Paulo Sousa was replaced by Di Livio who was immediately in the thick of the action. Vialli was at the heart of the Juventus attack and both he and Del Piero went close, and towards the end Vialli hit the bar. With four minutes to go, Padovano, on for an injured Ravanelli, sent in a cross which Vialli could only turn into the side netting.

The game went into extra time, with Deschamps heading wide and Peruzzi saving from Blind. Vialli escaped the attentions of Winston Bogarde only to shoot the ball at Van der Saar, while at the very end Del Piero fired a Jugovic pass straight at the Ajax keeper. Penalties would decide the destination of the trophy. Peruzzi kept his nerve and saved two Ajax efforts from Davids and Silooy, while Van der Saar let in four, the winner coming from Jugovic.

Juventus had won the Cup, and deservedly so.

The teams
Juventus: Peruzzi, Torricelli, Ferrara,Vierchowod, Pessotto, Conte (Jugovic), Paulo Sousa (Di Livio), Deschamps, Ravanelli (Padovano), Vialli, Del Piero (Manager: Lippi) [Ravanelli 12]
Ajax: Van der Saar, Silooy, Blind, F. De Boer (Scholten), Bogarde, R. De Boer (Wooter), Litmanen, Davids, George, Kanu, Musampa (Kluivert) (manager: Van Gaal) [Litmanen 41]
The penalties
Davids misses; Ferrara 0-1; Litmanen 1-1; Pessotto 1-2; Scholten 2-2; Padovano 2-3; Silooy misses; Jugovic 2-4.

THE *1996-97* SEASON

With the competition due for some dramatic changes next season, this was the last year in which there were only four league groups. The seeds were Juventus, AC Milan, Auxerre, Borussia Dortmund, Atlético Madrid, Ajax, Manchester United and Porto. In the qualifying round, Rangers disposed of Russian champions Alania Vladikavkaz helped by an incredible 7-2 victory in Russia, while Fenerbahçe struggled to beat Israel's Maccabi Tel Aviv 2-1. Rosenborg came back from a goal down in Greece to score two in extra time in Trondheim and secure a 3-1 win over the previous year's semi-finalists Panathinaikos.

GROUP A

Ajax, Auxerre, Grasshoppers Zurich, Rangers

Ajax had seen several players leave the club over the summer. Reiziger and Davids had gone to Milan, Finidi George to Seville and Kanu had departed to Inter, but midfielder Richard Witschge had come back home from Bordeaux and Marc Overmars had recovered from injury. They could also call on the goal-scoring abilities of Kluivert and Litmanen, the latter scoring a fine individual goal in the fourth minute against Auxerre in the opening game 1-0 victory. The same evening, two goals in Zurich from new signing Kubilay Turkyilmaz helped Grasshoppers secure three points from a disappointing Rangers.

Long-serving and popular coach Guy Roux had taken his provincial Auxerre team to the French 'double', and they put two past Rangers at Ibrox later in the month for a 2-1 win. Ajax were surprisingly beaten by a Murat Yakin 60th-minute strike in the new Amsterdam Arena to go 1-0 down to the Swiss champions. On the third match-day, Ajax easily overcame Rangers 4-1 at home, while Auxerre went joint top of the league with the Dutchmen thanks to a Thomas Deniaud goal against Grasshoppers just before the interval.

Grasshoppers, however, took over the top slot after the fourth round when they beat Auxerre 3-1 in Zurich, two of the goals coming from another new signing Romanian striker Viorel Moldovan. Ajax remained level on points when they beat Rangers 1-0 at Ibrox. On the fifth match-day, Auxerre surprised Ajax with a 2-1 win in Amsterdam, while Rangers finally got among the points with an Ally McCoist-inspired 2-1 victory over Grasshoppers.

On the last day, Ajax had to beat Grasshoppers in Zurich to qualify, and Kluivert brought relief to the Dutchmen with a 32nd-minute goal. Auxerre's home win over Rangers ended Zurich's hopes and the French novices qualified for the knock-out stage as group leaders.

Auxerre 0	Ajax 1
Grasshoppers 3	Rangers 0
Rangers 1	Auxerre 2
Ajax 0	Grasshoppers 1
Auxerre 1	Grasshoppers 0
Ajax 4	Rangers 1
Rangers 0	Ajax 1
Grasshoppers 3	Auxerre 1
Rangers 2	Grasshoppers 1
Ajax 1	Auxerre 2
Auxerre 2	Rangers 1
Grasshoppers 0	Ajax 1

	P	W	D	L	F	A	Pts
Auxerre	6	4	0	2	8	7	12
Ajax	6	4	0	2	8	4	12
Grasshoppers	6	3	0	3	8	5	9
Rangers	6	1	0	5	5	13	3

GROUP B

Atlético Madrid, Borussia Dortmund, Widzew Lódz, Steaua Bucharest

Coach Raddy Antic had built a strong Atlético Madrid side, and they had won the Spanish 'double'. In their Vicente Calderon stadium on the first day, they crushed Steaua Bucharest 4-0, two goals coming from Argentinian striker Juan Eduardo Esnaider and two from the head of midfielder Diego Simeone in the second half.

Borussia Dortmund, marshalled from midfield by Möller and Sammer and joined in the summer by Juventus's Paulo Sousa, were too good for Poland's Widzew Lódz, against whom striker Heiko Herrlich netted both goals in a 2-1 home win. In the second match-day, Atlético made their total eight goals in two games with a 4-1 away demolition of Widzew, two again coming from the head of Simeone. Borussia also recorded an impressive away win, this time 3-0 against Steaua. Lars Ricken scored in the sixth minute, and Heinrich and Stephane Chapuisat added the other two.

In October, a Stefan Reuter goal against Atlético ensured that Borussia took the halfway lead, while a Daniel Bogusz own goal gave Steaua a 1-0 win over Widzew and a slim remaining chance of qualifying. In the fourth round, Borussia, missing the injured Sammer and Kohler, went down 2-1 in Dortmund to Atlético, who went top of the group, while Lódz ended Steaua's hopes and gained their first points with a 2-0 home win. On the fifth match-day, a 65th-minute Kohler goal gave Borussia an away 2-2 draw in Poland, and Yugoslavian midfielder Milinko Pantic scored for Atlético in their 1-1 draw in Bucharest.

In their last game, a late goal again from Pantic gave Atlético a 1-0 victory over Widzew and the leadership of the group, in spite of Borussia's 5-3 defeat of Steaua in Germany.

Atlético 4	Steaua 0
Borussia 2	Widzew 1
Widzew 1	Atlético 4
Steaua 0	Borussia 3
Atlético 0	Borussia 1
Steaua 1	Widzew 0
Widzew 2	Steaua 0
Borussia 1	Atlético 2
Widzew 2	Borussia 2
Steaua 1	Atlético 1
Atlético 1	Widzew 0
Borussia 5	Steaua 3

	P	W	D	L	F	A	Pts
Atlético Madrid	6	4	1	1	12	4	13
Borussia Dortmund	6	4	1	1	14	8	13
Widzew Lódz	6	1	1	4	6	10	4
Steaua Bucharest	6	1	1	4	5	15	4

Fenerbahçe, Juventus, Manchester United, Rapid Vienna

As with Ajax, some familiar faces had departed from Juventus in the summer. Paulo Sousa, Vialli and Ravanelli had all gone, but new arrivals included the admired Croatian striker Alen Boksic, young French midfielder Zinedine Zidane from Bordeaux and forward Christian Vieri from Atalanta. They enjoyed a relatively simple 1-0 win over Manchester United at home in their first game.

Fenerbahçe manager Sebastiao Lazaroni had bought Bulgarian forward Emil Kostadinov and young Nigerian midfielder Jay Jay Okocha, but the Turks were outsiders to qualify. Against Rapid Vienna, however, Elvir Bolic put them in front after 31 minutes and, although Christian Stumpf headed Rapid level in the 70th minute, Fenerbahçe had the better of a 1-1 draw in Austria. In game two, a Boksic goal for Juventus in Istanbul was enough to beat Fenerbahçe, while United managed a 2-0 victory over Rapid at Old Trafford.

In October, a confident United won 2-0 in Istanbul. Vieri opened the scoring for Juventus in Vienna but Polish forward Andrzej Lesiak equalised for a 1-1 draw, leaving Juventus on top of the group above United. On the fourth match-day, Fenerbahçe shocked United by winning 1-0 at Old Trafford, while Juventus rocked Rapid with a 5-0 win in Turin, Boksic and Del Piero both scoring twice and the other coming from new defender Paolo Montero. Juventus qualified with one game to go in a thrilling 1-0 win at Old Trafford and Fenerbahçe moved one point ahead of United with a 1-0 home defeat of Rapid.

All now depended on the last two games. In a stirring performance in freezing Vienna, United won 2-0. In Turin, a weakened Juventus side faced Fenerbahçe and reserve forward Michele Padovano headed Juve into the lead late in the first half. Substitute Nicola Amoruso added a second with five minutes to go, his first for the club. United were through to the quarter-finals.

Rapid 1	Fenerbahçe 1
Juventus 1	United 0
United 2	Rapid 0
Fenerbahçe 0	Juventus 1
Rapid 1	Juventus 1
Fenerbahçe 0	United 2
United 0	Fenerbahçe 1
Juventus 5	Rapid 0
United 0	Juventus 1
Fenerbahçe 1	Rapid 0
Rapid 0	United 2
Juventus 2	Fenerbahçe 0

	P	W	D	L	F	A	Pts
Juventus	6	5	1	0	11	1	16
Manchester United	6	3	0	3	6	3	9
Fenerbahçe	6	2	1	3	3	6	7
Rapid Vienna	6	0	2	4	2	12	2

AC Milan, IFK Gothenburg, Porto, Rosenborg

Inevitably one of the favourites to win the tournament, AC Milan had strengthened their hugely talented squad with Ajax's Reiziger and Davids, and French striker Christophe Dugarry, under new coach Oscar Washington Tabarez. However, in a shocked San Siro in the opening game they threw away a 2-1 lead to crash 3-2 to Porto. Simone scored in the 14th minute and, although Porto equalised through Artur Oliveira, Weah restored Milan's lead in the 67th minute. Young Brazilian striker Mario Jardel took advantage of the absent Baresi and Costacurta to score twice for Porto in the last fifteen minutes. Rosenborg's Harald Brattbakk scored the winner against IFK in Denmark in a 3-2 victory.

A hat-trick from Simone and a goal from Weah gave Milan a 4-1 win over Rosenborg in the next game, while two from Oliveira disposed of IFK 2-1 in Portugal. In game three, Milan again stumbled. One-nil up through Weah against IFK in Gothenburg, they let in two goals in the last fifteen minutes, the winner coming from winger Niclas Alexandersson. A 90th-minute Jardel goal gave Porto a 1-0 victory over Rosenborg. At the halfway stage, unbeaten Porto were a full six points ahead of the other group members.

In their fourth match, Baggio scored the fourth in Milan's 4-2 home win over IFK in Italy, and Porto ensured their progress to the quarter-finals with a 3-0 victory over Rosenborg. In the fifth game, an Edgar Davids goal against Porto was equalised by Edmilson for a 1-1 draw, while a Bent Skammelsrud 66th-minute penalty gave Rosenborg a win over IFK and kept up their challenge on Milan.

Again, the second qualifying place depended on the last two games. Having dismissed Tabarez and brought back Arrigo Sacchi, Milan nonetheless failed again. Against Rosenborg at the San Siro, they fell behind to a 29th-minute Brattbakk strike, but equalised through Dugarry in the 45th minute. Vegard Heggem clinched the winner for Rosenborg with twenty minutes to go. Milan had dramatically lost out on second place and the delighted Norwegians were through to the quarter-final.

IFK 2	Rosenborg 3
Milan 2	Porto 3
Porto 2	IFK 1
Rosenborg 1	Milan 4
IFK 2	Milan 1
Rosenborg 0	Porto 1
Porto 3	Rosenborg 0
Milan 4	IFK 2
Porto 1	Milan 1
Rosenborg 1	IFK 0
IFK 0	Porto 2
Milan 1	Rosenborg 2

	P	W	D	L	F	A	Pts
Porto	6	5	1	0	12	4	16
Rosenborg	6	3	0	3	7	11	9
AC Milan	6	2	1	3	13	11	7
IFK Gothenburg	6	1	0	5	7	13	3

MANCHESTER UNITED 96/97

Manchester United had won last season's English 'double', but Alex Ferguson had continued to strengthen his squad over the summer. In came Romanian winger/midfielder Karel Poborsky, forward Jordi Cruyff, and two Norwegians, striker Ole Gunnar Solskjaer and defender Ronny Johnsen. With the commitment of Roy Keane and the ball play of David Beckham in midfield, and the sporadic genius of Eric Cantona, who had moved from Leeds, United appeared a real threat to the other big clubs of Europe.

There were few bigger than Juventus, who entertained United in Turin in the first league game. From the kick-off Juventus were in total command. Without Roy Keane, and with Cantona playing a lone role up front, United appeared disjointed and were no match for the athletic, quick passing of Zidane, Deschamps and Del Piero. Vieri missed two easy opportunities in the first half and Conte had a disallowed 'goal' in the 30th minute. Alen Boksic lashed Juve ahead in the 34th minute, and a 1-0 final scoreline disguised Juventus's dominance.

Two weeks later, Rapid Vienna were the opposition at Old Trafford. In an exciting, tactically intelligent performance, with Beckham outstanding in midfield, United outplayed Rapid and deserved their 2-0 victory. In the 20th minute, a Keane cross found the lively Solskjaer and United went ahead. Seven minutes later, Beckham seized on a mis-hit pass from Peter Stoger to keeper Michael Konsel and, although the keeper got his hands to the ball, Beckham scored on the rebound. In the second half, Cantona and Solskjaer went close, although Schmeichel had to be quick to save a long-range effort from Zoran Barisic.

In front of a menacing, partisan crowd in Istanbul, United faced Fenerbahçe in game three. Jay Jay Okocha and Elvir Bolic threatened a firmly defensive United in the first half, but the Turks could not penetrate the defensive pairing of Pallister and May. Within one five-minute period of the second half, United went 2-0 ahead. Firstly, Cantona sent a brilliant pass through the defence to Solskjaer who slipped the ball to an advancing Beckham. Beckham sent a low 15-yard shot past keeper Rustu. Then

Solskjaer back-heeled to Cruyff, who sent in a ball from the left to Cantona. The Frenchman sidefooted it into the net.

In the return match at Old Trafford, a game which United were expected to win, Fenerbahçe shocked the English club by winning 1-0 and becoming the first team to beat United at home in forty years of European competition. With Pallister injured, Jay Jay Okocha had a magnificent game in which he master-minded Fenerbahçe's creative movement, while central defender Uche Ukechuwku presided over a tight and disciplined defence. The goal came when, with just over ten minutes to go, an Elvir Bolic shot deflected off David May and went over Peter Schmeichel's head into the net. United were now in second place with two matches to play.

In the penultimate game, Juventus came to Old Trafford and, inspired by the class and vision of Zinedine Zidane, the Italians turned on a superb performance of skill and athleticism. Although Juventus only won 1-0, they should have scored more. Their goal came in the 36th minute when Nicky Butt fouled Del Piero in the box and Del Piero himself despatched the spot kick. This result, United's second 1-0 defeat in succession in Group C, left Fenerbahçe, 1-0 victors over Rapid Vienna, one point clear of United. In the final game against Rapid Vienna a draw would be sufficient for United to qualify, provided that Fenerbahçe lose in Turin, as their head-to-head results favoured United.

In Vienna, United began encouragingly, raining in shots on Rapid keeper Michael Konsel's goal, but Rapid came back into the game forcing some fine saves from Schmeichel. In the 24th minute United went ahead. Giggs collected from Keane, evaded a couple of tackles and passed to Cantona. The Frenchman slid a through ball into the path of the advancing Giggs and the winger finished off the move with a left-foot shot into the Rapid net. May, Pallister and Irwin were effectively holding off the Rapid attacks, and in the 72nd minute United scored again, Beckham sending in a low cross to Cantona who swept in the ball at the far post. Juventus had beaten Fenerbahçe 2-0 and United had qualified in second place.

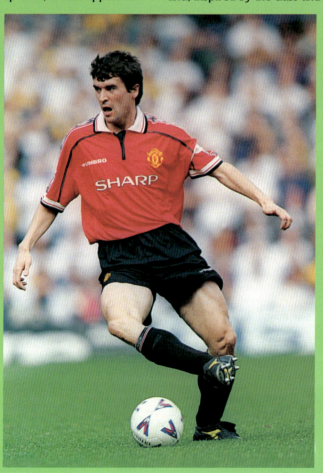

Roy Keane (1971). One of the toughest, most determined ball-winning midfielders in the British game, Keane also has abundant passing skills and the ability to score some memorable and important goals. A boy from Cork, he joined Nottingham Forest for £10,000 as an 18-year-old in 1990 and was transferred to Manchester United in 1993 for £3.75 million. In his career at United he has picked up four league titles and three FA Cups, including three 'doubles'. With the departure of Eric Cantona in 1997, the charismatic Keane was appointed captain but he spent most of season 1997/98 injured. He returned for the start of the 1998/99 season and captained United to the European Cup Final, which he missed due to suspension. His own goal in the 1999/2000 second leg quarter-final against Real Madrid at Old Trafford helped eliminate United from the tournament. He was first capped by Ireland in 1991 and played in the 1994 World Cup finals. He has represented his country 46 times.

RANGERS 1996/97

Scottish Player of the Year Paul Gascoigne's nineteen goals the previous season had, along with the efforts of Brian Laudrup and Gordon Durie, brought the 'double' to Ibrox.

In the preliminary round against the Russian champions from Chechneya, Alania Vladikavkaz, they went behind to an Igor Yanovsky's goal in the 29th minute at Ibrox. Substitute Derek McInnes equalised five minutes after the break. McCoist got the second in the 60th minute and defender Gordan Petric a third with ten minutes to go. In an extraordinary game in Russia, McCoist scored a hat-trick in the first eighteen minutes and, although by the 24th minute the Russians had pulled back two, Laudrup (twice), Van Vossen and Charlie Miller made the score 7-2, a 10-3 aggregate.

Zurich, the first league game, saw a humiliatingly inept performance against Grasshoppers. The speed and skill of the home side, particularly Turkish striker Kubilay Turkyilmaz, unsettled the Scots from the beginning. Ten minutes after an 18th-minute Murat Yakin header from a Turkyilmaz cross, he drove in a 20-yard free kick. Turkyilmaz headed in his second with eleven minutes to go.

Back at Ibrox against Auxerre, Rangers went on the offensive in the first half with French keeper Charbonnier kept busy by Gascoigne, van Vossen and Durie. Auxerre roused themselves in the second half and in the 55th minute, Bernard Diomede crossed to Thomas Deniaud whose well-flighted header evaded Goram. In the 68th minute, a Diomede corner again found Deniaud and Auxerre were two up. Gascoigne powerfully headed in a Laudrup cross two minutes later, but the score remained 2-1 and Rangers were in trouble.

In Amsterdam for game three, Laudrup nearly scored in the 5th minute when a clever chip went just wide. However, a Dani header from a Tijani Babangida cross in the 25th minute gave Ajax the lead, and three minutes later Gascoigne viciously kicked Bogarde and was ordered off. This was the turning point, and Dani headed another in the 41st minute from an Overmars cross. Rangers were powerless to prevent Babangida's goal in the 83rd minute, though substitute Ian Durrant managed an 88th-minute reply. Ajax substitute Nordin Wooter made the score 4-1 at the death.

With four players suspended – Gascoigne, Gough, Cleland and Moore – Rangers fielded a young, makeshift team at Ibrox. Again they began well, but the more experienced and skilful Ajax scored in the 39th minute, when Arnold Scholten sent a long-range, right-foot drive past keeper Snelders. In the second half, Laudrup and van Vossen were beating defenders but unable to find the net. The Ajax defence held firm, and Rangers had no chance of qualification.

Playing now only for honour, they met Grasshoppers at Ibrox. At last, Rangers put up a fighting performance with the visitors' keeper Pascal Züberbühler saving well from two Gough headers in the first half. Although the dangerous Turkyilmaz constantly threatened in the 65th minute McCoist scored from the spot after a handling offence, and within six minutes converted an Albertz pass with a 20-yard shot. Goram saved a Mats Gren penalty in the 75th minute, but was beaten by a volley from substitute Jan Berger two minutes later.

In the final game in France, a Goram mistake in the 20th minute allowed Lilian Laslandes in to score and, in the 32nd minute, Steve Marlet weaved past four defenders to make it two. Five minutes later, Gough, playing his last season for Rangers, headed in a Steven cross from the six-yard box.

Two years in succession, the Scottish champions had finished bottom of their group with a meagre three points.

Zinedine Zidane

Zinedine Zidane (1972). 'Zizou' is Platini's heir as the finest French footballer of his generation. Marseille born, he began his career with Cannes and moved to Bordeaux in 1992, from where he was transferred to Juventus in 1996. He played in two European Cup Finals in 1997 and 1998, being on the losing side both times, and his brilliant midfield play and finishing have brought Juventus two Italian league titles. He scored two headed goals in the 1998 World Cup Final, when France won the trophy for the first time, and was rewarded by the awards of European and World Footballer of the Year. To date, he has gained over 50 caps for his country, and he scored twice on his debut match against the Czech Republic in 1994.

UEFA moves the goalposts

For next year's tournament, UEFA revised the rules and format yet again, moving even further away from the original conception of the European Cup. The most important and controversial change was that the league runners-up of the top eight European countries, based on the country's club rankings in European competitions over the past five years, now enter the competition.

This meant that, for the first time, one country, Germany, had three teams – champions Bayern Munich, holders Borussia Dortmund and runners-up Bayer Leverküsen – in the tournament.

As before, the eight top seeds were to go direct to the group stage which was expanded into six groups of four clubs each. The winner of each group and the two best runners-up would then move on to contest the quarter-finals.

There are two preliminary, home and away knock-out rounds. The first is for the 30 lowest-ranked countries, and the seeded eight runners-up join the fray in the second round. The 16 winners then join the group stage. Teams knocked out in the first round are out of European competition, while those eliminated in round two go direct to the first round of the UEFA Cup as compensation.

Ajax v Atlético Madrid

Bogarde and Kluivert had announced their intentions to leave Ajax for Italy in the summer and Van Gaal was to take over at Barcelona. With Atlético striker Kiko suspended for the first leg in Amsterdam, the Spaniards nonetheless went ahead in the eighth minute through Esnaider but Kluivert equalised in the 53rd minute. A 1-1 full-time result gave the advantage to Atlético who went ahead through the restored Kiko in the 29th minute in Madrid. Ronald de Boer levelled the aggregate score in the 49th minute, and the tie went into extra time. Dani had come on for Litmanen in the last ten minutes of normal time, and he struck for Ajax in the 100th minute. Pantic scored five minutes later and, with one minute remaining, Tijani Babangida ensured Ajax's place in the semi-final,

Semi-finalist: Ajax (4-3 aggregate)

Borussia Dortmund v Auxerre

Karlheinz Riedle gave Borussia a 12th-minute lead in the first leg in Dortmund and substitute defender Rene Schneider made it two just after half-time. Midfielder Sabri Lamouchi pulled a goal back with fifteen minutes to go, but Andy Möller scored a third for Borussia in the 83rd minute. Without a suspended Stefan Reuter in the return leg, Borussia's Lars Ricken scored a 60th-minute goal to make the aggregate score 4-1 in Borussia's favour.

Semi-finalist: Borussia Dortmund
(4-1 aggregate)

Rosenborg v Juventus

Juventus had recently beaten Paris St-Germain 9-2 in the European Supercup and were on song. Rosenborg's success in the tournament had resulted in their losing two key players – winger Steffen Iversen to Tottenham and defender Bjorn Tore Kvarme to Liverpool. In the first leg in Norway, a goal from Trond Soltvedt in the 51st minute was equalised almost immediately by Christian Vieri and the score stayed 1-1. A Zidane goal in the 29th minute put Juventus ahead on aggregate but the Italian side suffered a nervous hour until a Nicola Amoruso penalty in the very last minute settled matters.

Semi-finalist: Juventus (3-1 aggregate)

Manchester United v Porto

In a superb performance at Old Trafford in the first leg, memorable for an unselfish and inspirational display by Cantona, United outplayed Porto to win 4-0. With 22 minutes gone, David May placed the ball past the inexperienced Porto keeper Hilario, and twelve minutes later Cantona scored the second with a low drive. An unstoppable shot from Giggs in the 60th minute made the score 3-0 and, with ten minutes to go, Cole latched on to a Cantona through pass to flick the ball over Hilario with his left foot.

In Porto, United played with intelligence to keep out the threat posed by Jardel, Edmilson and Rui Jorge. In the Das Antas stadium, they resisted the sustained bouts of pressure from Porto and launched quick counter-attacks through Solskjaer and Cantona, but neither side could score. United fans celebrated well before the final whistle. The club was to meet Borussia Dortmund in the semi-final.

Semi-finalist: Manchester United (4-0 aggregate)

Ajax v Juventus

Ajax, without injured striker Kluivert, started well in the first leg in Amsterdam. However, Juventus took advantage of some uncertain Ajax defending in the 13th minute when Amoruso touched in a Yugovic pass. Juventus were simply too fast and skilful for the Dutch, with Vieri confirming their superiority in the 41st minute. Juventus could have scored more in the second half, but instead Litmanen dribbled through the Juventus defence in the 66th minute to score an important goal for Ajax.

In Turin, Juventus destroyed Ajax and ended the Dutch team's three-year-old unbeaten away run in Europe. Although Ajax were on top for the first half-hour, the tie was over within three minutes. A Zidane corner in the 34th minute was met by Lombardo's head, and it was 1-0. Then, a Lombardo cut-back from the left of the penalty area found a stretching Vieri, whose left foot made it 2-0. Immediately after the interval, Boksic and Vieri could have added two more, but it was Ajax who were next to score, in the 76th minute, when defender Melchiot headed in a corner. Within three minutes, Zidane dribbled into the penalty area and flicked the ball to substitute Amoruso who could not miss. Two minutes later, Zidane, crowning an evening of personal triumph, rounded Van der Saar and the defence to shoot into an empty net.

Finalist: Juventus (6-2 aggregate)

Borussia Dortmund v Manchester United

An under-strength Borussia – missing the suspended Sammer and the injured Kohler, Cesar and Chapuisat – faced United, without Schmeichel, in Dortmund in the first leg. The weakened German side dominated an uncertain and unsettled United in the first half. After the interval, United briefly raised their game, and Nicky Butt hit the post while Beckham had a shot cleared off the line. In the 76th minute, however, Rene Tretschok dispossessed a below-par Cantona, shot from 25 yards, and saw his effort deflect off Pallister and past substitute keeper Raymond Van der Gouw for the only goal of the game.

At Old Trafford, a tremendous defensive display by Borussia, in particular by Wolfgang Feiersinger and Jürgen Kohler, kept out continuous, frenzied attacks by a young United side. Midfielder Lars Ricken had scored with a low, left-footed shot from a ball from Möller in the seventh minute, and United had no choice other than to go on the offensive. Throughout the game, United had several clear-cut opportunities but were guilty of poor and hasty finishing, the main culprits being Cole and Cantona. Giggs came on for Solskjaer in the second half, but Borussia's slick organisation and defensive obduracy kept out all United's efforts. Borussia Dortmund were to meet Juventus in this year's Final.

Finalist: Borussia Dortmund (2-0 aggregate)

Ricken and Riedle bring Cup to Dortmund

Borussia Dortmund 3 (2) Juventus 1 (0)

Olympic Stadium, Munich, 28 May 1997
Attendance: 60,000
Referee: Puhl (Hungary)

Juventus, the finest club side in Europe, were clear favourites. The Final, held in Juventus' centenary year, was to be a showcase for the awesome talents of Del Piero, Boksic and Zidane, and Borussia were simply a sideshow. What actually happened was one of the biggest upsets in the history of the tournament.

Sweeper and club inspiration Matthias Sammer was back for Borussia, and the German team contained no less than four ex-Juve players – Kohler, Möller, Paulo Sousa and Reuter. They needed to be at their best as the game began, as Juventus started in ominous form. With Di Livio and Jugovic pressing from midfield, and Boksic and Vieri threatening and stretching Borussia, the Germans were forced back into defence for the first 25 minutes.

In the 29th minute, however, Borussia forced a corner. Möller swung the ball in from the left, and it was half cleared by the Italian defence. It reached Paul Lambert who chipped it back into the box, where the waiting Karlheinz Riedle chested it down and fired it into the net with his left foot. Within five minutes, unfancied Borussia were two up. Möller again from the left corner spot found Riedle who outjumped the defenders to head it in at the near post.

Juventus had nothing to lose and surged forward, Zidane hitting the post with a low shot and Vieri scoring but using his hand, adjudged referee Puhl. At half time, Marcello Lippi threw caution to one side and replaced centre-back Sergei Porrini with Del Piero. Again, Juventus took the fight to Borussia, their pace and mobility posing all sorts of problems for Sammer's men. In the 56th minute, a deflected shot from Boksic beat keeper Stefan Klos, but bounced off the crossbar. Eight minutes later, however, Juventus made their breakthrough. Boksic left Kohler stranded on the wing and his near post cross was expertly flicked in the net past Klos by Del Piero.

Lars Ricken came on to replace Chapuisat in the 70th minute and within seconds of his arrival Borussia had scored a third. Möller passed to Ricken, accelerating in space through the centre, and Ricken, spotting Peruzzi off his line, sent a magnificent lob from 35 yards over the out-of-position keeper. Amoruso immediately replaced Vieri but Borussia held firm. At the final whistle, the Dortmund players threw themselves on top of each other on the pitch, while the Juventus team simply appeared stunned.

The trophy was back in German hands for the first time in fourteen years. Juventus had thrown all they had at the determined, intelligent and organised German side, but Borussia had tactically out-thought Juventus, taken their chances and deserved their victory. As coach Ottmar Hitzfeld said, 'I must thank all my players. They were magnificent'.

The teams

Borussia Dortmund: Klos, Sammer, Kree, Kohler, Reuter, Paulo Sousa, Lambert, Heinrich, Möller (Zorc), Chapuisat (Ricken), Riedle (manager: Hitzfeld) [Riedle 29, 34, Ricken 71]

Juventus: Peruzzi, Ferrara, Montero, Porrini (Del Piero), Juliano, Di Livio, Deschamps, Zidane, Jugovic (Tacchinardi), Boksic, Vieri (Amoruso) (manager: Lippi) [Del Piero 64]

Karlheinz Riedle (yellow shirt, 13) opens the scoring for Borussia Dortmund in the 1997 Final.

To accommodate the 55 clubs involved this season, the first preliminary round kicked off in late July. Steaua Bucharest were one big name who proved their worth with a fine 2-0 away win against CSKA Sofia. In the qualifying round, with the runners-up now appearing as seeds, tiny Skonto Riga were only beaten 3-2 in the Nou Camp by a 90th-minute Stoichkov penalty, and a Sonny Anderson goal in Riga put the nervous Catalans into the group stage. Kosice, the first Slovakian team since independence to compete, held Spartak Moscow in Russia 0-0 to go through 2-1, while Rangers failed again and went out 4-1 to IFK. Newcastle, English runners-up, battled hard against Croatia Zagreb and a last-minute, extra-time goal from Ketsbaia put the Geordies into the league. The first round began in mid September.

GROUP A

Borussia Dortmund, Galatasaray, Parma, Sparta Prague

Karlheinz Riedle had gone to Liverpool and been replaced by Aberdeen's Scott Booth, but otherwise Borussia Dortmund fielded the previous year's team. Under new manager Nevio Scala, they travelled to Istanbul on opening day without the injured Sammer, Möller and Reuter and the suspended Ricken and Sousa. A Stephan Chapuisat 73rd-minute goal got them the three points. Carlo Ancelotti's Parma had to settle for a goal-less draw with Sparta in Prague.

In Prague two weeks later, a 76th-minute strike from Horst Siegl restored a measure of decency to a 4-0 scoreline, with Chapuisat claiming two for Borussia. Argentinians Roberto Sensini and Crespo were the scorers for Parma in their home 2-0 win over Galatasaray. On the third match-day, Crespo struck again for Parma, giving them a 1-0 win in Italy to go top over Borussia and handing the Germans their first defeat in eight European Cup games. Sparta put three past Galatasaray, leaving the Turks with no points from three games.

In early November, Borussia were missing important players through injury against Parma but won 2-0, with Möller scoring both, one a penalty, and took over league leadership. Midfielder Tugay Kerimoglu brought Galatasaray among the points at last with the two goals in Gala's 2-0 win over Sparta. On the penultimate day, Borussia hammered Galatasaray 4-1 and took an unassailable lead in the group when Parma could only draw 2-2 with Sparta.

On the sixth match-day, a Chiesa goal just after the interval was cancelled by an Ilie strike for Galatasaray within five minutes, and the score stayed 1-1. Borussia beat Sparta 3-0 in Prague, substitute Booth scoring his first European goal for the club.

Galatasaray 0	Borussia 1
Sparta 0	Parma 0
Parma 2	Galatasaray 0
Borussia 4	Sparta 1
Parma 1	Borussia 0
Sparta 3	Galatasaray 0
Galatasaray 2	Sparta 0
Borussia 2	Parma 0
Parma 2	Sparta 2
Borussia 4	Galatasaray 1
Sparta 0	Borussia 3
Galatasaray 1	Parma 1

	P	W	D	L	F	A	Pts
Borussia	6	5	0	1	14	3	15
Parma	6	2	3	1	6	5	9
Sparta	6	1	2	3	6	11	5
Galatasaray	6	1	1	4	4	11	4

GROUP B

Feyenoord, Juventus, Kosice, Manchester United

The previous season's top Italian striker Filippo Inzaghi had joined Juventus for £8.5 million from Atalanta to compensate for the surprise departures of Boksic to Lazio and Vieri to Atlético Madrid. They started the competition in typically free-scoring style, slotting five past Feyenoord, who had sold keeper Ed De Goey to Chelsea and striker Henrik Larsson to Celtic in the summer. Del Piero scored two in the first eleven minutes, Inzaghi added a third and, in spite of a 57th-minute sending-off for Di Livio, they scored two more in the second half from Zidane and defender Alessandro Birindelli. Manchester United scored three away against a shaky Kosice.

In game two, Feyenoord beat a still-goal-less Kosice 2-0 in Holland while United beat Juventus in an epic at Old Trafford. On the third match-day, Juventus dominated Kosice in Slovakia but could only score through a Del Piero 34th-minute free kick. United continued winning with a 2-1 victory over Feyenoord at Old Trafford. In early November, Juventus were three up against Kosice in Turin – with goals from Del Piero, Amoruso and Fonseca – but the Slovaks retaliated twice in five minutes with Rusian Lubarskij and Dusan Toth. United won again, Andy Cole's hat-trick sinking Feyenoord in Holland.

On the fifth match-day, United qualified for the quarter-finals by beating Kosice 3-0 at Old Trafford, while Juventus went down 2-0 to Feyenoord in Holland, Julio Cruz doing the damage in the 66th and 88th minutes. On the last day, an Inzaghi 83rd-minute goal against United put Juventus into the quarter-finals as one of the two best second-placed teams, while Giovanni Van Bronckhorst's 81st-minute goal for Feyenoord in a 1-0 win left Kosice without a win, as well as point-less in the league.

Juventus 5	Feyenoord 1
Kosice 0	United 3
Feyenoord 2	Kosice 0
United 3	Juventus 2
United 2	Feyenoord 1
Kosice 0	Juventus 1
Feyenoord 1	United 3
Juventus 3	Kosice 2
Feyenoord 2	Juventus 0
United 3	Kosice 0
Kosice 0	Feyenoord 1
Juventus 1	United 0

	P	W	D	L	F	A	Pts
Manchester United	6	5	0	1	14	5	15
Juventus	6	4	0	2	12	8	12
Feyenoord	6	3	0	3	8	10	9
Kosice	6	0	0	6	2	13	0

Barcelona, Dynamo Kiev, Newcastle United, PSV Eindhoven

Ex-Ajax coach Louis Van Gaal had taken over from Robson as coach at Barcelona, and the squad had been further strengthened by the arrival of Brazil's Rivaldo from Deportivo for a staggering £17 million, as well as his countryman Sonny Anderson, a £13 million buy from Monaco. Much was expected of Van Gaal's side this season, although Newcastle and an Asprilla hat-trick at St James's Park gave Barca a bad start to their campaign in their first game.

Dynamo Kiev's young strikers Andrei Shevchenko and Sergei Rebrov fronted a strong, disciplined and experienced team, led from the midfield by captain Yury Kalitvintsev. Rebrov and Shevchenko both scored in their 3-1 away demolition of Dick Advocaat's PSV Eindhoven.

In Spain in October, PSV's Chris Van Der Weerden was sent off in the 35th minute, and Luis Enrique put Barca 1-0 ahead in the 61st minute. Enrique scored another, but striker Gilles De Bilde and midfielder Peter Möller earned PSV a point. Newcastle made a second-half comeback in Kiev to secure a 2-2 draw.

In the third match-day, Kiev stunned Barcelona in the Ukraine with a 3-0 drubbing. Barca keeper Ruud Hesp was sent off in the 60th minute for a professional foul, but Kiev were already 2-0 up through Rebrov and Yuri Maximov. Kalitvintsev added the third with a 20-yard shot in the 65th minute. Newcastle went down 1-0 in Holland against PSV. At the Nou Camp in game four, Kiev again humiliated Barcelona. Shevchenko scored a first-half hat-trick with two headers and a penalty, and Rebrov scored the fourth in the 79th minute to put Barcelona out of the tournament with one point from four games. Newcastle were defeated 2-0 at home by PSV.

A fifth-game 1-1 draw with PSV allowed Kiev to finish top of the league, Rebrov scoring in the 17th minute and De Bilde equalising in the second half to keep alive PSV's hopes of finishing best runner-up. An early Barcelona goal gave them a 1-0 win over Newcastle at the Nou Camp. A 2-0 Newcastle home win over Kiev in the final game was not enough to qualify. Goals from Wim Jonk and De Bilde within two minutes early in the second half in Holland could not prevent a 2-2 draw with Barcelona, and PSV were also out.

PSV 1	Kiev 3
Newcastle 3	Barcelona 2
Barcelona 2	PSV 2
Kiev 2	Newcastle 2
PSV 1	Newcastle 0
Kiev 3	Barcelona 0
Newcastle 0	PSV 2
Barcelona 0	Kiev 4
Barcelona 1	Newcastle 0
Kiev 1	PSV 1
PSV 2	Barcelona 2
Newcastle 2	Kiev 0

	P	W	D	L	F	A	Pts
Dynamo Kiev	6	3	2	1	13	6	11
PSV	6	2	3	1	9	8	9
Newcastle	6	2	1	3	7	8	7
Barcelona	6	1	2	3	7	14	5

Olympiakos, Porto, Real Madrid, Rosenborg

New Real Madrid manager Jupp Heynckes had plenty of attacking options in Raul, Davor Suker, Dani and Pedrag Mijatovic, reinforced by Fernando Morientes and Clarence Seedorf and Brazilian left wing-back Roberto Carlos. They easily disposed of Norway's Rosenborg 4-1 in the first game at the Bernabeu, while Olympiakos beat FC Porto in Greece.

Porto, with Ljubinko Drulovic the playmaker and Mario Jardel the main finisher, were beaten at home 2-0 by Real in the second game, Fernando Hierro and Raul the scorers. Rosenborg crushed Olympiakos 5-1 in Norway with Harald Brattbakk and Roar Strand scoring two apiece. In game three, it was Real's turn to put five past Olympiakos. Nikos Dabizas scored first for the Greek side, but two penalties from Suker, a goal each from Morientes and Victor, and a last-minute strike from Roberto Carlos, kept Real at the top of the table.

Real settled for a 0-0 draw in Greece in game four, while in Portugal a late equaliser from Strand cancelled out Jardel's 8th-minute goal, and Rosenborg stayed in second place. Real, however, were shaken in the fifth game in Norway when they were outplayed by Rosenborg. In a thrilling match, Strand and Brattbakk, soon to join Celtic, each scored to put Rosenborg level on points with Real, although behind on goal difference. Two goals from Jardel in a 2-1 win over Olympiakos were not enough to lift Porto off the bottom of the table.

In the last game, Real secured qualification with a 4-0 win over Porto at the Bernabeu, Suker again scoring two and Hierro and Roberto Carlos adding the others. Rosenborg ended in second place, but with not enough points to qualify, after a tough 2-2 away draw with Olympiakos.

Real 4	Rosenborg 1
Olympiakos 1	Porto 0
Porto 0	Real 2
Rosenborg 5	Olympiakos 1
Rosenborg 2	Porto 0
Real 5	Olympiakos 1
Porto 1	Rosenborg 1
Olympiakos 0	Real 0
Rosenborg 2	Real 0
Porto 2	Olympiakos 1
Real 4	Porto 0
Olympiakos 2	Rosenborg 2

	P	W	D	L	F	A	Pts
Real Madrid	6	4	1	1	15	4	13
Rosenborg	6	3	2	1	13	8	11
Olympiakos	6	1	2	3	6	14	5
Porto	6	1	1	4	3	11	4

GROUP E

Bayern Munich, Besiktas, IFK Gothenburg, Paris St-Germain

German league winners Bayern had bought Brazilian striker Giovanne Elber to replace Sampdoria-bound Jürgen Klinsmann and Bixente Lizarazu took over Ziege's wing back position. Coach Giovanni Trapattoni was confident he had the squad to reach the Final. Against John Toshack's Besiktas in the opening game, skipper Thomas Helmer and Mario Basler gave the Germans a 2-0 victory. Defender Bruno Ngotty put PSG ahead against IFK, and a Teddy Lukic own goal and a Rai penalty made the result 3-0 in France.

In October, Oktay scored twice for Besiktas and his substitute Ertegrul added another in their 3-1 win over PSG, and Bayern fired three past IFK in Gothenburg. A shaky performance from PSG keeper Christophe Revault helped Bayern to a 5-1 routing of PSG in the third game, with Elber and Carsten Jancker both scoring twice, and another goal from Oktay saw off IFK 1-0 in Istanbul.

In game four in Paris, two PSG goals in the last 20 minutes against Bayern gave PSG a 3-1 win and renewed hope of qualification. In Sweden, both the IFK keeper Thomas Ravelli and his Besiktas counterpart Marijan Mrmic were sent off in the second half, and Steffan Pettersson and Robert Andersson secured the points for IFK in a 2-1 victory. In the penultimate games, Bayern moved closer to qualification with Jancker and Helmer on target in their 2-0 win over Besiktas, and PSG remained in contention thanks to an 87th-minute goal from midfielder Eric Rabesandratana in a 1-0 result away to IFK.

In the last games, IFK picked up the points with a 1-0 away victory over Bayern, Babbel gifting an own goal to the Swedes. A 2-1 win by PSG against Besiktas, the winner coming from Simone, found the French side equal on points with Bayern but behind on goal difference. Other results that evening meant that PSG had come third-best runner-up, and would not be progressing in the tournament.

Bayern 2	Besiktas 0
PSG 3	IFK 0
IFK 1	Bayern 3
Besiktas 3	PSG 1
Besiktas 1	IFK 0
Bayern 5	PSG 1
IFK 2	Besiktas 1
PSG 3	Bayern 1
Besiktas 0	Bayern 2
IFK 0	PSG 1
Bayern 0	IFK 1
PSG 2	Besiktas 1

	P	W	D	L	F	A	Pts
Bayern Munich	6	4	0	2	13	6	12
PSG	6	4	0	2	11	10	12
Besiktas	6	2	0	4	6	9	6
IFK	6	2	0	4	4	9	6

GROUP F

Bayer Leverküsen, Lierse, Monaco, Sporting Lisbon

Leading Bundesliga striker Ulf Kirsten and Dutchman Erik Meijer spearheaded Bayer Leverküsen's attack, and the club had bought in two Brazilian midfielders – Emerson and Paulo Roberto Rink – in the summer. Skipper and *libero* Jens Nowotny kept control at the back. A penalty from Stefan Beinlich was enough for Bayer to claim three points from Belgian champions and first-time competition entrants Lierse in the first game.

Jean Tigana's Monaco had lost Manu Petit and Gilles Grimandi to Arsenal, but young French forwards Thierry Henry and David Trezeguet remained up front with the Nigerian Victor Ipkeba. Monaco had won the French title, and had hopes of at least reaching the semi-final, as they had done in 1994. Although they went down 3-0 to Sporting Lisbon in game one, they bounced back to beat Bayer in the next game 4-0, with two from outstanding prospect Henry and two from Ikpeba. Two goals in the last four minutes produced a 1-1 draw in Belgium between Lierse and Sporting.

Lierse were reminded of their outsider status in game three in Monaco when the French side scored five. Henry scored in the 33rd minute, then Scotland's John Collins, Ipkeba and Trezeguet twice in the last three minutes made it a dismal evening for the Belgians. An Emerson 80th-minute goal secured a 2-0 Bayer victory in Lisbon. A resilient display by Lierse against Monaco in the fourth game was not sufficient to prevent them going down 1-0 to an Ikpeba goal. The game in Germany between Bayer and Sporting saw Sporting down to nine men at the end and a 4-1 victory for the Germans.

In the fifth game, Monaco were 2-0 down to Sporting at half-time but Trezeguet and Henry twice, the last in the 90th minute, shot Monaco to a 3-2 win and leadership in the league. Bayer's 2-0 away victory over Lierse put them level on points with the French. In the last game, Sporting beat Lierse 2-1, while Henry's 81st-minute equaliser in Germany against Bayer ensured that Monaco won the League. Bayer's point also elevated them to the position of best runner-up, and they also qualified for the quarter-finals.

Sporting 3	Monaco 0
Bayer 1	Lierse 0
Lierse 1	Sporting 1
Monaco 4	Bayer 0
Monaco 5	Lierse 1
Sporting 0	Bayer 2
Bayer 4	Sporting 1
Lierse 0	Monaco 1
Lierse 0	Bayer 2
Monaco 3	Sporting 2
Bayer 2	Monaco 2
Sporting 2	Lierse 1

	P	W	D	L	F	A	Pts
Monaco	6	4	1	1	15	8	13
Bayer Leverküsen	6	4	1	1	11	7	13
Sporting Lisbon	6	2	1	3	9	11	7
Lierse	6	0	1	5	3	12	1

Filippo Inzaghi

Raul Gonzales

Filippo Inzaghi (1973). Inzaghi – 'Super Pippo', as he is known to the Juventus fans – is a fast, tricky striker who began his career with Piacenza, before moving to Verona, Parma and Atalanta. He was Serie A top scorer in 1996/97 when he scored 24 goals for Atalanta, and was bought by Juventus, for whom he has scored some memorable goals, including the two against Manchester United within ten minutes in the 1998/99 semi-final, although United won that match. His hat-trick in the Ukraine against Dynamo Kiev in the 1997/98 tournament put Juventus into the semi-final. He has represented his country 20 times. His brother Simone is a striker with Lazio.

Raul Gonzales (1977). Raul is currently the scoring star for Real Madrid and Spain. A technically gifted young player, he also possesses a powerful shot and an ability to deceive defenders with his subtle touch and his intuitive eye for goal. Originally a youth player for Atlético Madrid, he was signed by Real manager Jorge Valdano and made his first team debut at the age of 17 in 1994. With Real he has won two Spanish league titles, in 1995 and 1997, and the European Cup in 1998. In 1998/99 he was the top scorer in Spanish football with 25 goals. He made his international debut in 1996 against the Czech Republic and has already amassed over 30 international caps.

MANCHESTER UNITED 97/98

The influential Eric Cantona had left Old Trafford and his role had been taken over by Teddy Sheringham, bought from Tottenham. Henning Berg had joined from Blackburn in central defence, and Roy Keane had been appointed team captain. United were a young but increasingly experienced team who had qualified as English champions, and they were seeded into the group stage where they were drawn against last season's rivals, Juventus.

They began the tournament against Kosice in Slovakia. United were too good for the Slovakian novices, Irwin scoring from a tight angle on the half-hour and Berg finishing off after keeper Ladislav Molnar fumbled a Beckham free-kick on the hour. A well-placed Cole shot from 15 yards in the 88th minute made the final score 3-0.

The next game was a triumph for United, at home against favourites Juventus. Although Deschamps sent Del Piero through to evade Schmeichel and score after only 24 seconds, United stayed resolute in spite of some tough and provocative tackling by the Italians. Butt was replaced by Scholes, and in the 38th minute Giggs accelerated past two defenders and Sheringham headed his high cross past Peruzzi. Juventus were also down to ten men in the 63rd minute when Deschamps was red-carded, and in the 70th minute Scholes made full use of a Pallister pass to slide the ball into the net. In the last minute, Giggs collected a Sheringham ball and the score was 3-1. A Zidane free-kick added some respectability to the scoreline, but Old Trafford was ecstatic.

Feyenoord were next to visit Manchester. With the Dutch happy to sit back in defence in the first half, United went on the attack but wasted several chances until Paul

Scholes lobbed keeper Jerzy Dudek from 15 yards in the 32nd minute. After the interval, Feyenoord roused themselves but United scored again from an Irwin penalty in the 72nd minute after Sheringham's progress had been illegally impeded in the box. Paul Bosvelt split the United defence with eight minutes to go and Henk Vos ran on to score, but the game ended 2-1 to the home side.

In the fourth game in Rotterdam, in an unpleasant atmosphere and with tension running high on the terraces, United seized the initiative and their attacking play was rewarded with an Andy Cole strike in the 31st minute. Just before half time, a Beckham run on the right resulted in a low cross to Cole, who slotted in from ten yards. With United displaying maturity and level-headedness in the face of Feyenoord's increasingly cynical tactics, Pallister and Giggs combined to find Cole in the 74th minute, and the striker had an easy finish for his hat-trick. Igor Korneev scored a late consolation for the Dutch.

United had now qualified for the knock-out phase and met a defensively-minded Kosice in the fifth game. It was Cole again who opened the scoring in the 40th minute and, although Kosice were quick on the counter-attack, a Poborsky shot late in the game deflected into the net off Lubomir Faktor. Sheringham wrapped it up in the last minute with a powerful shot.

The last game in Turin against Juventus was crucial for the Italians, who had to win to have a chance of qualifying. Inzaghi was the main threat, nearly scoring three times in the first half. In the second half, Juventus powered forward with Fonseca hitting the post and Schmeichel turning away a fierce drive from Zidane. In the 84th minute, Zidane crossed into the six-yard box and Inzaghi gleefully tucked it in the net. With Rosenborg only managing a draw, Juventus were through to the quarter-finals with United.

NEWCASTLE 97/98

Deprived of star striker Alan Shearer through injury, Newcastle United manager Kenny Dalglish had to rely in the competition on veterans Ian Rush and John Barnes, and £7.5 million signing Colombian Faustino Asprilla. Qualifying as English league runners-up, and playing for the first time in the tournament, they met Croatia Zagreb at home in the first leg of the second qualifying round.

Although they were outplayed by the skilful Croatians, and particularly by the midfield pairing of Robert Prosinecki and Daniel Saric, Newcastle took the lead in the 22nd minute through John Beresford. Shortly after half-time, Croatia's leading striker Igor Cvitanovic equalised from the edge of the six-yard box. The Newcastle defence, the elegantly effective Alessandro Pistone, Philippe Albert and Stuart Pearce were stretched by the inventive Zagreb forwards, but 15 minutes from the end Beresford took advantage of an obvious but unpunished foul by Asprilla on keeper Drazen Ladic to slot the ball home. In Zagreb, a determined defensive performance from Newcastle kept Zagreb at bay. Just on the interval, a Goran Juric foul on Jon Dahl Tomasson in the box gave away a penalty and Asprilla converted. Simic pulled one back with a header in the 59th minute and, in the third minute of injury time, a defensive error by Pistone left Cvitanovic clear and he powered a low shot past young keeper Shay Given. In the last minute of extra time, Asprilla found Temuri Ketsbaia in space, and the Georgian scored from ten yards. Newcastle were through to the league stage.

Their first league game was against mighty Barcelona at St James's Park. In a fine performance from Newcastle, and notably from the pacy and inventive winger Keith Gillespie, they were deservedly two up by half time. Asprilla scored from the spot in the 21st minute when he collided with keeper Ruud Hesp in the area, and he converted a Gillespie cross ten minutes later. Just after the interval, Asprilla collected his hat-trick, connecting again with a Gillespie cross. Two late Barcelona goals, from Luis Enrique and Figo, could not dampen the Geordie jubilation.

In the second game against Dynamo Kiev in the Ukraine, Newcastle were lucky to escape with a 2-2 draw. Torn apart by the speed and passing of the Kiev forwards, Newcastle conceded a goal in the 4th minute to Rebrov and another twenty minutes later to a low shot from Shevchenko. However, towards the end of the game a tame shot from Beresford deceived keeper Alexandr Shevkovski, and with two minutes to go, another Beresford strike deflected into the net off Olexandr Holovko.

An excellent defensive display against PSV Eindhoven in Holland was breached by a Wim Jonk half-volley in the 38th minute to give PSV a 1-0 win. At St James's Park, Newcastle's quarter-final hopes virtually disappeared, with PSV in command throughout. With defender Jaap Stam in imperious form, and Luc Nilis and Gilles De Bilde cutting through almost at will, it was no surprise when Nilis scored in the 33rd minute and De Bilde added another with one minute to go. At the Nou Camp in game five, with only 26,000 braving the pouring rain, a long pass in the 18th minute from Guardiola to Giovanni beat the offside trap and the Brazilian lobbed reserve keeper Shaka Hislop for the only goal of the game.

Now out of the tournament, Newcastle entertained Dynamo Kiev in the last game. Kiev had already qualified and went through the motions without any apparent interest in the game. A 15-yard shot from Barnes in the tenth minute and a 25-yard free-kick from Pearce ten minutes later settled the game at 2-0, although Shaka Hislop made two superb saves from Kalitvintsev and Rebrov just before the interval.

RANGERS 97/98

Rangers had equalled Celtic's record of nine league titles in a row and had brought in Sergio Porrini to bolster the defence and Marco Negri to add to the attack of their cosmopolitan team. Given Scottish clubs' poor recent record in Europe, UEFA had placed the club in the first qualifying round, and they travelled north to the Faroe Islands to play Gotu in the first leg.

In front of 2,500 spectators on a wind-swept clifftop, an 18th-minute close-range volley from Negri marked his debut for the club and Durie headed another before half time. Durie scored again with twelve minutes to go, and substitute McCoist added two more in the last three minutes. In the return at Ibrox, with a rather larger attendance of 45,000, Durie and then Negri with a back-heel made the score 2-0 at the interval. Albertz came on and almost immediately created a headed goal for McCoist, and

he scored himself within ten minutes with a trademark 25-yard free kick. Ian Ferguson and Negri struck in the last five minutes, and the aggregate score was 11-0.

However, it was not quite so easy in Sweden against IFK Gothenburg in the second qualifying round. In temperatures of over 90F, and without Laudrup and central defender Craig Moore, Rangers slumped to a 3-0 defeat. Although they had the balance of the play in the first half, they were rocked by two goals in three minutes after the interval, Stefan Pettersson slamming the ball past Goram and then a shot from Per Karlsson to which Goram got his hand but could not hold. With a minute to go, Peter Eriksson put another past the despairing Goram. At Ibrox, Charlie Miller offered some hope with his 23rd minute opener, but Robert Andersson equalised shortly after the break. Laudrup, Durie and Albertz all came on but the odds were too heavily stacked in favour of IFK, and the game finished 1-1.

Rangers had failed in their European adventure again.

Stylish fight-back from PSG

Paris St-Germain, French runners-up, played Steaua Bucharest in Romania in the first leg of the second qualifying round, and came away with a creditable 3-2 defeat. It was soon pointed out, however, that defender Laurent Fournier had been ineligible to play, having received two yellow cards in last season's Cup Winners Cup, and the result was amended by UEFA to a 3-0 Steaua victory. Nothing daunted, PSG scored five goals in the first half in Paris, with a hat-trick from captain Rai and one each from Marco Simone and the young striker Florian Maurice, to beat the stunned Romanians 5-3 on aggregate.

Bayer Leverküsen v Real Madrid

Real's domestic form had been erratic but the arrival in January of French international Christian Karembeu promised to bring more stability to the midfield, and he was joined by Brazilian striker Savio to link up with Raul, Morientes and Mijatovic in the attack. In the first leg in Germany, midfielder Stefan Beinlich gave Bayer the lead in the 18th minute, while Karembeu made his mark for Real with an equaliser with fifteen minutes to go. At the Bernabeu, a header each from Karembeu and Morientes early in the second half and a last minute penalty from captain Hierro gave Real a 4-1 aggregate win.

Semi-finalist: Real Madrid
(4-1 aggregate)

Bayern Munich v Borussia Dortmund

With sweeper Sammer sidelined, and Paulo Sousa and Lambert having departed, Borussia faced Bayern in Munich in the first leg, where the two well-matched and similar German sides ground out a 0-0 draw, although Bayern had more chances. The return match continued in the same vein, with neither side able to break through the other's defence until a close range goal from Chapuisat in the 19th minute of extra time put Borussia through.

Semi-finalist: Borussia Dortmund
(1-0 aggregate)

Juventus v Dynamo Kiev

Valery Lobanovsky's Ukranian team were drawn against the favourites for the first game in Turin. New signing from Milan, Edgar Davids, beefed up an already top-class Juventus midfield and Del Piero and Inzaghi roamed dangerously in the Italian attack. Andri Husin put Kiev one up early in the second half, and Inzaghi equalised in the 70th minute. In Kiev, Juventus went out to win, and Inzaghi opened the scoring in the 30th minute. Kiev danger man Rebrov equalised after half time, but two more from Inzaghi and a late goal from Del Piero settled the tie.

Semi-finalist: Juventus (5-2 aggregate)

Monaco v Manchester United

Andy Cole and Teddy Sheringham were closely marked in the first leg in France and could not make their mark on the game, and Monaco strikers Henry and Ipkeba were having similar problems. The game ended in a 0-0 draw. At Old Trafford, missing Schmeichel, Pallister and Giggs, United went behind after only five minutes. The unpredictable French forward David Trezeguet took advantage of a sweetly-struck pass from Ali Benarbia to smash an unstoppable shot past keeper Van der Gouw. United pressed forward but Monaco's sweeper defence dealt admirably with the efforts of Cole, Solskjaer and Sheringham, while Monaco midfielder John Collins was launching some dangerous counter-attacks into United territory. United's persistence was rewarded in the 53rd minute when Solskjaer cleverly converted a Beckham cross at the far post, but the English side could not find their way through the Monaco defence a second time.

Semi-finalist: Monaco (1-1 aggregate)

Real Madrid v Borussia Dortmund

In a bizarre preamble to the first leg at the Bernabeu, the game was delayed for 75 minutes when some of Real's Ultra Sur hooligans brought down one of the goalposts by swinging on the fence behind the goal. When eventually a post was located, the game kicked off with Borussia playing under protest. Morientes pounced on a perfectly-weighted pass from Roberto Carlos in the 25th minute and Real were ahead. Karembeu added another midway through the second half. In a packed Westfalen Stadium in the return leg, Real were again on top although Borussia had an 'offside' goal disallowed, and the game finished goal-less. Real were through to their first Final for seventeen years.

Finalist: Real Madrid (2-0 aggregate)

Juventus v Monaco

In Turin, Juventus crushed Monaco 4-1. A thundering Del Piero free kick in the 34th minute started the rout and, although Monaco equalised through Francisco Da Costa just before half-time, Juventus went ahead moments later when Zidane was brought down in the box and Del Piero converted. In the second half, Monaco were reeling from the constant Juventus attacks, and a 62nd-minute trip on Inzaghi in the area gave Del Piero another penalty and his hat-trick. With two minutes to go, Zidane got the fourth.

In Monaco, Amoruso was substituted for Inzaghi early in the game and he scored the first in the 14th minute. Phillippe Leonard equalised with a free-kick before half-time and Henry put Monaco 2-1 up after the interval, but Del Piero volleyed home with fifteen minutes to go. Robert Spehar scored the winner for Monaco near the end, but Juventus were safely in the Final for the third year in succession.

Finalist: Juventus (6-4 aggregate)

Fernando Morientes
(1976). A fast and tricky striker, Morientes is Raul's striking partner with Real Madrid. He began his career with Albacete in 1993, then moved to Real Zaragoza in 1995. He joined Real in 1997, and played in the club's European Cup Final victory over Juventus. His blossoming talent saw him take over from Davor Suker, who eventually left the club, and in 1998/99 he scored 19 goals for Real. He had a sensational start to his international career, scoring twice in the first two minutes of Spain's game against Belgium.

Roberto Carlos

**Roberto Carlos
(Da Silva)** *(1973). A stocky, powerful attacking left-back, Brazilian-born Roberto Carlos is probably the best taker of a free-kick in the world. He played for Palmeiras from 1993 to 1995 and joined Inter Milan that year. He left Inter for Real Madrid the next year and has won the Spanish league and the European Cup with the Spanish club. Few who saw it will forget his incredible banana-shot free-kick for Brazil against France in the 1997 Tournoi. He made his international debut in Brazil's 3-0 defeat of the USA and played in the 1994 and 1998 World Cup finals.*

Rivaldo (right) in action for Barcelona against Newcastle in the Group C match at St James's Park which Newcastle won 3-2.

Real triumph after 32 years

Real Madrid (0) 1   Juventus (0) 0

Amsterdam Arena, Amsterdam, 20 May 1998
Attendance: 48,500
Referee: Krug (Germany)

As the spectators travelled to the new Arena on the edge of Amsterdam, they were anticipating an epic encounter between two of Europe's biggest and most famous clubs. With 21 internationals on the pitch, and a further six on the bench, the cream of European football was represented in the Final and, if there was ever to be a demonstration of football at its very finest, this match promised to be it.

Both teams lined up with three-men attacks – for Real, Morientes, Raul and Mijatovic while Juventus teamed up Del Piero, Inzaghi and Zidane, and the game began with both sides playing open, attacking football. In the early stages, Juventus were dominant and a shot from Di Livio deflected off Roberto Carlos into the side-netting, but they could not make the pressure pay.

Real, however, began to come back into the game, creating intricate and incisive passes and movement, many initiated by centre-half Hierro whose skill in releasing the ball to team-mates was matched by his fierce tackling ability and his acute positional sense. The game grew increasingly physical as first Davids and then Roberto Carlos were booked. Mijatovic, causing havoc on the left, was being hauled down by the Italian defenders, but midway through the half, he again evaded Torricelli to send in a cross which Raul wasted from seven yards. Real were in charge, but the half ended goal-less.

Juventus' Edgar Davids (right) and Real Madrid's Clarence Seedorf tussle for the ball during the 1998 Final.

Lippi took off Di Livio and replaced him with Tacchinardi at half time in an attempt to tighten up the centre of midfield and stifle the exuberant Mijatovic. At the other end Inzaghi untypically missed two simple chances, one a volley over the bar from a Davids cross, the other a shot at keeper Illgner when it would have been easier to score.

Then Real went ahead. In the 66th minute, Clarence Seedorf crossed from the right and the ball was collected by Roberto Carlos. He shot but the ball rebounded from Iuliano to Mijatovic who reacted instantly to skip round keeper Angelo Peruzzi and place the ball from a tight angle into the Juventus net. Juventus rallied and Del Piero, well policed by Hierro, Davids and Zidane all went close for Juventus. Conte came on for Deschamps with twelve minutes left but his introduction could not lift the Italian team into snatching the equaliser. The whistle went and Real had won the trophy for the first time in 32 years.

Lippi generously stated, 'Real Madrid deserved to win,' and thousands of Madrilenos took over the streets of Amsterdam to celebrate the long-awaited European Cup return of the trophy to the Bernabeu.

The teams
Real Madrid: Illgner, Sanchis, Panucci, Roberto Carlos, Raul (Amavisca), Hierro, Karembeu, Seedorf, Redondo, Mijatovic (Suker), Morientes (Jaime) (manager: Heynckes) [Mijatovic 66]

Juventus: Peruzzi, Torricelli, Montero, Iuliano, Di Livio (Tacchinardi), Deschamps (Conte), Davids, Pessotto (Fonseca), Zidane, Del Piero, Inzaghi (manager: Lippi)

THE 1998-99 SEASON

There were no real surprises in the first qualifying round this season, although Celtic were lucky to hold St Patrick's Athletic 0-0 at Parkhead. They did, however, win 2-0 away before being eliminated 3-1 in the next round by Croatia Zagreb. In the second round, Panathinaikos did well to beat Steaua Bucharest 6-3 in Greece after a 2-2 draw in Bucharest, and a strong fight-back from a 2-0 away defeat against Rosenborg saw Bruges win 4-2 at home but go out on away goals. An aggregate 2-2 draw between Athletic Bilbao and Dynamo Tbilisi was won by the Spaniards on away goals. The league games once again kicked off in mid-September.

GROUP A

Ajax, Croatia Zagreb, Olympiakos, Porto

Olympiakos travelled to Portugal in the first game and, with four minutes to go, were 2-0 down. Stylianos Giannakopoulos and then Sinica Gogic levelled the tie. Croatia Zagreb drew 0-0 at home with Ajax, who had the De Boer twins back from a contractual dispute with the club, and new signing Georgi Kinkladze came on as substitute. Two weeks later, an 86th-minute Litmanen penalty secured a 2-1 Ajax home win over Porto, while Olympiakos put two past Croatia in Athens, the second again coming from Gogic.

By the end of the halfway period, Olympiakos' 1-0 defeat of Ajax had them at the top of the league. Two goals from Zlatko Zahovic contributed to Porto's 3-0 defeat of Croatia. In the fourth game, a 33rd-minute goal from Richard Wittschge and a late strike from Dean Gorre gave Ajax a 2-0 win over Olympiakos, while Croatia scored three against Porto, top striker Jardel netting for the Portuguese in the 39th minute. On the penultimate day, Josip Simic gave Croatia maximum points against Ajax in Holland, and Olympiakos edged closer to the knockout stage with a 2-1 victory over Porto.

A 1-1 draw in Zagreb was enough for Olympiakos to finish top of the league, and a 3-0 win over Ajax put the Dutch at the bottom.

Croatia Zagreb 0	Ajax 0
Porto 2	Olympiakos 2
Ajax 2	Porto 1
Olympiakos 2	Croatia Zagreb 0
Olympiakos 1	Ajax 0
Porto 3	Croatia Zagreb 0
Ajax 2	Olympiakos 0
Croatia Zagreb 3	Porto 1
Ajax 0	Croatia Zagreb 1
Olympiakos 2	Porto 1
Croatia Zagreb 1	Olympiakos 1
Porto 3	Ajax 0

	P	W	D	L	F	A	Pts
Olympiakos	6	3	2	1	8	6	11
Croatia Zagreb	6	2	2	2	5	7	8
Porto	6	2	1	3	11	9	7
Ajax	6	2	1	3	4	6	7

GROUP B

Athletic Bilbao, Galatasaray, Juventus, Rosenborg

Italian champions Juventus entertained Galatasaray in the opening match and went ahead in the 17th minute through Inzaghi, scoring past Brazilian international keeper Claudio Taffarel. Juve keeper Angelo Peruzzi was sent off for handling outside the box shortly after, and Hakan Sukur and full-back Umit Davala scored for Galatasaray. Alessandro Birindelli equalised half way through the second period. Bilbao and Rosenborg drew 1-1 in Spain, Roar Strand levelling in the second half for the Norwegians. A fortnight later, Inzaghi again scored for Juventus in Norway but Bent Skammelsrud equalised for Rosenborg with a 69th-minute penalty. A last-minute goal by Hagi gave Galatasaray a narrow 2-1 victory over Bilbao.

In the third game, Juventus drew again, this time against Bilbao, and centre-forward Sigurd Rushfeldt scored a hat-trick in Rosenborg's 3-0 home win over Galatasaray. The score was reversed in Turkey, with Hakan scoring twice. Defender Paolo Montero saved a point for Juventus after Bilbao had gone ahead with a Julen Guerrero 45th-minute goal. On the penultimate day, two goals from Sorensen helped Rosenborg to a 2-1 win over Bilbao, while the game between Galatasaray and Juventus was postponed one week because of political tension between Turkey and Italy.

In the last game, Juventus finally won, with Inzaghi and Nicola Amoruso scoring against Rosenborg. Galatasaray, Rosenborg and Juventus all gained eight points, but Bilbao's 1-0 win over Galatasaray gave the Italian's leadership of the group and qualification.

Athletic Bilbao 1	Rosenborg 1
Juventus 2	Galatasaray 2
Galatasaray 2	Athletic Bilbao 1
Rosenborg 1	Juventus 1
Athletic Bilbao 0	Juventus 0
Rosenborg 3	Galatasaray 0
Galatasaray 3	Rosenborg 0
Juventus 1	Athletic Bilbao 1
Rosenborg 2	Athletic Bilbao 1
Galatasaray 1	Juventus 1
Athletic Bilbao 1	Galatasaray 0
Juventus 2	Rosenborg 0

	P	W	D	L	F	A	Pts
Juventus	6	1	5	0	7	5	8
Galatasaray	6	2	2	2	8	8	8
Rosenborg	6	2	2	2	7	8	8
Athletic Bilbao	6	1	3	2	5	6	6

GROUP C

Inter Milan, Real Madrid, Spartak Moscow, Sturm Graz

Inter had acquired Roberto Baggio and Nicola Ventola, and Ronaldo and Zamorano led the attack. They faced Real Madrid at the Bernabeu in the first game, and a 79th-minute Hierro penalty and a last-minute goal from Clarence Seedorf left Inter pointless. Spartak Moscow travelled to Austria to play Sturm Graz, and two goals in four minutes gave the Russians a 2-0 win. A Raul second-half header gave Real the lead in Moscow, but two goals from Spartak, the winner coming from Egor Titov in the 78th minute, meant the Russians were the only team in the tournament to have a 100% record after two games. Inter scraped through 1-0 against Sturm Graz with an injury-time goal from Djorkaeff.

Ventola and Ronaldo had Inter two up in Milan against Spartak in game three and the match finished 2-1. Real put six past Sturm at the Bernabeu with two apiece for Savio and new signing, Croatian wing-back Robert Jarni. In Moscow for game four, a 68th-minute Andrei Tikhonov strike had Spartak ahead against Inter until Diego Simeone headed in a 90th-minute equaliser from a Paulo Sousa free-kick. The game between Real and Sturm Graz was postponed because of heavy rain, but the following day Real ran up five goals. Spartak were now group leaders on goal difference.

In Milan for the penultimate game, Inter were drawing 1-1 with Real until Inter substitute Baggio scored in the 86th minute and then again in injury time. Spartak and Sturm drew 0-0 in Moscow, the Austrian team picking up their first point.

Real and Spartak played out a tense last game at the Bernabeu, both sides potentially likely to qualify as best runners-up. Real should have scored early on against the battling Russians, and finally found the net in the 33rd minute when Raul headed in from a Roberto Carlos corner. In the 60th minute, Savio flashed in a header from a Mijatovic cross, and Dimitri Khlestov's late goal for Spartak caused Real some anxious moments. However, they held on to their 2-1 advantage, and qualified. Inter went through as group leaders after their 2-0 win in Austria, Baggio again getting on the scoresheet.

Real Madrid 2	Inter 0
Sturm Graz 0	Spartak Moscow 2
Inter 1	Sturm Graz 0
Spartak Moscow 2	Real Madrid 1
Inter 2	Spartak Moscow 1
Real Madrid 6	Sturm Graz 1
Spartak Moscow 1	Inter 1
Sturm Graz 1	Real Madrid 5
Inter 3	Real Madrid 1
Spartak Moscow 0	Sturm Graz 0
Real Madrid 2	Spartak Moscow 1
Sturm Graz 0	Inter 2

	P	W	D	L	F	A	Pts
Inter Milan	6	4	1	1	9	5	13
Real Madrid	6	4	0	2	17	8	12
Spartak Moscow	6	2	2	2	7	6	8
Sturm Graz	6	0	1	5	2	16	1

GROUP D

Barcelona, Bayern Munich, Brondby, Manchester United

The so-called 'Group of Death' contained three of the strongest clubs in Europe. Louis van Gaal had added to his Dutch contingent with the acquisitions of Philip Cocu, Boudewijn Zenden and Patrick Kluivert, although Kluivert was ineligible for the competition. Barca fought out a thrilling 3-3 draw with Manchester United at Old Trafford. Bayern, now fielding Jens Jeremies alongside Steffan Effenberg in midfield, were surprisingly beaten away by Brondby. Marcus Babbel scored for the Germans in the 77th minute, but Bo Hansen and Allan Ravn scored in the last two minutes for a 2-1 Brondby victory.

Two goals from Brazilian Sonny Anderson at the Nou Camp saw off Brondby in the next round of games, and a late strike from Elber helped Bayern to a 2-2 draw at Old Trafford. In game three, Bayern achieved their first win, a tight-angle goal from Effenberg on half-time being the only goal at the Olympic Stadium. United demolished Brondby 6-2 in Denmark.

In Barcelona for game four, Giovanni converted a controversial penalty for Barca in the first half, but Bayern scored twice in the second half, through Alexander Zickler in the 47th minute and substitute Hasan Salihamidzic with three minutes to go. United again took apart Brondby, this time 5-0 at Old Trafford. In the penultimate matches, Barcelona and United staged another, equally enthralling 3-3 draw at the Nou Camp, while a goal each from Carsten Jancker and Basler gave Bayern a home 2-0 win over Brondby.

A 1-1 draw at Old Trafford was enough for United to qualify as second-best runner-up, thanks to Juventus' win over Rosenborg, and Bayern qualified as group leaders. Barcelona won 2-0 against Brondby in a largely meaningless game.

Brondby 2	Bayern Munich 1
United 3	Barcelona 3
Bayern Munich 2	United 2
Barcelona 2	Brondby 0
Bayern Munich 1	Barcelona 0
Brondby 2	United 6
Barcelona 1	Bayern Munich 2
United 5	Brondby 0
Bayern Munich 2	Brondby 0
Barcelona 3	United 3
Brondby 0	Barcelona 2
United 1	Bayern Munich 1

	P	W	D	L	F	A	Pts
Bayern Munich	6	3	2	1	9	6	11
Manchester United	6	2	4	0	20	11	10
Barcelona	6	2	2	2	11	9	8
Brondby	6	1	0	5	4	18	3

GROUP E

Arsenal, Dynamo Kiev, Lens, Panathinaikos

Dynamo Kiev fielded eight internationals and were a highly-regarded, attacking side who had won their league championship six years running. In the first game, their hopes of qualification suffered a knock when they were beaten by Panathinaikos in Greece. Sergei Rebrov opened the scoring in the 31st minute, but Erik Mykland and Nikos Liberopoulos scored for the Greeks in the second half. Arsenal drew 1-1 with Lens in France. Kiev then drew 1-1 with Lens in the Ukraine, a Shevchenko header in the 61st minute being levelled by a Vairelles strike less than one minute later. Arsenal won 2-1 against Panathinaikos at Wembley to go top of the group.

In the third games, an 80th-minute goal from substitute Wagneau Eloi gave Lens a 1-0 win over Panathinaikos, while Arsenal did well to hold Dynamo to a 1-1 draw at Wembley. Two weeks later, Dynamo were too good for Arsenal in Kiev, and won 3-1. A goal from Leonidas Vokolos in the 53rd minute gave Panathinaikos a 1-0 victory over Lens. With two games to go, Panathinaikos were top of the league.

At home in game five, Arsenal's fate was sealed by a 1-0 defeat by Lens. Dynamo beat Panathinaikos 2-1 in Kiev, through Rebrov and an Agelos Basinas own goal. A young Arsenal team travelled to Greece for the last game with no hope of qualifying, but beat Panathinaikos, who could still qualify, 3-1. Dynamo qualified as group leaders by beating Lens 3-1 in France, their last goal coming fittingly from their star striker Shevchenko.

Panathinaikos 2	Kiev 1
Lens 1	Arsenal 1
Arsenal 2	Panathinaikos 1
Kiev 1	Lens 1
Arsenal 1	Kiev 1
Lens 1	Panathinaikos 0
Kiev 3	Arsenal 1
Panathinaikos 1	Lens 0
Arsenal 0	Lens 1
Kiev 2	Panathinaikos 1
Panathinaikos 1	Arsenal 3
Lens 1	Kiev 3

	P	W	D	L	F	A	Pts
Dynamo Kiev	6	3	2	1	11	7	11
Lens	6	2	2	2	5	6	8
Arsenal	6	2	2	2	8	8	8
Panathinaikos	6	2	0	4	6	9	6

GROUP F

Benfica, HJK Helsinki, Kaiserslautern, PSV Eindhoven

New coach Bobby Robson's PSV had lost Cocu and Zenden to Barcelona, Arthur Numan to Rangers and big centre-half Jaap Stam to Manchester United, but he had the exciting young striking talent of Ruud Van Nistelrooy paired in attack with Luc Nilis. In the first game, a Bruggink goal in the 90th minute gave PSV a 2-1 win over HJK, the first Finnish team to qualify for the league stage, by virtue of a 2-1 aggregate win over Metz in the qualifying round. A 41st-minute Wagner goal gave the strong, athletic German champions Kaiserslautern a 1-0 win over Graeme Souness' heavily British-oriented Benfica.

In round two, the battle of the British managers produced a 2-1 win for Souness. Nuno Gomes chipped in for Benfica's first just after the interval, Dennis Rommedahl equalised in the second half, and Joao Pinto scored the winner with twelve minutes to go. HJK had a creditable 0-0 draw with Kaiserslautern. In the third games, HJK pulled out a shock, beating Benfica 2-0, while an 83rd-minute goal from Jürgen Rische gave Kaiserslautern a 2-1 victory at PSV.

In game four, PSV keeper Patrick Lodewijks was sent off early in the game, and Kaiserslautern capitalised with a 3-1 home win. HJK held Benfica 2-2 at home thanks to a Scott Minto own goal and a late strike from Luis Antonio. In the next game, Van Nistelrooy underlined his promise with a hat-trick in PSV's away defeat of HJK, while Nuno Gomes and Joao Pinto gave Benfica a 2-1 win over Kaiserslautern.

In the last game, Dimitri Khokhlov opened PSV's account in Holland against Benfica. Nuno Gomes scored twice for Benfica in the second half, but Van Nistelrooy equalised with two minutes to go, ending Benfica's hopes of qualifying as a runner-up. A hat-trick of headers from Uwe Rosler in a 5-2 win over HJK gave the German club the leadership of the league.

Kaiserslautern 1	Benfica 0
PSV 2	HJK 1
HJK 0	Kaiserslautern 0
Benfica 2	PSV 1
HJK 2	Benfica 0
PSV 1	Kaiserslautern 2
Kaiserslautern 3	PSV 1
Benfica 2	HJK 2
HJK 1	PSV 3
Benfica 2	Kaiserslautern 1
Kaiserslautern 5	HJK 2
PSV 2	Benfica 2

	P	W	D	L	F	A	Pts
Kaiserslautern	6	4	1	1	12	6	13
Benfica	6	2	2	2	8	9	8
PSV	6	2	1	3	10	11	7
HJK	6	1	2	3	8	12	5

ARSENAL 98/99

Manager Arsène Wenger had turned Arsenal into one of Britain's most cosmopolitan sides. French internationals Patrick Vieira and Emmanuel Petit were a powerful and effective midfield unit, while the two Dutchmen Marc Overmars and Dennis Bergkamp combined with young French striker Nicolas Anelka to fashion the goals. The famous Arsenal defence, with skipper Tony Adams at its heart, was still the strongest in the country, and the club had won the 'double'. Arsenal had decided to play all their European 'home' games at Wembley, apparently to allow more fans to see the games than could fit into Highbury.

Arsenal travelled to Lens, a small, coal-mining town in the north of France, for the first game in Group E. A nippy, attack-minded side, French champions Lens' quick movement and passing caused problems for the Arsenal defence in the first period, with Czech international Vladimir Smicer and Tony Vairelles plundering down the wings and Pascal Nouma moving through the centre. Arsenal, however, were squandering chances. In the second half, Arsenal upped the tempo. In the 51st minute, Petit passed to Overmars on the edge of the area and the Dutchman hit an excellent shot past keeper Guillaume Warmuz. Lens continued on the attack, hitting the crossbar with twenty minutes to go, and scored an equaliser through a close-range shot from Vairelles in injury time, which deflected in the net off Keown.

In the first game at Wembley, against Greek champions Panathinaikos, the game kicked off half an hour late to allow all of the 73,000 crowd to reach the stadium. Although Arsenal should have been three ahead within the first fifteen minutes, Panathinaikos' patient man-marking and controlled passing gradually denied space to the Londoners. Arsenal continued to miss good chances, with Anelka particularly culpable. Towards half-time, a 35-yard shot from Andreas Lagonakis nearly deceived keeper David Seaman and Nikos Liberopoulos missed two easy chances. However, Arsenal went ahead in the 64th minute when Adams hammered home a blocked Viera shot, and they scored again seven minutes later when Keown headed in a Petit corner. Brazilian substitute Mauro scored a consolation for Panathinaikos near the end.

Missing Petit and Vieira, Arsenal were outplayed by a sparkling Dynamo Kiev side in the next game at Wembley. Forwards Shevchenko and Rebrov demonstrated why they were the targets of Europe's super-rich clubs, and the first half was dominated by Kiev's speed, skill and movement. Only a magnificent Adams kept the game goal-less. Arsenal came out stronger in the second half and, against the run of play, went ahead in the 73rd minute. A long pass from midfielder Ray Parlour found Lee Dixon speeding down the right. Dixon powered over a cross and Bergkamp turned in a finely-taken, diving header. Justice was done, however, when Rebrov equalised in injury time.

Two weeks later in a freezing Ukraine, Kiev converted their superiority into victory. Without Adams, Anelka, Bergkamp and Overmars, Arsenal's chances of securing three points were slim. Parlour was outstanding in midfield, but he could do little to stem the waves of attacks which the masterful Ukranians were launching at the Arsenal defence. Rebrov scored from a penalty in the 29th minute and Olexandr Holovko headed in from an Oleh Luzhnyi free kick in the 62nd minute. Ten minutes later, Shevchenko curled in a wicked, 25-yard free-kick past Seaman. Although midfielder Stephen Hughes scored with a header with six minutes to go, the scoreline flattered a depleted but outplayed Arsenal.

In a match they had to win, they took on Lens at Wembley in the fifth game. Again under-strength, Arsenal moved into attack, with Adams shooting over the bar and Anelka having a bad miss. Lens, too, went for goal, and Seaman did well to tip over a 20-yard drive by Smicer. In the second half, Nouma and Smicer again both tested Seaman and, in the 72nd minute, Michael Debeve smartly converted a Smicer cross. Overmars should have equalised with two minutes to go, but fluffed his lob. Arsenal had failed to qualify for the knockout stage.

A young, inexperienced Arsenal side travelled to Athens to play Panathinaikos in the last game and produced a confident, adventurous performance. The Gunners had fourteen players ruled out for various reasons, and they played with a packed midfield with only Anelka up front. In the 64th minute, however, Alberto Mendez put Arsenal one up when his shot was deflected past keeper Jozef Wandzik. Substitute Igor Sypniewski levelled for the Greek side, but in the last ten minutes Anelka and Luis Boa Morte scored two more for Arsenal.

Celtic Stumble

As Scottish champions, Celtic entered the preliminary round and took on Ireland's St Patrick's Athletic. The game was new manager Josef Venglos' first in charge of the club, and they played the opening leg at their magnificent new 61,000-capacity stadium, the biggest and arguably the most impressive club ground in Britain. At the end of ninety minutes, Parkhead resounded with the sounds of booing and jeering as Celtic could only manage a goal-less draw with the Irish part-timers. A magnificent display from Irish keeper Trevor Wood compounded the Celts' inability to take the chances which came their way. In Ireland, an improved Celtic won 2-0 and moved into the qualifying round. Harald Brattbakk scored first in the 12th minute, and Henrik Larsson picked up a Paul Lambert through ball to find the net in the 74th minute.

They then met Croatia Zagreb, whose name had been changed from Dynamo in a deeply unpopular move by nationalist president Franjo Tudjman. The team contained six members of the Croatia squad which had reached third place in the 1998 World Cup finals. Before the game, there had been an unseemly squabble between Celtic's players and management over win bonuses, but a win was never on the cards. Although, in spite of Croatia's dominance, Celtic won the first leg in Glasgow when Darren Jackson slotted in a blocked Craig Burley volley after the interval, they were over-run in Zagreb. An effortlessly superior Croatia, led by the glittering skills of Robert Prosinecki, scored through Silvio Maric in the 22nd minute. Just before the break, Tommy Boyd fouled Maric in the area and Prosinecki rolled home the penalty. With twenty minutes left, Prosinecki scored from twenty yards to ensure that Celtic's next European game would be in the UEFA Cup.

MANCHESTER UNITED 98/99

In the qualifying round, a 2-0 win over Lodz at Old Trafford, and a 0-0 draw in Poland, took English league runners-up Manchester United into the league.

Their campaign began with a breathtaking game of football against Barcelona at Old Trafford. With Giggs and Scholes cutting swathes through the Spanish defence, the first goal came early on, Giggs soaring to connect with a Beckham cross in the 17th minute. Seven minutes later, Scholes stuck in a rebound from keeper Ruud Hesp. In the second half, Barcelona were irresistible. Rivaldo found Sonny Anderson, whose shot through the United defence eluded Schmeichel. In the 60th minute, Stam fouled Rivaldo in the area and Giovanni converted the penalty. 2-2. Beckham curved in a glorious 25-yard free-kick four minutes later, and Luis Enrique levelled with a penalty minutes later after Nicky Butt handled.

At the Olympic Stadium, Elber struck first for Bayern Munich in the 11th minute from what seemed an offside position. United fought back, and a Beckham cross in the 24th minute was met by a splendid diving header from Yorke which beat Oliver Kahn. Just after the break, a Yorke flick found Scholes and Kahn was beaten again. In the last minute, Bixente Lizarazu sent a long through ball into the box, Schmeichel failed to reach it, and Elber headed in the equaliser.

In game three in Denmark, played on a sodden pitch, United crushed Brondby. Defensive confusion allowed Giggs an easy goal in the 2nd minute, and Giggs again rose above the defence to head in a Jesper Blomqvist cross twenty minutes later. Giggs then turned provider, sending Cole down the pitch to sidefoot a shot past keeper Mogens Krogh. Brondby scored from a free-kick in the 34th minute, but United notched up three more within eight minutes in the second half. In the 54th minute, Keane headed in off the post, then Yorke headed in a Neville cross, and a Solskjaer drive from a Yorke lay-off took the tally to six. Ebbe Sand scored a last-minute consolation.

Now top of the league, United handed out more punishment to Brondby at Old Trafford, where the defensive Danes could not cope with the fast raiding of the United forwards. In the 6th minute, Beckham turned in a 30-yard free-kick, and Phil Neville and Cole, the latter with a delicate chipped shot from a tight angle, added to the scoreline. In the 28th minute, a mazy run from Blomqvist set Beckham free on the wing and his perfectly-judged cross was headed in by Yorke. Scholes added a fifth in the second half.

Another thrilling game took place at the Nou Camp. Barcelona, needing maximum points, dominated the opening spell with Anderson scoring in the first minute. Schmeichel saved well from Rivaldo and Anderson, and United replied in the 25th minute when Blomqvist passed from the left to Yorke and the striker's 20-yard effort beat keeper Hesp. Shortly after the break, a Cole and Yorke one-two was converted by Cole. In the 56th minute, a swerving, left-foot free kick from Rivaldo deceived an out-of-position Schmeichel, and twelve minutes later Yorke headed in a Beckham cross. Rivaldo's overhead kick in the 73rd minute levelled a frantic game, although the Brazilian still had time to hit the bar from 35 yards.

United now had to beat Bayern at Old Trafford to qualify as league leader. With Effenberg and Jens Jeremies dominating midfield, Elber and Zickler both headed just wide in the first half. However, United struck first when Giggs cut the ball back from the left and Keane sent a low shot past Kahn in the 43rd minute. Wing-back Thomas Strunz headed on an Effenberg corner in the 57th minute and the Bosnian striker Hasan Salihamidzic put the ball over the line. Towards the end, with both teams realising they had the points they needed to progress, the game turned into something of a charade. At the whistle, United had qualified as second-best runner-up.

Peter Schmeichel encourages his Manchester United defenders in his own inimitable style.

Ryan Giggs

Ryan Giggs (1973). Born in Cardiff, Giggs moved to England as a boy and signed professional forms for Manchester United in 1990. Since then, he has developed into one of the finest wingers in Europe, possessing astonishing pace, skill and an eye for goal. He made his league debut in 1991 and became a left-wing regular in 1991/92, and he has achieved five league medals, three FA Cups and the European Cup. His finest goal was probably in extra time in the 1999 FA Cup semi-final when he beat four Arsenal defenders before lashing the ball into David Seaman's net to put United through to the Final. He was the youngest ever player to play for Wales and he has gained 26 caps.

QUARTER FINALS

Manchester United v Inter Milan

The crossing skills of David Beckham and the accurate finishing of Dwight Yorke brought United victory in the first leg at Old Trafford in early March. Without Ronaldo, Inter nonetheless had attacking options in Zamorano, Ventola and Baggio, but it was United who went ahead as early as the 6th minute. Beckham whipped in a cross and Yorke neatly converted. Just before half-time, Beckham and Yorke repeated the move and United were two ahead. In the second half, Schmeichel had to make some excellent saves, once from Zamorano and twice from Ventola, but United maintained their two-goal lead.

In Milan, United survived a penalty claim from Zamorano and, four minutes after Ronaldo was substituted in the 59th minute, his replacement Ventola seized on a Keane error to pull back a goal. Paul Scholes ensured United's semi-final appearance with an 88th-minute goal from a pass by Cole.

Semi-finalist: Manchester United (3-1 aggregate)

Real Madrid v Dynamo Kiev

At the Bernabeu, under new coach John Toshack, Real went on the attack against a defensive Dynamo. Guti and Morientes should have scored in the first half but, against the run of play, Shevchenko scored a fine goal shortly after half time. Real replied through a curling, 20-yard free-kick from Predrag Mijatovic in the 67th minute. In Kiev, again against a defensive Dynamo looking for the counter-attack, Hierro scored a header late in the first half but it was disallowed for offside. In the 62nd minute, Shevchenko converted a rebound from a saved penalty and, after an excellent build-up with striking partner Rebrov, he scored again with eleven minutes to go.

Semi-finalist: Dynamo Kiev (3-1 aggregate)

Juventus v Olympiakos

In Turin, a dominant Juventus scored first through Inzaghi in the 38th minute, and Conte put them two up with eleven minutes to go. An Andreas Niniadis penalty in the very last minute gave Olympiakos an important away goal. In Athens, the opportunistic Sinica Gogic scored with a header for the Greeks in the 12th minute, and Juventus were struggling. Olympiakos defended in depth. Juventus had most of the possession but could not make it pay until, with five minutes remaining, Antonio Conte took advantage of keeper Dimitrios Eleftheropoulos' fumble of the ball to slot the winner on aggregate.

Semi-finalist: Juventus (3-2 aggregate)

Bayern Munich v Kaiserslautern

The all-German tie was something of a stroll for Bayern. They scored two goals in four minutes – from Elber and Effenberg – late in the first half in Munich and took a 2-0 lead to Kaiserslautern. In Kaiserslautern, a disputed foul in the area in the 9th minute resulted in Janos Hrutka's dismissal and Effenberg scored from the penalty spot. Big centre-forward Carsten Jancker scored two more in the first half, and Bayern were safe. Mario Basler added one more for Bayern in the 56th minute.

Semi-finalist: Bayern Munich (6-0 aggregate)

Manchester United v Juventus

At Old Trafford, United were outclassed by a thoroughbred Juventus performance. The Italian side controlled the first half with their flowing movement and immaculate touch, and Davids and Zidane were in superb form. A clever ball in the 24th minute from Davids to Conte through the United defence was controlled by Conte and shot low past Schmeichel's right. With Beckham and Giggs effectively policed by Di Livio and Conte, most of the play was in the United half. After the interval, United went in desperate search of a goal with Keane, Giggs and Scholes all having shots smothered and a Sheringham goal was ruled offside. In the very last minute of the game, Giggs smashed in a shot from a Beckham cross and United had levelled.

In Turin, United went two goals down in the first eleven minutes. In the 6th minute, Inzaghi knocked in a pass from Zidane and five minutes later Inzaghi scored another with a deflected shot off Stam. However, a much improved United performance saw Keane pull one back with a header from a Beckham cross in the 23rd minute and Yorke also with a header ten minutes later. The tie was now level. The stalemate continued through a tense second half until, with six minutes remaining, Yorke on the attack was brought down by keeper Angelo Peruzzi, the ball reached Cole and the striker coolly finished at the far post. United were in the Final but would be without Keane and Scholes, both of whom were booked.

Finalist: Manchester United (4-3 aggregate)

Bayern Munich v Dynamo Kiev

In a high-scoring game in the Ukraine in the first leg, Dynamo gave away a two-goal lead and allowed Bayern the security of three away goals. Shevchenko put away the first goal in the 16th minute from a Valiantsin Bialkevich pass, and he scored again two minutes before the interval with a deflected free-kick. On the stroke of half time, a low, 35-yard free-kick from Michael Tarnat made it 2-1. A Vitali Kossovskyi volley five minutes after the interval gave Kiev back a two-goal lead. Effenberg's free-kick with twelve minutes remaining reduced Kiev's margin, and Carsten Jancker in the last minute levelled the game.

Kiev began well in Munich but Bayern gradually assumed the dominant role as the game progressed. Oliver Kahn kept out the Kiev attack, saving well from Kossovskyi and at full stretch from Olexandr Khatskevitch. In the 36th minute, Basler took a corner for Bayern and the ball came back to him off the Kiev defence. He beat two defenders and sent a left-foot shot from the edge of the area inside the far post. That was the only goal, although Kahn had to make another fine save from Shevchenko near the finish. Bayern were through to the Final.

Finalist: Bayern Munich (4-3 aggregate)

David Beckham (1975). *Leytonstone-born Beckham had trials with Leyton Orient but signed trainee forms with Manchester United in 1991. He made his league debut in right midfield against Leeds in 1995, and by 1997 he was a regular in the United and England first teams. A masterful crosser of the ball, he is also a spot-kick expert with a powerful shot. He made his England debut in 1996 against Moldova, and played in the 1998 World Cup finals. He scored a magnificent 25-yard curling free-kick against Colombia in the tournament, but was sent off for retaliation in the following game against Argentina. His stunning goal against Real Madrid in the 1999/2000 European Cup quarter-final second leg was too late to save United from elimination. He has amassed over 30 caps in his career.*

David Beckham

United seize trophy in last seconds

Manchester United (0) 2   Bayern Munich (1) 1

Nou Camp Stadium, Barcelona, 26 May 1999
Attendance: 90,000
Referee: Collina (Italy)

Manchester United were in their first European Cup Final for 31 years, on what would have been Sir Matt Busby's 90th birthday. With Keane and Scholes suspended, Beckham was given the central midfield role, with Giggs moving out to the right wing. Schmeichel, on his last appearance for the club, was captain before his departure for Sporting Lisbon.

Bayern almost immediately took advantage of United's re-organisation. In the 6th minute Carsten Jancker powered towards goal, and a misunderstanding between Stam and Johnsen resulted in the Norwegian defender fouling Bayern's centre-forward twenty yards from goal. Babbel and Jancker peeled away from the wall as Mario Basler ran at the kick, and the ball sailed through the gap and over Schmeichel into the net.

As the half wore on, Michael Tarnat and Markus Babbel were containing the wingers Giggs and Blomvquist, and Lothar Matthäus and Samuel Kuffour in the centre were allowing little space for Cole and Yorke to operate. Effenberg and Jeremies were controlling the midfield, and efforts from Cole and Yorke were calmly saved by keeper Oliver Kahn. Bayern were dominating the game and dictating the pace but they could not add to their score.

Early in the second half Jancker forced a save from Schmeichel and Babbel missed a headed opportunity. In the 66th minute Sheringham replaced Blomqvist but Bayern remained on the attack. An Effenberg lob was tipped over by Schmeichel and substitute Mehmet Scholl's lob hit the bar. An increasingly desperate United substituted Solskjaer for Cole in the 80th minute, but time was nearly up and the Germans were preparing to celebrate their fourth European Cup victory.

In the 90th minute, United forced a corner. Schmeichel came running up to add his height to the attack. Beckham swung in the corner, and it was half-cleared to Giggs whose shot was knocked on by Sheringham into the Bayern net. The Germans were stunned and almost immediately conceded another corner. With the huge crowd in the Nou Camp expecting extra time, Beckham sent in the corner which was flicked on by Sheringham and deflected into the Bayern net by Solskjaer. Seconds later the whistle blew for full time.

In one of the most amazing reversals of fortune ever seen in the European Cup Final, United had won the trophy for only the second time in their history, and their last-gasp victory had brought them the 'treble' – European Cup, Premier League and FA Cup. There was little doubt that Bayern were the better team on the night but United had luck on their side. 'It is the greatest night of my life. It is a fairytale', exclaimed a delighted Alex Ferguson.

The teams
Manchester United: Schmeichel, Neville, Irwin, Johnsen, Stam, Beckham, Butt, Blomqvist (Sheringham), Giggs, Cole (Solskjaer), Yorke (manager: Ferguson) (Sheringham 90, Solskjaer 90)
Bayern Munich: Kahn, Babbel, Kuffour, Matthaus (Fink), Linke, Tarnat, jeremies, Effenberg, Basler (Salihamidzic), Zickler (Scholl), Jancker (manager: Hitzfeld) (Basler 6)

Ole Gunnar Solskjaer (centre) scores Manchester United's second goal in injury time in the 1999 Final.

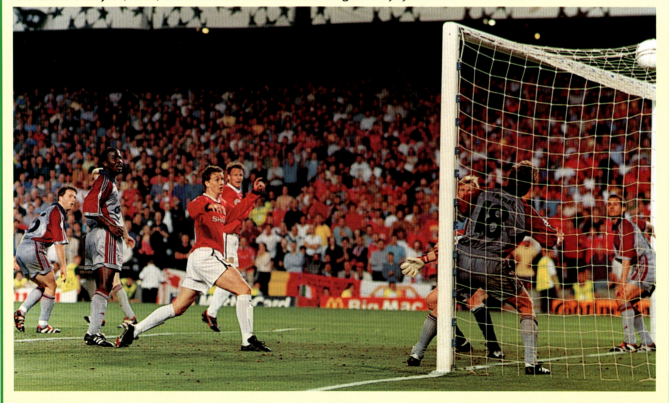

The Champions League expands

Media Partners, an Italian-based company, had proposed to the 'big' European clubs that they leave the competition for a new, breakaway Super League, with prize money of over £1 billion. UEFA countered with an expanded tournament and increased financial incentives. There are now no less than three qualifying rounds. The holders go straight into the league and join the top-ranked 15 clubs: the league winners from the nine highest-ranked countries and the runners-up from the six highest-ranked. Sixteen clubs also qualify from the preliminary rounds. The league is divided into eight groups of four, the top two from each group moving into a second league of four groups of four. The eight winners and runners-up then proceed to a two-leg, knock-out quarter-final, semi-final and single-leg Final, as before. All league matches are to be played on Tuesdays and Wednesdays to maximise TV income.

As a further incentive to the wealthy clubs, UEFA has reserved places in the UEFA Cup for all clubs eliminated in the third qualifying round as well as those placed third in the first group stage. With no more room for it in the crowded schedule, the Cup Winners Cup had been abolished at the end of the previous season after almost forty years. UEFA president Lennart Johansson averred, 'We have found a very good balance between sporting, political and commercial considerations'. Maybe, but the competition is now virtually unrecognisable from only ten years ago, and the profit motive has ousted the rather more Corinthian ideals of Gabriel Hanot and the pioneer clubs of the European Cup.

BRITISH CLUBS

Arsenal, second to Manchester United in the Premiership, moved straight into the first league in Group B. Away to Fiorentina, Arsenal's defence and offside trap frustrated the three-man attack of Chiesa, Batistuta and Mijatovic. Ljungberg should have converted an Overmars cross early on and both Adams and Kanu missed second-half chances. In the 80th minute, keeper Francesco Taldo then saved Kanu's feeble penalty to keep the score 0-0.

At Wembley, a defensive AIK kept Arsenal out until the 28th minute when Ljungberg scored from ten yards. Arsenal's second-half defensive lapse allowed Krister Nordin to beat Manninger from fifteen yards, but in the last minute substitute Henry made it 2-1 and then unselfishly laid off to Davor Suker for 3-1.

At the Nou Camp, Barcelona controlled the first half. In the 16th minute Cocu's shot was dropped by Manninger, and Luis Enrique nipped in to score. In the second half, although Giles Grimandi was sent off, Kanu equalised in the 81st minute.

At Wembley Barcelona produced some brilliant attacking football. Following a 13th-minute Rivaldo penalty, after an obvious dive by Cocu, a Figo header a minute later found Luis Enrique who scored from fifteen yards. Shortly after the interval, Bergkamp's trickery outwitted Abelardo and it was 2-1. In the 56th minute Luis Figo made it 3-1 and then Cocu added a fourth. Overmars scored Arsenal's second seven minutes from the end. In a critical fifth game at Wembley, Batistuta's beautifully-taken 75th-minute rocket took Fiorentina to the next stage and Arsenal into the UEFA Cup, the Wembley experiment over.

Gianluca Vialli's **Chelsea**, third in the Premiership, entered in the third qualifying round. Nervous at Stamford Bridge against Latvian side Skonto Riga, eventually they scored three goals in the last fifteen minutes through Babayaro, Poyet and Sutton. 0-0 in Latvia saw them through to league Group H.

Away to AC Milan, with Dennis Wise the only Englishman and Gianfranco Zola outstanding – flitting into space, teasing the Milan defence and nearly scoring twice – Chelsea's stirring display managed a point.

In Berlin, Dariusz Wosz masterminded Hertha, who went ahead in the 3rd minute, Iranian striker Ali Daei heading in a cross past Ed De Goey. Daei got the second in the 70th minute and Frank Leboeuf a consolation penalty in the 86th. Chelsea finally won at home to Galatasaray, helped by a 31st-minute sending-off for Galatasaray's Brazilian goalkeeper Taffarel. With Didier Deschamps controlling the midfield, Chelsea scored in the 51st minute when Dan Petrescu's low shot beat the substitute keeper from 15 yards.

In Istanbul, Zola yet again magnificent, a sparkling Chelsea crushed Galatasaray 5-0. In the 32nd minute, from Zola's long pass, Flo drilled in an angled shot. Just after half time, the tall striker added a second, and within five minutes Zola made it three. In the 79th minute Wise converted a Flo cross and with two minutes to go Gabrielle Ambrosetti scored the fifth. Chelsea went top.

The last game was against Hertha Berlin at home. Deschamps got the first, crashing in a 20-yard curling shot in the 11th minute, Ferrer shot home a Wise pass in the 44th, and Chelsea were through.

As Scottish champions, **Rangers** entered in the second qualifying round. A fairly simple 4-1 win away to Finnish champions FC Haka was followed by a 3-0 victory at Ibrox.

At home to Italy's Parma, Rangers dominated the first half and capitalised on Fabio Cannavaro's dismissal. They led in the 33rd minute when Tony Vidmar's right-foot shot deflected off Thuram over keeper Gianluca Buffon. Claudio Reyna's low shot added a second. In Parma, the home side had to attack, and Lassissi scored after 68 minutes, but Rangers were through 2-1 to Group F, one of the strongest.

In Spain Rangers survived Valencia's early onslaught until the 57th minute when Charbonnier could not hold Sanchez's shot and Kily Gonzalez converted. Gonzalez made it two in the 76th minute. At home to Bayern Munich, Rangers scored in the 22nd minute from Jorge Albertz's 20-yard shot. With Carsten Jancker on for Lizarazu in the second half, Bayern rallied and Michael Tarnat equalised in the very last minute.

In Holland, a nervous Amoruso almost gave away two goals to PSV but, although Luc Nilis and Ruud Van Nistelrooy threatened, Rangers were victorious with an 85th-minute volley from Albertz. At Ibrox, against a poor PSV, Rangers turned in a brilliant attacking display, and an early McCann corner met a fine header from Amoruso for the first. In the 38th minute Mols ran on for McCann's return ball, and headed in the second. Although Van Nistelrooy equalised from the spot at the end of the half, Rangers scored their third in the 55th minute when PSV keeper Ivica Kralj could not hold a Van Bronkhorst free kick and the ball was forced over by McCann. Mols made it 4-1 in the 80th minute.

At Ibrox, with Rangers qualifying if they won, Valencia's fast, flowing football had the Spanish club 2-0 ahead at half time, the first goal a 20-yard shot from captain Gaizka Mendieta and the second from Argentinian striker Claudio Lopez on half time. Craig Moore headed one back in the 59th minute, but 2-1 meant Valencia qualified and Rangers needed at least a point against Bayern in Germany.

In spite of a brave performance, Rangers hitting the woodwork three times and missing several chances, it was Bayern's Thomas Strunz whose disputed first-half penalty secured a 1-0 win, and Rangers again missed the final stage.

Manchester United, last year's European Cup holders, had won the Premier League and went straight into the relatively undemanding Group D.

Against Ossie Ardiles' Croatia Zagreb at Old Trafford, an injury-stricken United were unco-ordinated and the game ended goal-less. In Austria against a defensive Sturm Graz, Keane capitalised on a Beckham free kick in the 16th minute to send a thundering shot in off the crossbar. Then, in the 31st minute, Yorke headed in a Beckham corner and two minutes later Cole wrapped it up from a Yorke pass. Marseille came to Old Trafford next, unveiling a stiflingly defensive formation. In the first half-hour Yorke and Cole spurned easy chances, and Ibrahimi Bakayoya took advantage of Henning Berg's error to shoot in off the underneath of the bar. In the 79th minute, Cole scored with an athletic overhead kick, and Scholes got the winner from a Cole cross with seven minutes left.

In France United played a tactically defensive game against an attacking Marseille, and went down by the odd goal, scored by centre-back William Gallas in the 69th minute. United made sure of qualifying in Zagreb, Goran Juric fouling Scholes on the edge of the box in the 32nd minute and Beckham curling in a trademark free kick. Just after half time Keane met a Denis Irwin cross and the ball was deflected in, with Robert Prosinecki making the final score 2-1.

GROUP A

Bayer Leverküsen, Dynamo Kiev, Lazio, Maribor

The shock opening games saw Slovenians Maribor going top with a 1-0 away win over Dynamo Kiev, while Bayer drew with Lazio 1-1 in Germany. A 71st-minute Marcelo Salas goal against Kiev then put Lazio top, where they would remain. In the third game, despite having a defender sent off, Maribor held Lazio 0-0 at half time. Simone Inzaghi scored in the 60th minute, Sergio Conceicao added another two minutes later, and substitute Salas put away two within four minutes to consolidate Lazio's position. Bayer and Kiev drew 1-1 for Kiev's first point. Lazio again scored four past Maribor, two by Inzaghi, while Kiev beat Bayer 4-2 in the Ukraine. In the fifth game, a first-minute goal from Lazio's Pavel Nedved was equalised by Ulf Kirsten just before half-time to give Bayer an away draw, and two goals from Sergei Rebrov gave Kiev three points in Slovenia. Bayer could only draw at home against Maribor, meaning Kiev qualified even though they lost at home to Lazio.

Bayer Leverküsen 1	Lazio 1	
Dynamo Kiev 0	Maribor 1	
Lazio 2	Dynamo Kiev 1	
Maribor 0	Bayer Leverküsen 2	
Lazio 4	Maribor 0	
Bayer Leverküsen 1	Dynamo Kiev 1	
Maribor 0	Lazio 4	
Dynamo Kiev 4	Bayer Leverküsen 2	
Lazio 1	Bayer Leverküsen 1	
Maribor 1	Dynamo Kiev 2	
Dynamo Kiev 0	Lazio 1	
Bayer Leverküsen 0	Maribor 0	

	P	W	D	L	F	A	Pts
Lazio	6	4	2	0	13	3	14
Dynamo Kiev	6	2	1	3	8	8	7
Bayer Leverküsen	6	1	4	1	7	7	7
Maribor	6	1	1	4	2	12	4

GROUP B

AIK, Arsenal, Barcelona, Fiorentina

In Stockholm, AIK led Barcelona until the 86th minute when Abelardo equalised. Dani snatched a dramatic last-minute winner. Arsenal drew 0-0 with Fiorentina. In Spain, Fiorentina were two down within ten minutes. Gabriel Batistuta pulled one back in the 51st, but two in three minutes from Rivaldo ensured Barcelona's victory. Arsenal beat AIK 3-1 at Wembley. Both match-day-three games ended in draws. Arsenal were then well beaten by Barcelona at Wembley, putting the Spanish club five points clear at the top, and Fiorentina won 3-0 over AIK, Batistuta, Chiesa and Abel Balbo all scoring. Fiorentina confirmed their qualification beating Arsenal 1-0 at Wembley. Fiorentina and Barcelona fought out a 3-3 draw in the final match, Balbo and Rivaldo each scoring twice.

Fiorentina 0	Arsenal 0	
AIK 1	Barcelona 2	
Arsenal 3	AIK 1	
Barcelona 4	Fiorentina 2	
Barcelona 1	Arsenal 1	
AIK 0	Fiorentina 0	
Arsenal 2	Barcelona 4	
Fiorentina 3	AIK 0	
Arsenal 0	Fiorentina 1	
Barcelona 5	AIK 0	
AIK 2	Arsenal 3	
Fiorentina 3	FC Barcelona 3	

	P	W	D	L	F	A	Pts
Barcelona	6	4	2	0	19	9	14
Fiorentina	6	2	3	1	9	7	9
Arsenal	6	2	2	2	9	9	8
AIK	6	0	1	5	4	16	1

GROUP C

Boavista, Borussia Dortmund, Feyenoord, Rosenborg

Rosenborg opened in style, beating Boavista 3-0 in Portugal, while Feyenoord and Dortmund drew in Holland. Rosenborg stayed top drawing 2-2 with Feyenoord. A draw with Dortmund, and a 3-0 away win against Dortmund, with two goals from Jan Derek Sorensen, kept the Norwegians in pole position, while Feyenoord drew 1-1 with Boavista. A 2-0 win over Boavista sealed Rosenborg's qualification, and a 1-1 draw between Dortmund and Feyenoord left only one point between them. Dortmund were surprisingly beaten in Portugal, while Feyenoord's home 1-0 defeat of Rosenborg, thanks to Somalia's 86th-minute winner, saw them to the next stage.

Boavista 0	Rosenborg 3
Feyenoord 1	Borussia Dortmund 1
Rosenborg 2	Feyenoord 2
Borussia Dortmund 3	Boavista 1
Boavista 1	Feyenoord 1
Rosenborg 2	Borussia Dortmund 2
Feyenoord 1	Boavista 1
Borussia Dortmund 0	Rosenborg 3
Rosenborg 2	Boavista 0
Borussia Dortmund 1	Feyenoord 1
Feyenoord 1	Rosenborg 0
Boavista 1	Borussia Dortmund 0

	P	W	D	L	F	A	Pts
Rosenborg	6	3	2	1	12	5	11
Feyenoord	6	1	5	0	7	6	8
Borussia Dortmund	6	1	3	2	7	9	6
Boavista	6	1	2	3	4	10	5

GROUP E

Molde, Olympiakos, Porto, Real Madrid

Real escaped embarrassment at home to Olympiakos, when Raul equalised 3-3 in the 80th minute. Porto, having beaten Molde away, won 2-0 in Greece, both goals coming from Mario Jardell. Real beat Porto to go top. Porto gained revenge 2-1 in Porto, Jardel again the scorer, to take over leadership. Molde gained their first points vanquishing Olympiakos 3-2. Porto qualified with a 3-1 defeat of Molde, Deco scoring two. Real also qualified with goals from Raul, Fernando Morientes and Roberto Carlos in their 3-0 win over Olympiakos, watched by only 9,000 in the Bernabeu.

Olympiakos 3	Real Madrid 3
Molde 0	Porto 1
Real Madrid 4	Molde 1
Porto 2	Olympiakos 0
Real Madrid 3	Porto 1
Olympiakos 3	Molde 1
Porto 2	Real Madrid 1
Molde 3	Olympiakos 2
Real Madrid 3	Olympiakos 0
Porto 3	Molde 1
Molde 0	Real Madrid 1
Olympiakos 1	Porto 0

	P	W	D	L	F	A	Pts
Real Madrid	6	4	1	1	15	7	13
Porto	6	4	0	2	9	6	12
Olympiakos	6	2	1	3	9	12	7
Molde	6	1	0	5	6	14	3

GROUP D

Croatia Zagreb, Manchester United, Marseille, Sturm Graz

United were held 0-0 at home by Zagreb, while two first-half goals from Robert Pires and Fabrizio Ravanell against Sturm Graz put Marseille on top. Christian Perez scored a 77th-minute winner for Marseille in Zagreb and United beat Sturm Graz in Austria. United's 2-1 home win over Marseille gave them group leadership, while two goals from Tomislav Sokota helped Zagreb defeat Sturm Graz 3-0. Marseille's 1-0 defeat of United restored them to the top, and Sturm Graz finally picked up points with a 1-0 home win over Zagreb. United qualified with a 2-1 away win in Zagreb, and Marseille were beaten 3-2 away by Sturm Graz, Tomica Kocijan's 84th-minute winner coming after Dugarry had scored twice for the French. Marseille qualified by drawing 2-2 with Zagreb.

Manchester United 0	Croatia Zagreb 0
Marseille 2	Sturm Graz 0
Croatia Zagreb 1	Marseille 2
Sturm Graz 0	Manchester United 3
Croatia Zagreb 3	Sturm Graz 0
Manchester United 2	Marseille 1
Sturm Graz 1	Croatia Zagreb 0
Marseille 1	Manchester United 0
Croatia Zagreb 1	Manchester United 2
Sturm Graz 3	Marseille 2
Marseille 2	Croatia Zagreb 2
Manchester United 2	Sturm Graz 1

	P	W	D	L	F	A	Pts
Manchester United	6	4	1	1	9	4	13
Marseille	6	3	1	2	10	8	10
Sturm Graz	6	2	0	4	5	12	6
Croatia Zagreb	6	1	2	3	7	7	5

Jardel of Porto

GROUP F

Bayern Munich, PSV Eindhoven, Rangers, Valencia

Two goals from Sergio, in the 11th and 67th minutes, helped Bayern beat PSV in their first game and Rangers lost 2-0 to Valencia in Spain. A 4th-minute Claudio Lopez strike put Valencia 1-0 ahead of PSV but Ruud Van Nistelrooy equalised with a 71st-minute penalty, while Bayern held Rangers 1-1 at Ibrox. Valencia went top on goal difference, forcing a 1-1 draw with Bayern in Munich. A 6th-minute goal from Brazilian Giovane Elber was countered by Lopez ten minutes from time. Rangers beat PSV 1-0 in Holland. Another draw followed in Spain, Adrian Ilie scoring in the 11th minute and Stefan Effenberg's penalty equalising seven minutes later. Rangers achieved an impressive 4-1 win over PSV at Ibrox. Valencia's 2-1 defeat of Rangers sealed qualification, while PSV's Van Nistelrooy and Luc Nilis scored in a 2-1 win in Holland over Bayern, who finally qualified when they beat Rangers.

Bayern Munich	2	PSV	1
Valencia	2	Rangers	0
Rangers	1	Bayern Munich	1
PSV	1	Valencia	1
PSV	0	Rangers	1
Bayern Munich	1	Valencia	1
Rangers	4	PSV	1
Valencia	1	Bayern Munich	1
PSV	2	Bayern Munich	1
Rangers	1	Valencia	2
Bayern Munich	1	Rangers	0
Valencia	1	PSV	0

	P	W	D	L	F	A	Pts
Valencia	6	3	3	0	8	4	12
Bayern Munich	6	2	3	1	7	6	9
Rangers	6	2	1	3	7	7	7
PSV	6	1	1	4	5	10	4

GROUP G

Bordeaux, Spartak Moscow, Sparta Prague, Willem II

Sparta Prague and Bordeaux began with a 0-0 draw, and Spartak won in Holland. Bordeaux inflicted another defeat on Willem II in game two, and Prague drew again, this time with Spartak. Bordeaux went top by beating Spartak, Sylvain Wiltord in the 9th minute and Johan Micoud in the 56th their scorers. Bordeaux qualified by beating Spartak away 2-1. Willem II's 4-3 defeat by Prague left them still point-less. Prague qualified with a goal-less draw with Bordeaux, and Willem II picked up their first point in a 1-1 away draw with Spartak. Prague's 5-2 defeat of Spartak on the last day enabled them to win the group, as Bordeaux could only draw 0-0 with Willem II.

Sparta Prague	0	Bordeaux	0
Willem II	1	Spartak Moscow	3
Bordeaux	3	Willem II	2
Spartak Moscow	1	Sparta Prague	1
Sparta Prague	4	Willem II	0
Bordeaux	2	Spartak Moscow	1
Willem II	3	Sparta Prague	4
Spartak Moscow	1	Bordeaux	2
Bordeaux	0	Sparta Prague	0
Spartak Moscow	1	Willem II	1
Willem II	0	Bordeaux	0
Sparta Prague	5	Spartak Moscow	2

	P	W	D	L	F	A	Pts
Sparta Prague	6	3	3	0	14	6	12
Bordeaux	6	3	3	0	7	4	12
Spartak Moscow	6	1	2	3	9	12	5
Willem II	6	0	2	4	7	15	2

GROUP H

Chelsea, Galatasaray, Hertha Berlin, AC Milan

Hertha were 2-0 up against Galatasaray within thirteen minutes, but Hakan Sukur in the 24th minute and Gheorghe Hagi with an 89th-minute penalty saved a point. Chelsea had a goal-less draw with Milan. Hertha beat Chelsea and Milan won at home over Galatasaray, Leonardo and Andrei Shevchenko scoring for Milan in the two minutes before half time. Milan ran the third game, but Ali Daei put Hertha ahead in the 69th minute, Oliver Bierhof equalising four minutes later. Chelsea beat Galatasaray at Stamford Bridge, then thrashed Galatasaray 5-0 in Istanbul, and Hertha went top after their 1-0 defeat of Milan, Wosz's goal coming in the 41st minute. Galatasaray recovered to beat Hertha 4-1 away, two coming from Hakan, and Chelsea drew 1-1 with Milan in Italy. In the last game, Galatasaray shocked Milan with a 3-2 win in Istanbul, equalising with an 86th-minute Hakan strike and winning with Umit's 90th-minute penalty. Milan ignominiously finished bottom, their defeat meaning Hertha qualified despite losing 2-0 to Chelsea.

Chelsea	0	Milan	0
Galatasaray	2	Hertha	2
Milan	2	Galatasaray	1
Hertha	2	Chelsea	1
Milan	1	Hertha	1
Chelsea	1	Galatasaray	0
Hertha	1	Milan	0
Galatasaray	0	Chelsea	5
Milan	1	Chelsea	1
Hertha	1	Galatasaray	4
Galatasaray	3	Milan	2
Chelsea	2	Hertha	0

	P	W	D	L	F	A	Pts
Chelsea	6	3	2	1	10	3	11
Hertha	6	2	2	2	7	10	8
Galatasaray	6	2	1	3	10	13	7
Milan	6	1	3	2	6	7	6

MANCHESTER UNITED

United travelled to Fiorentina, to find their captain Batistuta, in particular, in top form, seizing on Keane's badly-directed pass in the 24th minute to beat Bosnich. In the 52nd minute, Henning Berg was dispossessed by Batistuta and Abel Balbo scored from the cut-back. At home to a fast, counter-attacking Valencia, United played more like English champions. In the 38th minute, Keane thumped in a clearance from twenty yards and seven minutes later Solskjaer converted a Beckham cross. A Scholes header from another in the 70th minute made it 3-0.

Bordeaux visited Manchester next, for a Giggs lesson in wing play. In the 41st minute, he sprinted into the box to score from a Beckham cross and he made the second with a perfect cross for Sheringham's header. In France, a Pavon 20-yard shot was helped into his own net by Raimond Van Der Gouw, but Lilian Laslande was sent off ten minutes later for fouling Beckham. In the 33rd minute Sheringham's pass was turned in by Keane and, with six minutes left, substitute Solskjaer scored with his first touch.

United qualified for the quarter-finals by beating Fiorentina 3-1 at Old Trafford, despite Batistuta's stunning, 30-yard swerving opener in the16th minute. Cole replied four minutes later with a deft, low shot past Francesco Toldo, equalling Dennis Law's club record of 14 goals in Europe. In the 32nd minute, Berg headed a Beckham cross against the bar and Keane scored from the rebound. With twenty minutes left, Yorke headed a Giggs cross down past Toldo.

Claudio Lopez of Valencia, playing against Manchester United in December 1999

GROUP A

Barcelona, Hertha Berlin, Porto, Sparta Prague

Porto beat Sparta 2-0, while Barcelona could only draw away with Hertha. Two goals each from Kluivert and Luis Enrique saw Barcelona hammer Sparta 5-0, and Porto won 1-0 against Hertha courtesy of a 79th-minute Drulovic goal. A polished and assured Barcelona saw off Porto 4-2, with a free-kick and brilliant individual goal from Rivaldo and one each from Kluivert and Ronald De Boer. Hertha drew 1-1 with Sparta. Barcelona qualified by beating Porto 2-0 in Portugal, Rivaldo scoring with another free kick, and a last-minute goal from Fukal saw Sparta beat Hertha. With Barcelona beating Hertha 3-1 and Porto drawing 2-2 with Sparta, runner-up qualification now depended on the last game. Two goals from Gabri gave Barcelona a 2-1 win over Sparta, and a 70th-minute strike from substitute Ferreira Clayton against Hertha got Porto through. Barcelona were the only team still unbeaten, and also the tournament's highest scorers with 36 goals.

Hertha	1	Barcelona	1
Sparta Prague	0	Porto	2
Porto	1	Hertha	0
Barcelona	5	Sparta Prague	0
Barcelona	4	Porto	2
Hertha	1	Sparta Prague	1
Porto	0	Barcelona	2
Sparta Prague	1	Hertha	0
Barcelona	3	Hertha	1
Porto	2	Sparta Prague	2
Hertha	0	Porto	1
Sparta Prague	1	Barcelona	2

	P	W	D	L	F	A	Pts
Barcelona	6	5	1	0	17	5	16
Porto	6	3	1	2	8	8	10
Sparta Prague	6	1	2	3	5	12	5
Hertha	6	0	2	4	3	8	2

GROUP B

Bordeaux, Fiorentina, Manchester United, Valencia

Fiorentina beat Manchester United 2-0 in Italy and a last-minute goal from Kily Gonzalez sealed Valencia's 3-0 win over Bordeaux. Bordeaux against Fiorentina was goal-less, and United scored three past Valencia. Predrag Mijatovic's 20th-minute penalty brought Fiorentina a 1-0 win over Valencia and a Giggs-inspired United put two past Bordeaux at Old Trafford. United won away in France while goals from Valencia's Adrian Ilie and Mandieta beat Fiorentina. United qualified with a 3-1 home win against Fiorentina, and Valencia kept up their challenge with a 4-1 away win over a ten-man Bordeaux. Three goals in seventeen minutes from Chiesa, Batistuta and Rui Costa helped Fiorentina draw 3-3 draw with Bordeaux, but Valencia's 0-0 draw with United in Spain saw the Spaniards qualify over the Italians.

Fiorentina	2	Manchester United	0
Valencia	3	Bordeaux	0
Bordeaux	0	Fiorentina	0
Manchester United	3	Valencia	0
Manchester United	2	Bordeaux	0
Fiorentina	1	Valencia	0
Bordeaux	1	Manchester United	2
Valencia	2	Fiorentina	0
Manchester United	3	Fiorentina	1
Bordeaux	1	Valencia	4
Fiorentina	3	Bordeaux	3
Valencia	0	Manchester United	0

	P	W	D	L	F	A	Pts
Manchester United	6	4	1	1	10	4	13
Valencia	6	3	1	2	9	5	10
Fiorentina	6	2	2	2	7	8	8
Bordeaux	6	0	2	4	5	14	2

GROUP C

Bayern Munich, Dynamo Kiev, Real Madrid, Rosenborg

Real Madrid opened with goals from Raul and Morientes beating Kiev 2-1 in the Ukraine, and Rosenborg held Bayern 1-1 in Norway. Carsten Jancker and Sergio scored in Bayern's 2-1 defeat of Kiev, Rebrov replying for Kiev. A last-minute Roberto Carlos goal eased Real through against Rosenborg 3-1. Rebrov scored what proved to be the winner in the 29th minute against Rosenborg, and Bayern humiliated Real 4-2 at the Bernabeu with goals from Mehmet Scholl, Effenberg, Thorsten Fink and Sergio. In the next round, Lothar Matthäus' last game for Bayern, they demolished Real again 4-1, Alexander Zickler scoring twice in the last ten minutes, and two goals from Rebrov ensured Kiev a 2-1 win over Rosenborg. Bayern's 2-1 victory over Rosenborg made the quarter-finals certain, and Real could only draw with Kiev. A 3rd-minute goal from Raul against Rosenborg secured Real's qualification, despite Kiev's better goal difference – the crucial factor was Real's head-to-head record against Kiev.

Dynamo Kiev	1	Real Madrid	2
Rosenborg	1	Bayern Munich	1
Bayern Munich	2	Dynamo Kiev	1
Real Madrid	3	Rosenborg	1
Real Madrid	2	Bayern Munich	4
Dynamo Kiev	2	Rosenborg	1
Bayern Munich	4	Real Madrid	1
Rosenborg	1	Dynamo Kiev	2
Real Madrid	2	Dynamo Kiev	2
Bayern Munich	2	Rosenborg	1
Dynamo Kiev	2	Bayern Munich	0
Rosenborg	0	Real Madrid	1

	P	W	D	L	F	A	Pts
Bayern Munich	6	4	1	1	13	8	13
Real Madrid	6	3	1	2	11	12	10
Dynamo Kiev	6	3	1	2	10	8	10
Rosenborg	6	0	1	5	5	11	1

GROUP D

Chelsea, Feyenoord, Lazio, Marseille

Chelsea started well, defeating Feyenoord 3-1, and Stankovic and Conceiacao scored in Lazio's 2-0 win in Marseille. Chelsea versus Lazio was goal-less, while Feyenoord defeated Marseille 3-0. Two late goals from Feyenoord's Jon Dahl Tomasson cancelled out Juan Veron's 37th-minute strike in an away win over Lazio, and Chelsea went down 1-0 at Marseille. A 26th-minute goal from Wise was enough for Chelsea to beat Marseille at home, and Feyenoord and Lazio drew 0-0. Chelsea beat Feyenoord 3-1, and four goals from Lazio's Simone Inzaghi and one from Alen Boksic destroyed Marseille 5-1. On the last day, Lazio's 2-1 win at Stamford Bridge meant they won the group and Chelsea finished second.

Marseille	0	Lazio	2
Chelsea	3	Feyenoord	1
Feyenoord	3	Marseille	0
Lazio	0	Chelsea	0
Lazio	1	Feyenoord	2
Marseille	1	Chelsea	0
Feyenoord	0	Lazio	0
Chelsea	1	Marseille	0
Lazio	5	Marseille	1
Feyenoord	1	Chelsea	3
Marseille	0	Feyenoord	0
Chelsea	1	Lazio	2

	P	W	D	L	F	A	Pts
Lazio	6	3	2	1	10	4	11
Chelsea	6	3	1	2	8	5	10
Feyenoord	6	2	2	2	7	7	8
Marseille	6	1	1	4	2	11	4

CHELSEA

Chelsea had an easy 3-1 win over a disappointing Feyenoord. Babayaro opened the scoring, and in the 67th minute Flo made it two, scoring again with three minutes to go. In Rome, midfielders Juan Veron and Diego Simeone were outstanding for Lazio but neither side could score. Manager Vialli was 'sent off' for protesting and given a touchline ban. In Marseille, with riot police moving in on crowd trouble, Chelsea went down 1-0 to a 16th-minute Robert Pires 15-yard shot.

The tables were turned when Marseille visited Stamford Bridge. With Dennis Wise a true captain, incisive in the tackle and deadly accurate in his passing, Chelsea dominated the first half. In the 26th minute, Wise scored with a fine half-volley. In the second half, Marseille attacked, and in the 80th minute Ivan De La Pena hit the post with a 30-yard free kick, but Chelsea held on. The Londoners qualified for the quarter-finals with a 3-1 away win over Feyenoord. After Leboeuf's penalty miss in the 8th minute, Zola bent in a shot past keeper Jerzy Dudek from the edge of the area in the 39th minute. Kalou equalised twenty minutes later, but a Wise header in the 64th minute and a Flo goal five minutes later finished off the Dutch.

Lazio came to London for the last game. Chelsea, with Wise absent, fielded a side without a single English player. Lazio, with their five-man midfield and Inzaghi up front, inflicted on Chelsea their first home European defeat in 42 years, to finish leaders by a point. Although Gus Poyet scored the first goal in the 44th minute, nine minutes later Pavel Nedved crossed and Inzaghi shot in from five yards. Sinisa Mihajlovic claimed the winner, curling in a free kick in the 66th minute.

Porto v Bayern Munich

With Bayern poor in the first leg in Portugal, Porto should have won. Porto dominated possession, and deserved their first goal, a magnificent Mario Jardel header in the 47th minute. Oliver Kahn's fine save from Jardel in the 77th minute denied the Brazilian a second but, against the run of play, Bayern scored a vital away goal with ten minutes left. An unmarked Paulo Sergio collected an Effenberg 30-yard free-kick, and fired past Henrique Hilario.

In Munich, Bayern missed the talismanic Effenberg and wing-back Bixente Lizarazu, but led in the 15th minute, Sergio converting a Michael Tamat cross. Jardel equalised with a downward header from a right-wing cross in the 90th minute but, in the third minute of injury time, Tamat headed in from a free kick, and Bayern had squeezed through.

Bayern 3 Porto 2 (aggregate)

Real Madrid v Manchester United

Real had most of the pressure in Madrid but could not score, largely due to the goalkeeping excellence of Mark Bosnich. Although Yorke had a 46th minute 'goal' disallowed and Cole missed an easy chance in the first half, Real were the stronger side and Bosnich had to be agile towards the end to save from McManaman and Bolic.

At Old Trafford, Real went ahead in the 21st minute when Keane slid the ball into his own net from a Real cross. The game was decided early in the second half when McManaman passed to Raul, who picked his spot. Two minutes later, an outrageous back-heeled nutmeg by Fernando Redondo on Berg gave the Argentine space to pick out Raul, who scored from close range. Beckham scored a stunning goal in the 64th minute from the edge of the box and Scholes converted a penalty two minutes from time, but the holders were out.

Real Madrid 3 Manchester United 2 (aggregate)

Chelsea v Barcelona

In a stirring performance at Stamford Bridge, three goals in eight minutes clinched victory for Chelsea. In the 30th minute, Zola drove in a superb free kick. Four minutes later, Flo outpaced defender Abelardo to score from a Zola pass and then in the 38th minute beat keeper Ruud Hesp again. Figo scored for Barcelona in the 64th minute.

At the Nou Camp Barcelona were imperious. In the 24th minute a Rivaldo free kick deflected off Babayaro and put them one up. Just on half time, Kluivert shot against the post and Figo calmly inserted the rebound. On the hour, however, Hesp fluffed a goal kick straight to Flo, who quickly curled the ball beyond the keeper's reach. With seven minutes remaining, Dani's header levelled the aggregate score, and Rivaldo missed a penalty. In extra time, Rivaldo atoned by making no mistake from the spot after Figo had been fouled. Kluivert finished Chelsea off five minutes later, heading home a Dani cross.

Barcelona 6 Chelsea 4 (aggregate)

Valencia v Lazio

In Spain, a brilliant, attacking performance from a young Valencia side, displaying quick movement and intelligent running, crushed the last Italian team in the tournament. Within the first four minutes they were two up through Miguel Angulo and a Gerard Lopez header. Inzaghi pulled one back in the 28th minute but Gerard headed another five minutes before the interval. In the 80th minute, Gerard claimed his hat-trick and, although Salas turned in a Boksic cross in the 87th minute, Claudio scored from the edge of the penalty area in injury time for an emphatic 5-2 win.

In Rome, Valencia continued to attack but Lazio's Veron was inspired and scored magnificently from 30 yards in the 52nd minute. In the second half, however, keeper Canizares kept Valencia in the game with a string of excellent saves.

Valencia 5 Lazio 3 (aggregate)

Real Madrid v Bayern Munich

Real avenged their two earlier defeats by Bayern in the tournament with a 2-0 win in Madrid. Dominant throughout, they led in the 4th minute when Anelka convincingly finished from a Raul pass. In the 33rd minute, Michel Salgado forced Jens Jeremies, a midfielder playing in defence, into an own goal.

In Munich, Real were without Hierro and Salgado, and centre-forward Jancker scored for Bayern in the 12th minute. In the 31st, Anelka, now forgiven his early-season histrionics, planted a superb header from a Savio cross past Kahn. Despite Elber flicking in a header after the interval, Real were in their 11th final.

Real Madrid 3 Bayern Munich 2 (aggregate)

Valencia v Barcelona

Hector Cuper's splendid Valencia were again unstoppable at home. Angulo put them ahead within ten minutes, although defender Mauricio Pellegrino deflected a Zenden shot into his net in the 27th minute. Angulo whipped a goal past Hesp from a Gonzales cross before half-time and captain Mandiate sent Hesp the wrong way from the spot two minutes later. In the third minute of injury time, Claudio Lopez capitalised on an Amedeo Carboni pass to shoot in off the post. Four-one down, Barcelona had a mountain to climb at the Nou Camp.

In Barcelona, Valencia's firm defending and quick counter-attacking restricted Barcelona to 2-1, ensuring their first-ever appearance in a European Cup Final. The Nou Camp waved white handkerchiefs in anger at Barcelona's stuttering performance.

Valencia 5 Barcelona 3 (aggregate)

Real win Spanish thriller

Real Madrid 3 (1)   Valencia 0 (0)

Stade de France, Paris, 24 May 2000
Attendance: 78,500
Referee: Braschi (Italy)

In a magnificent display, Real Madrid swept aside Valencia to prove they are the true champions of Europe. In the first ever European Cup Final between two teams from the same country, the match was won by three well-taken goals and the speed and flamboyant artistry of a superb Real side.

Steve McManaman was sensational in midfield, changing direction with a flick or a back-heel, sending deadly accurate passes to Raul and marauding wing-backs Roberto Carlos and Michel Salgado, and scoring the second goal. The Real midfield was supported by the three centre-backs – Ivan Campo, Ivan Helguera and Aitor Karanka – who dealt firmly with Valencia's Claudio Lopez and Kily Gonzales, and playmaker Gaizka Mandieta was reduced to a shadow by Real's pressing tactics.

Kitted out all in black, Real began ominously, with the tall Anelka's header saved in the 16th minute by Santiago Canizares, who did well to tip aside a McManaman strike fifteen minutes later. In the 39th minute, Real's pressure paid off. A Roberto Carlos free-kick from 35 yards was deflected to Anelka who whipped a low ball into the box. Salgado picked it up, found Fernando Morientes unmarked at the far post, and Morientes deftly headed in.

In the 63rd minute, the tireless McManaman was rewarded, connecting with a clearance on the edge of the box to crash in a second goal through a ruck of players, to become the first British player to score for a continental team in a European Cup Final. Now Real were rampant and, with fifteen minutes to go, and the entire Valencia team committed to attack, Silvio, on for Morientes, cleared to Raul inside his own half, who ran seventy yards to round Canizares and score.

At the whistle, Real changed into their normal all-white strip to receive the trophy. McManaman was Man of the Match and had probably never played better. Real had won their eighth European Cup in a manner which would have delighted the legendary team of the 1950s.

The teams
Real Madrid: Casillas, Salgado (Hierro), Ivan Campo, Helguera, Karanka, Roberto Carlos, McManaman, Redondo, Raul, Morientes (Savio), Anelka (Sanchis) (manager: del Bosque) [Morientes 39, McManaman 63, Raul 75]
Valencia: Canizares, Angloma, Djukic, Pellegrino, Gerardo (Ilie), Mendieta, Farinos, Gerard, Kily Gonzalez, Claudio Lopez, Angulo (manager: Cuper)

Steve McManaman lashes in the second goal for Real Madrid in the Final against Valencia.

Index

Page references in *italics* indicate illustrations

Aarhus 8, 10, 12, 18, 100
AB Copenhagen 38
Aberdeen 76, 77, 78, 90, 91-2, 94, 95, 114
AC Milan 7, 8, 10, 12, 13, 16, 22, 23, 24, 38, 39, 40, 42, 72, 103, 104, 105, 106-7, 108, 109, 110, 116, 117, 120, 121, 123-4, 125, 127, 129, 130, 138, 159, 162
Admira Vienna 30
AEK Athens 24, 38, 48, 49, 69, 71, 72, 106, 121, 127
AIK 159, 160
Ajax 7, 12, 18, 30, 32, 34, 38, 40, 45, 47, 48, 49-50, 51, 53, 54, 66, 72, 74, 76, 84, 87, 94, 127, 129, 130, 132, 135, 136, 137, 140, 141, 151
Akranes 48, 60, 63, 69, 90, 94
Akureyri 109
Alania Vladikavkaz 140
Alsteen 13
Altafini, José *6*, 23, *23*, 52
Anderlecht 8, 10, 16, 22, 23, 26, 28, 30, 34, 38, 39, 51, 57, 58, 80, 81, 95, 97, 100, 112, 113, 121, 123, 127
Anorthosis 24
Antwerp 12
Apoel Nicosia 28, 54, 76, 97, 109
Ararat Erevan 57
Archibald, Steve 94, *94*, 95
Ards 14, 15
Arges Pitesti 51, 72, 74
Aris Bonnevoie 26, 30, 51
Arsenal 6, 48, 49-50, 112, 114, 153, 154, 159, 160
ASK Linz 28
ASK Vorwaerts 16, 20, 22, 28, 30, 42
Aston Villa 80, 81, 83, 84, 85
Athletic Bilbao 10, 11, 87, 90, 151
Athlone Town 80, 87
Atlético Madrid 14, 30, 45, 54, 55, 56, 66, 67, 137, 141
Atvidaberg 54, 57
Austria Vienna 76, 80
Austria WAC 63, 69, 72
Auxerre 137, 140, 141
Avenir Beggen 42, 84, 90, 97
AZ Alkmaar 80, 82

Banik Ostrava 63, 76, 80
Barcelona 16, 18-19, 57, 94-5, 96, 113, 115, 116, 121, 122, 123, 125, 126, 129, 144, 147, 152, 155, 159, 160, 163, 165
Basle 34, 42, 45, 51, 54, 66, 76
Bayern Leverküsen 145, 148, 160
Bayern Munich 7, 42, 51, 54, 56, 59, 60, 61, 62, 63, 76, 77, 80, 83, 94, 97, 99, 100-1, 106, 107, 109, 121, 126, 129, 145, 148, 152, 155, 156, 157, 158, 159, 162, 164, 165
Beckenbauer, Franz 55, *55*, 56

Beckham, David 157, *157*, 158
Benfica 12, 18, 19, 20, 21, 22, 23, 24, 26, 27, 28, 34, 37, 38, 42, 48, 51, 52, 54, 60, 61, 63, 66, 67, 80, 87, 88, 90, 91, 100, 102, 106, 108, 112, 113, 114, 127, 129, 153
Beroe Stara Zagora 97
Besiktas 14, 18, 30, 34, 84, 85, 97, 109, 145
Best, George 29, *29*, 35, *35*
Bettega, Roberto *53*, 85, 86
Beveren 72, 90
BK Copenhagen 45, 48, 66
BK Odense 28
Blackburn Rovers 131, 133
Boavista 161
Boban, Zvonomir 128
Bohemians 60, 69
Bohemians Prague 87
Bologna 26
Boniek, Zbigniew 84, *84*
Boninsegna, Roberto 48, *48*
Bordeaux 90, 94, 100, 162, 163
Borussia Dortmund 10, 12, 24, 132, 134, 135, 137, 141, 142, 143, 148, 161
Borussia Moenchengladbach 45, 48, 49, 60-1, 63, 65, 66, 67
Brondby 97, 103, 106, 152, 155
Bruges 54, 63, 66, 67, 68, 69, 76, 103, 109, 116, 117, 119
Burnley 18, 19
Busby, Matt 12, *35*, 41, *41*
Butragueno, Emilio 100, *100*

Cagliari 45
Carl Zeiss Jena 24, 45
Case, Jimmy 66, *66*
CCA Bucharest 12, 20
CDNA Sofia 10, 12, 14, 16, 18, 20, 22
Celtic 7, 30, 31, *31*, 33, 34, 36, 38-9, 42, 43, 44, 45, 46, 48, 49, 51, 52, 54, 55, 57, 58, 66, 68, 72, 73, 80, 82, 84, 85, 97, 98, 103, 104, 154
Charlton, Bobby 11, 13, 29, *35*, 36, *36*, 37, *37*
Chelsea 8, 159, 162, 164, 165
Chemie Leipzig 26
Coleraine 57
Cologne 22, 23, 26, 69, 70, 71
Cork Celtic 57
Cork Hibernians 48
corruption 7, 88, 120, 124, 131
Cowans, Gordon 80, *80*, 81, 85
Croatia Zagreb 151, 154, 160
Crusaders 54, 55, 63, 64
Cruyff, Johann 32, 34, 38, 46, *46*, 47, 51, 53
Csepel 16
CSKA Moscow 48, 116, 117, 119
CSKA Sofia 30, 32, 42, 48, 51, 54, 60, 63, 76, 77, 80, 82, 84, 87, 100, 106, 109, 110
CWKS Warsaw 10

Dalglish, Kenny *5*, 67, 68, *68*
Davids, Edgar 134, *134*, *150*
Del Piero, Alessandro *133*, 134, 143, 148
Derby County 51, 52, 60, 62
Derry City 28, 106

Deschamps, Didier 120
Di Stefano, Alfredo 9, *9*, 12, *14*, 15, 17, 20, 21, 24, 25
Distillery 24-5
Djurgarden 8, 28, 34
Dnepr Dnepropetrovsk 90, 106
Drumcondra 14, 20, 28
Dukla Prague 12, 14, 20, 22, 24, 26, 30, 31, 66, 72, 84
Dundalk 24, 34, 63, 72, 73, 84, 103
Dundee United 22, 23, 87-8
DWS Amsterdam 26
Dynamo Berlin 72, 76, 80, 84, 87, 90, 94, 97, 100, 103
Dynamo Bucharest 10, 22, 24, 26, 28, 48, 54, 60, 66, 84, 85, 87, 88, 90, 109
Dynamo Dresden 48, 54, 63, 66, 67, 69, 106, 109
Dynamo Kiev 34, 36, 42, 51, 60, 63, 69, 80, 81, 84, 97, 98, 100, 101, 102, 112, 113, 121, 126, 131, 144, 147, 148, 153, 154, 156, 157, 160, 164
Dynamo Minsk 87, 121
Dynamo Tbilisi 72, 73-4, 124
Dynamo Tirana 76, 97, 109
Dynamo Zagreb 14, 84

Eintracht Brunswick 34
Eintracht Frankfurt 7, 16, 17
EPA Larnaca 45
Esbjerg 22, 24, 30, 76
Eusebio da Silva Ferreira 21, *21*, 26, 29, 34, 36, 37, 52
Everton 24, 25, 45

Facchetti, Giacinto 32, *32*, 33
Famagusta 134
FC Aarau 121
FC Copenhagen 121
FC Haka 159
FC Zurich 24, 30, 31, 38, 57, 60, 63, 64, 80
Fenerbahçe 16, 20, 26, 28, 38, 45, 57, 60, 61, 69, 87, 94, 106, 138, 139
Ferencváros 24, 28, 42, 63, 80, 132
Feyenoord 20, 22, 28, 42, 44, 45, 48, 57, 90, 143, 146, 161, 164
Fiorentina 10, 11, 42, 43, 159, 160, 163
FK Austria 20, 22, 24, 42, 45, 90, 91, 94, 97, 114, 116, 121
Floriana 22, 23, 38, 45, 54, 60, 66
Fram Reykjavik 54, 100, 106
Frederikstad 18, 20, 22
Futre, Paulo 98, *98*

Galatasaray 10, 22, 24, 42, 48, 51, 54, 100, 103, 122, 124, 126, 143, 151, 159, 162
Gardia Warsaw 12
Gento, Francisco 11, *11*
Giggs, Ryan 124, 139, 146, 155, 156, *156*, 157, 158, 163
Glenavon 12, 19
Glentoran 26, 34, 36, 38, 45, 66, 68, 80, 82, 103, 104, 107
Gonzales, Raul 146, *146*
Gornik Zabrze 20, 21, 24, 26, 28, 30, 34, 35, 48, 51, 94, 97, 100, 103

Gotu 147
Grasshoppers Zurich 10, 48, 69, 71, 84, 87, 90, 109, 112, 132, 137, 140
Gullit, Ruud 103, *105*, 107
Gwardia Warsaw 8

Hajduk Split 48, 57, 60, 72, 73, 127, 129
Halmstad 66, 76
Hamburg 18, 19, 72, 73, 75, 84, 86, 87
Hamrin, Kurt 38, 39, 40
Hamrun Spartans 87, 100, 103
Hanot, Gabriel 6
Hansa Rostock 112
Hearts 14, 15, 18, 19
Heighway, Steve 55, 64, *64*, 67
Helsinki Palloseura 14
Herrera, Helenio 16, 41, *41*
Hertha Berlin 159, 162, 163
Hibernian 6, 7, 8-9
Hibernians Malta 20, 34, 35, 42, 72, 80, 84
HJK Helsinki 18, 22, 28, 57, 72, 84, 97, 103, 106, 153
Honvéd 6, 10, 76, 90, 94, 97, 103, 104, 106
Hvidovre 34, 57, 84

IBK Keflavik 28, 45, 51, 57
IBV 76
IFK Gothenburg 14, 16, 20, 45, 87, 90, 94, 95, 103, 116, 117, 126, 129, 138, 145, 147
IK Start 80
Ilves 90
Innsbruck 48, 51, 54, 60, 66
Inter Milan 7, 24, 25, 26-7, 28, 30, 33, 48-9, 50, 76, 106, 107, 152, 156
Inzaghi, Filippo 146, *146*
Ipswich Town 22-3

Jeunesse Esch 14, 16, 18, 24, 34, 38, 45, 54, 57, 60, 63, 66, 68, 76, 87, 94, 100, 103
Johnstone, Jimmy 31, *31*, 32, *32*, 33, 39, 43, 55, 68
Juventus 14, 18, 20, 34, 51, 52, 53, 54, 60, 66-7, 69, 80, 82, 84, 85, 86, 90, 92, 93, 94-5, 97, 132, 134, 135, 136, 138, 139, 141, 142, 143, 146, 148, 150, 151, 156, 157

Kaiserslautern 112, 153, 156
KB Copenhagen 14, 42, 60, 80
Keane, Roy 139, *139*, 163
Keegan, Kevin 65, *65*, 72, 75
Kennedy, Alan 78, *78*, 85, 89
Kennedy, Ray 49, *49*, 64, 77
Kilmarnock 28-9
Kluivert, Patrick 127, 128, *128*, 130, *130*, 135, 137
Koeman, Ronald 102, 115, *115*
Koge BK 63
Kokkolan 45
Kopa, Raymond 8, 9, 11, 15, *15*
Kosice 143, 146
Koupia Palloseura 66
KR Reykjavik 26, 30, 42
Kuopian Palloseura 34, 60
Kuusysi Lahti 87, 94, 100, 109

La Chaux-de-Fonds 26
Labinoti 90
Lahden Reipas 26, 38, 48
Larissa 103
Laudrup, Michael 112, 114, *114*
Lausanne 28
Law, Denis 29, *35*, 39, *39*
Lazio 160, 164, 165
Lech Poznan 87, 90, 91, 109
Leeds United 42-3, 57, 58, 59, 118
Legia Warsaw 18, 42, 45, 131, 133, 135
Lens 153, 154
Levski Sofia 28, 121, 124
Levski Spartak 45, 57, 66, 72, 90
Lierse 18, 145
Lillestrom 66, 69, 100, 109
Limassol 38
Limerick 18, 76, 78
Linfield 16, 20, 22, 30, 32, 42, 48, 60, 69, 70, 72, 74, 76, 78, 84, 85, 87, 88, 90, 92, 94, 97, 100, 101, 106
Liverpool 26-7, 30, 32, 54, 55, 63, 64, 65, 66, 67, 68, 69, 71, 72, 73-4, 76, 77, 78, 79, 80, 82, 84, 85, 87, 88, 89, 90, 91, 92, 93
LKS Lodz 16
Lodz 155
Lokomotiv Sofia 26, 69
Lorimer, Peter 42, 58, *58*, 59
Lucerne 106
Lyn Oslo 24, 26, 28, 42
Lyngby 90, 116, 118

Maccabi Tel Aviv 116
McNeill, Billy 30, 31, *31*, *43*
Magdeburg 51, 57, 60
Maier, Sepp 58, 76
Maldini, Paolo 107, *107*
Malmö 18, 26, 30, 38, 48, 51, 60, 63, 69, 70, 100, 106, 107, 109
Manchester City 38
Manchester United 7, *7*, 10-11, 12, 13, 15, 28, 29, 34, 35, *35*, 37, 38, 39, 121, 124, 126, 138, 139, 141, 143, 146, 148, 152, 155, 156, 157, 158, 160, 161, 163, 165
Maribor 160
Marseille 48, 51, 106, 109, 110, 111, 112, 116, 117, 119, 120, 160, 161, 164
Mazzola, Alessandro 25, *25*
Mechelen 106-7
Michels, Marinus 41, *41*, 58
Molde 161
Monaco 20, 24, 69, 84, 103, 104, 122, 123-4, 145, 148
Morientes, Fernando 149
Moscow Torpedo 30, 66, 67
Moss 103
MTK Budapest 14, 100
1860 Munich 30

Nantes 28, 30, 31, 54, 66, 76, 87, 131, 135
Napoli 100, 109, 110
Neeskens, Johan 45, 52, *52*

17 Nentori Tirana 28, 29, 42, 45, 84, 103, 106
Neuchatel 100, 103
Newcastle United 144, 147
Nice 10, 16
Norrköping 10, 12, 22, 24
Nottingham Forest 69, 70, 71, 72, 74, 75, 76, 78
Nuremberg 20, 38

Odense 16, 20, 26, 69, 87, 109
Olympiakos 16, 30, 34, 54, 57, 60, 76, 80, 84, 87, 100, 144, 151, 156, 161
Olympiakos Nicosia 34, 42, 48
Omonia Nicosia 30, 51, 60, 63, 66, 69, 72, 80, 84, 87, 90, 94, 100, 106
Orgryte 97
Osters IF 42, 72, 74, 80, 84
Oulu Palloseura 76, 77, 80, 82

Paisley, Bob 78, *78*, 88
Panathinaikos 18, 20, 22, 26, 28, 42, 45-6, 47, 51, 66, 90, 91, 92, 97, 109, 112, 113, 131, 135, 153, 154
PAOK Salonika 63, 94
Papin, Jean-Pierre 110, *118*
Paris St-Germain 97, 126, 129, 145, 147
Parma 143, 159
Partizan Belgrade 8, 20, 22, 24, 28, 29, 63, 69, 87
Partizan Tirana 22, 24, 26, 48, 72, 73, 80, 100, 102
Petrolul Ploiesti 14, 16, 30, 32
Pezoporikos 103
Platini, Michel 92
Polonia Bytom 14, 22
Portadown 109, 111, 114
Porto 10, 16, 69, 72-3, 94, 97, 98, 99, 100, 103, 109, 110, 111, 117, 123, 131, 138, 141, 144, 151, 161, 163, 165
Progres Niedercorn 69, 80, 82
Prosinecki, Robert 109, *109*
PSV Eindhoven 8, 24, 60, 61, 63, 69-70, 97, 100, 101, 102, 103, 106, 107, 112, 116, 117, 144, 147, 153, 159-60, 162
Puskas, Ferenc 10, 14, 17, *17*

Rabat Ajax 94, 97
Rangers 10, 12, 16, 20, 24, 25, 26, 60, 61-2, 63, 69-70, 100, 101, 102, 106, 107, 109, 111, 112, 114, 116, 117, 118, 119, 124, 132, 134, 137, 140, 147, 159-60, 162
Rapid Bucharest 34
Rapid Heerlen 10
Rapid Vienna 8, 10, 12, 18, 19, 26, 34, 38, 39, 84, 87, 88, 100, 103, 138, 139
Real Madrid 7, 8, 9, 10, 11, 12, 13, 14, 15, 16, 17, 18, 20, 21, 22, 24, 25, 26, 28, 29, 30, 34, 35, 38, 42, 51, 60-1, 62, 63, 69, 72-3, 76, 78, 79, 97, 100-1, 103, 104, 106, 109, 110, 132, 135, 144, 148, 150, 152, 156, 161, 164, 165, 166

Real Sociedad 80, 84, 85, 121
Red Boys Differdange 72
Red Star Belgrade 10, 12, 13, 18, 26, 38, 39, 42, 45, 46, 54, 55, 66, 76, 80, 90, 97, 103, 109, 110, 111, 112, 113
Red Star Bratislava 16
Reims 8, 9, 14, 15, 18, 19, 22
Rep, Johnny 52, 53, *53*, 90
Rijkaard, Frank 103, *103*, *108*
Roberto Carlos Da Silva 149
Rocheteau, Dominique 61, *61*
Roma 87, 88, 89
Romario da Souza Faria 121
Rosenborg 38, 45, 51, 52, 97, 106, 131, 133, 138, 141, 144, 151, 161, 164
Rossi, Paolo 85, *85*
Rot Weiss Essen 8
Ruch Chorzow 57, 60, 72, 106
rule changes 34, 36, 104, 112, 122, 124, 140
Rummenigge, Karl-Heinz *60*, 61
RWD Molnebeek 60

Saarbrücken 8
St Etienne 12, 26, 34, 38, 42, 45, 57, 60, 61-2, 63, 64, 80
St John, Ian 26, 27, *27*, 32
St Patrick's Athletic 109, 154
Salzburg 127
Sampdoria 112, 113, 115
Sarajevo 34, 35, 94
Savicevic, Dejan 122, *122*
Schalke 04 14
Schnellinger, Karl-Heinz 40
Servette 8, 20, 22, 72, 94
Seville 12
Shamrock Rovers 12, 16, 26, 90, 94, 97, 98, 100
Shelbourne 22
Shilton, Peter 72, 74, *74*, 75
Sion 16
Skeid Oslo 34
Skonto Riga 121, 159
Slask Wroclaw 66
Sliema Wanderers 26, 28, 30, 48, 51, 63, 106
Sligo Rovers 66
Slovan Bratislava 10, 45, 57, 60, 62
Souness, Graeme 77, *88*, 101
Sparta Prague 28, 34, 90, 94, 100, 103, 106, 109, 112, 113, 114, 143, 162, 163
Sparta Rotterdam 16
Spartak Kralove 18
Spartak Moscow 45, 76, 103, 109, 110, 120, 121, 122, 126, 131, 133, 135, 152, 162
Spartak Plovdiv 24
Spartak Trnava 38, 39, 42, 48, 51, 52, 54
Spora Luxembourg 10, 20, 106
Sporting Lisbon 8, 14, 20, 22, 23, 30, 45, 57, 76, 84, 145
Stade Dudelange 12, 28
Stal Mielec 54, 63
Standard Liège 14, 20, 24, 42, 45, 48, 49, 84, 87, 88
Start Kristiansand 72
Steaua Bucharest 38, 63, 69, 94, 95, 96, 97, 100, 101, 103,

104, 105, 106, 121, 127, 132, 134, 137, 147
Stein, Jock 31, 33, 39, 41
Strasbourg 72
Stromsgodset 48, 49
Sturm Graz 152, 160, 161
Stuttgart 90, 118
Szombierki Bytom 76

Tirol 106, 109
Torino 63
Tottenham Hotspur 20-21
Trabzonspor 63, 64, 66, 72, 76, 80, 90
Trakia Plovdiv 34, 94, 95
Turun Palloseura 42, 51, 54, 63

Ujpest Dózsa 18, 45, 48, 49, 51, 52, 54, 57, 58, 60, 61, 69, 72, 109
Universitatea Craiova 57, 76, 80
US Luxembourg 22, 48, 109, 116
UT Arad 42, 45
Utrecht 14

Valencia 48, 159, 160, 162, 163, 165, 166
Valerengen 30, 32, 84, 90, 94
Valkeakosen Haka 20, 24, 30, 69
Valletta 24, 57, 69, 76, 90, 109
Valur 34, 38, 66, 72, 80, 81, 97, 103
Van Basten, Marco *103*, 105
Vardar Skopje 100
Vasas 12, 20, 22, 30, 34, 66
Vasas Gyor 26, 84, 87
Vejle 51, 54, 72, 94
Verona 94
Vialli, Gianluca 114, *114*
Viking Stavanger 54, 57, 60, 63, 76, 87, 116
Vikingur 84, 87, 116
violence 59, 89, 92, 101
Vitkovice 97
Vitosha 103
Vllaznia 69, 87
Voest Linz 57
Vogts, Berti 60, 63, 65, *65*
Vojvodina 30, 31, 106
Voros Lobogo 8

Waterford 30, 38, 39, 42, 45, 51, 54
Werder Bremen 28, 103, 121, 123
Widzew Lódz 80, 84, 85, 137
Wiener Sport-Club 14, 16
Willem II 162
Wisla Krakow 69
Wismut Karl-Marx-Stadt 12, 14, 18, 34
Withe, Peter 82, 83, *83*
Wolverhampton Wanderers 6, 14, 15, 16

Young Boys Berne 12, 14, 16, 18, 97

Zarja Voroshilovgrad 54
Zbrojovka Brno 69
Zeljeznicar Sarajevo 51, 52
Zenit Leningrad 94
Zidane, Zinedine *140*, 14